The Roots of Southern Populism

The Roots of Southern Populism

Yeoman Farmers and the Transformation of the Georgia Upcountry, 1850–1890

STEVEN HAHN

New York   Oxford
OXFORD UNIVERSITY PRESS

First published by Oxford University Press, New York, 1983
First issued as an Oxford University Press paperback, 1984

Library of Congress Cataloging in Publication Data
Hahn, Steven, 1951–
The roots of southern populism.
Bibliography: p.   Includes index.
1. Georgia—Politics and government—1775–1865.
2. Georgia—Politics and government—1865–1950.
3. Populism—Georgia.   4. Cotton trade—Georgia—
History—19th century.   I. Title.
F290.H33   1983   975.8'041   82-12584
ISBN 0-19-503249-7
ISBN 0-19-503508-9 (pbk.)

Printing (last digit): 9 8 7

Printed in the United States of America

For my Parents
Who Kept the Faith

Preface

This book is about the social origins of rural radicalism in the late-nineteenth-century South—specifically about the origins of Southern Populism, the most dramatic manifestation of rural unrest and the most vibrant component of America's greatest third-party movement. As such, it tells a story at once familiar and still remarkably obscure. For longer than the past three decades, there has been considerable interest in what is known as the "Populist revolt" and, to be certain, no lack of important scholarship. Although historians initially focused on the Midwestern variant, their attention increasingly shifted southward. Studies of Southern Populist ideology, state parties, and leaders now abound, as do more general treatments of the post-Reconstruction period. Together, they have stirred lively debate and have enormously enriched our understanding of national unification, economic development, and political conflict; the best of them deserve inclusion among the seminal contributions to American historical literature. Yet, when we turn to the thousands of Southern rural folk who made Populism a mass movement and a challenge to the dominant institutions, relations, and ideas of that time, the shadows rapidly steal forth.

I have attempted to lift some of those shadows by exploring the process through which white yeoman farmers—who would pre-

dominate in the rank-and-file—came to embrace the Populist alternative. A close examination of the yeomanry's experiences over a lengthier
period of time than is customarily accorded, it seemed to me, might help
explain not only the emergence of political disaffection and protest but
also the nature and meaning of Populism itself. And so, I have selected
an appropriate locale, pressed back into the antebellum period,
reconstructed many relations of social and political life, and elaborated
the momentous changes brought forth by the Civil War and
Reconstruction. As might be expected, the undertaking required that I
piece together bits of information from a wide variety of sources, for my
subjects rarely left detailed accounts of their lives and thoughts. It also
required that I range out and consider the people, classes, and events
that touched their lives in significant ways from near and far. The story,
therefore, is both small and large in scale: one involving planters and
merchants, slaves and freedpeople, artisans and laborers, tenants and
croppers as well as yeoman farmers; one involving a locality, a region,
and a nation. It is not, I should hasten to add, the full story of the
Southern yeomanry or of the making of Southern Populism, by any
means. There are many more settings, experiences, and roads to
rebellion. Much still remains in the shadows. In dispersing some,
nonetheless, I hope to extend our field of vision while shedding new
light on areas long illuminated.

It once was thought that written expressions from Southern common
people were virtually non-existent. I have discovered otherwise, but
that discovery has also posed problems of presentation. Excerpts from
letters, diaries, and even newspapers are often awkward in grammar,
inconsistent in spelling, and limited in punctuation—so much so that
they can demand several close readings. To preserve the integrity and
flavor of this material, however, I have, for the most part, chosen simply
to reproduce it, making relevant corrections only when the meaning
could be in serious doubt.

Studying the experiences of the Southern yeomanry has, among
many other things, continually reminded me about—indeed launched
me into—the complex thicket of pecuniary and personal indebtedness.
As for the pecuniary debts accumulated in the course of preparing this
book, they are being repaid on a quarterly basis, although, thanks to the
now-defunct National Direct Student Loan program, at a rate of
interest the yeomanry would have thought just. Thanks, also, to grants
from the American Council of Learned Societies, the National

Endowment for the Humanities, and the University of Delaware, those debts are far smaller than they would have been and the book is finished far sooner.

Other debts are in many ways more substantial, but nevertheless impossible to repay. Thus, with considerable gratitude, I should like to acknowledge them here. For their assistance, patience, and kindness, I owe much to the staffs at the Sterling Memorial Library, Yale University; the Baker Library, Harvard University; the National Archives, Washington D.C.; the Emory University Library and Archives; the Duke University Archives; the Southern Historical Collection, University of North Carolina; the University of Georgia Archives; the Rome (Georgia) Public Library; the Carrollton (Georgia) Public Library; the Jackson County and Carroll County (Georgia) Courthouses; the Atlanta Historical Society; and particularly, the Georgia Department of Archives and History, where I spent a great amount of time over the past few years. Special thanks go to Ira Berlin, Joseph Reidy, and Leslie Rowland of the Freedmen and Southern Society Project for their warmth, expertise, and guidance through the valuable civil and military records housed in the National Archives.

A fellowship from the Newberry Library's Summer Training Institute in Quantitative History enabled me to spend a rewarding month learning the promises and pitfalls of quantitative methods and sharing ideas with an exceptional collection of scholars in attendance. Thereafter, I faced the numbers alone, though I did have some help in compiling them from Maxine Freifeld, Kathy Foxen, Vicky Gunn, and Barbara Sculz, and in the latter stages received incalculable assistance at the computer terminal from Thomas Dublin.

This book has its own roots in a senior honors essay completed at the University of Rochester under the direction of Christopher Lasch, whose penetrating criticisms forced much fruitful re-thinking. Rochester was quite a splendid place to learn history, for I had the unusual opportunity of also working with Eugene Genovese, Herbert Gutman, Leon Fink, Bruce Palmer, and Bruce Levine. All taught me a great deal, not only about history but about the relation of scholarship and political commitment. And Professors Genovese, Gutman, and Fink have continued to be special sources of encouragement.

Since commencing this study, I have benefited immeasurably from a group of historians who have shared their thoughts and materials, read my work, and pushed me on. Charles Flynn, William Harris, Robert

McMath Jr., Joseph Reidy, Barton Shaw, and David Weiman are all
rapidly finishing related studies of nineteenth-century Georgia and
have, from the first, exchanged their ideas, leads, and good cheer.
Edward Ayers, Richard Bushman, David Brion Davis, Barbara Fields,
Thomas Fleming, William Freehling, Alice Kelikian, Michael
Merrill, Clarence Mohr, Earl Pomeroy, and Jonathan Wiener read
portions or versions of the manuscript and provided extremely useful
suggestions on content, style, and organization. And Thomas
Fleming launched what proved to be a most remarkable series of
events.

For the time, energy, and care they devoted to my manuscript, I owe
an especially large debt to Ira Berlin, Thomas Dublin, Stanley
Engerman, Drew Faust, Eric Foner, David Montgomery, and Harold
Woodman. They raised searching questions, proposed new avenues of
inquiry, helped clarify my arguments, and generally speeded my
progress. Whatever its shortcomings, this book is far, far better for their
involvement.

Rachel Klein, Lawrence Powell, Jonathan Prude, Michael Wayne,
and Barbara Weinstein performed yeoman service by suffering through
years of brain-picking and more manuscript pages than I would care to
admit. Along with Florencia Mallon, Steve Stern, and Emilia Viotti da
Costa, they taught me more than can be imagined and set a standard of
friendship, scholarship, and integrity that I can only hope to emulate.

Dun and Bradstreet and the Greenwood Press have, respectively,
permitted me to quote from archival sources and to utilize some
material from a previously published essay. The Academic Senate of
the University of California, San Diego, allocated funds for final
manuscript preparation, and Patricia Rosas of the History
Department, with great forbearance, introduced me to the word
processor. My copy-editor, Otto Sonntag, helped me better say what I
wished to; my Oxford editors, Nancy Lane, Leona Capeless, and
Sheldon Meyer offered sound advice and welcome enthusiasm. And, at
a very crucial moment, the Society of American Historians honored the
doctoral dissertation on which this book is based with the Allan Nevins
Prize.

Lastly, two special acknowledgments are in order. C. Vann
Woodward directed this study during its early stages. Indeed, his work
inspired my interest in the subject well before I arrived at Yale
Graduate School. During my years there, Professor Woodward asked
hard questions, steered me away from unpromising scholarly paths, and

held out an example of learning and historical imagination to which I, like all his students, aspired. The merits of this book owe much to his influence. Upon Professor Woodward's retirement, Howard Lamar kindly assumed supervisory responsibilities. Professor Lamar's close readings, excellent insights, and unfailing encouragement helped me over many rough spots and lifted my spirits at difficult times—and all this despite the burdens imposed upon him by new duties as Dean of Yale College. It is typical of Professor Lamar's generosity that when I first approached him about advising the project he said, "Sure," and then, after a discussion of procedural technicalities, asked almost sheepishly, "By the way, what is your dissertation?" The last time we had spoken at length, I had just completed a paper on Jefferson's agrarian social theory. Like the Populists, Professor Lamar could appreciate the connection.

San Diego, California   S.H.
November 1982

Contents

List of Maps

List of Tables

List of Abbreviations

The Roots of Southern Populism

Introduction

Amid widening social upheaval in the 1880s, the United States Senate launched the first comprehensive investigation of the "relations between labor and capital."[1] The senators were not alone in their assessment of the forces threatening to rupture the nation. They joined newspaper editors, ministers, local politicians, and other members of the elite in making "class conflict" part of the American political vocabulary as never before. And with good reason. From the turbulent railroad strike of 1877 to the Pullman strike of 1894, from the Greenback-Labor party of the late 1870s to the Knights of Labor tickets that vied for power in scores of cities and towns during the 1880s, the social and political thrust of the Gilded Age met staunch popular challenges.[2] But none assumed the proportions of the rural Populist revolt, and nowhere did Populism sink deeper roots than in the South.[3]

Populism shared more with labor struggles than temporality. While resting upon different constituencies, both movements advanced a

1. Committee on Education and Labor, *Report of the Committee of the Senate Upon the Relations Between Labor and Capital*, 5 vols. (Washington, 1885).

2. Leon Fink, *Workingmen's Democracy: The Knights of Labor and American Politics* (Urbana, Ill., 1983).

3. C. Vann Woodward, *The Burden of Southern History*, rev. ed. (Baton Rouge, 1970), 150.

critique of the emerging social order imbued with a common spirit: they lashed out at the increasing concentration of wealth and power in the American economy; they decried the new conditions of dependency that came to define productive relations; they assailed what they believed to be the attendant corruption of the democratic process; and they held out a vision of a cooperative commonwealth of producers to be realized through public regulation of production and exchange. The Populist program owed much, in fact, to Greenback-Labor radicals. And as a measure of its broad appeal, the People's party won the allegiance of some industrial workers in the overwhelmingly rural South along with substantial support from miners and timber workers in the Midwest and the Rocky Mountain states.[4]

Populism's ideological kinship with labor radicalism and its critique of the dominant economic and political relations of industrial capitalism raise serious questions about standard appraisals of its character. Generally speaking, historians have viewed the agrarian rebellion as a manifestation either of backward-looking rural "status-anxiety" infused with political paranoia, or, more commonly, of interest-group agitation within the liberal tradition.[5] Like all typologies, these contain elements of truth and speak to many of Populism's complex and ostensibly contradictory features. Invoking Jefferson, Populists harked back to a halcyon world of independent cultivators and voiced deep suspicion of centralized authority; anticipating the exigencies of a mass society, they advocated government ownership of the means of transportation and communication. At times they could express both sentiments in the same breath. But however irreconcilable these ideas may seem from the vantage point of the late twentieth century, they were thought to be quite compatible by contemporaries. The ideas embodied strains of a preindustrial republicanism—still vital in the

4. Lawrence Goodwyn, *Democratic Promise: The Populist Moment in America* (New York, 1976), 9–24; William Warren Rogers, *The One-Gallused Rebellion: Agrarianism in Alabama, 1865–1896* (Baton Rouge, 1970), 274–75; James E. Wright, *The Politics of Populism: Dissent in Colorado* (New Haven, 1974); David Montgomery, "On Goodwyn's Populists," *Marxist Perspectives*, I (Spring 1978), 169–71.

5. See, among others, Richard Hofstadter, *The Age of Reform: From Bryan to F. D. R.* (New York, 1955), 60–93; John D. Hicks, *The Populist Revolt: A History of the Farmers' Alliance and the People's Party* (Minneapolis, 1931); Walter T. K. Nugent, *The Tolerant Populists: Kansas Populism and Nativism* (Chicago, 1963); Sheldon Hackney, *Populism to Progressivism in Alabama* (Princeton, 1969). C. Vann Woodward has called Populism "agricultural interest politics," but his work also places heavy emphasis on class dimensions. See Woodward, *Burden*, 153, and *Origins of the New South, 1877–1913* (Baton Rouge, 1951), 175–290.

1880s and 1890s—which linked freedom and independence with control over productive resources and portrayed the state as defender of the public good, as protector of communities of petty producers. The cooperative ideal, captured by the subtreasury plan of credit and marketing, lay at the heart of Populism, offering an alternative to established economic structures that sought to pair small-scale production with the realities of an industrial age.[6] Those historians who equate radicalism with socialism and have found Populism wanting overlook other forms of popular radicalism that challenged the hegemony of the marketplace throughout the nineteenth century.

Scholarly assessment of Populism as a variant of liberalism reflects a broader perspective on American social and economic development, one based on the assumption that market relations and values took hold very early and set the stage for widely shared aspirations and behavior. With no vestiges of a feudal past to dismantle, most historians argue, capitalism encountered only technological barriers; the formation of a national economic system hinged solely on the advance of transportation networks, the accumulation of financial and material resources, and the advent of labor-saving machinery. Whether emphasizing consensus or conflict as the central theme of our history, these historians take a capitalist framework as their starting point.[7]

That America did not carry the burden of a feudal legacy there can be no doubt. The colonies had their origins in the commercial expansion of western Europe. But while trade figured prominently in the early American economy, it coexisted with or, indeed, proved an integral component of productive systems organized along noncapitalist lines. A tradition of precapitalist relations and customs of the shop enabled artisans to celebrate craft pride, mutual endeavor, and production for use as late as the 1830s, even as they serviced and supplied bustling urban centers.[8] Farming communities featuring a

6. Lawrence Goodwyn's *Democratic Promise* has been of signal importance in bringing the Populist vision of cooperative commonwealth to the fore and thus in rehabilitating Populism as a radical force. But also see Bruce Palmer, *"Man Over Money": The Southern Populist Critique of American Capitalism* (Chapel Hill, 1980).

7. Historians with as differing perspectives as Carl Degler and Douglas Dowd can share this assumption. See Carl N. Degler, *Out of Our Past: The Forces That Shaped Modern America* (New York, 1970), 1-8 and passim; Douglas Dowd, *The Twisted Dream: Capitalist Development in the United States Since 1776* (Cambridge, Mass., 1974), 45-48, 152-54.

8. Sean Wilentz, "Artisan Republican Festivals and the Rise of Class Conflict in New York City, 1788-1837," in Michael H. Frisch and Daniel J. Walkowitz, eds., *Working-Class America: Essays on Labor, Community, and American Society* (Urbana, Ill., 1982).

wide distribution of landownership, household and cooperative labor, and a primary orientation to semisubsistence agriculture and local exchange could be found in many parts of the North during the eighteenth century and the first half of the nineteenth. If they shipped more than a few goods to market, the goods normally represented "surpluses."[9] And although westward migration encouraged commercial and speculative impulses, it also led to the reproduction of these communities in new settings, giving shape to emerging political alignments. During the Jacksonian period, for example, hard-money Democrats attracted their greatest support in areas that resisted full absorption into the market economy.[10]

The South presents perhaps the most compelling case of social formations diverging from the capitalist mold. Without question, cotton production decisively linked the region to national and world markets and fueled the burgeoning industrial revolution in the North and in Europe. Yet the staple owed its vitality to slave, not free, labor and its soil was ruled by an elite increasingly scornful of bourgeois relations and values. Furthermore, the South itself saw the growth of dual societies: alongside the commercialized Plantation Belt arose areas characterized by small farms, relatively few slaves, and diversified agriculture.[11] Comprising hilly terrain, sandy soil, or pine-flats, these nonplantation districts remained on the periphery of the export economy until the Civil War. Thereafter, they were swept into the cotton kingdom. Economic dislocations, changing social relations, and spiraling tenancy accompanied the shift. And here Populism would plant its firmest foothold.

The important role of yeoman-dominated areas in the Populist revolt is, by now, quite well established, but historians have been accustomed to explaining it in largely economic terms: impoverishment and

9. Christopher Clark, "Household Economy, Market Exchange, and the Rise of Capitalism in the Connecticut Valley, 1800–1860," *Journal of Social History*, XIII (Summer 1979), 169–89; Michael Merrill, "Cash Is Good to Eat: Self-Sufficiency and Exchange in the Rural Economy of the United States," *RHR*, III (Winter 1977), 42–66; Clarence H. Danhof, *Change in Agriculture: The Northern United States, 1820–1870* (Cambridge, Mass., 1969), 1–48.

10. James R. Sharp, *The Jacksonians Versus the Banks: Politics in the States After the Panic of 1837* (New York, 1970), 160–210.

11. Eugene D. Genovese, *The Political Economy of Slavery: Studies in the Economy and Society of the Slave South* (New York, 1965); idem, "Yeoman Farmers in a Slaveholders' Democracy," *AH*, XLIX (April 1975), 334; Morton Rothstein, "The Antebellum South as Dual Economy: A Tentative Hypothesis," *AH*, XLI (October 1967), 373–82.

dependency at the hands of a cotton market suffering from chronic, and at times severe, depression during the postbellum years.[12] The argument, of course, is neither badly taken nor wrongheaded. By all accounts, the material conditions of most white family farmers deteriorated steadily. They increasingly failed to raise adequate foodstuffs for household consumption, became heavily indebted for the purchase of supplies, lost their land in growing numbers, and faced declining prospects of reattaining the status of freeholders. Economic tribulation does not necessarily spark political insurgency, however. It may just as easily sap resistance, and it dispenses no inherent ideology to its victims. If, according to the conventional wisdom, Southern yeomen were touchy and isolated individualists, petty entrepreneurs with their backs to the wall by the 1890s, there is no clear reason why they would have been lured by the Populist vision of cooperative commonwealth. Small wonder that much of the historiography finds Populism so perplexing.

Limitations of research and conceptualization have contributed to the interpretive debacle. Despite the existence of a vast and imposing regional literature, we know remarkably little about those Southern whites who would fill the ranks of the People's party: the small slaveholders and nonslaveholders of the antebellum era; the family farmers and tenants of the postbellum era. To be sure, impressive statistical work beginning in the 1940s has effectively dispelled the notion, first popularized by nineteenth-century abolitionists, that the majority of Southern whites were poverty-stricken, marginalized, and degraded. There is, at present, wide agreement that the social order, although dominated by a planting elite, included large numbers of respectable yeomen as well as the landless and the poor.[13] We have also come to recognize that most yeoman farmers resided outside the areas

12. Hicks, *Populist Revolt*, 36–95; Rogers, *One-Gallused Rebellion*, 222–24; Hackney, *Populism to Progressivism*, 25–31; Roger W. Shugg, *Origins of Class Struggle in Louisiana: A Social History of White Farmers and Laborers During Slavery and After, 1840–1875* (Baton Rouge, 1939), 269–313; William Ivy Hair, *Bourbonism and Agrarian Protest: Louisiana Politics, 1877–1900* (Baton Rouge, 1972), 199–200, 209–10. Hair also points to divisions within the elite as a significant influence.

13. See, especially, Frank L. Owsley, *Plain Folk of the Old South* (Baton Rouge, 1949); Blanche H. Clark, *The Tennessee Yeomen, 1840–1860* (Nashville, 1942); Herbert Weaver, *Mississippi Farmers, 1850–1860* (Nashville, 1945); Fabian Linden, "'Economic Democracy' in the Slave South: An Appraisal of Some Recent Views," *JNH*, XXXI (April 1946), 140–89; Gavin Wright, *The Political Economy of the Cotton South: Households, Markets, and Wealth in the Nineteenth Century* (New York, 1978).

where plantations and slavery loomed prominently.[14] But we are still very much in the dark about their lives and livelihoods at any point in the nineteenth century—about their farming practices, social relations, economic priorities, cultural and political sensibilities, or place in Southern politics.

These gaps in our knowledge help account, at once, for the economic explanation of the Populist revolt and for the periodization on which that explanation rests. For while acknowledging the pivotal role of the Civil War in fostering the preconditions for agrarian unrest, historians of Populism have confined their studies exclusively to the postbellum years—often to the post-Reconstruction years—and have offered only sweeping generalizations about the contours of antebellum life.[15] Such chronological boundaries most easily lend themselves to interpretations based on shorter-term dysfunctions and distress rather than on longer-term process and transformation. There are, it should be said, new efforts to break out of this mold, to refashion the traditional antebellum/postbellum historiographic dichotomy, but they focus primarily on the Black Belt and have yet to influence treatments of Populism.[16]

This study, therefore, is informed by two interrelated propositions: first, that Populism, or any other political movement, can best be understood by analyzing how its participants directly experienced social change; and second, that this experience can become most meaningful by tracing it back into the antebellum period. The Populists did not simply "react" to economic stimuli. Ideas about justice, independence, obligation, and other aspects of social and political life, rooted in specific relationships and refracted through historical experiences, shaped their responses to the postwar era. Nor did Populism represent the only episode of social and political conflict in the nineteenth-century South. Antagonisms between rich and poor, black and white, plantation and nonplantation districts long buffeted the region and erupted with particular force during the secession crisis, the

14. Genovese, "Yeoman Farmers," 333–36; Robert R. Russel, "The Effect of Slavery Upon Nonslaveholders," *AH*, XV (April 1941), 54–71; Ira Berlin, "White Majority," *Social History*, V (May 1977), 653–59.

15. Roger Shugg's pioneering *Origins of Class Struggle in Louisiana*, published in 1939, embraced the prewar and postwar periods, but his conceptual lead attracted few, if any, followers.

16. See, for example, Jonathan M. Wiener, *Social Origins of the New South: Alabama, 1860–1885* (Baton Rouge, 1978); Michael Wayne, *The Reshaping of Plantation Society: The Natchez District, 1860–1880* (Baton Rouge, 1983); James L. Roark, *Masters Without Slaves: Southern Planters in the Civil War and Reconstruction* (New York, 1977).

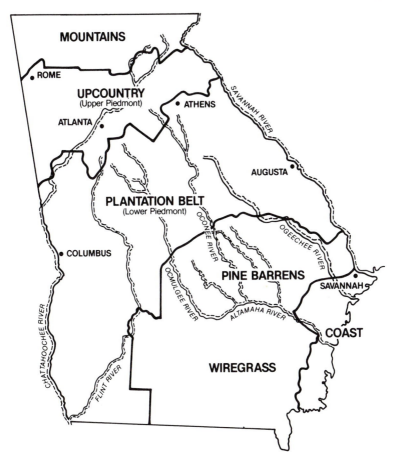

GEORGIA REGIONS

Civil War, Reconstruction, and the Independent battles of the 1870s and early 1880s. If Populism marked a qualitative leap, that leap must be explained by considering the dimensions of previous confrontations.

Ideally, a study of the origins of Southern Populism should be regional in scope, for the movement displayed important variations. In some states, the party won consistently substantial electoral support and adhered closely to the full spectrum of national demands. In others,

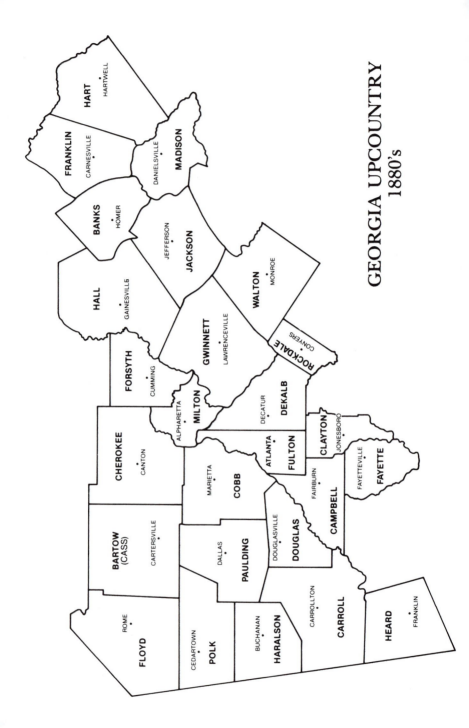

GEORGIA UPCOUNTRY
1880's

support fluctuated and the leadership came to abandon much of the party platform for the free-silver panacea. Relations with white and black Republicans also differed from state to state. And even within states, certain areas followed their own roads to rebellion. Yet, a local study that speaks to larger issues is both feasible and desirable. On the one hand, the requisites of a detailed social history can, at this stage, be met only through a localized approach. On the other hand, an experience common to many of Populism's strongholds can make such an approach valuable. Those nonplantation counties that contributed sizable blocks of votes to the People's party underwent a transition from semisubsistence to commercial agriculture between the late antebellum period and the last decade of the nineteenth century.[17]

Georgia emerged as a vibrant center of Populism and its Upper Piedmont—or Upcountry—as particularly fertile political terrain. A stretch of piedmont plateau counties north of the Plantation Belt and south of the Mountains, this area and its yeoman farmers will serve as our focus.[18] Predominantly white, the Upcountry provides an excellent example of a region that moved from the periphery into the mainstream of the cotton economy between 1850 and 1890. Boasting roughly one-fourth of Georgia's white population, the area raised less than one-tenth of all the state's cotton before the Civil War; by the 1880s it raised almost one-quarter, as total cotton production nearly quadrupled. Politically, the Upcountry also trod a path familiar to nonplantation districts, from its strong leanings toward hard-money Democracy during the 1840s and 1850s to its enthusiastic response to the Southern Farmers' Alliance during the late 1880s.

Two Upcountry counties have been selected for very close scrutiny: Jackson County in the east and Carroll County in the west. Although

17. Significantly, the two states of the cotton South in which Populism failed to establish much of a foothold—South Carolina and Mississippi—lacked substantial Hill Countries that made this transition.

18. The Upcountry includes the following counties: Franklin, Hart, Madison, Banks, Jackson, Hall, Forsyth, Walton, Gwinnett, Milton, Cobb, Campbell, Paulding, Carroll, Heard, Haralson, Floyd, Bartow (Cass), Cherokee, Douglas, Rockdale, Fayette, and Clayton. Some of these were created between 1850 and 1890. Although Fulton and Dekalb counties were also part of the geological region, they have not been included, because they embraced Atlanta and its immediate environs and were therefore somewhat atypical. The Mountain counties north of the Upcountry were small farming areas before the Civil War as well. But they were not absorbed into the cotton economy during the postbellum period and gave little support to the Populists despite long-standing anti-planter politics.

not "typical" in any statistically demonstrable way, these counties do
have much to recommend them. They shared a history with other
Upcountry counties during the period under consideration while
capturing some of the intraregional diversity. Jackson County, for
instance, claimed one of the largest black populations and Carroll one
of the smallest. Furthermore, they offer some geographical balance,
they are interesting politically, and they have among the most complete
runs of local records.[19] Both counties had Populist officeholders, sent
Populists to the state legislature, and delivered substantial votes to
Populist congressional candidates, yet in neither did Populism prove
overwhelming. Hence, it will be possible to explore developing
alignments in microcosm.

This study will not include a thorough treatment of Populism itself.
Nor will it trace the origins of discrete issues and programs upon which
the People's party stood. Rather, the concern is with social change and
popular consciousness; with the materials and dynamics of a political
culture; with class and race; with the roots, the promise, and the limits of
certain forms of radicalism. The concern, in short, is with those
experiences leading to and, indeed, informing what has appropriately
been called the Populist "moment." I hope to show that the experiences
had less to do with deteriorating conditions or spreading poverty, per se,
than with the transformation of social relations and particular sorts of
confrontations—with the penetration of market relations into a society
of different organization and sensibility, and with the conflicts provoked
thereby. In social terms, those conflicts arrayed town against countryside, merchants and landlords against yeomen and tenants of both
races; in cultural terms, the conflicts arrayed the values of the free
market against the republicanism of petty producers. A legacy of the
eighteenth century that the popular classes claimed for their own after
the Civil War and Reconstruction,[20] this republicanism gave Populism
its ideological force and political vitality. Thus, if the story is confined to
a small geographical locale, its implications reach far beyond. It links

19. Many of the counties suffered courthouse burnings, for one reason or another, during
the nineteenth century and had at least some of their records destroyed. Jackson and
Carroll counties avoided this, although like most of the other counties in the region, they
did not have local newspapers until the 1870s.

20. Eric Foner, *Tom Paine and Revolutionary America* (New York, 1976); David
Montgomery, *Beyond Equality: Labor and the Radical Republicans, 1862–1872* (New York,
1967); Leon Fink, "Class Conflict in the Gilded Age: The Figure and the Phantom,"
RHR, III (Fall–Winter 1975), 56–73.

not only rural folk in Georgia with their counterparts throughout the South, but also the South with much of nineteenth-century America, and much of nineteenth-century America with much of the industrializing world. It is a story that needs to be told.

PART ONE
"The Poor Man's Best Government"

I

"Society in the up Country"

I

Shortly before his marriage to Eugenia DuBignon, the daughter of a Sea Island planter, the young slaveowning lawyer Archibald T. Burke journeyed to Carroll County in northwestern Georgia, where he planned to settle with his new bride. Surveying the area, Burke wondered whether she would feel comfortable in one of Georgia's last frontiers. "I am sometimes fearful that you will not be pleased with the Society in the up Country," he wrote her in 1853. "You will think it strange . . . to see white people living in Log Cabins . . . [and] you will find all sorts of Society here except Aristocracy."[1] Burke's misgivings, to be sure, reflected the class attitudes of wealthy slaveholders, yet his point was never lost on the planting elite. The "Free State of Carroll," as early inhabitants brashly dubbed the county, had few slaves and few plantations, hardly resembling the Georgia Low Country to which Eugenia had been accustomed and perhaps less than receptive to a haughty master class. Their qualms notwithstanding, the couple chose to remain, and Burke began a law practice in the small town of

1. Burke, quoted in James C. Bonner, *Georgia's Last Frontier: The Development of Carroll County* (Athens, 1971), 72.

15

Carrollton, though not before hiring out his slaves to coastal rice planters. But the contrasts between Low and Upcountry, to which Burke drew attention, highlight a division significant in marking the South's social, economic, and political, much as its physical, terrain.

The geographic expansion of the slave South during the early nineteenth century broadened the base and strengthened the foundation of the slaveholding class. The natural reproduction of the slave population, the opening of hinterlands and the Old Southwest, and the upland cotton boom brought planters into a common export market and thrust the plantation economy and culture out to an extent unparalleled in the Western Hemisphere. From the seaboard into the piedmont, across the fertile soils of the Gulf states, through the Mississippi Valley, and into eastern Texas, the regime spread, drawing into its orbit many small farmers who could feasibly grow the new staple, and linking their destinies with those of the upper class.[2]

Yet, this very process of consolidation had its own internal contradictions. The disruptive tendencies of plantation agriculture, which followed the path of sugar cane in the Caribbean and Brazil, stalked the trail of the cotton plant as well. The availability of cheap western lands, the utilization of slave labor, the low level of technological development, and the aristocratic vision of many planters encouraged methods of land cultivation and accumulation that served at once to exhaust the soil and to strain class relations by crowding out smallholders. Over time, land and slave prices rose considerably, thereby narrowing prospects for social mobility. Evidence suggests that the Cotton Belt witnessed a growing concentration of wealth and increasing social stratification between 1830 and 1860: plantations claimed an ever larger share of farmland while proportionately fewer white families came to own slaves. If complex ties of kinship and quasi-dependent relationships, nurtured by the staple economy and the planters, eased social tensions, those tensions did occasionally surface and raise nagging doubts about the allegiances of lower-class whites. It was no accident that Southerners initially led the congressional battle for homestead legislation and then made their final stand on the territorial issue.[3]

2. Lewis C. Gray, *History of Agriculture in the Southern United States to 1860*, 2 vols. (Gloucester, Mass., 1958), II, 691–720; Ulrich B. Phillips, *Life and Labor in the Old South* (Boston, 1963), 91–111.

3. Eugene D. Genovese, *The Political Economy of Slavery: Studies in the Economy and Society of the Slave South* (New York, 1965); Gavin Wright, *The Political Economy of the Cotton South: Households, Markets, and Wealth in the Nineteenth Century* (New York, 1978), 26–37;

At the same time, the diversity of terrain and patterns of settlement spawned regions into which slavery and the plantation failed to penetrate significantly. Although Tidewater planters led the earliest migration into the interior, by the fourth decade of the eighteenth century a steady stream of German and Scots-Irish immigrants flowed south from Pennsylvania into the Great Valley of Virginia and ultimately into the uplands of the Carolinas and Georgia. Around the time of the Revolution, the "Backcountry," where small farms and free labor predominated, boasted a substantial population and offered a cultural, as well as political, challenge to the gentry.[4] Here the "evangelical revolt"·first took root, then moved eastward into the slaveholders' domain, where the Baptists scorned the pretensions of the elite and created forms of community which called traditional notions of authority and hierarchy into question.[5] Here, too, planter control of the political system initially came into dispute. And here the few, and short-lived, Southern antislavery societies had their home.[6]

As slavery pushed across the South, the plantation economy absorbed some of these areas. The Backcountry of one generation could become part of the Cotton Belt in the next. The South Carolina piedmont, for example, made the transition between the 1760s and the first decade of the nineteenth century, and the process ran its course

---

James C. Bonner, "Profile of a Late Antebellum Community," in Elinor Miller and Eugene D. Genovese, eds., *Plantation, Town, and County: Essays in the Local History of American Slave Society* (Urbana, Ill., 1974), 30–49.

4. Carl Bridenbaugh, *Myths and Realities: Societies of the Colonial South* (Baton Rouge, 1952), 120–24; Thomas P. Abernethy, *Three Virginia Frontiers* (Baton Rouge, 1940), 29–62.

5. Rhys Isaac, "Evangelical Revolt: The Nature of the Baptists' Challenge to the Traditional Order in Virginia, 1765–1775," *WMQ*, 3rd ser., XXXI (July 1974), 345–68; Donald G. Mathews, *Religion in the Old South* (Chicago, 1977), 7–38.

6. Political conflicts erupted in the North and South Carolina Backcountry during the third quarter of the eighteenth century, and while they had complicated dimensions and differed substantially in each colony, they revealed a common strain of opposition to colonial administration, unequal representation in assemblies, and forms of taxation. See Rachel N. Klein, "Ordering the Backcountry: The South Carolina Regulation," *WMQ*, 3rd ser., XXXVIII (October 1981), 661–80; James P. Whittenburg, "Planters, Merchants, and Lawyers: Social Change and the Origins of the North Carolina Regulation," *WMQ*, 3rd ser., XXXIV (April 1977), 219–35. On Southern antislavery, see David Brion Davis, *The Problem of Slavery in the Age of Revolution, 1770–1823* (Ithaca, 1975), 209–10; Donald L. Robinson, *Slavery in the Structure of American Politics, 1765–1820* (New York, 1971), 49.

elsewhere in what became the cotton South.[7] But, owing to topography, inaccessibility, and strong local customs, numerous regions resisted the trend. Western North Carolina, eastern Tennessee, the hilly sections of Georgia, Alabama, and Louisiana, as well as southeastern Mississippi and Georgia, among others, remained isolated enclaves or on the periphery of the staple economy. Known variously as the Backcountry, Upcountry, Hill Country, Pine Barrens, and Piney Woods, and inhabited principally by small farmers and herdsmen owning few or no slaves, these locales presented the planters with thorny political problems throughout the nineteenth century. While their political loyalties varied from state to state and county to county, nonplantation districts generated the stiffest opposition to secession, the highest desertion rates in the Confederate army, the greatest number of white Republicans and Independents, and many of Populism's strongholds.[8]

The Georgia Backcountry of the eighteenth century, populated largely by Creek and Cherokee tribes, included the entire piedmont plateau as well as the Hills and Mountains to the north and the Pine Barrens and Wiregrass separating the coast from the fall line. Indian cessions of 1763, 1773, and 1783 promoted settlement northward along the Savannah River and westward to the Oconee where the counties of Wilkes, Franklin, and Washington were established. Following the Revolutionary War, migrants from Virginia, but especially from North and South Carolina, began to flock into the state. Some came in groups, like the Virginians who settled on the fertile banks of the Broad River or the Scots-Irish who moved from the Anderson district of South Carolina to the piedmont counties of Franklin and Washington; others scattered through the hinterlands, often among the Indians, where they cleared small patches, hunted, fished, and traded. For many families, Georgia was the culmination of a protracted journey originating in England, Scotland, and Wales with stops of varying duration in western Virginia and North Carolina.[9]

Before the turn of the nineteenth century, the state distributed land

7. Eugene D. Genovese, "Yeoman Farmers in a Slaveholders' Democracy," *AH*, XLIX (April 1975), 333–36; Rachel N. Klein, "The Rise of the Planters in the South Carolina Backcountry, 1767–1808" (Ph.D. diss., Yale University, 1979).

8. Carl N. Degler, *The Other South: Southern Dissenters in the Nineteenth Century* (New York, 1974).

9. W. B. Jones, "L. B. Jones Family History" (Typescript, UGa.); George R. Gilmer, *Sketches of Some of the First Settlers of Upper Georgia* (New York, 1855), 1–137; Garnett Andrews, *Reminiscences of an Old Georgia Lawyer* (Atlanta, 1870), 72–73.

under the headright system, allotting 200 acres to every family head, with an additional 50 acres for each child and slave up to the number of ten, thus laying the foundation for the emergence of large estates. With the Creek cession of a strip of territory between the Ocmulgee and Oconee rivers in 1802, however, came the land lottery. Newly created counties were henceforth divided into land districts and then sub-divided into square tracts of 202.5 acres. Every free white male over the age of twenty-one who could prove American citizenship and had paid taxes in Georgia for a year was entitled to one draw; those with wives and children were permitted two. The government then granted title upon receipt of a small fee.[10]

The lottery system served as the basis for distributing other tracts of land that came under state control during the 1820s and 1830s, and it helped widen the base of property ownership. But several features made the accumulation of substantial landholdings possible. First, those obtaining grants under headright were not excluded from the lottery. Furthermore, many drawees failed to take out their lots, and the land reverted to the government for resale. One official estimated that this may have been the case for nearly one-quarter of the land lots. Finally, some of the land hungry arranged to have others draw lots and then turn over title for a nominal sum.[11]

The eradication of the last Creek claims in 1826 and the expulsion of the Cherokees opened the remainder of northern and western Georgia to white settlement.[12] Geography and climate, however, helped make for variegated social and economic settings. Stimulated by the cotton boom, the rich loams and gently rolling hills of the middle and lower piedmont gave rise to large land and slaveholdings—a development intensified by the construction of railroads linking the flourishing cotton country to the coast. Black majorities could be found in most eastern

10. Enoch Banks, *The Economics of Land Tenure in Georgia* (New York, 1905), 15–17; Amanda Johnson, *Georgia as Colony and State* (Atlanta, 1938), 230; James C. Bonner, *A History of Georgia Agriculture, 1732–1860* (Athens, 1964), 34–35.

11. Banks, *Economics of Land Tenure*, 18–20; Sarah Blackwell Temple, *The First Hundred Years: A Short History of Cobb County in Georgia* (Atlanta, 1935), 46; Rev. Lloyd G. Marlin, *The History of Cherokee County* (Atlanta, 1932), 36.

12. On the history of Indian removal, see Ulrich B. Phillips, *Georgia and State Rights* (Antioch, Ohio, 1968), 39–86; Charles S. Sydnor, *The Development of Southern Sectionalism, 1819–1848* (Baton Rouge, 1948), 182–84; Michael P. Rogin, *Fathers and Children: Andrew Jackson and the Subjugation of the American Indian* (New York, 1975).

counties by the 1830s and 1840s, forming a belt that would soon stretch west and south to the Alabama line.[13]

In the upper section of the piedmont, on the other hand, a different configuration emerged. Although highly fertile lands hugged numerous waterways, generally hilly and broken terrain as well as a cooler climate, which shortened the growing season, discouraged cotton planting and focused agriculture on grain crops.[14] Farms were smaller and the region's population overwhelmingly white. In 1850, fewer than one-quarter of the denizens were black. Parts of middle and south-western Georgia also had white majorities in this period, but those majorities shrank and often disappeared during the 1850s, as the plantation economy took shape. By contrast, the racial composition of the Upper Piedmont, or Upcountry, maintained a remarkable stability.[15] What is more, save for the Western and Atlantic Railroad, connecting Atlanta and Chattanooga, and a feeder to Rome, the region had no rail lines. Although the Upcountry later became a major staple-producing area, and although its southernmost tier blended into the Plantation Belt, it remained very much a backwoods throughout the antebellum era.[16]

II

Archibald T. Burke proved a more perceptive observer than his slighting tone would lead us to believe. For when he told his wife-to-be that she would "find all sorts of Society" in Carroll County "except Aristocracy," he suggested not only that the Upcountry lacked a significant planter element but also that it had an entire social structure of its own. If the conventional portrait of nonplantation districts as

13. Robert P. Brooks, *The Agrarian Revolution in Georgia, 1865–1912* (Madison, Wis., 1914), 82–86; Bonner, *History of Georgia Agriculture*, 47–56; Ulrich B. Phillips, *A History of Transportation in the Eastern Cotton Belt to 1860* (New York, 1908), 20, 221–36.

14. *Seventh Census of the United States, 1850* (Washington, 1853), 210, 216. Grain accounted for about 90 percent of the cropland and for about 80 percent of the value of all crops on Upcountry farms.

15. Of the 153,533 Upcountry inhabitants in 1850, some 77.9 percent were white. By 1860 the population had grown to 192,940, some 75.2 percent of whom were white. See *Seventh Census*, 367–68; *Eighth Census of the United States, 1860* (Washington, 1864), Population, 72–73.

16. Brooks, *Agrarian Revolution*, 74–76; Milton S. Heath, *Constructive Liberalism: The Role of the State in the Economic Development of Georgia to 1860* (Cambridge, Mass., 1954), 276–77.

relatively homogeneous zones of smallholding cultivators contains more than a shred of truth, it is far too simple, too static—it speaks of isolated individuals rather than of a society. Like the Plantation Belt, the Upcountry had its rich and poor, its landed and its landless, its slaveholders and nonslaveholders. But taken as a whole, the distribution of wealth, the organization of production, the division of labor, and the social relations they engendered constituted a distinct socioeconomic formation which reflected and shaped the lives and aspirations of its numerically preponderant yeomanry.

Consider the occupational spectrum. While most of the Upcountry's free household heads were "farmers," evidence from two counties reveals that roughly one-quarter had different occupations. Included were a small number of merchants, lawyers, and physicians, a few miners scattered through the mineral-rich areas, and, most prominently, artisans and laborers. In Carroll County during the 1850s, fully half of this group consisted of craftsmen and more than three-quarters were either craftsmen or laborers. Jackson County presents a comparable picture, though laborers outnumbered artisans (see Table 1.1). These householders, to be sure, were inextricably tied to the agricultural economy, and many combined farming with their profession or trade. Thus John Park, a Jackson County blacksmith who possessed 100

Table 1.1 Occupations of White Household Heads, Jackson and Carroll Counties, 1850–1860

	Percentage of Household Heads			
	Jackson County		Carroll County	
Occupation	1850	1860	1850	1860
Farmer	75.4%	69.2%	74.7%	78.3%
Trade	1.5	0.7	2.4	2.1
Professional	2.4	3.7	2.6	3.0
Service	0.3	0.0	0.0	0.2
Artisan	8.1	11.0	12.6	11.5
Laborer	11.7	15.4	7.5	5.0
Other	0.6	0.0	0.2	0.0
Total	100.0	100.0	100.0	100.0
Number	332	428	454	430

Sources: Manuscript Census, Georgia, Jackson and Carroll Counties, Schedule I, 1850, 1860. For a more complete occupational breakdown, see Appendix, Table I.

acres in 1850, and Baxter McPherson, a Carroll County sawyer who possessed 200, typified the experience of between one-third and one-half of the craftsmen in owning land. Others, like Baron Maynard, a carpenter in Carroll County, appeared to rent small parcels on which to set up their shops and supplement their earnings. And all serviced the farm sector. Some laborers found jobs in the tiny Upcountry towns and villages, but most worked in the countryside.[17]

These laborers formed part of a larger nonlandowning segment among the farming population. About three of ten household heads listed as "farmers" in 1850 owned no real estate. But they did not make up a floating body of dispossessed, claiming few if any ties to the property-holding community. Some may have been scarcely more than farm laborers, residing in separate dwellings on the plantations or farms they worked. The majority probably entered into one of several forms of tenancy.[18] Although precise figures are unavailable and even estimates involve a good deal of guesswork, it may be that tenants accounted for at least 15 percent (and in some counties more) of all those claiming agricultural occupations.[19] A number of these tenants, particularly in

17. Manuscript Census, Georgia, Jackson and Carroll Counties, Schedule I, 1850. On rural artisans and laborers, see Carl Bridenbaugh, *The Colonial Craftsman* (Chicago, 1961), 1–32; George B. Hudson Store and Farm Account Book, Gwinnett County, 1856, Mrs. Don G. Aiken Collection, GDAH; James Washington Watts Farm Diary, Cass County, 1855, James Washington Watts Papers, GDAH.

18. For an extended discussion of landlord-tenant relations in the antebellum Upcountry, see Chapter Two.

19. The census did not record the land tenure of farm units until 1880. But some of the farm operators on the agricultural schedule of the census did not own real property, almost all of whom had their occupations reported as "farmers" on the population schedule. If one includes as tenants only those "farmers" who appear on the agricultural schedule with both acreage and crop production, the number is quite small: under 5 percent of the agricultural population (those with occupations such as farmer, farm laborer, and overseer) and of the total farm units. Yet in Carroll County in 1850 about 70 percent of the other "farmers" who did not own real estate appeared on the agricultural schedule with only crop production, not acreage. In all probability they, too, were tenants of some sort, bringing the proportion of tenants in the agricultural population to about 21 percent. Although the Jackson County census taker did not include landless "farmers" on the agricultural schedule with only crop production, I believe that the situation in Carroll County gets us closer to reality. Thus, I estimated as tenants in Jackson County all landless "farmers" who appear on the agricultural schedule along with 70 percent of those who do not appear, which brings the proportion of tenants to about 18 percent of the agricultural population. My confidence in this as a reasonable, if slightly low, estimate is strengthened by information from another Upcountry county, Paulding. There, the census taker in 1860 used more precise occupations: along with "farmers" owning no real

the more recently settled western Upcountry, farmed land owned by Georgians who had drawn lots but lived elsewhere in the county and state and wished to have the lots cleared and improved. Others were new arrivals who lacked the resources to purchase land and looked to renting as a means of necessary accumulation. Most commonly, tenants and landless "farmers" of ambiguous status were linked by kinship to the landowners whose property they tilled. Sons of Upcountry farmers normally did not remain in their parents' household after marriage: they moved out, established their own households, and usually either continued to work the homestead or made such arrangements with neighboring relatives. So it was with Middleton Brooks, Jr., of Jackson County. Reported as a "farmer" having no real estate in 1850, Brooks lived near if not on his elderly father's farm, which he undoubtedly helped cultivate. During the 1850s Brooks's father died, and by 1860 Brooks owned land worth $1,200.[20]

Most Upcountry whites farmed their own land or resided in households that did so. More than half of the household heads in both sample counties were landholding farmers, and to these may be added the professionals, craftsmen, and occasional "laborers" who cultivated their own tracts as well. In all, approximately six of ten household heads were landed proprietors. Yet, as was true in other rural areas during the mid-nineteenth century, such property was by no means evenly distributed. The richest landowners held a disproportionately large share of the real-estate wealth in their counties. In 1850, the top tenth controlled over 40 percent of the real wealth, while the top quarter controlled well over 60 percent. Poorer landholders, on the other hand, came up much shorter, for the entire bottom half of the ladder

estate, he designated "tenants," "renters," and "croppers." Aggregating all of these occupations, I found that the "tenants," "renters," and "croppers" composed 95 percent of the group. In Paulding County, farm tenants of some kind hence made up about 30 percent of the agricultural population. See Manuscript Census, Georgia, Jackson, Carroll, and Paulding Counties, Schedules I and II, 1850, 1860. Also see Appendix, Table I.

20. Manuscript Census, Georgia, Jackson County, Schedule I, 1850, 1860. Brooks was listed next to his 93-year-old father on the population schedule. The large number of landless "farmers" either listed on the agricultural schedule with crop production and no acreage (Carroll County) or not listed on the agricultural schedule at all suggests the prevalence of informal tenancy arrangements. And about 25 percent of the landless "farmers" in both counties were listed next to or near a landowning household head with the same surname on the population schedule, a considerable underestimate of potential kinship ties.

Table 1.2 Distribution of Real Wealth Among Real-Property Owners, Jackson and Carroll Counties, 1850 (by Decile of Real Wealth)

Rank	Jackson County		Carroll County	
	Value	Share	Value	Share
Top Decile	$131,270	41.4%	$213,700	53.2%*
Second Decile	62,410	19.8	59,400	14.8
Third Decile	35,600	11.2	38,400	9.6
Fourth Decile	23,600	7.4	26,500	6.6
Fifth Decile	20,480	6.5	20,100	5.0
Sixth Decile	14,400	4.5	14,450	3.6
Seventh Decile	11,440	3.6	12,600	3.1
Eighth Decile	8,850	2.8	8,500	2.1
Ninth Decile	6,085	1.9	5,600	1.4
Tenth Decile	3,005	0.9	2,360	0.6
Total	$317,140	100.0%	$401,610	100.0%
Number		232		275

* The distribution is slightly exaggerated due to the presence of one extremely large landowner in the sample.

Source: Manuscript Census, Georgia, Jackson and Carroll Counties, Schedule I, 1850.

controlled less than 15 percent of the total real wealth (see Table 1.2).

Whatever the fortunes of those who owned land and those who did not, of those who farmed and those who plied a craft, of those who tended stores and those who earned their keep, none fared worse than a small, albeit not insignificant, group of Afro-Americans, almost all of whom were slaves. Owning neither property nor their persons, the blacks made up something over one-fifth of the Upcountry's total population in 1850. They could be found in greater numbers in several long-settled eastern counties and in the counties bordering the Western and Atlantic Railroad and major navigable rivers. Within counties, they could be found in greater numbers in districts boasting richer soils and larger farms.[21] But the variations were not substantial. Virtually everywhere the blacks were outnumbered by at least two or three to one, and virtually everywhere they came under the direct command of only a small minority of whites. In Jackson County nearly seven of ten white households contained no slaves in 1850; in Carroll County nine of

21. *Seventh Census*, 367–68; Manuscript Census, Georgia, Jackson and Carroll Counties, Schedule III, 1860.

ten were slaveless. And of all white slaveowners, whether or not they owned land, about half had fewer than five slaves while well under one-tenth had more than twenty. In short, the overwhelming majority of whites were either nonslaveholders or small slaveholders.[22]

Most of the Upcountry slaves, however, lived among ten or more of their peers and worked for the largest landholders in the region. If Jackson and Carroll counties are indicative, the wealthiest tenth of the entire free population owned upwards of 60 percent of the slaves and the wealthiest quarter owned upwards of 80 percent. Among only land-holders the distribution was similar, though not quite as skewed. Which is to say that slaveownership, together with landownership, made for an economic hierarchy.[23]

A comparative glimpse at the Black Belt casts that hierarchy into sharper relief, for there the setting was rather different. To begin with, the richest landowners held a larger while the poorest held a smaller share of the total real wealth. Indeed, the Upcountry bore a closer resemblance to much of the rural North in this regard. Even more striking were geographical distinctions in absolute wealth: the Black Belt elite was far more imposing than its Upcountry counterpart. Real-estate holdings among the top tenth of Black Belt landowners normally averaged well over $20,000; in the Upcountry they averaged well under $10,000. A few Upcountry planters, like Zaddock Bonner of Carroll County, who owned $50,000 of real property in 1850, shared the economic status and lifestyle of the Black Belt upper class. Most did not.[24]

Just as the Black Belt was more clearly the domain of large landowners, so it was also more clearly the domain of slavery and slaveholders. In the southeastern Black Belt, for example, more than 70 percent of the farm operators owned slaves in 1850, among whom nearly half owned over ten and roughly one-fifth owned twenty or more. About one-third of the farm operators, that is, depended largely on slave labor. Some areas of the Upcountry, like Jackson County, came nearer to approximating this pattern than did others, but even in

22. Appendix, Table III.

23. Appendix, Table IV.

24. Wright, *Political Economy of Cotton South*, 24–29; Jonathan M. Wiener, *Social Origins of the New South: Alabama, 1860–1885* (Baton Rouge, 1978), 15. The mean real-estate values for the top tenth of real-property owners in Jackson and Carroll counties were $5,707 and $7,632 respectively. For Northern comparisons, see Merle Curti et al., *The Making of an American Community: A Study of Democracy in a Frontier County* (Stanford, 1959), 78.

Jackson County half the farmers had no slaves and a far smaller proportion of the slaveowners had more than ten. In Carroll County over three-fourths of all farmers had no slaves, while almost 80 percent of those who did had fewer than ten. And as Black Belt slaveholdings became increasingly concentrated during the 1850s, something of the reverse occurred in the Upcountry.[25]

John Horton would have sat atop the economic hierarchy almost anywhere in the antebellum South. One of Jackson County's wealthiest residents in 1850, Horton owned twenty-five slaves and 1,100 acres of land, 500 of which were under cultivation. He grew substantial crops of wheat, corn, oats, peas, beans, and sweet potatoes, had more than a hundred head of livestock, including fifty hogs and twenty-five sheep, and raised seventeen bales of cotton. Isaac Cobb of Carroll County did not quite measure up to the stature of John Horton, but he was undeniably a man of some means. Master to twelve slaves in 1850, Cobb improved 200 of his 700 acres, which yielded 2,000 bushels of grain and potatoes along with twelve bales of cotton. In addition, he owned five horses, ten cows, and a sizable number of other cattle, sheep, and hogs.[26]

More typical of the standing of most Southern farmers were Charles Brock of Jackson County and Richard White of Carroll. In 1850 Brock, his two sons, and five slaves worked 130 acres, growing about 700 bushels of grain, 100 bushels of sweet potatoes, and only two bales of cotton. A large herd of hogs, sheep, and cows supplied Brock's family with meat, wool, milk, and butter. During the same year, White farmed 50 of his 100 acres with only the aid of his children and perhaps an occasional hired hand. He devoted his attention entirely to the cultivation of grains, peas, beans, and potatoes and to the raising of livestock. Although his farm was comparatively small, White owned several cows, a couple of horses and oxen, almost two dozen sheep, and fifty hogs.[27]

However different they were statistically, Horton, Cobb, Brock, and White—indeed, white farm proprietors throughout the South—had

25. James D. Foust, *The Yeoman Farmer in the Westward Expansion of United States Cotton Production* (New York, 1975), 115, 135; Appendix, Tables II–III. For more detailed statistics on the distribution of slaveownership, see my doctoral dissertation, "The Roots of Southern Populism: Yeoman Farmers and the Transformation of Georgia's Upper Piedmont, 1850–1890" (Ph.D. diss., Yale University, 1979), 414–16.

26. Manuscript Census, Georgia, Jackson and Carroll Counties, Schedule II, 1850.

27. Ibid.

important things in common. All owned their land and farming implements, all made day-to-day decisions about farming operations themselves, all exploited the labor of nonowning household members and perhaps other legal dependents, all produced substantial food crops, all had much of their clothing and necessaries made at home, and all had a considerable number of livestock. By virtue of their relations to the means of production and their claims to the services, if not the persons, of family and slaves, all, in sum, stood on one side of a great historical divide. Yet, at the same time, divergent interests and experiences could set set certain proprietors apart from others; and the divergent interests and experiences fell most clearly along geographical lines.

For it was not simply that men like John Horton and Isaac Cobb—men who cultivated more than 200 acres (and often more than 500 acres), who relied primarily upon the labor of slaves, and who had close ties to the export market through the production of sizable cotton crops—were more numerous in the Black Belt than in the Upcountry. Nor was it simply that men like Charles Brock and Richard White—men who cultivated fewer than 200 acres (and often fewer than 100 acres), who relied primarily upon their own labor and that of their kin, and who had limited ties to the export market because they produced little if any cotton—were more numerous in the Upcountry than in the Black Belt. Rather, it was that men like Horton and Cobb, planters large and small, owned most of the land and slaves and grew most of the crops in the Black Belt, while men like Brock and White, yeomen large and small, owned most of the land and grew most of the crops in the Upcountry. During the 1850s, farms in Jackson and Carroll counties containing fewer than 200 improved acres (about 90 percent of all units) embraced at least 60 percent of the total improved acreage and produced at least 70 percent of the foodstuffs. They even raised more than 60 percent of the relatively small cotton crop (see Table 1.3). In the Black Belt, by contrast, farms of this size (over 60 percent of all units) embraced only 20 percent of the improved acreage and produced only 20 percent of the cotton and less than 30 percent of the foodstuffs. Most of the cropland and output fell, in fact, to those farm units containing 500 or more improved acres.[28] Black Belt yeomen lived in a society dominated by planters and plantations; Upcountry yeomen in a society dominated by farmers and farms. If they shared a broadly similar economic status, they resided in very different worlds.

28. Foust, *Yeoman Farmer*, 110–12.

Table 1.3 Distribution of Farms, Improved Acreage, and Crop Production, Jackson and Carroll Counties, 1850–1860

| | Percentage Combined County Total | | | | | | | | | | | |
| Farm Category | % Total Farms | | % Total Improved Acres | | % Total Food Production* | | % Total Cotton Production | |
	1850	1860	1850	1860	1850	1860	1850	1860
Under 200 Improved Acres	87.8%	93.6%	58.8%	76.4%	71.1%	76.1%	61.9%	77.1%
Over 200 Improved Acres	12.2	6.4	41.2	23.6	28.9	23.9	38.1	22.9
Total	100.0%	100.0%	100.0%	100.0%	100.0%	100.0%	100.0%	100.0%
Number	403 Farms	456 Farms	36,400 Acres	32,792 Acres	223,389 Bushels	508,537 Bushels	946 Bales	1,519 Bales

* Includes wheat, corn, oats, peas and beans, and sweet potatoes.

Source: Manuscript Census, Georgia, Jackson and Carroll Counties, Schedule II, 1850, 1860.

III

The world of Upcountry yeomen was one in which production and consumption focused on the household, in which kinship rather than the marketplace mediated most productive relations, in which general farming prevailed and family self-sufficiency proved the fundamental concern, and in which networks of exchange proliferated. It was a world, therefore, that renders somewhat artificial the neat categories of subsistence and commercial agriculture, pointing instead to an entire system of productive organization—paralleled elsewhere in early America—that combined features of each within an overriding logic of its own.[29]

Providing for the short- and long-term independence of the family governed the logic of this system, and the household economy rested at the heart of the undertaking. Yeoman families looked to securing most of life's necessities through their own efforts. To this end, the household evinced a clear, though by no means rigid, division of labor based principally on sex and age. Husbands took charge of the fields where, with sons who had entered early adolescence, they cleared, plowed, planted, and hoed, devoting most of their farm land to foodstuffs—to wheat, oats, sweet potatoes, and above all to corn, invariably the largest crop. A farmer who worked sixty-five acres in 1850 would very likely give between twenty and thirty of them over to corn, another ten or fifteen to wheat and oats, and perhaps one or two to sweet potatoes, common fare in the Upcountry diet. Much of the remainder would lie fallow, with small additional portions sown in other vegetables and possibly a little fruit and tobacco; an acre or so would be planted in cotton. It is, in fact, probable that cotton could be found growing on virtually all farms during the early 1850s, although only about half of the yeomen raised it for sale. Those who did raised but a bale or two or three.[30]

29. For Northern comparisons and important theoretical treatments, see Michael Merrill, "Cash Is Good to Eat: Self-Sufficiency and Exchange in the Rural Economy of the United States," *RHR*, III (Winter 1977), 42–66; Christopher Clark, "Household Economy, Market Exchange, and the Rise of Capitalism in the Connecticut Valley, 1800–1860," *Journal of Social History*, VIII (Summer 1979), 169–89; James A. Henretta, "Families and Farms: *Mentalité* in Preindustrial America," *WMQ*, 3rd ser., XXXV (January 1978), 3–32.

30. Appendix, Tables V–VI. The census does not record acreage in specific crops until 1880. My broad estimate here is based on average levels of crop production and on information regarding crop yields and field systems from George M. White, *Statistics of the*

Harvest brought wives and daughters into the fields. More regularly they might tend to the garden and to some of the livestock. For the most part, however, theirs was the sphere of domestic chores and production. As the son of a farmer who owned 200 acres and three slaves in a comparable area of Tennessee put it, he and his father "did all kinds of farm work [while] my mother cooked sewed, spun thread, wove clothes, and clothed the family of eleven children with the fruits of her labor." Another wrote similarly that his nonslaveholding father cultivated the fields and his mother "worked in the house cooking spinning weaving [and doing] patch work."[31] The same could have been said for the Georgia Upcountry, as census and estate records demonstrate that most yeoman families had spinning wheels and looms, that many raised sheep for the wool, and that at least some of the cotton crop went to fill home needs.[32] Complementing the labors of the men, women played a pivotal role in assuring that the household produced much of what it consumed.

The vast majority of yeoman households included only the immediate family, though at some point an elderly parent might be present. Wills often stipulated that one of the male heirs care for the widow as a condition of inheritance. On occasion, these households took in young relatives, a neighboring child, or, less frequently, a locally unattached boarder who would work on the farm. And then there were the slaves who could be found on between one-fifth and one-half of the yeoman farms and who were important participants in the household economy, if rather ambiguous members of the household itself. There is little doubt that slavery on smaller farms had an easier social atmosphere and promoted distinctive forms of racial interaction. Whites and blacks shared a close living environment, worked side by side at similar tasks, might attend the same church, and could engage in casual fraternization. Thus, David M. Highfield, who farmed $500

State of Georgia (Savannah, 1849), 101–617; Gray, History of Agriculture, II, 807–20; and Georgia Department of Agriculture, Supplemental Report of the Commissioner of Agriculture for the Year 1878 (Atlanta, 1878), 6–8.

31. J. Press Abernathy of Giles County, Stokely Acuff of Granger County, and John S. Allen of Rutherford County, all in John Trotwood Moore, Civil War Questionaires, Reel 1, Tennessee State Archives. See also Julia Cherry Spruill, Women's Life and Work in the Southern Colonies (Chapel Hill, 1938), 80–84.

32. Of 159 inventories probated in Jackson and Carroll counties during the 1850s, 115 (72.3 %) reported spinning wheels and looms. See Ordinary Estate Records, Inventories and Appraisements, Carroll County, Vols. C–D, GDAH; Court of Ordinary, Inventories and Appraisements, Jackson County, Vol. A, GDAH. Also see Appendix, Tables V–VI.

worth of land in Jackson County during the early 1850s, traded, drank, and gambled with some of the local blacks.[33] What is more, in the patriarchal household economy, relations of legal and customary dependency, not equality, linked all to the male head. Women could not vote and surrendered rights of property to their husbands upon marriage; children also stood juridically subordinate and were expected to live and labor on the homestead without remuneration until they started families of their own. If slavery was the most extreme and neatly defined relation of dependency, it nonetheless occupied the extreme end of a racially mixed continuum.[34]

But that extreme form of dependency, amplified by community norms, did set the slaves apart from other dependent household members. With rare exceptions, slaves lived in separate dwellings on yeoman farms, and although quite a number resided in family settings, or at least with a mate, the generally small size of yeoman slaveholdings commonly made such arrangements impossible.[35] Many slaves, then, depended on forming bonds with peers on other farms—perhaps to a greater extent than in the Plantation Belt—making for a subcommunity within the household economy, and one distinguished by more than color. For unlike dependents in white households, slaves were not tied

33. Superior Court Minutes, Jackson County, February 1850, August 1850, GDAH; Cabin Creek Baptist Church Minutes, Jackson County, May 1, 1852, GDAH; Eden Primitive Baptist Church Minutes, Carroll County, 1853–1860, GDAH; Daniel Robinson Hundley, *Social Relations in Our Southern States* (New York, 1860), 193–94; Eugene D. Genovese, " 'Rather Be a Nigger Than a Poor White Man': Slave Perceptions of Southern Yeomen and Poor Whites," in Hans L. Trefousse, ed., *Toward a New View of America: Essays in Honor of Arthur C. Cole* (New York, 1977), 85–89.

34. Lawrence M. Friedman, *A History of American Law* (New York, 1973), 184–86; Anne Firor Scott, *The Southern Lady: From Pedestal to Politics, 1830–1930* (Chicago, 1970), 46–79. Thus it was not uncommon, as Scott notes, for women to compare their lot with that of the slaves.

35. Manuscript Census, Georgia, Jackson and Carroll Counties, Schedule III, 1850, 1860. The slave schedules of the census list neither the names of slaves nor their relationship with other slaves in the unit. But the schedules do list the sex and age of each slave owned by each slaveholder as well as the number of slave houses. In Carroll County in 1860, for example, about 80 percent of the slaveholders reported separate dwellings for their slaves. Of those who did not report separate dwellings, roughly one-third owned only teenagers or children, although it is by no means certain that these slaves resided in their masters' dwellings. Furthermore, fewer than half of the slaveholders had slaves who could be living in some sort of complete family setting, or at least with a mate (by virtue of the age and sex of the slaves they owned), and this probably overestimates the number of slaves living in nuclear-family settings.

by kinship to property holders and could never expect, through the life cycle or inheritance, to attain such independence. Indeed, they were objects in the process of property transmission. The slaves remained permanent, propertyless dependents in a society that looked upon such a status with fear and contempt.[36] Daily discipline might be more relaxed and racial mingling somewhat more egalitarian in the Upcountry, but rumors of slave risings intermittently percolated and brought out the patrols. And a man like David M. Highfield might have rubbed shoulders, socially and economically, with the slaves, but he was indicted for the "offense."[37]

Whether or not they owned slaves, yeoman farmers normally raised more than enough grain and meat for their own sustenance.[38] They certainly did not rely on the small Upcountry stores for essential foodstuffs, buying primarily supplemental items. Local merchants kept stocks of sugar, coffee, and molasses along with shirting, yarn, ribbon, shoes, and hats. They also carried nails, needles, dishes, utensils, paper, pencils, cotton cards, and tobacco. James Wellborn of Jackson County, for example, bought $8.12 of merchandise from Jackson Bell in 1858, including six pounds of coffee, several pounds of tobacco, a hat, a pair of cotton cards, some paper, and two pairs of shoes. In Floyd County, Cicero White purchased hoes, cups, shoes, and sundries worth $24.07 in 1850, while Phillip Barrow of Carroll County ran up a bill of $22.23 at the store of J. Long and Son in 1853 for nails, candles, shirting, and muslin, among other things. When food crops did change hands, it was usually the merchants who took them in as payment, later selling to the neighboring landless or to buyers in larger market towns outside the region.[39]

Thus, if yeoman households tended toward a basic self-sufficiency, it is apparent that self-sufficiency was not simply a household enterprise.

36. Edmund S. Morgan, "Slavery and Freedom: The American Paradox," *JAH*, LIX (June 1972), 5–29; J. Mills Thornton III, *Politics and Power in a Slave Society: Alabama, 1800–1860* (Baton Rouge, 1978), 20–58.

37. Superior Court Minutes, Jackson County, February 1850, August 1850; Cassville *Standard*, August 15, 1860, August 30, 1860.

38. According to a "self-sufficiency index," 74 percent of the slaveless farmers in Jackson and Carroll counties cultivating fewer than 200 improved acres in 1850 raised grain surpluses. See Appendix, Tables V–VI.

39. Court of Ord., Inv. and App., Jackson County, Vol. A, 722; Fain Account Books, Floyd County, 1850, GDAH; Ord. Est. Recs., Inv. and App., Carroll County, Vol. C, 123; Lewis E. Atherton, *The Southern Country Store, 1800–1860* (Baton Rouge, 1949), 71–80.

That yeomen raised surplus cotton and grain and had dealings with merchants nearby suggests that an orientation to subsistence farming and home manufactures did not—and could not—preclude exchange. At issue is the nature and extent of exchange and its social and cultural ramifications. Most Upcountry yeomen participated in a market, but one decidedly local in character and regulated by custom. Although it is difficult to determine the relative importance of custom and circumstance in the formation and vitality of such markets, they had deep roots in rural America and particularly in areas of the South whence came many Upcountry settlers.[40]

Circumstances surely reinforced custom, and the relevant circumstances were those combining to leave the Upcountry on the periphery of the staple economy. The dominant market structures in the antebellum South had their origins in the relations and exigencies of cotton production for export. Large planters shipped their crops to factors in Southern ports or to commission merchants in interior market towns who, in turn, sold it and often purchased supplies needed on the plantations. Yeomen and small planters in the Black Belt who failed to raise sufficient quantities of the staple to make such connections viable, marketed their crops through large plantation owners or small country merchants like William A. Cobb of Thomaston, Georgia. In November 1850, for instance, Cobb bought a bale of cotton from Nathaniel Waller and then resold it.[41] To a lesser extent, small farmers traded with traveling peddlers such as H. Hirschfield, who wended through Jasper County during the late 1850s with "no vis[ible] means but his wagon of goods." Hirschfield fared better than most of his counterparts, for according to an R. G. Dun and Company credit agent, he "seem[ed] to be getting along well." The construction of railroads into the Black Belt in the 1830s and 1840s undermined the position of many other peddlers by extending the factorage system and eventually leading to the rise of itinerant buyers who speculated in cotton with the backing of the factors themselves. While providing planters with an opportunity to strike a

40. Henretta, "Families and Farms," 12–17; John T. Schlotterbeck, "Plantation and Farm: Social and Economic Change in Orange and Greene Counties, Virginia, 1716–1860" (Ph.D. diss., Johns Hopkins University, 1980), 64–68.

41. William A. Cobb Daybooks, Thomaston, Book 5, November 14, 1850, UGa; Harold D. Woodman, *King Cotton and His Retainers: Financing and Marketing the Cotton Crop of the South, 1800–1925* (Lexington, Ky., 1968), 3–71; Atherton, *Southern Country Store*, 45–46, 51, 105.

good bargain or make a quick sale, these speculators also helped draw Black Belt yeomen into the market.[42]

Hilly terrain and a cooler climate weighed against cotton culture in the Upcountry. Home to roughly one-fourth of Georgia's white population in 1850, the region produced less than one-tenth of the state's cotton crop. Marketing of other produce, moreover, was circumscribed both by a trend toward self-sufficiency within the Black Belt and by poor means of transportation linking the two areas. Upcountry grand juries perpetually complained about the "bad order" of county roads which made hauling goods by wagon slow and costly. Journeys to and from towns like Augusta and Columbus could take at least six weeks. Farmers living along major waterways had better luck, but most resided in relatively isolated locales.[43] Conceding that "little has been made in our new country for market," the editor of Rome's *Georgia Courier* saw "the distance to markets" as "the great drawback upon our prosperity," for "the profits of whatever we might make has been consumed in the cost of carriage." A railroad, he believed, would "in great measure" remedy the problem and open up "the interior of the state [to] our excess produce." Yet, except for the state-owned Western and Atlantic, completed in 1850, no rail lines penetrated the Upcountry before the Civil War. And even this project, having won the strong endorsement of Governor Wilson Lumpkin, passed over the opposition of some Black Belt planters who had little desire to subsidize potential competitors and over the objections of representatives from the eastern Upcountry and southeastern Wiregrass and Pine Barrens whose regions would derive scant benefit.[44]

The *Georgia Courier*'s enthusiasm for economic "improvement" was shared by certain groups in other sections of the Upcountry. Throughout the 1850s, wealthy farmers, planters, and merchants in many counties attempted to charter railroad companies and raise stock

42. R. G. Dun and Company, Credit Reporting Ledgers of the Mercantile Agency, Georgia, XII, 58, Baker Library, Harvard University; Woodman, *King Cotton*, 76–97.

43. *Seventh Census*, 210, 216, 367–68; Grand Jury Presentments, Superior Court Minutes, Jackson County, August 1852; Grand Jury Presentments, Superior Court Minutes, Carroll County, April 1857, GDAH; John W. Baker, *History of Hart County* (Atlanta, 1933), 56; Marlin, *History of Cherokee County*, 48.

44. Rome *Georgia Courier*, June 6, 1843, in Ulrich B. Phillips Collection, Box 37, Folder— Cotton, YU; *Journal of the Senate of the State of Georgia* (Milledgeville, 1833), 15–16; *Journal of the House of Representatives of the State of Georgia* (Milledgeville, 1836), 256–58; *Journal of the Senate* (Milledgeville, 1836), 240; Heath, *Constructive Liberalism*, 269.

subscriptions for construction. They pointed to the importance of developing "the agricultural interests and mineral resources of this region" and of "uniting [it] by rail with the principal markets of the State." They also warned representatives from Athens, Augusta, and Savannah that Charleston would tap the trade of northeastern Georgia if they did not act quickly and lend financial assistance to incipient undertakings.[45] Meetings in Jackson, Gwinnett, Franklin, Madison, and Hall counties during this period pressed for feeder lines to Athens or other points on the Georgia Railroad, which ran from Augusta to Atlanta through the northern tier of the Black Belt. The Jackson County planters John Horton, Alfred Brooks, Green R. Duke, Samuel Watson, Madison Strickland, D. M. Burns, and Robert Moon, as well as the merchants William S. Thompson and Jackson Bell, who owned land and slaves themselves, assumed a prominent role in agitating the issue. Similar gatherings in the western Upcountry sought to link their counties with the Western and Atlantic, the Atlanta and LaGrange, or with railroads in Alabama. The Carroll County merchants Appleton Mandeville and John T. Meador, along with the well-to-do planters Zaddock Bonner, his son Thomas, and D. M. Bloodworth, incorporated the Carrollton Railroad Company in 1852.[46] In all, the Georgia legislature chartered seven companies to build railroads in the Upcountry between 1850 and 1860. But few got off the ground and none was completed during the antebellum years.[47]

For one thing, Upcountry railroad promoters had great difficulty raising sufficient capital. Part of the problem was local competition. Many inhabitants initially supported railroad construction, expecting that lines would pass through their towns or districts, and "in view of possible obstacles imposed by conflicting local interests," promoters left "discussion of the precise locality of the road to the future decision of the company."[48] Charters, therefore, often failed to specify routes, and when decisions ultimately came down, disappointed parties backed out.

45. Athens *Southern Banner*, July 20, 1854; Athens *Southern Watchman*, October 7, 1858.

46. Athens *Southern Banner*, May 12, 1853, July 20, 1854, August 17, 1854, October 5, 1854; Rome *Weekly Courier*, February 5, 1852, February 26, 1852, October 26, 1859; Cassville *Standard*, July 9, 1857; Newnan *Independent Blade*, September 30, 1859; *Acts of the General Assembly of the State of Georgia, 1851–1852* (Milledgeville, 1852), 131.

47. *Acts of the General Assembly, 1851–1852*, 121, 130, 148; *Acts of the General Assembly, 1853–1854* (Savannah, 1854), 202–3, 320; *Acts of the General Assembly, 1859* (Milledgeville, 1859), 310–15.

48. Athens *Southern Banner*, September 7, 1854.

Subscribers in Franklin and Hall counties, to cite one example, had been led to believe that the Georgia Air Line Railroad, incorporated in 1856, would run through their counties. A year later they discovered otherwise and met to protest "a great injustice done them by not having their claims fully represented," recommending that no citizens take stock in the road and resolving to discontinue subscription payments unless the railroad was resurveyed "as near as possible to the originally proposed route."[49]

Perhaps more important, many potential supporters of railroad development doubted whether lines could be profitable. "Railroads are not built so much from patriotic motives as for the purpose of making money," one newspaper reminded its readers, "[and] to accomplish this object they must connect some important points of trade, or form a link in the chain of communication." Growing small quantities of cotton, the Upcountry had little to market, for by all indication the Black Belt raised ample foodstuffs. Opinion was, indeed, widespread that northern Georgia "was a bleak and sterile region, not capable of producing much," prompting the Atlanta backers of the Air Line Railroad, in one instance, to repudiate their stock subscriptions and turn their energies to a new enterprise which promised to build westward to Jacksonville, Alabama.[50]

That local men of wealth played leading roles in attempting to stimulate railroad construction should not be surprising; few others had the resources to invest. Yet, proclivity as much as economic status distinguished these promoters. The railroad issue, in fact, hinted at emerging cultural divisions in Upcountry communities, for many eyed the road with suspicion, if not outright hostility. Yeoman farmers, like rural peoples in other traditional settings, did not easily accept the pitch of "economic development," seeming to recognize that its offerings might be less than advantageous. Railroad building could, and did, generate "right of way" controversies; speculative land dealings might lead to dispossession or make it difficult to keep landed property in the family; and increasing attention to market production could well undermine self-sufficiency and independence.[51] As a "Native

49. Ibid., March 12, 1857.

50. *Sunny South*, quoted in Rome *Weekly Courier*, June 10, 1852; Atlanta *American*, quoted in Athens *Southern Banner*, June 23, 1859; Athens *Southern Banner*, July 19, 1860.

51. The construction of a feeder line from Rome to the Western and Atlantic Railroad, for example, led to a growing concentration of wealth in the affected areas of Floyd County. See David Weiman, "Petty Production in the Cotton South: A Study of Upcountry Georgia, 1840–1880" (Ph.D. diss., Stanford University, 1983), chap. 1.

Georgian" thundered: "The people have rights still to be respected and it were better for us to lose the benefits of our railroads than to have those rights trampled upon." "Upon what principle," he asked, "is my land taken and given to a Railroad Company?" Others feared that locomotives would run over their children and livestock, that sparks from engines might set their fields and homes ablaze, and that the noise would frighten horses and disturb the general tranquility. Scattered attacks on railroad property suggest the existence of deep resentments.[52]

And yeomen were not alone in their concern for the consequences of "progress." Small-town merchants who depended on the wagon trade as well as rural craftsmen who supplied the needs of local inhabitants saw the railroad, and the flow of goods and commerce it would bring, as a threat to their livelihoods. Residents of Decatur, a flourishing wagon town near Atlanta, bitterly opposed rail lines and successfully petitioned against granting a right of way through its corporate limits. Apprehensive about the "confusion and bustle which attend those places through and by which [the railroad] passes," the Cassville *Standard* warned that commercialism brought mixed blessings. "Where you see a town possessed of too much of the spirit of enterprise when the resources are too limited to authorize it," the paper remonstrated, "you may set that place down as having attained the zenith of its glory . . . but [it] will remain a monument of . . . folly for succeeding generations." For a great number of farmers, artisans, and shopkeepers, whose interdependencies created complex cultural ties, the railroad loomed as a disrupter of customary relations and values.[53]

Freight rates charged by the Western and Atlantic Railroad, which discriminated against local traffic, further disinclined farmers to the roads and steered them away from shipping crops. Although the Western and Atlantic moved substantial quantities of corn, wheat, and bacon down toward Atlanta, most of it came from Tennessee; Upcountry shipments represented but a small fraction of accessible produce.[54] Such high transportation costs may also have reinforced the

52. Athens *Southern Banner*, January 10, 1850; Joseph B. Mahan, Jr., "A History of Old Cassville, 1833–1864" (M.A. thesis, University of Georgia, 1950), 32–33; Cassville *Standard*, April 15, 1858.

53. Cassville *Standard*, November 22, 1855; Thomas H. Martin, *Atlanta and Its Builders: A Comprehensive History of the Gate City of the South* (Atlanta, 1902), 21–23.

54. In 1860, for instance, the Western and Atlantic Railroad carried 909,991 bushels of corn from Chattanooga to Atlanta, but at least 627,517 bushels (69%) came from Tennessee depots. Furthermore, while the two counties (Cass and Cobb) in which the eight Upcountry depots were located produced 743,447 bushels of corn in that year, only

disposition of yeoman families to provide for themselves by hiking the price of store-bought goods, much to the chagrin of local merchants who did "not do a considerable business." The lack of growth and high turnover rate among mercantile establishments attests to their precarious status and to the general boundaries of economic life. In Carroll County almost half the stores that opened during the 1850s failed to survive until the decade's end, and many had a rather short life span. One Carrollton dry-goods firm started up in 1852 with an inventory worth about $2,000. By 1854 the R. G. Dun and Company credit agent reported that "business [was] not good" and that the firm had "closed up." Another merchant had even worse luck with his small concern at the crossroads hamlet of Liberty Plains, for within a year his "business failed" and he was being "sued a great deal." The total number of storekeepers operating at any one time in Carroll and Jackson counties changed little between 1850 and 1860. Those keeping their heads above water combined farming with trading.[55]

Thus, while yeomen had some contact with more distant markets— selling off small cotton crops and, perhaps, taking surplus produce to Atlanta, Columbus, Athens, and Augusta by way of railroad, wagon, or pole boat[56]—their predominant networks of exchange were local and often skirted merchants. Tiny courthouse towns and hamlets served as the primary marketplaces. However difficult it is to determine just how much a farmer set aside for sale, household and agricultural needs brought all into a complex of trade relations distinguished largely by direct transactions between various producers. Shoemakers, carpenters, blacksmiths, and millers, some of whom owned farms, proffered

45,648 bushels (6.1 % of the total) were shipped. And this is an overestimate of the proportion of accessible produce shipped, since a good many farmers in Paulding and Cherokee counties resided relatively near to the road. See "Principal Articles of Transportation From Stations, Year Ending September 1860," Western and Atlantic Freight and Income Expenses, 1849–1868, GDAH; *Eighth Census*, Agriculture, 23–27.

55. Dun and Company, Credit Ledgers, Georgia, V, 108–9, 111, 113, and generally 101–22. In Jackson County the total number of stores dropped from nineteen to fifteen between 1850 and 1860; in Carroll County the number rose from fourteen to twenty-one. Also see John M. Allman, "Yeoman Regions of the Antebellum Deep South: Settlement and Economy in Northern Alabama, 1815–1860" (Ph.D. diss., University of Maryland, 1979), 270–75.

56. William H. Sims to Stephen D. Heard, Rome, January 28, 1859, Stephen D. Heard Papers, SHC; James Washington Watts Farm Diary, November 3, 1855, James Washington Watts Papers, GDAH; Dun and Company, Credit Ledgers, Georgia, XVI, 104; Baker, *History of Hart County*, 56.

essential goods and services for their neighborhoods.[57] Yeomen raising grain surpluses, moreover, found buyers among landless farmers and laborers and among newly arrived settlers who required provisions until they could plant and harvest their crops. Court days were not reserved exclusively for politics and litigation. Farmers met their neighbors, visited shops, and exchanged the produce they commonly brought to town on their wagons and carts. In Carroll County, husbandmen customarily assembled on the "First Tuesday" of the month to attend public sales, swap horses, and trade other goods.[58]

These local markets were hardly immune from the influence of prices and terms of credit established elsewhere. Merchants, as well as other storekeepers, craftsmen, and farmers, traded in major commercial towns, perhaps as far away as Charleston. "Our streets are again assuming the appearance of business," the Athens *Southern Banner* announced in October 1853, "the up-country wagons are rolling in and the coming fall and winter trade bids fair to be good." More substantial merchants might even travel to Baltimore or New York to purchase their stocks of supplies.[59] But currency always remained scarce in the Upcountry, and communications with larger commercial centers were often circumscribed. The frustration of one Hart County planter, while not that of the less well-to-do, speaks to the point nonetheless. "I was altogether ignorant of the Augusta cotton market," he moaned to his factor who was about to receive a shipment, "as we failed to get our papers (as we frequently do from some unknown cause to us) hence I could not say what I desired in reference to the selling of it. . . ."[60] Such staggered interchange left trade significantly shaped by yearly levels of crop production and local custom, the nature of which will be explored in the next chapter. To the extent that yeomen produced most of what they consumed and supplemented household production with exchange in the community, the market served their interests rather than dominated their lives.

The history of the mass of white farmers throughout the South is

57. Foster and King Mill Account Book, Cherokee County, 1857–1858, GDAH; Job Bowers Account Book, Hart County, 1832–1836, GDAH.

58. Andrews, *Reminiscences*, 73; Bonner, *Georgia's Last Frontier*, 27; Atherton, *Southern Country Store*, 69.

59. Dun and Company, Credit Ledgers, Georgia, XII, 249; Athens *Southern Banner*, October 13, 1853.

60. Richard J. D. Durrett to Simpson and Heard, Hart County, December 6, 1858, Heard Papers.

undeveloped, to say the least. But what little we know suggests that the social and economic experience of yeomen in the Black Belt and Upcountry differed substantially. The predominance of the plantation in major staple-growing areas reduced the size of yeoman farms, at times to the marginal. And there, yeomen appear to have devoted a more considerable portion of their improved acreage to cotton, thereby producing more heavily for external markets. Consequently, many Black Belt yeomen failed to attain the levels of self-sufficiency common to the Upcountry.[61] These divergent economic configurations would have critical implications for the texture of regional social relations and ultimately for political behavior.

IV

Favorable conditions in the cotton market, together with internal improvements, encouraged commercial expansion throughout the Lower South during the 1850s. Population, acres in farms, land and slave values, track mileage, and market production all registered notable increases. Foreshadowing the postbellum era, a trend toward economic integration within the South seemed to be under way.[62] Yet, symptomatic of the different logics of plantation and household economies, the structural gap between Black Belt and Upcountry also widened during the same period. Shifting patterns of land and slaveownership distinguished the regions even more in 1860 than in 1850, with effects both strengthening and weakening the political hegemony of the planter class. The response of Upcountry yeomen to social change sheds added light on their values and aspirations and on emerging contradictions in their society as the antebellum era drew to a close.

61. Weiman, "Petty Production," chap. 1; William Harris, "Cotton in the Georgia Piedmont: A Social History, 1860–1880" (Paper, Johns Hopkins University, 1976), 10–11; Sam B. Hilliard, *Hogmeat and Hoecake: Food Supply in the Old South, 1840–1860* (Carbondale, Ill., 1972), 151; Foust, *Yeoman Farmer*, passim. Gavin Wright has recently argued that small farmers in the Black Belt raised little cotton, and there is no question that the bulk of the cotton crop was produced on plantations. The more detailed work of David Weiman and William Harris on Georgia, however, indicates that relative to their Upcountry counterparts, Black Belt yeomen not only grew more cotton but had a less diversified crop mix. See Wright, *Political Economy of Cotton South*, 55–56.

62. Allman, "Yeoman Regions," 321; Schlotterbeck, "Plantation and Farm," 302–9; Robert W. Fogel and Stanley L. Engerman, *Time on the Cross: The Economics of American Negro Slavery* (Boston, 1974), 59–106.

In the Black Belt, land and slaveholdings became further concentrated. While the very richest planters lost a small share of the total real wealth, substantial landowners made the greatest gains at the expense of poorer farmers and the planting elite.[63] At the same time, the number of large plantations and the proportion of improved acreage they held rose significantly, particularly in South Carolina and Georgia. In 1850, planters owning 500 or more improved acres controlled about 35 percent of all the cropland in the southeastern Black Belt; by 1860 they controlled well over 50 percent. Similar tendencies were evident in the distribution of slaveholdings: the number of nonslaveholders and the number of large slaveholders among the agricultural population both increased during the 1850s, with the wealthiest landowners enlarging their share of the black labor force. Although developments in the more recently settled states of Alabama, Mississippi, Louisiana, and Texas proved somewhat less favorable to the big planters, for the staple-producing region as a whole the gulf between rich and poor, between planter and yeoman, widened.[64]

A different portrait emerges for the Upcountry. Among those engaged principally in farming, the percentage of landowners remained reasonably stable. In both sample counties, roughly seven of these household heads in ten owned land in 1850 and 1860. For the entire free population, however, real-property ownership broadened considerably. In 1860 more than six of ten household heads possessed real estate, a marked jump over the ten-year period.[65] While it is difficult to know with certainty, a relative decline in tenancy also appears to have taken place, though the institution retained more importance in western Carroll County, where settlement had not begun until the third decade

63. Wright, *Political Economy of Cotton South*, 30; Wiener, *Social Origins*, 15; Fabian Linden, "'Economic Democracy' in the Slave South: An Appraisal of Some Recent Views," *JNH*, XXXI (April 1946), 140–89.

64. Foust, *Yeoman Farmer*, 106, 110, 128, 131; Wright, *Political Economy of Cotton South*, 29–37.

65. Thus, in Jackson County the percentage of real-property owners among those reporting agricultural occupations grew from 70.9 percent to 71.7 percent between 1850 and 1860, while the percentage of real-property owners among all household heads grew from 58 percent to 66.9 percent. In Carroll County the percentage of real-property owners declined from 70.2 percent to 66.4 percent among those reporting agricultural occupations but increased from 59.8 percent to 64.4 percent among all household heads. Manuscript Census, Georgia, Jackson and Carroll Counties, Schedule I, 1850, 1860.

of the nineteenth century and where a great deal of land was still unimproved.[66]

Like their counterparts in the Black Belt, the richest Upcountry planters saw part of their share of real wealth slip away over the course of the 1850s. But the redistribution was more extensive in the Upcountry: the entire top quarter of real-property owners lost ground, to the advantage of the second and third quarters. The poorest farmers made gains as well, albeit minimal ones (see Table 1.4). A similar pattern is to be found in slaveownership. No dramatic alterations in the proportion of slaveholders occurred, but among them the percentage of households owning between two and four slaves increased substantially, at the expense of smaller and larger units. Fewer slaveowners with fifteen or more slaves and fewer with only one slave appeared in 1860 than in 1850. This was due, in part, to the natural increase of the black population; to inheritance, which broke up large holdings; to the geographical mobility of some big slaveholders, who may have moved to more economically promising locales; and to additional purchasing among smallholders. John Magarity of Carroll County, master to one slave in 1850, for example, owned three in 1860. And the trend was replicated among farmers alone, where the number of small slave-owners increased and that of large slaveowners decreased. In Jackson County, residence of quite a few planters in 1850, the decline was particularly impressive.[67]

If plantations dominated the Black Belt to an even greater extent in 1860 than in 1850, their role in the economic life of the Upcountry receded. By the eve of the Civil War, small farms had grown in number and come to control most of the region's cropland (see Table 1.5). In 1850 almost half the improved acreage in Jackson County and well over half in Carroll County lay in farms containing fewer than 200 improved

66. By a generous estimate of possible tenants (landless "farmers" appearing on the agricultural schedule with acreage and crops plus 70 percent of those who did not appear), the proportion of tenants in the agricultural population of Jackson County declined from about 18 percent to about 8 percent between 1850 and 1860, as the percentage of landless "farmers" in the agricultural population declined from about 25 percent to about 10 percent. In Carroll County a similar estimate would leave the proportion of tenants in the agricultural population relatively unchanged during the 1850s, but significantly, whereas about 70 percent of the landless "farmers" appeared on the agricultural schedule with only crops in 1850, just 18 percent did in 1860. It is, therefore, likely that tenancy declined somewhat in Carroll County as well. Also see Appendix, Table I.

67. Appendix, Table III.

Table 1.4 Distribution of Real Wealth Among Real-Property Owners, Jackson and Carroll Counties, 1850–1860 (by Decile of Real Wealth)

Rank	Jackson County			Carroll County		
	Value 1860	Share 1860	Change 1850–60	Value 1860	Share 1860	Change 1850–60
Top Decile	$198,828	39.1 %	−2.3 %	$185,788	42.0 %	−11.2 %*
Second Decile	88,484	17.4	−2.4	73,975	16.6	+ 1.8
Third Decile	60,055	11.8	+0.6	48,700	11.0	+ 1.4
Fourth Decile	44,700	8.8	+1.4	36,800	8.3	+ 1.7
Fifth Decile	34,700	6.8	+0.3	28,175	6.4	+ 1.4
Sixth Decile	28,920	5.7	+1.2	23,250	5.3	+ 1.7
Seventh Decile	21,705	4.3	+0.7	18,271	4.2	+ 1.1
Eighth Decile	15,790	3.1	+0.3	13,782	3.1	+ 1.0
Ninth Decile	10,727	2.1	+0.2	8,900	2.0	+ 0.6
Tenth Decile	4,621	0.9	+0.0	4,821	1.1	+ 0.5
Total	$508,530	100.0 %		$442,462	100.0 %	
Number	299			279		

* The decline in the share of real wealth for the top decile in Carroll County is inordinately large because of an exaggeration in the 1850 distribution. The distribution for 1860 appears to be more accurate, as the figures for Jackson County indicate.

Source: Manuscript Census, Georgia, Jackson and Carroll Counties, Schedule I, 1850, 1860.

acres. Ten years later, these farms embraced about three-fourths of the improved acreage in both counties and produced an increasing proportion of the grain and cotton crops.[68] Though large farms and plantations continued to hold a disproportionate share of land, slaves, and livestock, and though they continued to produce a disproportionate share of food and fiber, their shares declined. During the 1850s the Upcountry became more of a yeoman stronghold.

Certain links between Upcountry and Black Belt helped bridge the widening social and economic divide and extend the political influence of the planter class. The relatively broad distribution of landed property and the availability of slave labor in the Upcountry were especially important in giving yeomen a stake in the slave regime. Furthermore, a small but steady stream of migrants filtered into northern Georgia from the plantation districts, some of whom boasted considerable wealth.

68. See above, Table 1.3. For more detailed statistics, see Hahn, "Roots of Southern Populism," 422–23.

Table 1.5 Distribution of Farms and Improved Acreage, Jackson and Carroll Counties, 1850–1860

Farm Size (Imp. Acres)	Jackson County				Carroll County			
	1850		1860		1850		1860	
	% Farms	% Imp. Acres	% Farms	% Imp. Acres	% Farms	% Imp. Acres	% Farms	% Imp. Acres
1–24	0.6	0.1	8.0	1.7	31.6	7.8	11.6	2.6
25–49	12.9	3.1	31.7	14.2	28.8	18.1	35.8	18.1
50–99	28.8	13.3	34.2	29.4	22.5	26.4	32.4	31.5
100–199	34.4	31.2	18.9	28.9	12.5	26.1	15.0	27.2
200–299	12.3	20.1	3.2	8.7	2.9	11.4	3.9	11.7
300–499	6.1	14.5	4.0	17.1	1.7	10.2	0.9	5.3
500+	4.9	17.7	—	—	—	—	0.4	3.6
Total	100.0	100.0	100.0	100.0	100.0	100.0	100.0	100.0
Number	163 Farms	23,215 Acres	249 Farms	18,868 Acres	240 Farms	13,185 Acres	207 Farms	13,524 Acres

Source: Manuscript Census, Georgia, Jackson and Carroll Counties, Schedule II, 1850, 1860.

Thus, G. A. McDaniel resided in Elbert and Spalding counties before relocating during the early 1850s to Carroll, where he owned a good many acres and slaves.[69] Finally, more than a handful of Upcountry inhabitants had landed interests in the Black Belt, particularly in the rapidly developing counties of southwest Georgia. N. H. Pendergrass, for one, owned 250 acres in Jackson County as well as a 200-acre lot in Stewart County.[70]

Other emerging regional links eventually proved less conducive to social and political harmony, and none was more significant than the extension of cotton culture in the counties bordering the Western and Atlantic Railroad and throughout the western Upcountry in general. During the 1850s, staple production nearly doubled in Paulding, Heard, Cass, Campbell, and Carroll counties, and in Floyd County, where Rome was located, it nearly quadrupled.[71] The Rome *Weekly Courier* pointed approvingly to the large number of bales shipped in 1852 and predicted more business for the next year. By 1859 a correspondent for the *Southern Cultivator* could speak of the "fiery trail of the cotton plant" between Rome and its rail link to the Western and Atlantic. Small farmers and large took part in what appeared to be something of a cotton boom. In 1850 fewer than half of Carroll County yeomen raised cotton for sale; a decade later more than three-quarters did.[72]

Greater access to transportation networks and rising cotton prices, along with the very dynamics of the household economy, help explain the surge in cotton cultivation. It did not reflect a shift away from the customary "security first" orientation. Emphasizing the minimal impact

69. Southern Historical Association, *Memoirs of Georgia*, 2 vols. (Atlanta, 1895), I, 432–33; II, 431. The overwhelming majority of land transactions during the 1850s, however, involved only county residents. See Superior Court Deeds and Mortgages, Jackson County, Vols. M–N, P–Q, GDAH; Superior Court Deeds and Mortgages, Carroll County, Vols. F, I, GDAH.

70. Jackson County Tax Digests, 1850, 1859, GDAH. Among those Jackson County residents listed on the tax rolls in 1850, 169 owned land in other counties and, of them, 79, or almost half, owned land in the Black Belt. In 1859, 116 Jackson County taxpayers owned land in other counties, 43 of them in the Black Belt. There are no extant tax records for Carroll County during this period.

71. *Seventh Census*, 210–16; *Eighth Census*, Agriculture, 23–27. Total cotton production for these counties in 1850 was 13,467 bales; in 1860 it was 29,535 bales. But even in 1860, Upcountry cotton production paled in comparison with that of the Black Belt.

72. Rome *Weekly Courier*, June 10, 1852; *Southern Cultivator*, quoted in Rome *Weekly Courier*, October 12, 1859; Appendix, Table II.

of soil exhaustion in the Upcountry, a Georgia statistician concluded that a farmer could produce almost two bales per acre. Although this estimate probably exaggerated yields for all save the best lands, it indicated that smallholders could raise a few bales of cotton without jeopardizing their general self-sufficiency. Substantial yeomen might grow even more. And a report issued in 1857 by the Cass County Agricultural Society, a planter club, seemed to highlight the reluctance of many farmers to shift their energies to the market. Summarily dismissing the claim that "Cherokee Georgia" was "not a cotton country," it declared that cotton culture, the "most important branch of agriculture," should be "impressed upon the Southern people" because it "aids in the extension of civilization." Ridiculing fears about oversupply and challenging the cant of those who warned about the perils of monoculture, the society implored farmers "to extend the cotton planting area . . . until every foot of land throughout the cotton growing region shall be brought into cultivation."[73]

Yeomen apparently needed to be "impressed" with the "civilizing" influence of full-scale commercial agriculture, for however much aggregate cotton production rose, they continued to devote by far the greater portion of their cropland to foodstuffs and most continued to raise small grain surpluses. The overall crop mix did undergo some alteration, as yeomen raised larger quantities of wheat and fewer bushels of corn, oats, and sweet potatoes.[74] Doubtless related to this development, they had fewer head of livestock in 1860 than in 1850. The decline in the number of hogs and cattle on farms containing under 200 improved acres was considerable, and while smallholders still had sheep, here too the number fell, to which a concurrent drop in the value of household manufactures may partly be attributed.[75] But these trends were not peculiar to the counties affected by the expansion of cotton culture; they were evident throughout the Upcountry and reflected a process inherent in the region and the household economy—declining yields and the subdivision of farms—which spelled serious long-term

73. White, *Statistics of Georgia*, 147; Cassville *Standard*, January 8, 1857.

74. The increased production of wheat (which normally was planted in the fall and winter months) may have been part of an effort to compensate for the lower production of corn and sweet potatoes (which were planted in the early spring and thus shared a growing season with cotton). But it is worth noting that 1850 was a bad year for wheat in the South, so that the larger output in 1860 may have reflected a better harvest rather than expanded cultivation.

75. Appendix, Tables V–VI.

consequences. General farming remained dominant. Increasing attention to cotton in some areas simply did not transform the lives of most
yeoman farmers. In this way, the yeomanry of the western Upcountry
continued to share an experience common in the eastern Upcountry,
where cotton production had stabilized at a rather low level.[76]

Geography and limited economic horizons clearly had roles in
shaping yeoman priorities. A hilly terrain and cooler climate made
extensive cotton cultivation difficult without the aid of fertilizers, and
until transportation facilities became more widely available, access to
the market would be circumscribed. That many smallholders looked
upon railroad construction with jaundiced eyes and evinced little
inclination to avail themselves of commercial fertilizers, however,
suggests that the obstacles to staple agriculture ran deeper. The
prospects for amassing considerable wealth could not have appeared
encouraging. Only a handful of Upcountry Georgians had large land
and slaveholdings and, with rare exception, even they did not measure
up to the stature of Black Belt planters. "Rags-to-riches" stories,
moreover, were in decidedly short supply. In Carroll County, farmers
persisting from one census year to the next occasionally acquired
additional land and perhaps a slave or two, but virtually none did well
enough to become planters. The number of plantation-size units, in
fact, declined during the decade.[77] In a society in which families were
large, manual labor a necessity for almost all, and freehold independence a mark of status, acquisitiveness had its own rationale. Unlike
their counterparts in the Black Belt, for whom the planter frequently
served as the social ideal, Upcountry yeomen seemed to opt for the
safety of diversified agriculture rather than risk the uncertainties of the
export market.

Indeed, Upcountry yeomen may have viewed a cash crop, especially
with high cotton prices during the 1850s, as a convenient means of
establishing themselves in general farming, acquiring material comforts, and accumulating property to pass on to their children and

76. Ibid.; *Seventh Census*, 210–16; *Eighth Census*, 23–27.

77. In Jackson County, farms containing 300 or more improved acres accounted for 11
percent of all farms in 1850 but for only 4 percent of all farms in 1860. In Carroll County,
farms with 300 or more improved acres accounted for less than 2 percent of all farms in
both census years. See above, Table 1.4. The mobility findings for Carroll County are
based on a survey which took the entire sample for 1850 and traced it through to 1860,
using an alphabetized list of slaveholders for the latter year in Bonner, *Georgia's Last
Frontier*, 204–12.

thereby reproduce their experience. An unusual case may help illustrate the point. Hamilton Hogan, a nonslaveholder, had a 200-acre farm in Carroll County in 1850. At that time he cultivated only sixteen acres and planted most of it in cotton—exceptional for the year and area—producing thirteen bales and a scant thirty bushels of corn. Perhaps he hoped to pay off a mortgage on his farm or purchase a slave, which he did. Yet he was no budding entrepreneur. While he tripled his cropland by 1860, he reduced his cotton crop by more than half and turned primarily to the cultivation of corn, oats, wheat, and sweet potatoes. Few farmers made such a dramatic transition, but numbers appear to have followed the general pattern. Elisha Bailey of Jackson County, for example, working twenty-two acres as a tenant with the assistance of one slave in 1850, raised a little cotton. During the 1850s he managed to buy a ninety-acre farm, but grew only food crops in 1860. More generally, an age profile of yeomen who grew cotton and those who did not shows the latter to be older than the former.[78] In the absence of an exploitative credit system oriented to commercial agriculture, farmers could enter and withdraw from the cotton market with relative ease. And apparently they did.

Yeomen beginning to cultivate cotton or enlarging their output during the 1850s may have done so for similar reasons. Land values climbed in the Upcountry. Real estate selling for a dollar or two an acre in 1850 often sold for five or six dollars an acre ten years later. Population growth, farm improvements, and possibly the expectation of a railroad may account for such a trend even in an area minimally touched by commercial farming.[79] Property accumulation offering added security for the household and for the children thus increasingly required a cash crop.

That the effort to maintain their independence, to avoid subjection to, as one farmer put it, the "fluctuations of commerce," led many yeomen into the market signaled developing contradictions not simply

78. Hamilton Hogan in Manuscript Census, Georgia, Carroll County, Schedule II, 1850, 1860; Elisha Baily in ibid., Jackson County. Farmers cultivating fewer than 200 improved acres and growing cotton in Jackson and Carroll counties averaged forty-five years of age; those not growing cotton averaged forty-seven years of age. But for farmers cultivating fewer than 50 improved acres, the average ages were forty-one and forty-six respectively. For a more detailed breakdown, see Hahn, "Roots of Southern Populism," 427.

79. For land values, see Superior Court Deeds and Mortgages, Jackson County, Vols. M–N, P–Q; ibid., Carroll County, Vols, F, I.

between the household economy and "external forces" but within the household economy itself.[80] A growing population gradually pressed the resources of Upcountry farm families. While the free population increased by almost one-fourth between 1850 and 1860, the number of acres in farms increased by less than one-fifth; the average size of yeoman farms declined from 240 to 198 acres, or by nearly 20 percent.[81] If not of crisis proportions, these contradictions intensified as land values rose and fewer farm units could be parceled out viably among several heirs. And they left the household economy vulnerable when the structure and relations of staple farming changed in the postwar era.

The contradictions emerged, however, in a society that had a logic and resiliency rooted, not only in geographical isolation, but in a complex of social relations which served as the foundation of a broad cultural, as well as economic, experience: ownership of productive resources, control over farming operations, reliance on household labor, an emphasis on family self-sufficiency, and a distinctive sort of contact with the marketplace. Thus, Upcountry yeomen shared something with small producers in the preindustrial North and with peasantries in certain areas of the world.[82] And their culture found further vitality in a constellation of relations and customs that governed the workings of the market and other spheres of social life, mediating inherent tensions, reaffirming an intricate set of values, and providing means for the reproduction of a historical experience.

80. Cassville *Standard*, November 26, 1857.

81. *Seventh Census*, 210–16, 367–68; *Eighth Census*, Population, 72–73, Agriculture, 22–29; Manuscript Census, Georgia, Jackson and Carroll Counties, Schedule II, 1850, 1860.

82. Merrill, "Cash Is Good to Eat," 42–66; Clark, "Household Economy," 169–89; Henretta, "Families and Farms," 11–32; Clarence H. Danhof, *Change in Agriculture: The Northern United States, 1820–1870* (Cambridge, Mass., 1969), 1–48; Teodor Shanin, "The Nature and Logic of the Peasant Economy," *Journal of Peasant Studies*, I (October 1973), 67, 74; Harriet Friedmann, "Household Production and the National Economy: Concepts for the Analysis of Agrarian Formations," *Journal of Peasant Studies*, VII (January 1980), 158–84.

2

Bounds of Custom

I

When yeoman farmers came to the Georgia Upcountry, they brought
more than their families, furnishings, farm implements, livestock, and
land titles. They also brought distinct notions and understandings
about the dynamics of production, exchange, and social interaction—
about social relations and community. Patterns of migration and
settlement, of working the land, of defining property rights, and of
facing one another in the marketplace sprouted from a soil nourished by
rich historical traditions. In short, farmers brought cultural as well as
material resources. These were not entirely specific to the region; in
many respects they were shared by small farmers throughout preindustrial America, giving early popular appeal to a republican
ideology that associated freedom and independence with landownership. In the South, slavery itself strengthened claims to this cultural
baggage, not only by serving as a stark reminder of the consequences of
dependency, but also by limiting the development of directly exploitative, market relations between whites.[1]

1. On slavery's role in shaping white class relations and attitudes, see Edmund S.
Morgan, *American Slavery, American Freedom: The Ordeal of Colonial Virginia* (New York,

Yet, as the South spawned an increasingly dual economy and social structure, the cultural formations diverged as well. There was, in an important sense, more than one yeomanry. In the staple-producing areas, planter and plantation shaped the landscape and the texture of social relations. If, as Frederick Law Olmsted insisted, many of the Big Houses "belonged to men who had come into the country with nothing within twenty years," the road to wealth and refinement took these men far from their humble roots and symbolized possibilities even as it narrowed over time.[2] The propensity of Black Belt yeomen to participate in the cotton economy reflected, at least in part, shared aspirations. And the exigencies of staple agriculture encouraged dependence on local planters for a variety of services. Few small farmers could afford cotton gins or raise enough cotton to sustain direct links with factors in Southern ports. Hence, they turned to wealthy planters who would gin and market their crop for a reasonable fee, or sold the cotton to mercantile establishments nearby, often owned or backed by the planters themselves. Such attention to cotton culture, moreover, left some Black Belt yeomen with food shortages while the planters normally had surpluses. Yeomen might then rely on well-to-do neighbors for essential supplies.[3] These class relations had explosive qualities, particularly as the prospects for mobility grew dim,[4] but along with ties of kinship they also pulled yeoman farmers into the economic and cultural orbit of the planter class, bolstering the planters politically.

The experience of Hancock County's Benton Miller is illustrative. Marriage in 1858 to Matilda Womble, daughter of a wealthy slaveholder, brought Miller three slaves and an eighty-five acre farm,

1976), 295–387; J. Mills Thornton III, *Politics and Power in a Slave Society: Alabama, 1800–1860* (Baton Rouge, 1978); James McGowan, "Planters Without Slaves: Origins of a New World Labor System," *Southern Studies*, XVI (Fall 1977), 5–26.

2. Frederick Law Olmsted, *The Cotton Kingdom: Traveler's Observations on Cotton and Slavery in the American Slave States* 2 vols. (New York, 1861), II, 59.

3. Eugene D. Genovese, "Yeoman Farmers in a Slaveholders' Democracy," *AH*, XLIX (April 1975), 336–38; Sam B. Hilliard, *Hogmeat and Hoecake: Food Supply in the Old South, 1840–1860* (Carbondale, Ill., 1972), 151; Robert Gallman, "Self-Sufficiency in the Cotton Economy of the Antebellum South," *AH*, XLIV (January 1970), 5–23. The mercantile credit ledgers compiled by the R. G. Dun and Company show that many Black Belt firms had active or "silent" planter partners.

4. For examples of class antagonisms, see the recollections of ex-slaves in George P. Rawick, ed., *The American Slave: A Composite Autobiography*, 19 vols. (Westport, Conn., 1972), VII, 354; XVIII, 215; XV (2), 273–4, 319; XVII, 13, 328.

and enabled him to "plant cotton for myself . . . [for] the first time,"
thereby "making a commencement in life." Miller worked in the fields
with his slaves but could always depend on his father-in-law, who lived
close by, to lend a hand when extra labor was needed. On one occasion,
"Mr. Womble sent all of his hoe gang over . . . to help me finish
chopping [cotton] the first time and we got don." Another substantial
slaveowner, a Mr. Harrison, gave Miller access to additional slave labor
and paid for his subscription to the *Southern Countryman*. In return,
Miller did odd jobs for his neighbors or kin, or lent them his own slaves.
Thus, on November 27, 1858, "Harry and Clark went to Mr. Wombles
to pay back Lige's time." Several days later, "Harry [was] at Mr.
Harrison's [killing hogs]." Miller raised eleven bales of cotton that year
and hoped to double his output the next. Womble and Harrison set the
social standard for Miller and many of his counterparts.[5]

Such patterns could, of course, be found in areas like the Upcountry
where some planters and large slaveholding farmers shared the outlook
and affected the style of their class in the plantation districts. And these
wealthy landowners would exert an important political influence. But
narrower economic horizons, a less significant concentration of wealth,
and a much smaller slave population in the Upcountry diminished the
planters' social and economic power. Resident yeomen, therefore, were
able to plant and nurture a more distinctive culture of their own, whose
features raise serious questions about the conventional image of rural
folk. For although the organization of production on yeoman farms—
based on the household and fee-simple landownership—fostered the
bourgeois traits of individualism, acquisitiveness, and deep adherence
to private property, the Upcountry's economy and society circumscribed their development and generated strong countervailing tendencies. Indeed, the independence to which Upcountry yeomen
aspired hinged on social ties, on "habits of mutuality" among
producers, that imparted to their culture a communal, prebourgeois
quality whose egalitarian proclivities sharply distinguished it from that
of the planters.

II

Upcountry farmers did not live in closed corporate villages, as did
peasantries in certain areas of the world. The system of land distribution
had more of a scattering effect on residences and farms. But neither did

5. Benton H. Miller Farm Journal, Hancock County, 1858–1859, GDAH.

settlement lead to the proliferation of isolated homesteads. Settlers normally migrated with neighbors or kin, partly to mitigate the hardships, dangers, and loneliness of frontier life. At times, they were bound together by religious or ethnic ties, and they tended to search out locales with familiar terrain and soil types, thereby reproducing their previous social and economic experience.[6] "[F]rom earliest settlement the community idea was highly developed," an Upcountry inhabitant recalled in a fit of romantic fancy that made a point nonetheless. "[T]hese pioneers grouped themselves into 'settlements' whose motto might well have been 'one for all and all for one.'"[7]

Families seemed particularly inclined to locate near one another. At least a quarter of the farmers in any district, in fact, would have one or more neighboring relatives. Thus, Hugh McElhannon, who owned $1,200 of real estate and three slaves in Jackson County in 1850, was in good company. Living close by were Hezekiel McElhannon, owner of two slaves and real estate worth $1,000; the widow Elizabeth McElhannon, left slaveless with $300 of real property; John McElhannon, a landless farmer; and Frederick McElhannon, a propertyless laborer. A short distance away were Steward McElhannon, a more substantial farmer and master to two slaves, and William McElhannon, a nonslaveholder with $400 in real estate.[8] On occasion, bonds of kinship embraced a considerable spectrum of wealth. William Park, also of Jackson County, owned $8,000 of land and twenty slaves in 1850. In the neighborhood were the relatives Garrett W. and William M. Park, both laborers; Garrett D. Park, a slaveless yeoman; and

6. Frank L. Owsley, *Plain Folk of the Old South* (Baton Rouge, 1949), 50–77; John M. Allman, "Yeoman Regions in the Antebellum Deep South: Settlement and Economy in Northern Alabama, 1815–1860" (Ph.D. diss., University of Maryland, 1979), 92–110, 162; Robert W. Ramsay, *Carolina Cradle: Settlement of the Northwest Carolina Frontier, 1747–1762* (Chapel Hill, 1964).

7. Judge William A. Covington, quoted in Rev. Lloyd G. Marlin, *A History of Cherokee County* (Atlanta, 1932), 83.

8. Manuscript Census, Georgia, Jackson County, Schedule I, 1850. This description is based on proximity of names in the population schedule of the census. Hugh, Hezekiel, Elizabeth, Frederick, and John McElhannon, all household heads, thus appear on pages 16 and 17; Steward and William McElhannon are on pages 8 and 23 respectively. Using the 1860 census, which breaks counties down by militia district, I found that as many as 35 percent of the farm operators shared surnames with at least one other farm operator in the same district. Although it is by no means certain that individuals with the same surname were related, the figure is probably an underestimate since it does not include relatives with different surnames.

Robert G. Park, a farmer who probably worked the planter William's land with the aid of four slaves. In the same county but in another locale lived William J. and Robert Park, a miller and carpenter respectively, neither of whom owned real estate. Doubtless some of these relatives would inherit property when William died.[9] More often than not, however, Upcountry families did not contain members who could be considered planters.

Sound reason steered kin to settle in the same vicinity if possible. Life held many uncertainties in the Upcountry, as it did in other rural areas during the nineteenth century. Sickness was common, droughts, floods, and windstorms jeopardized crops and property, and labor needs, especially in regions with relatively few slaves, exceeded available household supply at several points during the year. Neighboring kinfolk, whether or not they owned slaves, could lend a hand and, perhaps, make the difference between subsistence and want. When family did not reside nearby, yeomen reached out to other farmers in the area, creating bonds of community even when homes were dispersed. "In the tasks of the individual citizen which transcended his powers," Judge William Alonzo Covington of Cherokee County declared, "the neighbors were called in to help." Indeed, according to Hiram Bell, who lived in Jackson County, "each neighborhood had its circle of fifteen or twenty" ready to be summoned. Some of these occasions, such as logrollings, corn shuckings, and house-raisings, are familiar to rural lore. But they were not merely sporadic affairs confined to a single farm.[10]

Logrollings, for example, which occurred during the winter and early spring, took place in a series until the logs on every neighbor's farm were piled. So with many other chores, for cooperative patterns of work formed an integral part of productive organization. "Farmers swapped work so that families could work together and enjoy the company," Jess Hudgins, also of Cherokee County, wrote. "If Willis Howell's fodder was ready to pull before Ernest Cowart's both families pulled fodder together on the Howell farm . . . [and] after a farmer gathered his corn, he invited his neighbors to come to a corn shucking." When hardship or calamity struck, relief, too, was a local enterprise. As Hudgins put it, "All the charity in the settlement came from friends and neighbors." He

9. Manuscript Census, Georgia, Jackson County, Schedule I, 1850, 15, 21–2, 51, 60.

10. Covington, quoted in Marlin, *History of Cherokee County*, 83; Hiram P. Bell, *Men and Things* (Atlanta, 1907), 6.

told of one incident when lightning killed a farmer's two cows and the neighbors took up a collection and bought him two more. If a family's home, furniture, or barn burned, "the neighbors came bearing gifts, food, dishes and clothes and quilts and even furniture. They contributed logs and lumber, helped to rebuild the house and barn, and brought wagon loads of fodder to feed the stock." "Borrowing . . . was 'neighboring,'" Hudgins proclaimed, adding that "it was a long trip to the store and often a family had no money and nothing to barter."[11]

In some cases, as in the Black Belt, social custom and economic necessity brought Upcountry yeomen into quasi-dependent relations with planters. Thomas Maguire, who owned 950 acres and twenty-six slaves in Gwinnett County during the 1850s, served as captain of his militia district and local postmaster and was frequently called upon to act as an appraiser of estates and to draw up deeds and wills for his less literate neighbors. Maguire also had a threshing machine and a cotton gin to which farmers brought their crops for a toll.[12] Living near the Western and Atlantic Railroad in Cass County, James Washington Watts performed similar services for the yeomen Elijah Johnson, Samuel Lockridge, and John McKelvey. By early August 1854, for example, Watts had received fifty-four and three-quarters bushels of wheat "by threshing for toll." In addition, he marketed some of the cotton he ginned, as on November 3, 1855, when he "went to Cartersville in the morning and sold 2 bales of cotton for Joseph Smith to Robert Towers for $7\frac{1}{4}$ ¢ per pound." Watts "kept $14.94 for toll, bacon, and the am[oun]t of an order I gave him last summer."[13]

These relations were most common in sections of the Upcountry such as southeastern Carroll County, bordering the Chattahoochee River, where the highest concentrations of slaves and cotton production could be found.[14] But for many yeomen, reliance on large slaveholding

11. Hudgins, quoted in Floyd C. Watkins and Charles H. Watkins, *Yesterday in the Hills* (Chicago, 1963), 103–4. Also see Rebecca Latimer Felton, *Country Life in Georgia in the Days of My Youth* (Atlanta, 1919), 52–53; Owsley, *Plain Folk*, 104–17.

12. Thomas Maguire Farm Journal, Gwinnett County, 1859, 1861, Thomas Maguire Family Papers, AHS.

13. James Washington Watts Farm Diary, Cass County, 1854–1855, James Washington Watts Papers, GDAH. Johnson, Lockridge, and McKelvey owned $1,000, $500, and $800 of real estate respectively in 1850. Joseph Smith was a farmer and blacksmith with $300 in real estate. See Manuscript Census, Georgia, Cass County, Schedule I, 1850.

14. James C. Bonner, *Georgia's Last Frontier: The Development of Carroll County* (Athens, 1971), 39.

farmers and planters was neither extensive, feasible, nor necessary. Plantation-size units were few and far between. Small farmers grew little for supralocal markets and generally managed to raise sufficient grain and meat for home consumption. They could also turn to neighboring millers, blacksmiths, carpenters, shoemakers, and merchants for various supplies and services, and when harvesting required equipment like threshers, neighbors might arrange to rent them collectively.[15]

Community standards and interdependencies governed other relations of production. Many yeomen employed white labor, usually for short stints and specific tasks, to supplement the work force provided by family and neighbors. Nathaniel Reinhardt of Cherokee County remembered one year when his father "made a large crop of corn [and] hired a great deal of work done on the farm." Some of these laborers were freeholders themselves attempting to make ends meet or raise extra cash to pay taxes or purchase goods; many were sons of farmers who worked for others in the hope of eventually acquiring farms or as they waited to inherit them. Twenty-three-year-old Thomas J. Stapler, for instance, was a laborer in 1850. His father, Thomas L. Stapler, owned $1,500 of real estate. Ten years later, Thomas J. farmed land worth $200. For their services, laborers received payment in cash or kind at a customary rate equivalent to about fifty cents per day. Thus, when a Gwinnett County landowner hired a hand for eleven and one-half days in the spring of 1856, he paid $5.75.[16] Furthermore, yeomen occasionally boarded laborers or children who did farm chores in return for food, clothing, and schooling. Almost one yeoman household in ten included such persons, suggesting additional ways in which Upcountry settlements allocated labor, took charge of the offspring of poorer neighbors and kin, and cared for orphans.[17]

Hiring of slaves offered yeomen another source of labor and provided further links among Upcountry whites while strengthening the

15. Federal Writers' Project, "Folklore: Wheat Threshing," Folder 24, Reel 2, 280, University of North Carolina Library.

16. "Diary of Nathaniel Reinhardt," in Marlin, *History of Cherokee County*, 51; George B. Hudson Store and Farm Account Book, Gwinnett County, 1856, Mrs. Don G. Aiken Collection, GDAH; Manuscript Census, Georgia, Jackson County, Schedule I, 1850, 1860.

17. Manuscript Census, Georgia, Jackson and Carroll Counties, Schedule I, 1850, 1860; Superior Court Writs, Carroll County, April 1853, 32–34, CCC. About 7 percent of the yeoman households had farm laborers, and if children with different surnames are added, the figure comes closer to 10 percent.

"peculiar institution." It is difficult to tell how extensive the practice was. Few localities could boast either large numbers of slaveowners or large numbers of slaves: in Carroll County, six of thirteen militia districts averaged under one slave per household in 1860.[18] Much of the evidence for hiring, moreover, comes from wealthier slaveowners like James Washington Watts. In March 1854, Watts "sent Jerry to help Alex P. Millain roll logs." Several months later he "sent two hands to help Dr. Young put in a fish trap" and received "$65 [from Dr. Anderson] to pay the hire of the girl Dorces belonging to my sister." Thomas Maguire, the Gwinnett County planter, reported in 1861 that "Albert [had] gone to help Mr. Campbell pick cotton." But some smaller farmers seem to have hired out their slaves, as Milton Wood, who owned $600 worth of land in Jackson County, did in 1859. M. Charles had the services of Wood's "Negro man Matt" for $20.10; Terrea and Will, both "Negro boys," worked for John C. Bramlett for $15; and D. S. Jarrett hired Wood's "Negro girl Nina" for $11.05.[19] Yeoman slaveholders also brought their slaves to corn shuckings, logrollings, and other community gatherings associated with farming, where nonslaveholders reaped the benefit of black labor free of charge.

Relations such as these did not prove to be the sinews of tightly knit, harmonious communities, whatever nostalgic reminiscences might suggest. A considerable level of geographical mobility circumscribed cohesiveness and pointed to limited opportunities and difficult times for numerous denizens. Personal conflicts often erupted as well. In 1847, for example, David Blalock of Carroll County sent his son Thomas to Zion Cantrell's farm, where he was to work for "$5 per month in schooling or clothing or in money." Cantrell apparently failed to live up to his end of the bargain, for in 1853 Blalock brought suit for $300.[20] County court records were cluttered with cases of a similar sort, unavoidable manifestations of the tensions within Upcountry society: the corporate and the individualistic, self-subsistence and the market,

18. Jackson County had a greater average number of slaves per household, but the number was small nevertheless: five of twelve districts had fewer than two slaves per household, while ten of twelve districts had fewer than three. Manuscript Census, Georgia, Jackson and Carroll Counties, Schedules I and III, 1860.

19. Watts Farm Diary, Cass County, March 27, 1854, October 23, 1854, October 30, 1854, Watts Papers; Maguire Farm Journal, Gwinnett County, October 10, 1861, Maguire Papers; Court of Ordinary, Inventories and Appraisements, Jackson County, February 1, 1859, Vol. A, 591–92, GDAH.

20. Superior Court Writs, Carroll County, April 1853, 32–3.

reciprocity and the cash nexus. Yet, if customs of mutuality did not constitute the elements of a halcyon "world we have lost," neither did they represent merely one side of a cultural coin. Rather, they served as means of absorbing social antagonisms, as resources that brought stability in an environment of uncertainty and established standards for social behavior. Although many farmers settled, stayed for a time, and moved on, they carried these customs along wherever they went, reproducing cultural institutions across the South. In the Black Belt, such relations tended to reinforce the prestige of the planter class and bolster their paternalism; in the Upcountry, they strengthened bonds among yeomen and deepened a commitment to local autonomy.

III

"Good fences make good neighbors." So Robert Frost gave immortal expression to the contradictions between community and private property. The Southern lower classes had their own version of the adage, as wealthy planter William Elliott grumbled in 1859: "Though it is the broad common law maxim, 'that everything upon a man's land is his own' . . . and he can shut it out from his neighbor without wrong to him, yet custom with us, fortified by certain decisions of the court, has gone far to qualify and set limits to the maxim."[21] In a society with unequally distributed agricultural resources, independence for small-holders demanded a broad definition of property rights, linking the culture of yeomen and poorer whites throughout the South. Hunting and fishing were important means for procuring subsistence, and travelers never ceased to marvel at the region's abundance of game.[22] But the woods and streams frequently ran through privately owned land, as most of the acreage on farms was unimproved. Public access to such land was therefore vital, and before the Civil War custom and law sanctioned appropriate common rights. "The right to hunt wild animals is held by the great body of the people, whether landholders or otherwise, as one of their franchises," Elliott observed, bemoaning that the land one purchased "is no longer his . . . unless he encloses it. In other respects, it is his neighbor's or anybody's."[23]

21. William Elliott, *Carolina Sports by Land and Water Including Incidents of Devil-Fishing, Wild-Cat, Deer, and Bear Hunting, etc.* (New York, 1859), 254–55.

22. Hilliard, *Hogmeat and Hoecake*, 71–83.

23. Elliott, *Carolina Sports*, 254–55; Donald B. Dodd and Wynelle S. Dodd, *Historical Statistics of the South, 1790–1970* (Tuscaloosa, Ala., 1973), 2, 18, 26, 34, 38, 50, 54, 58.

A court case, which Elliott disdainfully recounted, strikingly attests to the nature and tenacity of popular opinion on hunting rights. An action for trespass, growing out of the conflicting claims of hunter and landholder, came to trial in South Carolina. One of the hunters, himself a landowner, took the stand and was asked by the prosecuting attorney whether he would pursue a deer into his neighbor's enclosure. The defendant nodded, adding that "I should follow my dogs where they might!" The judge then intervened, warning the defendant that he would be committing "a trespass" and "would be mulcted in damages," and charging that "there is no law for such an act!" "It is hunter's law, however!" came the defendant's reply. "And hunter's law is likely somewhat longer to be the governing law of the case in this section of the country," Elliott groaned, "for the prejudices of the people are strong against any exclusive property in game. . . ."[24]

Elliott and like-minded planters feared that unregulated common rights would lead to a depletion in the supply of game, thereby threatening one of their favorite sports. Hunting, with its occasional pageantry and display, reinforced the cultural prestige of the planter class. And during the 1850s some planters began agitating for the passage of game laws. Legislation was local, and the greatest inroads came in Maryland and Virginia, but several counties in Mississippi, Alabama, and Georgia also established hunting seasons for deer, turkey, partridge, and quail.[25] Overall, however, the impact of game laws remained quite limited, for they met with deep popular resistance. As Elliott could again note, the "laboring emigrants" from Britain brought a profound "disgust at the tyranny of the English game laws. . . . The preservation of game is thus associated in the popular mind, with ideas of aristocracy—peculiar privileges to the rich, and oppression toward the poor."[26]

Common right to unenclosed land had even more significance for

24. Elliott, *Carolina Sports*, 257–58. Also see "Fox Hunting Fever," in B. A. Botkin, ed., *A Treasury of Southern Folklore: Stories, Ballads, Traditions, and Folkways of the People of the South* (New York, 1949), 610–11.

25. *Fur, Fin, and Feather: A Compilation of the Game Laws of the Principal States and Provinces of the United States and Canada* (New York, 1871), 112, 141–47. In Georgia, the Black Belt counties of Burke, Richmond, and Worth passed game laws during the early 1850s. Carroll County also had one passed, but it was repealed quickly. See *Acts of the General Assembly of the State of Georgia, 1851–1852* (Macon, 1852), 448–49; *Acts of the General Assembly, 1853–1854* (Savannah, 1854), 336–38.

26. Elliott, *Carolina Sports*, 250–53, 260.

livestock raising. From earliest settlement, Southerners had customarily turned their hogs, cattle, and sheep out in the woods to forage rather than provide pasture. "The cows graze in the forest . . . [and the hogs] go daily to feed in the woods, where they rove several miles feeding on nuts and roots," the traveler John Pinkerton observed of mid-eighteenth-century North Carolina.[27] And reports of the prevalence of the "open-range" came from all geographical areas of the nineteenth-century South. "Many people [in the Piney Woods of Mississippi] are herdsmen," J. F. H. Claiborne recorded, "owning large droves of cattle . . . [which] are permitted to run in the range or forest." Northern Alabama, a United States Patent Office correspondent wrote in 1851, had "no system of raising stock . . . of any sort. The cattle live half the time on Uncle Sam's pasture." So, too, in the South Carolina piedmont. "We really raise [cattle] with so little care, that it would be a shame to charge anything for their keep up to three years old," one resident claimed. "We raise our hogs by allowing them to range in our woods, where they get fat in the autumn on acorns."[28]

Widespread in Britain, continental Europe, and Africa before capitalist agriculture fully penetrated the countryside,[29] these grazing practices entered Southern statute books during the colonial period in the form of fence laws. An act passed in 1759 set guidelines that endured throughout the antebellum period in Georgia. It required farmers to enclose their crops, thereby permitting livestock to roam freely on uncultivated land. The specifications were detailed and precise:

> all fences or enclosures . . . that shall be made around or about any
> garden, orchard, rice ground, indigo field, plantation or settlement

27. Pinkerton, quoted in Rupert P. Vance, *Human Geography of the South: A Study in Regional Resources and Human Adequacy* (Chapel Hill, 1932), 146–47; Lewis C. Gray, *History of Agriculture in the Southern United States to 1860*, 2 vols. (Gloucester, Mass., 1958), I, 146.

28. J. F. H. Claiborne, "A Trip Through the Piney Woods," *Publications of the Mississippi Historical Society*, IX (Oxford, Miss., 1906), 521; U.S. Patent Office, *Report to the Commissioner of Patents for the Year 1851* (Washington, 1852), 331; *Report to the Commissioner of Patents for the Year 1850* (Washington, 1851), 233–34. Also see J. Crawford King, "The Closing of the Southern Range: An Exploratory Study," *JSH*, XLVIII (February 1982), 53–70.

29. Forrest McDonald and Grady McWhiney, "The Antebellum Southern Herdsman: A Reinterpretation," *JSH*, XLI (May 1975), 156; Terry G. Jordan, *Trails to Texas: Southern Roots of Western Cattle Ranching* (Lincoln, Neb., 1981), 1–15; Jerome Blum, *The End of the Old Order in Rural Europe* (Princeton, 1978), 123–25, 149–50.

in this province, shall be six feet high from the ground when staked or ridered and from the ground to the height of three feet of every such fence or enclosure, the rails thereof shall not be more than four inches distant from each other; and that all fences or enclosures that shall consist of paling shall likewise be six feet from the ground and the pales thereof not more than two inches asunder: *Provided always*, that where any fence or enclosure shall be made with a ditch or trench, the same shall be four feet wide, and in that case the fence shall be six feet high from the bottom of the ditch.

Although the Assembly reduced the legal height of fences by a foot during the early nineteenth century, the other provisions stood. Should animals break into a farmer's field, his fencing had to measure up to these standards if he hoped to collect damages. "If any trespass or damage shall be committed in any enclosure, not being protected as aforesaid," the *Georgia Code* decreed, "the owner of such animal shall not be liable to answer for the trespass, and if the owner of the enclosure shall kill or injure such in any manner, he is liable in three times the damages."[30] Other Southern states incorporated remarkably similar laws.[31]

Dissident voices could be heard. As the antebellum era wore on, agricultural reformers and "progressive" planters blamed the custom of open-range foraging for the poor quality of Southern livestock. They also argued that the fence laws worked a special hardship on farmers as expanded cultivation led to timber shortages and made fencing unduly expensive, not to mention laborious and time-consuming. "In some parts," one critic insisted, "timber is becoming so scarce that it will be a serious question how we are to provide fences for our fields." Another complained that "custom and the example of our fathers have riveted upon us practices, which although . . . injurious to our interests, are nevertheless unnoticed, because they are familiar." In the words of a Virginia planter, the prevailing fence laws represented the "heaviest of all taxes on farmers." The *Southern Cultivator*, an agricultural journal, suggested the use of wire fencing or thorn hedges, but agitation soon

30. Thomas R. R. Cobb, *A Digest of the Statute Laws of the State of Georgia* (Athens, 1851), 18–19; R. H. Clark, T. R. R. Cobb, and David Irwin, *The Code of the State of Georgia* (Atlanta, 1861), 271–72.

31. See, for example, David J. McCord, *The Statutes at Large of South Carolina* (Columbia, S.C., 1839), 331–32; A. Hutchinson, *Code of Mississippi, 1798–1848* (Jackson, Miss., 1848), 278–80; John J. Ormond, Arthur Bagby, and George Goldwaite, *Code of Alabama* (Montgomery, Ala., 1852), 250–51.

turned to a call for new statutes requiring the enclosure of livestock rather than crops.[32]

Appeals to the general interests of agriculture notwithstanding, the issue highlighted conflicting notions of use rights. "Justice and policy have concurred in fixing as a general principle in the laws of civilized nations, that every individual should be compelled to refrain from trespassing on the property [of] . . . other person[s]," a petitioner reminded the Virginia Assembly, but in the case of fencing "the rule is just reversed . . . [and] every individual shall guard and protect his property from depredators and everyone is permitted to consume or destroy all that may not be well guarded." More succinctly, another proponent asked, "Why . . . should my land which I choose to turn out to improve by rest, be taken possession of and impoverished by other people's stock?" Poorer farmers, he admitted, thought differently, as they tenaciously held to and gained considerable benefit from claims to the "commons." "It is notorious," he sneered, "that those frequently have the largest stock who have the least land to graze." The Committee on Agriculture and Manufactures in the Virginia General Assembly made the same point in a different way when rejecting petitions for a "Change of the General Law of Enclosures": "Many poor persons have derived advantage from grazing their stock . . . on the common and unenclosed lands, and to whom the obligation to confine them, or a liability to damages if not confined, would operate as a great hardship." Several Virginia counties managed to obtain adjustments in the fence law, but limited progress was made there, or elsewhere in the South, before the Civil War.[33] The desire of the planter class to mitigate social conflict within the region as the sectional crisis deepened doubtless contributed to the protection of these popular customs.

Yeoman farmers in the Upcountry often owned sizable tracts of unimproved land and therefore did not confront the same problems of those in more commercialized areas. The distribution of land in relatively substantial lots, later settlement, and minimal attention to staple agriculture helped facilitate such a situation. In 1860, farms

32. *Southern Agriculturist*, quoted in *Southern Cultivator*, II (October 1844), 173; *Farmers' Register*, I (January 1834), 450–52; I (December 1833), 396–98; I (March 1834), 633–34; I (May 1834), 753–54; *Southern Cultivator*, III (January 1845), 10; VIII (April 1850), 55–56.

33. *Farmers' Register*, I (December 1833), 396–98; I (January 1834), 450–52; II (April 1835), 712.

containing fewer than 50 acres of cropland had, on average, roughly 100 acres lying wooded or uncultivated. Larger farms had even more.[34] In the Upcountry, as in other locales, of course, the fence laws could stir conflict. For while the *Code* spelled out procedures for branding, marking, and taking up strays, farmers occasionally accused one another of illicitly appropriating their stock. Thus, in 1851 John Stewart of Carroll County petitioned the Superior Court for recovery of the value of five head of cattle which he charged John Hately "came into the possession of . . . by finding . . . but contriving and fraudulently intending . . . to deceive and defraud your petitioner in this behalf hath not as yet delivered said cattle. . . ." Hately denied the allegation. In a similar case a year later, John Snow was imprisoned for the apparent "crime of stealing a hog," though he soon won release because "in the opinion of the Court the Evidence was not sufficient."[35]

Despite such unavoidable skirmishes, yeomen supported the fencing statutes and common rights. For men like John McEver, who farmed 40 of his 200 acres in Jackson County, the open range had real benefits. Enclosing 160 acres of unimproved land would be costly and difficult, especially since he owned no slaves; enclosing a smaller area might reduce the number of livestock he could raise or force him to use more of his food crop for feed. Farmers normally let their stock forage in the woods during the spring and summer months, then turned them loose in the fields after harvest. Systematic fattening, when done, focused on a short period of time in late fall before the animals were slaughtered. Since Upcountry yeomen marketed few of their hogs and cattle, hefty stock merited no premium. For farmers like William Morris of Carroll County, who tilled almost all of his 110 acres, and for tenants and farm laborers, who often had livestock of their own, access to the commons offered special advantages and created a cultural bond that would be carried into the New South.[36]

---

34. Appendix, Tables V–VI.

35. John F. Steward v. John Hately, Carroll County, April 1851, Superior Court Writs, 5–6; Petition of John Snow, Carroll County, February 1852, Inferior Court Minutes, 1851–1854, GDAH.

36. John McEver in Manuscript Census, Georgia, Jackson County, Schedule II, 1850; William Morris in ibid., Carroll County, 1860. On foraging and feeding practices in the South, see Hilliard, *Hogmeat and Hoecake*, 100–101, 122–24, 136–40.

IV

In January 1847, George B. Hudson, a substantial farmer and merchant in Gwinnett County, "rented [his] field on the right hand side of the Jones plantation to Buckner and Jackson Kimbrill for 1/4 cotton, 1/3 corn and 1/3 oats." Almost a decade later, a tenant in Gordon County, on the northern fringe of the western Upcountry, agreed to "giv [the landowner] one third of what he makes . . . or one half . . . if [the landowner] will furnish one horse and feed for two horses. . . ." These arrangements seem to bear close resemblance to patterns of tenancy associated with the postbellum era, and suggest that labor relations after the war built upon antebellum precedents. Widespread in early Virginia and Maryland, farm tenancy declined during the first half of the nineteenth century but could be found in all Southern states during the 1840s and 1850s.[37]

A more detailed examination of tenancy in the Georgia Upcountry, however, reveals both great variations and qualitative distinctions between the prewar and postwar periods. And it indicates that the aspirations and experiences of yeoman farmers were broadly shared by groups entering, at least temporarily, into different social relations. At the same time that George Hudson rented out part of his land for a share of the crop, for instance, he "let John Bush have use of the Jones house and patches for ten dollars per year." Richard Thurmond, who owned well over 400 acres in Carroll County, also set leasing terms in cash. John Thurmond, presumably a relative, rented a "dwelling garden and house lot and lot around the house and 30 acres of land" along with an orchard field in 1857 for $71; W. W. Roberson farmed "8 acres south of the bridge" for $11; and C. K. Hearn agreed to pay $30 for "20 acres on [the] north side of [the] road." In Bartow County, William Franks leased land from William Solomon, who lived in Atlanta, for $150 in 1863, consenting "to take care of and manage [the] farm in good and husband like man[ner]."[38] Undoubtedly, many of these tenants

37. Hudson Store and Farm Account Book, Gwinnett County, January 13, 1847, Aiken Collection; Michael Frix to John Dobbins, Gordon County, November 17, 1856, John S. Dobbins Papers, Reel 2, EU. On Southern tenancy before the Civil War, see Gray, *History of Agriculture*, I, 406–8; Gregory A. Stiverson, *Poverty in a Land of Plenty: Tenancy in Eighteenth Century Maryland* (Baltimore, 1977); Joseph D. Reid, "Antebellum Share Rental Contracts," *Explorations in Economic History*, XIII (January 1976), 69–83; Frederick A. Bode and Donald E. Ginter, "Farm Tenancy and the Census in Antebellum Georgia" (Unpublished ms., 1980).

38. Hudson Store and Farm Account Book, Gwinnett County, January 13, 1847, Aiken

ultimately made their payments in kind, at customary cash equivalents, but contracts did not include crop stipulations.

Perhaps more frequently, farmers rented out tracts of land to have them cleared and improved. With settlement beginning only in the late 1830s in many sections of the Upcountry, much of the land remained densely wooded. Thus, Joseph Brown, soon to be governor of Georgia, had Reuben F. Daniel "clear a field of ten acres [in Cherokee County] . . . and put a good ten rail fence around it." In return, Daniel had "use of said ten acres for agricultural purposes . . . as he may think proper" for a period of two years. Similarly, John A. Rhea rented "a certain lot of land in the thirteenth district of originally Carroll now Heard Co. known . . . as Lot No. 122" from Lucius H. Featherston "for the space of two years during which time . . . Rhea binds himself to clear ten acres of land on the said lot and put it in good repair." Rhea was "allso to build a common log house[,] a smoke house[,] a corn crib and stable and such other improvements as he . . . should neade for convenience during the time specified." The landlord Featherston apparently gave Rhea control of the cropland and bound "himself to keep said John A. Rhea in peaceable possession" for the term of the lease.[39] Jesse Windsor became a tenant on "a plantation of land embracing six forty acre lots known as the 'Fisher Place'" in Cass County for twelve months during the late 1850s. "[I]n consideration of use, occupancy, and rent of land," Windsor agreed "to build a plank fence around the yard, build a well house and new frame for the well . . . put in the sash and glass of all windows in new and unfurnished buildings on [the] premises . . . and take good care . . . and prevent all 'waiste' upon [the] premises." Three years later a new tenant, A. J. Cooper, had use of the "Fisher Place" in lieu of "tak[ing] special care of said premises in protecting Houses and fences from fire, and . . . keep[ing] out all intruders and trespassers." In addition, Cooper was "not to abandon or leave premises during term of

Collection; Ordinary Estate Records, Inventories and Appraisements, Carroll County, March 25, 1857, Vol. C, GDAH; Leasing Agreement: C. Dodd, Agent for William Solomon of Atlanta, and William Franks, Bartow County, September 9, 1863, Chunn-Land Family Papers, Box 2, Folder 22, GDAH.

39. Leasing Agreement: Joseph E. Brown and Reuben F. Daniel, Cherokee County, May 4, 1854, Joseph E. Brown Papers, Box 1, Folder 11, UGa; Leasing Agreement: Lucius H. Featherston and John A. Rhea, Heard County, November 6, 1837, Lucius H. Featherston Papers, Box 1, Folder 4, EU.

rent without first giving [the landowners] at least 20 days notice. . . ."
Failure to meet the provisions of the lease would cost Cooper $500 "for
use and occupancy of premises."[40]

Some rental agreements covered longer periods of time. John Ray of
Coweta County owned land in Gordon and in October 1853 leased
twenty acres of it to James and J. P. Kennedy, who "as tenants, agree[d]
to clear [the] land . . . and enclose it with a good fence." Ray also
permitted the Kennedys to "clear 3 acres of land around the house,"
instructing them to fence the patch, and he consented to pay for all
improvements made if he chose to sell the land before the lease expired.
The Kennedys had to complete all tasks within five years or surrender
the crop they raised in 1858 "or a sufficiency thereof." On the same day,
Ray made identical arrangements with five other tenants.[41]

Under leases such as these, tenants retained control over the day-to-
day operations of the farm and had scant outside supervision to contend
with. In part this was a product of sheer distance, for renters often
cultivated land in a county different from the one in which their
landlord resided. Landowners like John S. Dobbins, who lived in
eastern Habersham County while having tenants in western Gordon
County, might arrange for neighboring farmers to keep an eye on the
renters. Dobbins's agents reported on the progress of the crops, but
commonly complained about the tenants' touchiness and summoned
him on occasion to settle disputes over stipulations in the lease.[42] While
some landlords furnished their tenants with supplies, many others left
the tenants to deal with local merchants instead. G. C. Reese and R. M.
Heard of Carroll County, for example, rented land from Israel Hendon
and purchased goods from the mercantile firm of Davis, Kolb, and
Manning. Furthermore, renters working under share agreements did
not always cultivate cotton. The tenant Israel Boalk was not unusual in
paying "one third of all the corn and one third of all the oats" for use of a

40. Leasing Agreement: William Solomon and Nathan Land and Jesse Windsor, Cass
County, May 27, 1858, Chunn-Land Papers, Box 2, Folder 17; Leasing Agreement:
William Solomon and Nathan Land and A. J. Cooper, Cass County, January 1, 1861,
ibid.

41. Leasing Agreement: John Ray and James and J. P. Kennedy, Gordon County,
October 11, 1853, Dobbins Papers, Reel 2. Also see the agreements between Ray and
A. P. Cobb, Nathaniel Cook, Newton Cook, Eaton Brown, and Samuel Mallet.

42. Michael Frix to John Dobbins, Gordon County, June 15, 1856, October 19, 1856,
June 27, 1856; Joseph Printup to Dobbins, Gordon County, June 21, 1856, March 29,
1858, all in Dobbins Papers, Reel 2.

tract of land in Cass County. In this way, tenants were able to raise a substantial portion of their own foodstuffs.[43]

Indeed, more systematic evidence shows that farming practices among Upcountry tenants closely approximated those of yeomen. Although some renters did grow relatively large quantities of cotton, most devoted their acreage primarily to wheat, sweet potatoes, and especially to corn. Dilmer J. Lyle, who farmed thirty acres of rented land in Jackson County, typified many of his counterparts: in 1860 he produced 25 bushels of wheat, 30 bushels of sweet potatoes, 350 bushels of corn, and only two bales of cotton. Lucius J. Patrick and Sanford Wages, tilling thirty-five and forty acres respectively, followed a similar pattern, as did Thomas Black and Joseph King during the same year in Carroll County. A few, like Rolen Tolbert, who worked seventy-five acres, grew no salable cotton.[44]

With some exceptions, tenant farmers, like yeomen, owned their tools and livestock. John Haynie, renting twenty-eight acres in Jackson County, had $6 worth of farming equipment along with a couple of horses, cows, and cattle, twelve sheep, and sixteen hogs in 1860. Nearby, Thomas Whisler had a horse, three cows, four head of cattle, and twenty-five hogs, as well as farm implements valued at $50. In Carroll County, the tenant A. J. Cole owned tools worth $15, a horse, two cows, four head of cattle, ten sheep, and twelve hogs. Similar conditions are revealed by leasing agreements from other Upcountry counties. Unlike their postbellum counterparts, antebellum landlords rarely furnished tenants with animals and "farming utensils." Eaton Brown, who agreed to "giv [his landlord] half of what he makes . . . if [the landlord] supplied one horse and feed for two horses," was the atypical case. What is more, tenants and their families generally made clothing and other necessaries. L. J. Williams, a Carroll County tenant, reported $25 in home manufactures in 1860; numerous others reported even greater amounts. In domestic economy as in crop production, tenants differed little from freeholders.[45]

43. Israel Hendon v. G. C. Reese and R. M. Heard, Carroll County, February 1855, Inferior Court Minutes, Court and County Purposes, 1852–1862, GDAH; Leasing Agreement: William Solomon and Nathan Land and Israel Boalk, Cass County, January 26, 1859, Chunn-Land Papers, Box 2, Folder 18.

44. Manuscript Census, Georgia, Jackson and Carroll Counties, Schedule II, 1860; Appendix, Tables VII–VIII, V–VI.

45. Ibid.; Frix to Dobbins, Gordon County, November 17, 1856, Dobbins Papers, Reel 2.

Whether tenancy provided an effective stepping-stone to landownership is a question that awaits closer study. To be sure, some tenants were the sons of substantial landholders and would eventually inherit real estate. A few, in fact, only appear to be tenants, for they worked farms bequeathed by their fathers although legal title was not conveyed for years. Green M. Duke of Jackson County, for instance, was a landless farmer in 1850, but his father, Green R. Duke, stood as one of the wealthiest men in the county. By the end of the decade, the younger Duke could boast $2,500 in real property. A more extensive survey suggests a high rate of geographical mobility coupled with fair prospects for those who remained to acquire land. Slightly over one-third of Jackson County landless farmers in 1850 resided in the county ten years later. Among them, 60 percent had become landholders; the others were reported as farm laborers.[46]

Whatever the reality, tenants appear to have viewed their status as a temporary stage in the process of becoming landowners. As John Dobbins's agent wrote in 1856, "all your tenants hav got good crops of corn . . . and are wanting to go to the west anctious to sell out to you crops and all[,] there object is to settle where tha can get land cheap. . . ."[47] During their careers in tenancy, they sought to maintain as much of their independence as the situation allowed. The relatively undeveloped state of the Upcountry economy and, particularly, tenant ownership of farm tools and livestock provided essential room. While relinquishing a portion of their crops or performing other services to gain access to the land, tenants still tended to follow farming practices of the region's yeomanry. They also laid claim to the common grazing rights enjoyed by landowners, which enabled them to control some of the means of production and subsistence.

Yet, these very claims to independence on the part of individuals who worked for others as well as for themselves created frictions that surfaced in far greater proportions when the Upcountry became a major staple-producing area after the Civil War. Several of John Dobbins's tenants, for example, wished to sell their leases during the late 1850s and move to Alabama. Dobbins refused to pay the asking price, but another of his tenants, a Mr. Chanler, agreed to buy one of them himself. Declining the bid, Dobbins had to bring the matter to court, where he obtained

46. Manuscript Census, Georgia, Jackson County, Schedule I, 1850, 1860.

47. Frix to Dobbins, Gordon County, June 15, 1856; A. N. Edmundson to Dobbins, Gordon County, March 31, 1857, all in Dobbins Papers, Reel 2.

a favorable judgment. Chanler then promptly picked up and "left . . . for the west," though not before he "took care to cut up his old flat. . . ." The transfer of leases by tenants apparently was common, since some landowners specifically prohibited it. Dobbins had further difficulty with a few tenants who insisted upon using timber from land not directly allotted to them. In Cherokee County, Joseph Brown sought to establish more leverage over a troublesome tenant by refusing him the right "to pasture the land with any kind of stock." While such a provision appeared very infrequently, it anticipated developments of the 1870s and 1880s, when commercial agriculture more fully penetrated the region.[48]

During the antebellum period, therefore, tenancy retained many of the features of farm ownership, and tenants seemed to share the culture and outlook of yeomen. Thus, when land values rose and some sections of the Upcountry became more involved in the market during the 1850s, the number of tenants appeared to decline while the number of farm laborers increased. And in an important sense, this process accelerated after the Civil War, for as tenancy grew in significance, it changed in character. Contracts would specify crop acreage, supervision would become more extensive, and tenants would *receive* rather than *pay* a share of the crop. When Harvey D. Lemmings arranged to work twenty acres on John H. Dent's plantation in Floyd County in 1873, Dent furnished the livestock, implements, and feed, and Lemmings was "to plant cultivate and harvest 15 acres of corn . . . [and] 5 acres of cotton and receive 1/2 corn and fodder and 1/2 cotton." In effect, and ultimately in law, types of tenancy were transformed into a system of wage labor and many tenants were transformed into rural proletarians.[49]

---

48. Frix to Dobbins, Gordon County, July 27, 1856, October 19, 1856, Dobbins Papers, Reel 2; Leasing Agreement: Joseph E. Brown and Ralph L. Kinnett, Cherokee County, October 29, 1857, Brown Papers, Box 1, Folder 14.

49. Cottage Home Farm Journal, Floyd County, December 1873, John H. Dent Papers, GDAH. On postbellum sharecropping as a form of wage labor, see Harold D. Woodman, "Post–Civil War Southern Agriculture and the Law," *AH*, LIII (January 1979), 321–27. Joseph D. Reid, in an analysis of fifty-nine rental agreements made by two North Carolina landlords during the antebellum era, places heavy emphasis on the continuities between the prewar and postwar periods. While he is right in arguing that "the forms and arrangements applied after the war had been tried and found workable long before emancipation," he mistakenly equates share rental with sharecropping. See Reid, "Antebellum Share Rental Contracts," 69–83.

V

At his death, in 1851, Henry S. Butler, who owned 640 acres and thirteen slaves in Jackson County, had at least 104 notes worth $1,783.25 owed to his estate. This should not surprise us, for Butler was a man of wealth and doubtless something of a creditor and merchant in his neighborhood. More striking is the case of John J. Long of Carroll County. Deceased in 1862, he left an estate appraised at just over $600. It included 50 acres of land, eighteen head of livestock, farm tools, crops of corn and fodder, and a few dollars in cash, all of which came to $400. The remaining $200 were in notes owed to him. So, too, with James B. Woody, also of Carroll County. He owned 40 acres of land, several animals including a mule, some household furniture, foodstuffs, and a spinning wheel. The most substantial part of his estate, however, accounting for almost half its value, was "notes on hand" totaling $595.09. Then there was Mathew Scott, who owned neither land nor slaves but held outstanding debts amounting to $24. In all, more than seven of ten probated inventories from Jackson and Carroll counties during the 1850s showed such assets.[50]

That farmers, rich and poor, often had sizable debts owed to their estates suggests the formation of a wide network of exchange governed by its own system of credit. Many of the transactions occurred during market days when cultivators brought surplus produce into the small Upcountry towns and villages; others were conducted irregularly among farmers in the countryside when an extra bushel of corn or a few pounds of bacon were needed. In either case, there was no middleman: relations were directly between different producers, and most involved the extension of credit. Few farmers had ready cash, especially in the spring and summer months before crops could be harvested and sold. Probated inventories, in fact, show that well over half of the deceased had no currency whatsoever, and those who did usually had very little. Thus, when Benjamin Beal died, in 1855, he had a scant $2.50, while John J. Long could claim "cash on hand" amounting to only $18. Small

---

50. Court of Ord., Inv. and App., Jackson County, Vol. A, 126–28; Ord. Est. Recs., Inv. and App., Carroll County, Vol. E, 254; Vol. D, 133–34, 588–89. Of 159 inventories probated in Jackson and Carroll counties during the 1850s, 115 (or 72 percent) listed debts owed. Unfortunately, neither the inventories nor the notes usually specify what the debt was for.

wonder that year's end normally brought settlements in kind or labor services.[51]

Some of these persons were artisans who rented dwellings and shops, owned small lots, or combined farming with a craft. They assumed a particularly important place in the grid of local trade. Millers ground grain into flour, grits, and meal; blacksmiths made and repaired farm tools, horseshoes, and harnesses; coopers, carpenters, and wagonmakers put up houses and barns, made furniture, constructed barrels for storage and shipment, and built animal-drawn vehicles; shoemakers, hatters, and tailors made various articles of clothing. Bricklayers, stonecutters, cabinetmakers, tinners, carriage makers, saddlers, sawyers, weavers, harness makers, wheelwrights, gunsmiths, potters, and mechanics also found a niche in the Upcountry economy.[52] But it was not for an anonymous public that they plied their crafts. Artisans did custom work in their settlements—perhaps making the rounds from farm to farm—and generally on a credit basis. A. F. Upchurch, a Carroll County shoemaker, had fifty-eight accounts totaling $628.28 when he died, in 1856. Benjamin S. Merrill, a tanner or saddler, who owned sixty acres of land, left notes and accounts amounting to over $80 at his death three years earlier. And like farmers, artisans were often reimbursed in kind or by the performance of some task.[53]

The account books of Job Bowers, a Hart County blacksmith, offer a lucid portrait of this mode of exchange. William Cheek, for instance, ran up a bill of $1.25 at Bowers's shop for services that included "pointing plow," "making plow," "making small hoe," and "sundry work," but did not settle until the end of the year, when he paid "500 shingles." John P. Gaines paid Bowers for similar jobs by handing over "100 lbs seed cotton" and by "splitting 100 rails." Samuel Hymer, who owed $10.96 for the repair of assorted farm tools, paid with fifteen pounds of flour, buttons, four bushels of corn, and $7.30 in cash. For Sincler Self, farmer and craftsman, Bowers worked on an ax and trace chain, made bridle bits, sharpened a plow, and mended traces over the

51. Ord. Est. Recs., Inv. and App., Carroll County, Vol. C, 117; Vol. E, 254. In Carroll County only 22 percent of the inventories probated during the 1850s reported "cash on hand"; in Jackson County 40 percent of the inventories did.

52. Manuscript Census, Georgia, Jackson and Carroll Counties, Schedule I, 1850, 1860.

53. Ord. Est. Recs., Inv. and App., Carroll County, Vol. C, 15–16, 287–90. Also see John T. Schlotterbeck, "Plantation and Farm: Social and Economic Change in Orange and Greene Counties, Virginia, 1716–1860" (Ph.D. diss., Johns Hopkins University, 1980), 67–68, 214–35.

course of a year for which he charged $8. Self began to settle the bill in February by "making pair shoes."In June he made Bowers another pair; in October he was "half soling shoes"; in December he paid $3 cash; and the following January he made three additional pairs of shoes and a harness. Other artisans operated in a similar fashion, and millers took a certain portion of the grain they ground for toll.[54]

Yet if the structure of indebtedness points to a market broad in base, the size of individual debts indicates that the market was nonetheless quite shallow. The estate of Thomas B. Williams, owner of 150 acres in Carroll County, had notes due worth $115.02 in 1856, but almost all were for sums under $10. A few years later the inventory for the craftsman George A. Henderson listed twenty-five notes and eighty-one accounts, sixteen and sixty-two of which, respectively, involved similarly small amounts. Of over one hundred notes held by Henry Butler of Jackson County at his death, roughly one-half were for less than $5, about three-quarters were for less than $10, and virtually all were for less than $20.[55] Debts involving far more substantial sums can, of course, be found, boosting the average value of notes in Jackson and Carroll counties to well over $30. But such debts were exceptional. Exchange supplemented yeoman household subsistence rather than provided the measure of it.[56]

Store ledgers of Upcountry merchants reveal almost identical patterns. Most of the merchandisers carried stocks of goods valued at considerably under $5,000 and had limited operations. An R. G. Dun and Company credit agent said as much when he took care to note that a merchant in the Carroll County town of Villa Rica did "a large business for the up country." Farmers, too, usually purchased supplies on credit and paid interest only if accounts remained open at the end of the year. William Beall of Carroll County, for example, accumulated a

54. Job Bowers Account Book, Hart County, 1832–1836, GDAH; Foster and King Mill Account Book, Cherokee County, 1857–1858, GDAH; Watkins and Watkins, *Yesterday in the Hills*, 59. Although Bowers's records come from the 1830s, there is every reason to believe that the patterns were common throughout the antebellum period. For early Northern parallels, see Michael Merrill, "Cash Is Good to Eat: Self-Sufficiency and Exchange in the Rural Economy of the United States," *RHR*, III (Winter 1977), 55–56; James A. Henretta, "Families and Farms: *Mentalité* in Preindustrial America," *WMQ*, 3rd ser., XXXV (January 1978), 15–16.

55. Ord. Est. Recs., Inv. and App., Carroll County, Vol. C, 273–74, 287–90; Vol. E, 233–35; Court of Ord., Inv. and App., Jackson County, Vol. A, 126–28, 132–33.

56. Thus, in Carroll County the average value of notes during the 1850s came to $33.25, but 61 percent of those who held notes averaged less than $30 per note, and most of them averaged less than $20 per note.

bill of $4.30 at the establishment of J. Long and Company in 1851. When he died, in 1854, the debt was still on the books, and the administrators of his estate had to pay an extra forty-five cents for "interest 19 months."[57] When settlements came, moreover, few were exclusively in cash. Indeed, though stores in the Black Belt generally advertised goods for "cash or cotton," those in the Upcountry often announced that "all kinds of country produce" would be accepted. Francis C. Byron of Franklin Country paid the storekeeper Thomas Morris in corn and fodder for the merchandise he bought in 1847, while Thomas Scott came to terms with Morris by doing odd jobs for a ten-day period. In Floyd County, Cicero White squared his debt of $24 with a merchant named Fain by hauling logs and giving Fain three pairs of socks, one grindstone, and a note for $6. Others combined payments in cash, kind, and labor.[58]

Chronic currency shortages in the region at once reflected and contributed to the viability of these exchange relations—relations which represented more than mere proxies for strict cash restitutions and did not resemble other local trading arrangements by coincidence. The quasi-barter transactions that characterized much of the exchange between various producers sprang from complex interdependencies in Upcountry neighborhoods— a communitywide division of labor and community-based self-sufficiency—and from the household uses the goods satisfied. Farmers traded corn for tools, wheat for furniture, meat for leather. And because these dealings had a face-to-face quality, goods and services symbolized the embodiment of labor and specific use values. This configuration helped govern the terms of trade and shaped understandings of the proper workings of the marketplace. Although the price and credit structures in Athens, Atlanta, Augusta, and Charleston exerted an impact, yeomen in effect turned this system into a standard for all exchange activities. In so doing, they expressed a certain labor theory of value—a notion that the worth of goods was determined by the effort required to produce them—and circumscribed the power of the market and the merchant.[59]

57. R. G. Dun and Company, Credit Reporting Ledgers of the Mercantile Agency, Georgia, V, 102, Baker Library, Harvard University; Ord. Est. Recs., Inv. and App., Carroll County, Vol. C, 229.

58. Thomas Morris Store Ledger, Franklin County, 1847, GDAH; Fain Account Book, Floyd County, 1850, GDAH; Lewis Atherton, *The Southern Country Store, 1800–1860* (Baton Rouge, 1949), 49.

59. For Northern parallels, see Merrill, "Cash Is Good to Eat," 55–56; Henretta, "Families and Farms," 15–16.

However much debt linked Upcountry denizens in an intricate network of social relations, it also provoked tensions and conflicts, especially as ties to external markets became more extensive. In an area where cash was in short supply, where crop surpluses were not routinely large, and where the whims of nature could spell disaster, credit placed everyone in potentially precarious circumstances. Farmers not only had debts owed to them; they owed debts to others as well. A bad year for one, which prevented settlement, could have serious consequences for several neighbors. Similarly, merchants had to contend with the demands of creditors in commercial towns where they obtained their goods. A generally poor harvest could push many to the wall. Thus, the court records are filled with actions for debt. As the Jackson County grand jury complained in 1851, "our Superior Courts are litterally weighed down with suits creating litigation in which some portion from the amount involved is either unworthy of consideration or founded in shear malice. . . . " A year later the Cassville *Standard* observed that "there is more business on the docket than has ever been before. Times are hard and creditors harder—and a great many are sued. . . . "[60]

Court suits could be costly encounters in more ways than one. First, the losing party assumed responsibility for expenses, and when this was the defendant, interest on the debt was also charged, which together could easily double the original sum at issue. When, for example, P. H. Field brought Gilbert Gay before the Carroll County Inferior Court in 1855 for failing to pay a debt of $3.50, the justices decided in Field's favor and assessed Gay an additional $5.38 to cover interest and court costs.[61] Furthermore, suits might bring temporary confinement for the defendant if he neglected or refused to report his property holdings to the court for the purpose of establishing his solvency. Thomas Word of Carroll County, "having failed to comply with the statute by notifying his creditors and filing a full and fair schedule of his property" in 1851, was not alone in being "imprisoned in the common jail . . . until he satisfy . . . his principal, interest, and cost or until he otherwise discharge [the debt]."[62]

60. Grand Jury Presentments, Superior Court Minutes, Jackson County, 1851, 54; Cassville *Standard*, March 11, 1852.

61. Inferior Court Minutes, Court and County Purposes, Carroll County, 1855–1862, 52–3, 55–6. Also see Justice of the Peace Appearance Docket, Jackson County, 1855–1860, GDAH.

62. Inferior Court Minutes, Carroll County, June 1851.

Property attachments and ultimate dispossession could also be the result of these proceedings if the debt was sufficiently large. Most often this did not happen. For a closer look at the adjudication of these cases reveals the extent to which custom and law recognized debt as a fundamental aspect of social life and gave a strong measure of protection to the productive property of smallholders. That the statute requiring submission of a property schedule was entitled "An Act for the Relief of Honest Debtors" provides a clue to the workings of the system: while it shielded creditors from fraudulent claims of insolvency, it offered the court evidence with which to make "equitable" adjustments. And in numerous instances debts were scaled down. During the early 1850s, Thomas Campbell of Carroll County had "bound [himself] to Gallington Coke" for the sum of $40. By 1855 the debt remained unpaid and Coke brought suit. Campbell then asked the benefit of the "Honest Debtors" law, and after due consideration the court awarded Coke "$20 principal, $1.60 interest, and $6.56 cost." Many other cases of this sort had similar outcomes.[63]

The "Act for Relief of Honest Debtors" facilitated the scaling down of debts in large part because a law passed in 1841 and amended twice thereafter, commonly known as the homestead exemption, limited the amount of property liable for levy and sale. Proclaiming that "it does not comport with the principles of justice, humanity, or sound policy to deprive the family of an unfortunate debtor of a home and means of subsistence," the act entitled every white household head to exempt from judgment fifty acres of land and an additional five acres for each child under the age of fifteen, "provided that the same or any part thereof not be the site of any town, city, or village or of any cotton or wool factory, saw or gristmill, or any other machinery propelled by water or steam." Also immune from liability were one horse or mule, ten hogs, and $30 of provisions. During the 1850s the list grew to include one cow and calf; beds and bedding for the family; one spinning wheel and loom, two pairs of cotton cards, and 100 pounds of lint cotton; common tools of trade; equipment and arms of the militia; ordinary cooking utensils and table crockery; the family's wearing apparel; a Bible; religious, work, and school books; a family portrait; and the library of professionals.[64]

63. Ibid., March 12, 1855, June 1856, and generally 1855–1860.
64. Cobb, *Digest of Statute Laws of Georgia*, 389–90; Clark, Cobb, and Irwin, *Code of Georgia*, 398–99.

The homestead exemption doubtless accounted in good measure for the low incidence of mortgaging for credit in the antebellum Upcountry. In 1850 the Jackson and Carroll County ordinaries recorded only four and seven mortgages respectively. Most were held by merchants, involved real property or slaves, and secured notes for substantial sums, averaging nearly $300. Mortgaging became somewhat more common during the 1850s, but remained relatively unimportant and showed similar patterns. In Carroll County, where staple agriculture had expanded, a few mortgages securing lesser debts covered livestock or "the corn and cotton crop," anticipating the postwar crop lien. Neither in extent nor in character, however, did antebellum mortgages serve as devices through which one social class extracted surpluses from another.[65]

Protections afforded by law and the general operation of the credit system notwithstanding, foreclosures and attachments did take place. Yet, considering the volume of litigation, they occurred infrequently. During the entire year of 1851, for instance, only nine sheriff sales were carried out in Jackson County, and most involved fairly large amounts of property, suggesting that the original debts were sizable. Joshua Wimberly had 250 acres sold off to satisfy a creditor, Stewart Floyd 200 acres, James Nabers a house and lot in the town of Jefferson. Louis Hubbard, who surrendered five pounds of wool and 100 pounds of feathers, proved to be the exception rather than the rule. Moreover, many debtors who faced levy had at least two plaintiffs to settle with. These patterns were also evident in Carroll County, and little changed by 1860. Most debtors who went to court and lost ultimately came to terms with their creditors without recourse to the auction block.[66]

However many "complaints for debt" came before the local justices, far more settlements were made outside their jurisdiction. Estate

65. Superior Court Deeds and Mortgages, Jackson County, Vol. N, 407–53, GDAH; ibid., Carroll County, Vol. F, 338–446; ibid., Jackson County, Vol. P, 236–427; Superior Court Deed Record, Carroll County, Vol. I, 379–595, CCC. Also see Chunn-Land Family Papers, Bartow County, September 9, 1863, Box 2, Folder 22. In 1860, Jackson and Carroll counties reported only twelve and twenty-one mortgages respectively.

66. Athens *Southern Banner*, 1851, 1860; Superior Court Deeds and Mortgages, Carroll County, Vol. F, 358–464. The Inferior Court Records for Jackson County list only three cases of attachment for debt throughout the 1850s. See Inferior Court Minutes, Jackson County, 1847–1862, 124–270, GDAH. In 1860 Jackson County saw only seventeen sheriff sales, fifteen of which involved real property. Also see Superior Court Deed Record, Carroll County, Vol. I, 430–31; Superior Court Deeds and Mortgages, Jackson County, Vol. P, 314.

records clearly show that debts commonly ran for years, at times with little expectation that they would ever be repaid in full. Fennell Hendrix of Jackson County had seven notes owed to his estate when he died, in late 1850: one was due in 1848, two were due in 1849, and three in early 1850. Henry S. Butler carefully distinguished "solvent" from "insolvent" outstanding notes.[67] To be sure, the magnitude of litigation, to which newspapers and grand juries felt compelled to draw attention, spoke to the tensions pervading the Upcountry during the 1850s—tensions leading, as several contemporaries put it, to "an unpleasant state of morals in our community." That a county body regarded legal actions "in which some portion of the amount involved is . . . unworthy of consideration" as a "social evil," nevertheless, tells us something about the nature of local custom.[68]

The structure of credit and debt, in short, was more an indication of community interdependencies, which unquestionably had discordant features, than an index of class power. Notions that social relations were not governed simply by the marketplace and laws that protected the property of petty producers set limits to the economic leverage that any social group, however wealthy, could hold over the mass of the white population. Little wonder that when Emancipation altered labor relations, planters and merchants would launch an attack on the homestead exemption, that this attack would exacerbate class tensions, and that the homestead exemption's repeal would be disastrous for the yeomanry.

VI

The vitality of local custom, the value that Upcountry yeomen placed on the control and perpetuation of productive property within the family, and the contradictions besetting the household economy during the 1850s emerge strikingly in the patterns and practices of inheritance. Although historians of the South have paid this subject scant attention, scholars of rural Europe and early America, among others, have demonstrated that inheritance is part of a wider process whereby social structure and social relations are reproduced over time. It is thus a

67. Court of Ord., Inv. and App., Jackson County, Vol. A, 126–28, 132–33.

68. Grand Jury Presentments, Superior Court Minutes, Jackson County, February 1851, February 1856. Also see Grand Jury Presentments, Superior Court Minutes, Carroll County, October 1857; Cassville *Standard*, March 11, 1852.

critical measure of a society's character and of the world views of groups within it.[69] In the mid-nineteenth-century South, where few alternatives to agriculture offered viable livelihoods, the transmission of real and personal property assumed a special importance, even as geographical mobility held out one solution to the problem of providing for the next generation—a solution testifying as much to the precarious status of smallholders in a commercializing world as to the fluidity of the social order.

Ostensibly, distinctive class patterns of inheritance are not readily evident in the antebellum South. Primogeniture and entail, the props of many European landed elites, had been abolished by the late eighteenth century. Even as Thomas Jefferson railed against the institutions in the mid-1770s, putting bills for their eradication before the Virginia House of Delegates with the alleged intention of destroying the foundation of the aristocracy, they had fallen into disuse among many planters. By practice and law of intestacy, partible inheritance served as the principal mode of property transmission.[70] Such a system, however, encouraged planters to engross extensive tracts of land and seek marriage partners for their children among other planter families, thereby contributing to the proliferation of kinship networks among the well-to-do. In the plantation districts, the system also made for the development of kinship ties across class lines, for in a society where much of the wealth rested in relatively few hands, "good connections," as men like Benton Miller well knew, proved the surest avenues for social mobility. Upcountry yeomen along with many Black Belt counterparts, on the other hand, relied more heavily upon the resources of their households and the customs of the marketplace. For them, inheritance symbolized the intimate relationship between family, community, and freehold independence.

Farmers, rich and poor, who left wills normally made their wives direct heirs of the estate—so long as they did not remarry—and provided for equal division among the children upon her death.

69. Jack Goody, Joan Thirsk, and E. P. Thompson, eds., *Family and Inheritance: Rural Society in Western Europe, 1200–1800* (Cambridge, 1976), 1 and passim; Henretta, "Families and Farms," 21–30. Also see Bertram Wyatt-Brown, "Religion and the Formation of Folk Culture: Poor Whites of the Old South," in Lucius F. Ellsworth, ed., *The Americanization of the Gulf Coast, 1803–1850* (Pensacola, Fla., 1972), 23.

70. Dumas Malone, *Jefferson and His Time: Jefferson the Virginian*, 6 vols. (Boston, 1948–1980), I, 253–56; C. Ray Keim, "Primogeniture and Entail in Colonial Virginia," *WMQ*, 3rd ser., XXV (October 1968), 545–86.

William Thurmond of Jackson County, for example, bequeathed "unto my beloved wife all of the lands whereon I now live together with all of the household and kitchen furniture all of my negro property, and horses, cows, hogs, stock of all sorts, with the farming or plantation tools to have during her natural life or widowhood." Thurmond gave his wife the right "to divide any of the aforesaid property . . . equally between all of my children" should she "see cause at any time," and determined that all of his offspring would receive equal shares after she died. Ephraim Jackson of Carroll County, who owned 202 acres, followed a similar tack, leaving his wife, Ann, "with all the rights and appurtenances to said lot of land during her natural life . . . [and] all of my household and kitchen furniture together with all my perishable property," and declaring that at her death the property would be distributed equitably among his children. So, too, for Solomon Holoway, proprietor of "40 acres of land more or less . . . stock consisting of one horse cow and hogs . . . household and kitchen furniture . . . [and] one carriage and harness."[71]

Variations could, of course, be found. Particularly if the widow was elderly, property might pass directly to the children, though usually accompanied by strict provisions for her care. Joel Woods of Carroll County willed a tract of land to his sons Nathan and Joel with specifications for dividing it between them and instructions not to sell it during his wife's lifetime and to give her "a comfortable house and decent support . . . of 1/4 of the proceeds of said land." In the same county, Levi Gunter received 100 acres of land "in consideration of . . . his attention [to his mother] during her sickness and in consideration of his paying all her debts and taking care of her for the rest of her life."[72]

Partition among the offspring, moreover, was not always equal. Reflecting the social and legal grid of the household economy, the sons commonly acquired the land while the daughters received personal property or cash. James Wheeler, for instance, distributed real estate to each of his two sons and gave his daughter, Charity, his "bay mare, one cow and calf, five of the first choice of hogs, one feather bed and bedstead and furniture all my kitchen furniture of all kinds together

71. Ord. Est. Recs., Wills, Jackson County, Vol. A, 425, GDAH; ibid., Carroll County, Book A, February 1852, September 1855, GDAH. Also see ibid., May 1854; ibid., Jackson County, Vol. A, 393, 395; John S. Pool Will, Paulding County, UGa.

72. Ord. Est. Recs., Wills, Carroll County, Book A, July 1860; Superior Court Deeds and Mortgages, Jackson County, Vol. P, 238.

with all the cotton and half the corn and wheat that I may have at my death in field and gathered." William and Calvin Barron of Jackson County each inherited land from their father, Thomas, then extended a legacy to their married sisters and accepted responsibility for finding another sister "a Descent [sic] support as long as she shall live as single. . . . "[73] Distribution of property among male heirs might be uneven as well. James Barr's will in Jackson County provided his son James H. with "the plantation he now lives on, a Negro man, and one cow," with the "balance of the property to be sold and equally divided among the children including James H. Barr." In Carroll County, John T. Carr bequeathed 187 acres to his son Allen, 165 acres to son John J., and 63 acres to son Joseph. Doubtless the eldest son or sons, like Allen and John J. Carr, often came into the largest shares, but this was not uniformly true.[74]

Substantial farmers, such as Carr, bought up extensive tracts of land in their own or in other counties, which they expected to pass on to their children. And in numerous cases death merely conveyed legal title to property on which their offspring, who had married and moved out of the household, already resided. Thus, before Jacob Brooks of Jackson County died, his sons John, James, and Moses farmed "land in Banks [county] worth $500," his sons Zenny and Essau lived on property of the same value in Gwinnett and Hall counties respectively, his son David obtained land in Jackson County, and his son Jacob was granted "right of possession to and using of my farm as may not be needed for support of myself and family." When Brooks and his wife died, Jacob would become the owner outright. Brooks also instructed that his slaves be distributed among his wife and daughters and that the remainder of the estate be sold and equally divided among all his children.[75]

For poorer farmers, partible inheritance frequently meant sale of the entire estate. Smallholdings could not easily be parceled out among several heirs and remain viable economic units. Hence, after the widow's death, sons and daughters usually sold the land and appurtenances and split the proceeds. Furthermore, yeomen often died intestate, and the division of the estate then fell subject to the dictates of law. According to the *Georgia Code*, an administrator was to be appointed to

73. Ord Est. Recs., Wills, Jackson County, Vol. A, 356–57.

74. Ibid., 253; ibid., Carroll County, Book A, 4–5.

75. Ord. Est. Recs., Wills, Jackson County, Vol. B, 129–33. Also see ibid., Carroll County, Book A, 4–5.

appraise the value of real and personal property, whereupon a year's support would be set aside for the widow and offspring and the rest put up for auction, in part to expedite the repayment of debts. Wives and children were entitled to equal shares. As the *Code* of 1861 put it: "Children stand in first degree from the intestate and inherit equally all property of every description. . . . [T]he wife shall have a child's part, unless the shares exceed five in number, in which case the wife shall have one fifth part of the estate."[76]

Yet, while seemingly a market institution, the public auction had a decidedly nonmarket character, for closed rather than open bidding prevailed. When Thomas B. Williams of Carroll County died, his livestock, farming equipment, household furniture, spinning wheel, and loom were sold at the courthouse on the customary day. Most of the articles were purchased by his widow, Hannah, and by J. H. Williams, John T. Williams, E. M. Williams, and E. R. Williams, presumably sons or other relatives. After William A. Hendon's death, in early 1854, his perishable property was taken to auction, where "widow Hendon" reclaimed plows and hoes, a chisel, three axes, a cow, a saddle, and a bedstead, while "widow Stallings," perhaps a relation or needy neighbor, bought one of Hendon's heifers. Real property also appeared to be redistributed in this manner. Upon the death of Henry Pike of Jackson County, in 1860, his wife, Ann, put 146 acres of land up for sale. At the auction one Marcus Lay purchased the tract. But Lay probably was asked to do the bidding, for he promptly transferred title to the widow.[77]

Family members retrieved this property at much reduced prices. James Eskew's personal estate in Carroll County was appraised at $678.45. At the sale, his wife, Lucy Ann, obtained one of the horses, some of the livestock, fifty bushels of corn and wheat, saddles, cooking utensils, and other household furnishings. She bought the spinning wheel, valued at $2.50, for fifty cents and paid half value for the beds and tables. The total bill for all property sold came to $461.35. Lucy Ann then rented out her husband's land for the support of the family. When George Wright died in Jackson County, his property was also auctioned on the appointed day. Save for a steel ax, all of it was acquired by

76. Clark, Cobb, and Irwin, *Code of Georgia*, 464–88. It is worth noting that Georgia law was less favorable to women in this regard than was the common law which prescribed the "widow's third."

77. Ord. Est. Recs., Inv. and App., Carroll County, Vol. C, 7, 273–74. Also see ibid., 253–64, 315–16; Superior Court Deeds and Mortgages, Jackson County, Vol. P, 348.

Robert J. and E. A. Wright, the latter buying a cupboard appraised at $8 for $1, a shotgun valued at $12 for $7, and a spinning wheel for half the price set by the administrator.[78]

These practices bear a striking resemblance to somewhat more ritualized forms of estate transmission evident as late as the 1960s in relatively isolated areas of the South. Following a couple's death, according to the student of one Tennessee ridge community, the children had all the property sold and divided the money equally, which they used to buy back the home property or to purchase other local real estate at auction. The heirs let it be known who wanted the land, and there was a communitywide understanding as to how the property would be distributed. An auctioneer, who lived elsewhere but was familiar with the locality and customs, then came to supervise the sale, though he learned of the preferences in advance. Through the process of bidding the community set the "fair" price, thereby providing a safe clearing ground and guarding against hard feelings between seller and buyer. The details of one such auction are particularly revealing:

> . . . a group of five siblings (three brothers and two sisters) were heir to their grandfather's land that had been in the possession of their bachelor uncle who died. The siblings put the sixty-five acre farm up for auction, and two of the brothers let it be known that they wanted the land. The older brother already had a farm including part of his parents' land. The younger brother Bill was a tenant and community talk favored him, but he lacked the means to buy the land. Bill's second cousin and a group of more distant kin went to see a banker and offered to stand with Bill in debt for the amount they thought would be the winning bid.
>
> Some eighty men and women were present at the auction. A neighbor to the piece of property opened the bid, after which Bill and his brother were the only bidders. The older brother's bid went beyond what Bill was able to borrow. At this point the auctioneer called an intermission . . . during [which] . . . three local residents who hauled walnut timber stepped to Bill's side and expressed desire for the cedar on the property being auctioned, offering to pay for it immediately if Bill raised the bid. He did so and was the successful bidder.

78. Ord. Est. Recs., Inv. and App., Carroll County, Vol. D, 250–51; Court of Ord., Inv. and App., Jackson County, Vol. A, March 26, 1859.

These inheritance customs apparently extended back more than a century.[79]

Although similar descriptions of auctions in the Georgia Upcountry are not available, it is clear that farmers turned this small marketplace into a mechanism for controlling the redistribution of property and maintaining it within the family. They directed tools, livestock, and furniture into the hands of those getting a start in life and those for whom the death of a husband or father might bring great hardship. The custom did not follow strict class lines. Wealthy farmers frequently engaged in the practice, as did James Carr, a substantial landholder, who instructed his eldest sons "to advertise and bring to sale my property both real and personal[,] such heir allowed to bid for himself except my two daughters who I want . . . to choose an agent to bid for them if they wish to buy any of the property if still single. . . ."[80] Even the well-to-do in the Upcountry rarely had the resources to set several children up as small planters. Thomas Bonner of Carroll County, who inherited a sizable tract of land and over twenty slaves, proved to be unusual. Therefore, large landowners relied on closed auctions to effect a fair division of the estate, compensating in part for the varying fates of their children. For yeoman farmers, who often failed to leave wills and whose property holdings were far more limited, this customary method of transmitting property had a special significance; and they seized upon it to protect their families from destitution and to provide the next generation with a material foundation for the attainment of freehold independence.

But while popular customs afforded yeomen means for defending their way of life, trends of the late antebellum period presented complications. Population growth outpaced the number of acres being brought into farms: on average, yeoman farms shrank in size during the 1850s. Inheritance practices thus made it increasingly difficult for smallholders to transfer land directly to their offspring, and as land prices rose, sons would have a harder time using their share of the estate to purchase farms. The Civil War and the expansion of commerical agriculture thereafter would only make matters worse. So it was that in the 1870s a man like John M. Stapler, whose father owned $800 worth of real estate and died during the 1850s, would be landless and his

79. Elmora Matthews, *Neighbor and Kin: Life in a Tennessee Ridge Community* (Nashville, 1965), 14–19.

80. Ord. Est. Recs., Wills, Carroll County, Book A, 4–5.

brother Richard would have left the county.[81] However "egalitarian", partible inheritance may have contributed to the long-term "unmaking" of the Southern yeomanry.

VII

No small irony surrounded the abolitionist argument that slavery degraded and oppressed the Southern white lower classes, as Northern labor spokesmen who assailed the emerging "wage-slavery" in their own region took occasion to note. For the elevation of the marketplace as the fundamental arbiter of social relations, to which the abolitionists lent moral force, was predicated upon the separation of petty producers from control over productive resources and their consequent dependence on capital for their livelihoods—a process that artisans and rural peoples in the North saw as degrading and oppressive in its own right.[82] The abolitionists had a point, to be certain. Over time, slavery disadvantaged yeomen and landless whites, especially in the plantation districts, by limiting opportunities, creating ties of dependency, and promoting social and economic backwardness. Yet, in its Southern setting, slavery also provided economic, social, and cultural space for independent, non-market-oriented freeholders.[83]

That space did not evolve at the slaveholders' behest. It grew out of conditions specific to slavery and the Old South and out of the sensibilities, aspirations, customs, and ongoing struggles of those who inhabited it. On the one hand, white class divisions in the South, broadly considered, fell primarily along geographical lines. Most small farmers and other nonslaveholders resided in nonplantation areas. Their claims to the means of production, their penchant for semi-subsistence agriculture, and their commitment to local autonomy did not clash directly with the exigencies of the plantation order. Afro-American slaves produced the surpluses that underwrote great fortunes; the planters had no need to accumulate and discipline a white labor

81. Manuscript Census, Georgia, Jackson County, Schedule I, 1850; Jackson County Tax Digest, 1873, GDAH.

82. Williston H. Lofton, "Abolition and Labor," *JNH*, XXXIII (July 1948), 250–70; David Brion Davis, *The Problem of Slavery in the Age of Revolution, 1770–1823* (Ithaca, 1975), 242, 246, 349–50, 357–61, 489–501.

83. For an interesting historical precedent when slavery provided for the "coexistence of a nobility with an indigenous free peasantry," see Perry Anderson's discussion of Viking Scandinavia in *Passages From Antiquity to Feudalism* (London, 1974), 173–81.

force. Indeed, the planters' own experience led them to share a distaste for the power of the marketplace as well as a profound localism with the mass of Southern whites. And it was precisely on slavery's role in mitigating the centralization of authority and the development of market relations—expressed in the ideology of state rights—that the planters sought to establish their political and cultural hegemony, their command of civil society.

But the very space which helped to define its character also cast the planters' hegemony in precarious balance. The relations of production and exchange, the habits of mutuality, the common use-rights, and the customs of inheritance—the cultural web of social life—in the Upcountry, not only encouraged anticommercial sentiments and an attachment to small communities of producers. They also encouraged a general antiauthoritarianism easily turned against wealthy slaveholders whose haughty airs, demands for subservience, and increasingly undemocratic tendencies became widely recognized. To the extent that the Upcountry remained on the periphery of the staple economy and to the extent that the planters evinced little desire to have it any other way, direct confrontations might be avoided. Yet the Upcountry, and other nonplantation regions, formed part of a larger political system in which the planters sought to advance interests that could, at least symbolically, threaten the yeomanry's independence and way of life. If the planters disdained the forces of the market, their own stature hinged on the protection and expansion of a commercial economy that promised to promote even greater concentrations of wealth and power, the potential scope of which broadened during the 1850s, as staple agriculture began to penetrate the Upcountry. As the sectional crisis deepened, furthermore, a unified response to "Black Republicanism" became a pressing concern. In parading evidence of the white citizenry's common stake in slavery, the planters implicitly questioned the loyalties of the lower classes and exposed their fears of social conflicts. While yeomen had complex reasons of their own for taking up arms against the North, the requirements of defending a nascent slaveholders' republic brought those conflicts to the surface.

3
The Politics of Independence

I

"Slavery," Georgia Governor Joseph E. Brown proclaimed, "is the poor man's best Government." Trumpeting familiar refrains from the score of proslavery doctrine, Brown argued that, despite the inequalities of wealth in Southern society, black bondage served as the foundation of white social and political democracy: "Among us the poor white laborer is respected as an equal. His family is treated with kindness, consideration, and respect. He does not belong to the menial class. The negro is in no sense his equal. . . . He belongs to the only true aristocracy, the race of white men." With special reference to Upcountry yeomen, Brown acknowledged that "some contemptible demagogues have attempted to deceive [them] by appealing to their prejudices and asking them what interest they have in maintaining the rights of wealthy slaveholders." But he felt that such efforts were to little effect. "They [the yeomen] know that the Government of our State protects their lives, their families, and their property," he announced, "that every dollar the wealthy slaveholder has may be taken by the Government of the State, if need be, to protect the rights and liberties of all." And Brown assured skeptics that the yeomanry "will never consent to submit to abolition rule. . . . " "When it becomes necessary to defend our rights against so foul a domination," the governor insisted, "I would call upon the mountain boys as well as the people of the lowlands, and they would come down like an avalanche and swarm around the flag of Georgia."[1]

More than many other defenders of slavery, Joseph Brown had some claim to speak for the sentiments of the Southern white majority. Like Mississippi's Albert Gallatin Brown, he catapulted to political prominence after building a power base in a nonplantation district. But Brown simply added an influential voice to a growing chorus whose very resonance betrayed its ostensibly confident tone. Along with such widely circulated and closely reasoned essays as J. D. B. DeBow's *The Interest in Slavery of the Southern Non-Slaveholder*, Brown's address capped three decades of expositions that filled the pages of newspapers and agricultural journals and emanated from the hustings. Emphasizing the white egalitarianism that the chattel institution made possible, indeed asserting "that a republican government can only be maintained upon the basis of domestic slavery," spokesmen for the master class sought to create a political consensus across class lines while they implicitly exposed the deepest contradictions of their society.[2]

Yet, the racial appeals of proslavery theorists can easily obscure the underlying tenets of their argument and, perhaps, the very meaning of race to different social groups. For whether one considers the doctrines of George Fitzhugh and Henry Hughes or those of others who offered less of a challenge to bourgeois sensibilities, the defenders of slavery ultimately rested their case, not so much on the innate inferiority of blacks—though they never hesitated to make this point—but on the inevitability of class distinctions and the consequent moral superiority of a system whose social relations were not beholden to the whims of the marketplace. Thus South Carolina's James Henry Hammond taunted his Northern colleagues in the United States Senate, "In all social systems there must be a class to do menial duties, to perform the drudgery of life . . . or you will not have the other class which leads

---

1. Allen D. Candler, ed., *The Confederate Records of the State of Georgia*, 6 vols. (Atlanta, 1909), II, 483–88; Milledgeville *Federal Union*, December 11, 1860.

2. Joseph H. Parks, *Joseph E. Brown of Georgia* (Baton Rouge, 1977), 1–40; James B. Ranck, *Albert Gallatin Brown: Radical Southern Nationalist* (New York, 1937), 7–25; George M. Fredrickson, *The Black Image in the White Mind: The Debate on Afro-American Character and Destiny, 1817–1914* (New York, 1971), 58–70; James D. B. DeBow, *The Interest in Slavery of the Southern Non-Slaveholder* (Charleston, 1860); Candler, ed., *Confederate Records*, II, 118–23.

progress, civilization, and refinement. It constitutes the very mudsill of society and of political government." In its most extreme form, the argument questioned the premise, as Chancellor Harper put it, that "all men are created equal," but for the entire spectrum of the Southern ruling class, which lorded over a plantation society, the notion that "there must be a class . . . to perform the drudgery of life" proved inescapable. "Fortunately for the South," Hammond added, "she found a race adapted to that purpose at hand."[3]

The moral and political justifications of slavery turned on identical points. Given the necessary social distinctions rooted in the division of labor of plantation agriculture and, for that matter, of all societies, slavery provided the only humane alternative to insecurity and destitution in the labor market. Assailing capitalism in the North and in Europe for casting the laboring poor upon their own meager resources, the slaveowners' representatives ridiculed the "freedom" that market societies pretended to advance. Whereas industrialization pitted the interests of labor against capital and offered its "wage slaves" an experience of isolation and material deprivation, slavery in the rural South linked master and dependent in an organic relationship which conferred upon laborers protection from want as a reward for their toil.[4]

To the extent that it limited the development of market relations, slavery also served the interests of poorer whites, or so the institution's outspoken supporters vehemently claimed as they paraded evidence touching the concerns of all strata of nonslaveholders. Because the significant element of the region's work force was black and enslaved, propertyless whites received higher wages for their labor than did Northern counterparts; because the elite invested in slaves as well as real estate, landownership was widely distributed; and because Upcountry farmers grew nonstaple crops, they did not have to compete with the slave-based plantations. Warning of the consequences of Eman-

3. James Henry Hammond, quoted in Eric L. McKitrick, ed., *Slavery Defended: The Views of the Old South* (Englewood Cliffs, N.J., 1963), 122; *DeBow's Review*, VIII (March 1850), 235–37; ibid., XXII (May 1857), 487–90; George Fitzhugh, *Sociology for the South; or the Failure of Free Society* (Richmond, 1854), 84–85, 163–68.

4. C. Vann Woodward, "A Southern War Against Capitalism," in *American Counterpoint: Slavery and Racism in the North-South Dialogue* (Boston, 1971), 107–39; Eugene D. Genovese, *The World the Slaveholders Made: Two Essays in Interpretation* (New York, 1969), 156–234; William Sumner Jenkins, *Pro-Slavery Thought in the Old South* (Gloucester, Mass., 1960), 296–302. Also see Drew Gilpin Faust, *A Sacred Circle: The Dilemma of the Intellectual in the Old South, 1840–1860* (Baltimore, 1977), 112–31; John McCardell, *The Idea of a Southern Nation: Southern Nationalists and Southern Nationalism, 1830–1860* (New York, 1979), 49–90.

cipation, Joseph Brown wove these threads into an ominous tapestry. There are always rich and poor men, he stated, and "if we had no negroes the rich would still be in a better position to take care of themselves than the poor. They would still seek the most profitable and secure investment for their capital." "What would this be?" Brown asked rhetorically. "It would be land. The wealthy would soon buy all the lands of the South worth cultivating [and] . . . the poor would all become tenants . . . as in all old countries where slavery does not exist." "It is sickening to contemplate the miseries of our poor people under these circumstances," Georgia's governor concluded. "They now get higher wages for their labor than the poor of any other country on the globe. Most of them are now landowners, and they are now respected. . . . Abolish slavery . . . and you very soon make them all tenants and reduce their wages to the smallest pittances that will sustain life." By shielding the lower classes from what one contributor to the Cassville *Standard* termed the "fluctuations of commerce," slavery proved to be the guardian of their personal and local independence. As the Atlanta *Daily Intelligencer* chimed in 1856, "It is a fact well known in the South, but which is surprisingly hard to beat into the heads of the Yankees, that it is to preserve their own independence that the nonslaveholding voters of the South have ever been staunch supporters of slavery. They well know that wealth always commands service and that there can be no such thing as equality between a boot-black and his master."[5]

Yeoman farmers, especially in nonplantation areas, did not need to accept—and generally did not accept—the paternalist underpinnings of the proslavery argument to feel a certain affinity with its social and cultural premises. Fundamentally committed to producing for household consumption and local exchange, wary of "economic development," and often hostile to outside authority, they shared important ideological ground with wealthy planters. As small property holders born into a society sanctioning racial bondage, they saw blacks as symbols of a condition they most feared—abject and perpetual dependency—and as a group whose strict subordination provided

5. Milledgeville *Federal Union*, December 11, 1860; Cassville *Standard*, November 26, 1857; Atlanta *Daily Intelligencer*, in Ulrich B. Phillips Collection, Box 37, Folder—Artisans and Town Labor, YU; DeBow, *Interest of the Non-Slaveholder*, 5–7; Montgomery (Alabama) *Advertiser*, November 13, 1850, quoted in J. Mills Thornton III, *Politics and Power in a Slave Society: Alabama, 1800–1860* (Baton Rouge, 1978), 273–74.

essential safeguards for their way of life.[6] Whatever the differing milieu of slavery on farms and whatever the force of racism in its own right, the attitudes of the yeomanry toward Afro-Americans must be understood, historically, as attitudes of petty property owners toward the property-less poor—attitudes which at certain junctures led smallholders to join with the upper class in defining the dispossessed out of the political community.[7]

But while the planters and their spokesmen prated about the common stake all Southern whites had in slavery, their continuing pronouncements seemed to reveal nagging doubts. The yeomanry, and nonslaveholders in general, they occasionally admitted, would likely be the very people most receptive to free-labor ideology. Wealthy slaveholders certainly could not fail to recognize that yeomen and poorer whites rarely had patience for their haughty pretensions. Indeed, the planters might pose as much of a threat to the independence of small farmers as did the slaves, for it required no keen analytical mind to see that the dependency of the blacks and the domineering, aristocratic stance of the masters went hand in glove. Racism and anti-planter sentiment, in short, could represent two sides of the same coin, with potentially explosive repercussions by the 1850s.[8]

The sources of class cohesion and conflict in the antebellum South, which the proslavery argument sought to enunciate and resolve, found special expression in the structure and dynamic of local and state politics. In a region embracing diverse physical and economic settings, the political process provided the means through which social and

6. Frederick Law Olmsted, *A Journey in the Backcountry* (New York, 1860), 203; idem, *A Journey in the Seaboard States* (New York, 1859), 573.

7. During the English Revolution, for example, the Levellers, who represented the interests of small property, sought a considerable extension of the franchise, but one that still excluded servants and almstakers. As C. B. Macpherson has written, the Levellers assumed that only "free men" whose living was not dependent on the wills of others were entitled to the franchise. Although Christopher Hill has recently shown that the Levellers were a more diverse lot and that some supported an even more democratic commonwealth, Macpherson's main point stands. See C. B. Macpherson, *The Political Theory of Possessive Individualism: Hobbes to Locke* (Oxford, 1962), 107–93; Christopher Hill, *The World Turned Upside Down: Radical Ideas During the English Revolution* (New York, 1972), 86–120.

8. Michael P. Johnson, *Toward a Patriarchal Republic: The Secession of Georgia* (Baton Rouge, 1977), 39–46; James L. Roark, *Masters Without Slaves: Southern Planters in the Civil War and Reconstruction* (New York, 1977), 20–24; Eugene D. Genovese, "Yeoman Farmers in a Slaveholders' Democracy," *AH*, XLIX (April 1975), 336.

cultural tensions as well as social and cultural power found public articulation, display, and reinforcement. It was in the workings of the county courthouse that the social relations of the Black Belt and Upcountry took political form, while it was in the statehouse and party system that conflicting claims within the elite, between the elite and other social groups, and between different geographical locales were mediated. And, as the core of the proslavery argument suggested, the issues of independence and the role of the marketplace served as the bridges of political consensus and as the elements of political discord.

II

Politics in the Georgia Upcountry had a distinctive flavor—local in orientation, at once democratic and deferential in substance—that complemented the relations of social and economic life. In an era of limited transportation and communication, the courthouse, not the state legislature, the Congress, or the presidency, stood as the symbol of political authority; local, rather than state or national, concerns elicited the greatest popular attention. And that attention was considerable. By the 1840s, a series of reforms stretching back into the eighteenth century had broadened the suffrage to include all adult white males and expanded the number of elective offices on every level of government. This process of democratization grew out of extended agitation, much of which originated in the Upcountry, but in many ways it bolstered instead of challenged the influence of the well-to-do.[9] For although reflecting and contributing to the yeoman commitment to local autonomy and political independence, the contours of local politics also mitigated class conflict by encouraging the formation of patron-client relations.

Local politics meant county- and district-level politics. Not townships, as in New England, but counties served as the primary political units in the South. Here public affairs were ministered to, civil cases tried, and

9. Fletcher M. Green, *Constitutional Developments in the South Atlantic States, 1776–1860* (Chapel Hill, 1930), 151–52, 233–40; Albert B. Saye, *A Constitutional History of Georgia, 1732–1945* (Athens, 1948), 159, 162, 171–72; Lucien E. Roberts, "Sectional Factors in the Movement for Legislative Reapportionment and Reduction in Georgia," in James C. Bonner and Lucien E. Roberts, eds., *Studies in Georgia History and Government* (Athens, 1940), 94–110; Donald A. DeBats, "Elites and Masses: Political Structure, Communication, and Behavior in Antebellum Georgia" (Ph.D. diss., University of Wisconsin, 1973), 320–28; Genovese, "Yeoman Farmers," 339–40.

representation in the state legislature determined. In Georgia the Inferior Court, consisting of five popularly elected justices, constituted the local governing body, though it often acted upon the recommendations of the countywide grand jury, which met twice yearly. Among other things, the Inferior Court supervised the maintenance of roads, bridges, and public buildings, the licensing of liquor retailers, the operation of slave patrols, the allocation of pauper relief and the poor-school fund, and the levying of county taxes. While technically subject to the authority of the General Assembly through special legislation, the court had achieved virtual autonomy by the 1850s.[10] Seven additional officials, also elected, attended to the dictates of the court and other vital local matters: the ordinary oversaw probate, apprenticeship, commissions of lunacy, and registration of free blacks; the sheriff executed court orders, conducted public sales, and took charge of the county jail; and the tax collector, tax receiver, surveyor, coroner, and clerk of the Inferior Court performed the duties that befit their titles. The counties were further subdivided into militia districts, which doubled as election precincts, under the control of a popularly mandated justice of the peace if not the militia captain.[11]

Local officeholding demanded no property qualification, but profiles of over 100 individuals who filled some post in Jackson and Carroll counties during the 1850s reveal that landownership brought political, much as social, respectability. Almost nine of ten county officials owned real estate. Most reported their occupations as "farmers," though a sprinkling of merchants, artisans, and teachers could be found among them. Save for two physicians, no professionals were represented. More significantly, the size of property holdings demonstrates a decided yeoman presence. About three-fourths of the identifiable officers owned land valued at under $2,500, while over nine-tenths owned land valued at under $5,000 (see Table 3.1).[12]

10. Inferior Court Minutes, Carroll County, March 6, 1852, GDAH; Grand Jury Presentments, Superior Court Minutes, Jackson County, February 1850, August 1851, GDAH; Melvin C. Hughes, *County Government in Georgia* (Athens, 1944), 13–16; Ralph A. Wooster, *The People in Power: Courthouse and Statehouse in the Lower South, 1850–1860* (Knoxville, 1969), 82–85.

11. R. H. Clark, T. R. R. Cobb, and David Irwin, *The Code of the State of Georgia* (Atlanta, 1861), 67–75, 161–64, 680–81, 685–87, 721–25.

12. Executive Department, County Officers, Jackson and Carroll Counties, 1850–1860, GDAH; Secretary of State, Justice of the Peace Commissions, Jackson and Carroll Counties, 1850–1860, GDAH; Manuscript Census, Georgia, Jackson and Carroll Counties, Schedule I, 1850, 1860, GDAH.

Table 3.1 Real-Property Holdings of County Officers, Jackson and Carroll Counties, 1850–1860

A. Real-Property Ownership Among All Officials

	Percentage of All Officials	
	Jackson County	Carroll County
Real-Property Owners	88.7%	87.7%
Own No Real Property	11.3%	12.3%
Total	100.0%	100.0%
Number	53	57

B. Distribution of Real Property Among Owners

	Percentage of Owners	
Category	Jackson County	Carroll County
Under $1,000	41.2%	40.8%
$1,000–2,499	33.3%	32.7%
$2,500–4,999	19.6%	16.3%
$5,000–9,999	3.9%	8.2%
$10,000+	2.0%	2.0%
Total	100.0%	100.0%
Number	47	49
Mean Real-Estate Value	$2,068.40	$1,791.90

Sources: Executive Department, County Officers, Jackson and Carroll Counties, 1850–1860, GDAH; Secretary of State, Justice of the Peace Commissions, Jackson and Carroll Counties, 1850–1860, GDAH; Manuscript Census, Georgia, Jackson and Carroll Counties, Schedule I, 1850, 1860.

Slaveownership also proved more common among county office-holders than among the white population at large, the proportion varying in Carroll and Jackson counties from 15 percent to 40 percent respectively. Yet here again, small slaveholdings predominated. Most of the slaveowning officials had fewer than five slaves, and virtually all had fewer than ten. Eli Benson, who served two terms as Carroll County's sheriff and owned $4,000 of real estate and twenty-two slaves in 1860, was the exception. The more influential political offices such as ordinary and sheriff did tend to be filled by wealthier individuals, and, as a group, the countywide officials boasted greater property holdings than did the district-level justices of the peace. This was not uniformly the case, however, and in any event the distinctions were by no means substantial. For both groups in both counties, the average real-estate value fell below $2,500, and the least well-off collection of officers—the Jackson County justices of the peace—averaged about $1,500 in real property.[13]

Much more needs to be known about local politics in different regions of the South. The little evidence available suggests that county officers in the Black Belt tended to be considerably wealthier, in terms of land and slaveholdings, than were their Upcountry counterparts. This, of course, is not terribly surprising, nor does it tell the full story. Small farmers assumed county posts in plantation areas, at times in large numbers, and it would be a mistake to assess the social ramifications of politics merely by tabulating economic profiles of officeholders.[14] Social structure and social relations very much shape the political terrain.

In rural societies containing weak commercial and industrial bourgeoisies, such as the South, smallholders often surrender political leadership to their richer neighbors. A common concern for the protection of property, the need to discipline a labor force, and the visibly higher cultural attainments of the economic elite help explain this phenomenon. Yet, as the experience of the Black Belt indicates, this pattern of deference is ultimately founded upon the prestige of wealthy landowners in the spheres of production and exchange and upon the relations they enter into with other social groups. That Black Belt yeomen frequently depended on the planters for various services enormously strengthened the planters' claims to authority beyond the bounds of their plantations, and nurtured networks of patronage which account, in large sum, for local political alignments and the personal factionalism that undergirded much of the political discord in the antebellum era. In a social order that conferred status upon the ability to command the allegiances of lesser men, intracounty rivalries often reflected competition among members of the elite and their followers

13. The mean real-estate values for different groups of county officeholders were as follows: Jackson County-wide—$2,431.50; Jackson County J.P.'s—$1,472.10; Jackson County Combined—$1,791.90; Carroll County-wide—$2,119.00; Carroll County J.P.'s—$2,030.40; Carroll County Combined—$2,068.40. See Executive Dept., County Officers; Secretary of State, Justice of the Peace Commissions; Manuscript Census, Georgia, Jackson and Carroll Counties, Schedules I and III, 1850, 1860.

14. Wooster, *People in Power*, 101–2; Roberta G. O'Brien, "War and Social Change: An Analysis of Community Power Structure, Guilford County, North Carolina, 1848–1882" (Ph.D. diss., University of North Carolina, 1975); D. Alan Williams, "The Small Farmer in Eighteenth Century Virginia Politics," *AH*, XLIII (January 1969), 92–101.

for influence. Thus, the electoral process offered poorer whites the advantages and favors that good connections might bring, while it reinforced the political and cultural hegemony of the master class.[15]

Consider the nature of officeholding itself. For planters, election to a county post could be an affirmation of their personal power, a means of enlarging their patronage, and perhaps a stepping-stone to bigger things. Aspiring planters doubtless saw political preferment as a possible avenue for social mobility. But for yeoman farmers, local office held a special lure—a steady source of income. Given the uncertainties of agriculture, this was no small attraction, especially since the salary could easily equal the annual earnings derivable from the farm, if not surpass them. Men, in fact, commonly announced their candidacy by emphasizing circumstances of hardship, and political contests normally drew large numbers of office seekers. Yet, whatever their local popularity, these individuals could rarely hope to win unless they had a wealthy sponsor who wielded some leverage in other districts. The legal requirements for officeholding made such relations particularly compelling. According to Georgia law, all county officials had to post bond as part of their oath, and the bonds were rather substantial. Sheriffs had to put up $20,000, tax receivers and collectors had to put up double the taxes due the state from their county, and even the clerk of the Inferior Court had to put up $3,000. Clearly, few smallholders had the resources to stand for these sums, so they turned to neighboring planters who would sign as security. This loosely organized, but nonetheless widespread, patron-client structure strengthened the slaveholders' political influence in the Black Belt and in the South as a whole.[16]

The stipulation that county officers post bond, along with the provision that grand jurors be "able, discrete, and qualified citizens" selected from the tax roles, had a conservative bearing on politics in the Upcountry, as it did in the Black Belt. When, for example, Benjamin Park, owner of $600 in real estate and two slaves, became Jackson County surveyor in 1852, he was backed by the wealthy planter-

15. Barrington Moore, Jr., *Social Origins of Dictatorship and Democracy: Lord and Peasant in the Making of the Modern World* (Boston, 1966), 117; Genovese, "Yeomen Farmers," 340. On patron-client politics, see Eric J. Hobsbawm, *Primitive Rebels: Studies in Archaic Forms of Social Movement in the 19th and 20th Centuries* (New York, 1965), 13–56; Eric J. Hobsbawm, "Peasants and Politics," *Journal of Peasant Studies*, I (October 1973), 3–22; Anthony Hall, "Patron-Client Relations," *Journal of Peasant Studies*, I (July 1974), 506–8.

16. Salaries were derived from a variety of court fees or as a percentage of collected taxes. See Clark, Cobb, and Irwin, *Code of Georgia*, 69–70, 161–64, 680–87.

merchants William S. Thompson and Samuel D. Watson. And the grand jurors, on average, tended to be even more well-to-do than the elected officials.[17] Still, a numerically preponderant yeoman constituency largely committed to the maintenance of the social relations of semisubsistence agriculture and to the exercise of their political rights gave local politics a distinctive texture and limited the cultural authority of the planters. One student of the Georgia bench captured the spirit when he contrasted the greater "dignity and . . . similarity to the English customs" of the courthouse milieu in the older plantation counties with the "rough and tumble manner" found in newer areas. The conservative jurist Garnett Andrews, who rode the north Georgia circuit during this period, said much the same when he decried the popular propensity to "look upon all the imposing forms and ceremonies—not to say pomp—with which official station is, and once in this was, clothed, as empty parade. . . . "[18] Andrews perhaps underestimated the deferential behavior that enabled men like R. J. Daniel, D. M. Burns, Robert Moon, and J. C. Hays, all owners of more than twenty slaves, to represent Jackson County in the General Assembly and play leading roles in local political life. But in a region where the turnout for elections could exceed 80 percent of the eligible voters, where literacy was widespread, and where partisan leanings expressed an ideological stance, these individuals had to pay keen attention to the sentiments of the yeomanry, if they did not share those sentiments themselves.[19]

17. Executive Department, Record of Bonds, Officers, Jackson County, 1850–1853, GDAH; ibid., Carroll County. The mean real-estate holding for the Jackson County grand jury of February 1850, for instance, was $2,835.29. See Superior Court Minutes, Jackson County, February 1850; Manuscript Census, Georgia, Jackson County, Schedule I, 1850.

18. Warren Grice, *Georgia Bench and Bar* (Macon, 1939), 237; Garnett Andrews, *Reminiscences of an Old Georgia Lawyer* (Atlanta, 1870), 18.

19. Taking the county votes in the gubernatorial election of 1859, for example, and comparing them with the total number of adult males over the age of twenty listed in the federal census for 1860, we find that the turnouts ranged from 75 percent in Franklin County to 92 percent in Heard County. Jackson and Carroll counties had turnouts of 82 percent and 83 percent respectively. And this figure underestimates the real turnout, for twenty-year-old males were ineligible to vote. See Athens *Southern Banner*, October 13, 1859; Athens *Southern Watchman*, October 20, 1859; *Eighth Census of the United States, 1860* (Washington, 1864), Population, 58–61. Literacy rates among white adults in the Upcountry ranged from 60 to 98 percent, averaging out at about 85 percent. See *Seventh Census of the United States, 1850* (Washington, 1853), 375–76.

Local political divisions and conflicts reflected these patterns. While scattered evidence suggests something of a town-country split, especially in counties with growing commercial centers like Rome and Marietta, by and large the split had limited significance. In most areas the towns were little more than glorified hamlets having populations numbering in the low hundreds and distinguished solely by the presence of small trading establishments and the county courthouse. And their impact on local affairs was not extensive. It might be expected that a substantial number of county officials would find their homes in or near the town districts, for the sake of convenience in a region where travel was slow, if for no other reason. But the majority lived elsewhere. In Carroll and Jackson counties, 69 percent and 53 percent of the respective county officeholders resided in rural districts.[20] Rather, district rivalries for county influence seemed to provoke the most heated contests. Thus, citizens of both Cass and Hart counties wrestled over the location of the county seat, with opposing sides protesting efforts to situate it "at a spot inelligible, inconvenient, and destructive to the permanent interest of the people." Greater access to the county seat, where decisions concerning the repair of roads and bridges, the allocation of poor relief, and the assessment of taxes were made and where market day often took place, could be particularly meaningful.[21]

But if county residents locked horns over certain matters, they could unite when the larger integrity of the county was threatened. The establishment of the Georgia Supreme Court during the late 1840s, for instance, touched a raw popular nerve as it menaced the authority of the state Superior Court, which was organized by circuits and was far more subject to local control. Gatherings in Franklin and Jackson counties, among others, demanded its abolition, branding the new court as "unconstitutional, organized against the express will of the people, and forcing upon the people an increase of taxes without furnishing corresponding beneficial results."[22]

Such sensitivity to external power and authority had deep roots and emerged with special force in state politics. As early as the first decades

20. James Washington Watts Farm Diary, Cass County, January 11, 1856, James Washington Watts Papers, GDAH; Executive Department, County Officers, Jackson and Carroll Counties, 1860; Manuscript Census, Georgia, Jackson and Carroll Counties, Schedule I, 1860.

21. Cassville *Standard*, February 5, 1857, May 7, 1857, December 3, 1857, June 10, 1858; Athens *Southern Banner*, June 8, 1854, June 29, 1854.

22. Athens *Southern Banner*, March 24, 1853, May 26, 1853, September 16, 1858.

of the nineteenth century, representatives from the Upcountry joined with rising slaveholders in Georgia's central Cotton Belt in a concerted attempt to loosen the hold of Low Country planters on the legislature. Apportionment on the basis of the federal ratio and the creation of new coastal counties had given the seaboard gentry sway in both the state house and the senate even as the hinterlands rapidly boasted a substantially larger white population. Reform forces succeeded in enlarging the franchise, abolishing property qualifications for most offices, and facilitating the popular election of the governor, who previously had been selected by the seaboard-dominated senate; they fared worse in attacks on the federal ratio, which the old elite managed to keep firmly entrenched. Under threat of ad hoc action, however, the legislature consented to a formal constitutional convention in 1833.[23]

This movement for political democratization may not have involved a clear-cut class confrontation, but neither was it a mere "clash of tin swords." For conservative planters, an entire conception of politics along with the security of their property appeared to be at stake. From their vantage point, the fight over legislative apportionment threatened to remove considerations of wealth from the allocation of representation, and, as Eugenius Nisbet argued at the convention, the federal ratio offered essential protection to plantation counties against the "assaults of those [regions] unsuitable to slavery." Nisbet shared with many large slaveholders the belief that the "West and Pine Barrens" were "anti-slaveholding." Furthermore, the alliance of Upcountry and Cotton Belt soon began to dissolve. As a proliferating slave population turned the federal numbers to their advantage by the early 1830s, delegates from middle Georgia abandoned support for a new scheme of apportionment based on white population alone and shifted their energies to reducing the size of the assembly, thereby bolstering their strength in the state senate. The convention then deadlocked until a compromise, which, ironically, joined the Upcountry and the coast in a plan to guarantee each county representation, narrowly passed. But disappointed delegates from the Cotton Belt helped defeat it when it was submitted for popular ratification, despite the strong backing it received from Upcountry and Mountain counties.[24] A similar scenario

23. Roberts, "Sectional Factors," 94–110; Green, *Constitutional Developments*, 151–52, 233–40; Saye, *Constitutional History*, 159, 162, 171–72; DeBats, "Elites and Masses," 320–28.

24. DeBats, "Elites and Masses," 330; Roberts, "Sectional Factors," 118–19.

unfolded in 1839, though the intervening years saw the enactment of bills abrogating the last property qualifications for state office and establishing elective Superior Court judgeships. Reapportionment and reduction remained divisive questions throughout the antebellum period.[25]

Conservative fears notwithstanding, political democratization was possible only because slavery did not present itself as an issue. The few antislavery societies that appeared in western Virginia and North Carolina during the eighteenth century had long since been squelched, and there is no indication that they ever commanded a following in the Lower South. By insisting upon the inclusion of the three-fifths clause in the Constitution and later by formulating a sophisticated state rights position during the Nullification crisis, the master class sought to reinforce its power in national politics while effectively removing the peculiar institution from the domain of national authority. In the context of an expanding slave society, the reform agitation ultimately strengthened the hands of the planters at home by creating room at the top and by absorbing diverse geographical and economic locales into a political system that the planters were able to control. The radical voices of men like Franklin Plummer of Mississippi and John Jacobus Flournoy of Georgia were quickly silenced within party circles. The path to political prominence for aspiring politicians of the Upcountry as well as of the Black Belt clearly began at the altar of slavery.[26]

Yet, the class and regional divisions that surfaced during the battle for political reform became very much a part of Southern politics in the 1840s and 1850s. There is no need to accept the simplified equation of Whiggery with planters and the Black Belt and Democracy with yeomen and the Upcountry in order to recognize that each party appealed to certain constituencies. In Georgia and other states of the Lower South, a distinct correlation could be found between high per capita wealth, commercial agriculture, large slaveholdings, and strong support for the Whig party. Indeed, from the personal factionalism of the 1820s to the formation of the Union and State Rights parties during

25. Roberts, "Sectional Factors," 110–22; Green, *Constitutional Developments*, 233–40; Saye, *Constitutional History*, 175–78.

26. William W. Freehling, *Prelude to Civil War: The Nullification Controversy in South Carolina, 1816–1836* (New York, 1964); Edwin Miles, "Franklin Plummer: Piney Woods Spokesman of the Jackson Era," *Journal of Mississippi History*, XIV (January 1952), 6–32; E. Merton Coulter, *John Jacobus Flournoy: Champion of the Common Man in the Antebellum South* (Savannah, 1942).

the Nullification controversy, to the linkages with emerging national parties in the late 1830s and 1840s, to the realignments of the 1850s, and eventually to the movement for secession, political rifts in Georgia often tapped antagonisms between plantation and nonplantation areas.[27]

In defending slavery and assuming, at least, a broad state rights position, both Whigs and Democrats served the larger interests of the planter class. And the political grid in Georgia, as elsewhere, did not follow neat social and geographical lines. Loyalties built upon personal prestige and patronage helped shape voting behavior, and each party embraced numerous factions frequently at odds with one another. Elections in the Black Belt and in parts of the Upcountry usually were closely contested, and while the Democrats generally attained predominance statewide, their margin of victory was not substantial until the late 1850s. But it was no accident that the locus of Whig and Democratic support dovetailed geographically and economically. Whigs marshaled their greatest strength in the Plantation Belt and in counties with sizable commercial centers; the Democrats did so in the Upcountry and Pine Barrens. Between 1836 and 1856, for instance, the Upcountry stood as a Democratic stronghold. Some counties consistently delivered over 80 percent of their votes to the party; most delivered over 60 percent. Only in the counties of Madison and Gwinnett, bordering the Black Belt and containing a significant small planter element, could the Whigs command an occasional majority. During the same period in the Black Belt, on the other hand, the Whigs received approximately 60 percent of the votes cast.[28]

At bottom, partisan divisions reflected deeper cleavages between those social groups and locales participating extensively in the market economy and those on the periphery or virtually isolated from it. On issues such as banking, credit, and internal improvements, party stances diverged. The Whigs hoped to facilitate and expand commercial interchange, while the Democrats, certainly by the 1840s, sought to

27. Arthur C. Cole, *The Whig Party in the South* (Gloucester, Mass., 1962); Ulrich B. Phillips, *Georgia and State Rights* (Antioch, 1968), 104, 127, 140, 145–46, 205–6; Richard H. Shryock, *Georgia and the Union in 1850* (Philadelphia, 1926), 71–72, 93–99, 105–7; James R. Sharp, *The Jacksonians Versus the Banks: Politics in the States After the Panic of 1837* (New York, 1970), 89–109; Paul Murray, "Economic Sectionalism in Georgia Politics, 1825–1855," *JSH*, X (August 1944), 294–305.

28. Phillips, *Georgia and State Rights*, 143–70; Johnson, *Patriarchal Republic*, 66–71; Murray, "Economic Sectionalism," 305; Paul Murray, *The Whig Party in Georgia, 1825–1853* (Chapel Hill, 1948), 185.

limit or regulate it. Both parties spoke to the ideal of independence and defined it in economic terms, but as the Whigs believed that independence required the accumulation of wealth, the Democrats contended that it could survive only by circumscribing involvement in the market. The Democrats' suspicion of and hostility toward corporate power and the cash nexus in general appealed to many planters who resented outside authority, feared industrial development, and groaned about Northern and Southern middlemen and the fluctuations of cotton prices. As election returns strikingly illustrated, however, the party also captured the spirit of Upcountry yeomen.[29]

The bank question offers a cogent example of the nature of social and political discord. During the first decades of the nineteenth century, alignments remained hazy, partly because of the constitutional issues surrounding the Bank of the United States. But by the 1830s, and especially after the Panic of 1837, battle lines in Georgia crystallized between supporters of independent commercial banking—generally Whigs in the Black Belt and market towns—and a broad spectrum of reformers—congregating primarily in the Democratic party—who pressed for strict regulation, state control, or the outright abolition of banks. As early as 1823, Governor John Clark, a hard-money man whose following would eventually side with the Democrats, favored restricting banks to major marketing cities, where convertibility of paper into specie would be required, and the establishment of a state-owned institution. Although the ensuing years saw the multiplication of commercial banks, as the plantation economy spread through middle Georgia, Clark's recommendation for a public corporation designed to extend long-term loans came to fruition in 1828 with the founding of the Central Bank.[30]

A more firmly entrenched banking system in Georgia mitigated both the effects of economic depression and the rise of vehement antibank sentiment that took hold in the southwest during the late 1830s. Nevertheless, some legislative representatives from small farming areas

29. Murray, *Whig Party*, 101–4, 109–11; Thornton, *Politics and Power*, 56–58. Thornton's work offers the best appraisal of the distinctions between Whig and Democratic ideology, and though his study is confined to Alabama, I think he is correct in arguing that his conclusions are applicable, at least, to the other states of the Lower South.

30. Milton S. Heath, *Constructive Liberalism: The Role of the State in Economic Development in Georgia to 1860* (Cambridge, Mass., 1954), 190–92; Murray, *Whig Party*, 13–14; Thomas P. Govan, "Banking and the Credit System in Georgia, 1810–1860" (Ph.D. diss., Vanderbilt University, 1937), 119.

argued that commercial banking should be confined to the wholesale trade, and hard-money Democrats played a leading role in agitating for debtor relief and bank regulation. They inspired a series of laws demanding the issuance of semiannual reports detailing bank transactions, preventing the circulation of small notes, and penalizing banks for failing to make specie redemptions. One measure passed by the assembly in 1840 sought to enforce strict convertibility with the threat of immediate suit for foreclosure and liquidation. Amid a widespread conservative response to the commercial panic, the 1840s witnessed a halt to bank charters in Georgia and, under Democratic auspices, the virtual prohibition of banking in two other Southern states.[31]

During the prosperous 1850s, commercial banking in Georgia expanded once again, with twenty-seven new institutions chartered between 1850 and 1856. But a new crisis accompanied the Panic of 1857, for while state banks operated on a relatively stable basis, they defied the law and suspended specie payments. Although the out-going governor, Herschel V. Johnson, took no action, his successor, Joseph E. Brown, who spoke for the hard-money wing of the Democratic party, issued a scathing attack and warned that when he received evidence of a bank's transgression, he would "order proceedings for the forfeiture of its charter." Moving to forestall such retribution, the banking interest obtained enabling legislation from the General Assembly; Brown then summarily vetoed it. "The people [will] sustain him," the Upcountry Clarksville *Georgian* proclaimed, and meetings in several north Georgia counties which passed resolutions in support of the governor's stand seemed to bear testimony to the paper's prediction. An intensive lobbying campaign waged by the banks ultimately won enough legislators to the side of moderation to override Brown's veto, but the controversy continued to bristle in the press.[32]

For the Whiggish Athens *Southern Watchman*, "Brown was strictly carrying out Democratic principles in opposing banks, railroads, factories, and internal improvements." And as another paper of similar disposition sneered: "By his Bank Veto Message [Brown] . . . got his name up with the 'wool hat boys' and that class of our *Democratic* friends,

---

31. Sharp, *Jacksonians Versus the Banks*, 110–22, 277–80; Govan, "Banking and the Credit System," 175–79; Heath, *Constructive Liberalism*, 207–10.
32. Govan, "Banking and the Credit System," 179; Parks, *Brown of Georgia*, 45–52; I. W. Avery, *The History of the State of Georgia From 1850 to 1881* (New York, 1881), 60–67; Herbert Fielder, *A Sketch of the Life and Times and Speeches of Joseph E. Brown* (Springfield, Mass., 1883), 119–30.

who have little or no correct knowledge of the practical science of Banking. . . ."[33] Yet, neither a flat rejection of commercial intercourse nor a muddled understanding "of the practical science of Banking" led Brown's supporters, the staunchest of whom resided in the Upcountry, to join his "war" on the banks. Rather, notions about the proper relations of production and exchange and the threat that banks posed to those relations fueled the agitation. Through the "unguarded grant of corporate powers and privileges" denied to "the laboring masses," the hard-money forces thundered in the language of Jacksonianism, the banks had become "monied monopolies" exercising inordinate power in the marketplace. By "extend[ing] their paper circulation . . . in a wild spirit of speculation," they were also responsible for the frequent cycles of economic dislocation. "The great fundamental defect of our present banking system," an Upcountry representative told the state legislature, "is that the office or province of furnishing a circulating medium and of supplying our commercial exchange is vested in the same institution."[34]

Perhaps more importantly, commercial banking challenged the deepest popular sensibilities by divorcing wealth from productive labor. "What is the use of money?" a contributor to the Cassville *Standard* asked. "Money is not bread to eat nor clothes to wear. Money is not wealth—it is only the representation of wealth. . . . Bread is wealth, clothes is wealth; a bed to lie on; a horse to ride, to plow—whatever meets man's necessities is wealth. . . ." Unfortunately, he lamented, "the idea . . . has extensively obtained, that . . . money is wealth . . . that just as money is multiplied, so is wealth increased, and shrewd and far-seeing men have taken advantage of this popular delusion, upon which to engraft the banking system—a system which *makes the money* and *avoids the labor*. . . ."[35]

Corporate domination of the marketplace, the antibank forces insisted, lay only a short step from corporate domination of the political process. "It is already claimed by some," Governor Brown charged, "that [the banks] now have the power by combinations and free use of large sums of money to control the political conventions and elections of our State and in this way to crush those who may have the

33. Athens *Southern Watchman*, January 7, 1857; Rome *Weekly Courier*, February 3, 1858.

34. Athens *Southern Banner*, November 11, 1857, December 23, 1858; Fielder, *Life and Times*, 121–28.

35. Cassville *Standard*, November 26, 1857.

independence to stand by the rights of the people in opposition to their aggressive power. . . ." Acknowledging the "sudden shock" that "harsh [and] . . . radical . . . measures" might precipitate, Brown nonetheless counseled that "we should do all in our power to bring about [the] complete reformation . . . of our banking system . . . and if this not be possible, we should abandon it entirely. . . ." He and his supporters in the General Assembly suggested the rigid regulation of charters or the establishment of a state subtreasury. "Let it not be forgotten . . . by those who have watched with anxiety the growing power of corporate influence," the governor reminded his constituents, "that the price of Republican liberty is perpetual vigilance."[36]

The strong backing that Brown received from the Upcountry in the gubernatorial election of 1859, when the opposition attempted to make political capital out of the bank issue, further evidenced the yeomanry's identification with the governor's point of view. In county after county, Brown mustered well over 60 percent of the votes, and in several counties he won over 80 percent. Only in those areas blending into the Black Belt or containing large commercial centers did Brown's margin of victory prove less than overwhelming.[37] For most Upcountry yeomen, to be sure, the "monied monopolists" could have appeared, at worst, a distant threat. No county north of the Black Belt had a chartered bank, circulating currency always remained scarce, and few cultivators had more than limited involvement with the export market and its attendant financial structure. But at a time when commercial agriculture was expanding, railroad development being promoted, and court dockets being cluttered with actions for debt, the bank question had a special symbolic importance.

Upcountry resistance to the power of consolidated wealth not only sharpened partisan divisions; it stirred added dissension within the ranks of the Democratic party. Angered by previous conflicts over legislative apportionment, north Georgia Democrats complained, as late as the 1850s, of the "aristocratic minds in the older sections of our state" who "with not more than one-fifth of the Democracy exercise a controlling influence in the nomination of candidates." "It seems never to have occurred to the politicians of middle and lower Georgia," one disgruntled party member roared in 1857, "that we in the mountains were fit for anything else than to vote. . . . Mention the claims of the

36. Athens *Southern Banner*, November 11, 1858.
37. Ibid., October 13, 1859; Athens *Southern Watchman*, October 20, 1859.

Upcountry, intimate there are talents and statesmanship among us, and you are stared at as if you were green." "The people of the Up Country intend no longer to be cajoled by the spurious pretext of party harmony," a writer under the pseudonym "Cherokee" warned, "[and] they intend to have their interests represented by someone they know . . . someone who is adverse to making the state government a mere machine for transfering the earnings of one class or section into the pockets of another, someone who does not consider the Georgia and Central Railroads as the only interests of the State."[38] Resentments such as these provoked bitter showdowns in congressional districts that crossed regional lines. In the northeastern Sixth, for example, the nomination of Clarke County's candidate in the wake of a controversy over the seating of rival delegations in 1857 led to a walkout of Upcountry representatives and the entrance of an independent into the race. "The people of the upcountry," the bolters cried, "are beginning to feel and believe and know that there *is* a clique, which has exercised and still exercises a most despotic influence. . . ." Small wonder that Democratic chieftains settled on the dark horse Joseph Brown of Cherokee County after a similar wrangle disrupted the gubernatorial convention that year.[39]

III

If the confrontations over legislative apportionment, selection of candidates, and banking did not manifest a direct challenge to the material base or, indeed, to the legitimacy of the slaveholders' rule, the independent spirit evinced by the Upcountry proved worrisome to the planter class as the sectional crisis intensified and the need for Southern unity became increasingly urgent. When a Southern Rights paper insisted that the then moderate Howell Cobb's election to the governorship in 1851 provided evidence of a "considerable anti-slavery party in Georgia" which found its strength in "the jealousies of the poor who owned no slaves, against the rich slaveholder," it exuded more than simple partisanship. The paper expressed the elite's deepest fear that the controversy over slavery, which ignited national politics, could

38. North Georgia *Times*, quoted in Cassville *Standard*, May 14, 1857; Cassville *Standard*, April 16, 1857, March 5, 1857; Marietta *Union*, quoted in Cassville *Standard*, October 14, 1852.

39. Athens *Southern Banner*, June 16, 1857, July 9, 1858; Athens *Southern Watchman*, April 16, 1857; Parks, *Brown of Georgia*, 20–26.

be played out within the South itself. Marshaling a coalition of Union Democrats and Whigs after the Compromise of 1850, Cobb, in fact, swept to an impressive victory distinguished by strong support throughout the state. Mindful of South Carolina's abortive defiance of the federal government some twenty years earlier, few Georgians were ready to embrace extreme actions. But while numerous considerations promoted hesitancy among a large segment of the ruling class, the recognition that areas like "Cherokee Georgia" were "for the Union and against any measure that will place the State in a hostile attitude to the Federal government" surely stood as one of them.[40]

It would, however, be a mistake to exaggerate the Unionist sentiment in Georgia or to view the response of the Upcountry as monolithic. Secession as a possible recourse to Northern threats achieved widespread acceptance in the Lower South during the congressional turmoil of 1850. And Cobb's Constitutional Union party adhered to the "Georgia Platform," drawn up at a state convention that same year, which announced that "we hold the American Union secondary in importance only to the rights and principles it was designed to perpetuate." While grudgingly accepting the compromise, the Platform maintained that "the preservation of our much-beloved Union" hinged on congressional nonintervention with slavery in the states and territories and on the "faithful execution" of the fugitive-slave law. It was, in short, a conditional Unionism resting upon the "safety . . . the rights, and the honor of the slaveholding states."[41]

Although the militant Southern Rights faction of the Democratic party had its base in the Plantation Belt, and particularly in developing areas, it won some support in the Upcountry. Charles J. MacDonald, Howell Cobb's opponent in 1851, hailed from Cobb County and received popular majorities there and in two other Upcountry counties, including Carroll.[42] The moderate Constitutional Unionists, on the

40. Augusta *Constitutionalist and Republic*, quoted in Augusta *Daily Chronicle and Sentinel*, October 23, 1851; Athens *Southern Banner*, October 16, 1851; John H. Lumpkin to Howell Cobb, Rome, October 5, 1860, in the Ulrich B. Phillips, ed., *The Correspondence of Robert Toombs, Alexander Stephens, and Howell Cobb* (Washington, 1913), 214–15; David M. Potter, *The Impending Crisis, 1848–1861* (New York, 1976), 125–29.

41. *Journal of the State Convention Held in Milledgeville, December, 1850* (Milledgeville, 1850), 18–19; Potter, *Impending Crisis*, 122, 128.

42. Athens *Southern Banner*, October 16, 1851; John Jones to Hugh A. Haralson, Villa Rica, August 26, 1850, Hugh A. Haralson Letterbooks, 278, AHS; Charles Rodahan to Haralson, Carrollton, August 4, 1850, ibid., 226.

other hand, rolled to victory elsewhere in northern Georgia, but there Unionism ranged from uncompromising allegiance to the national government to the qualified commitments proposed by the state leadership. A meeting in Cass County, for example, denounced the extremist Southern convention, "cherishing as we do a strong attachment to the Union," yet denied that Congress had any authority to prohibit slavery in the territories and resolved that the restoration of peace and harmony required a "settle[ment] on what is known as the Missouri Compromise." This seeming patchwork of political identifications became even more complicated as the two-party system ruptured during the 1850s, though Upcountry yeomen generally remained within the broadly defined ranks of the Democratic party which reemerged in 1852.[43]

The apparently divided loyalties of yeoman farmers in the Upcountry can easily obscure the values and political perspectives they shared. Southern Rights or Unionism could be two sides of the same coin—the coin of local autonomy beholden to a particular social, economic, and political experience. The revolutionary republican heritage with which smallholders often identified through kinship and cultural affinity was not that of an expansive, centralized, industrializing nation, but rather that of a commonwealth of independent producers for whom political liberty and personal freedom were inseparable from the patterns of mutuality in their settlements. In the same way, a state-rights stance could be attractive, less because it represented a constitutional protection for slavery than because it expressed a broader commitment to defending local affairs and institutions against the intrusions of outsiders. Issues such as Indian removal, which saw the state of Georgia back the claims of Upcountry settlers against those of the Cherokees and the dictates of the federal government, played important roles in determining specific political allegiances, as did the outlook and judgment of trusted leaders. Whereas yeomen in nonplantation areas increasingly tied to Northern markets, like western Virginia, could cast their fate with the free states, their counterparts in Georgia, who produced primarily for their own consumption and whose economic horizons rarely extended beyond the county, could find much of the planters' rhetoric appealing.[44]

43. Athens *Southern Banner*, March 15, 1850; Arthur Hood to Hugh A. Haralson, Rome, March 17, 1850, Haralson Letterbooks, 45.

44. Genovese, "Yeoman Farmers," 335; U.S. Patent Office, *Report to the Commissioner, 1850* (Washington, 1851), II, 247–48.

And it was not simply a penchant for local autonomy that enabled yeomen to feel a certain commonality of interest with the elite. Whatever the complex meanings of state rights, all parties clearly recognized that, as a political ideology, it served to defend slavery. That numerous Upcountry farmers owned slaves and that nonslaveholders occasionally hired them explains part of this proslavery sentiment. That others who had little direct involvement with the institution followed suit suggests that the slavery issue tapped deeper concerns and fears. Those concerns and fears reflected the status of yeoman farmers as petty property holders and their staunch belief that property ownership formed the foundation of their independence. Thus, the planters struck a responsive chord when they argued that abolitionism threatened not only slave but all property. As a Hart County public meeting charged shortly after Lincoln's election: "a party has arisen at the North, founded in bigotry and fanaticism, whose sole ambition is directed against the institutions of the Southern states . . . [with the intention of] excit[ing] discontent and insurrection among our slaves, disturbing our peace, destroying our property, and jeopardizing the lives of our wives and children. . . ."[45]

The power of racism as a source of white social cohesion must be understood in this context. Yeomen and poorer whites acquired a wide reputation for rough attitudes toward, and rough dealings with, Afro-Americans. The ex-slaves themselves left ample testimony of the less-than-charitable treatment they received at the hands of overseers, patrollers, and the neighboring poor.[46] Travelers and other contemporary observers, to be sure, noted the more relaxed atmosphere of slavery on smaller farms. So far as the planter ideologue Daniel Robinson Hundley could see, yeomen exercised "but few of the rights of ownership over their human chattels, making so little distinction between master and man, that their negroes invariably become spoiled . . . and in all things [are] treated more like equals than slaves."

45. Athens *Southern Banner*, December 13, 1860. Also see Milledgeville *Federal Union*, December 11, 1860; Athens *Southern Banner*, December 6, 1860, December 20, 1860, December 27, 1860; Athens *Southern Watchman*, December 12, 1860; Carroll County Secession Resolutions, Executive Department, Incoming Correspondence, 1861–1865, Letters, Box 5, GDAH.

46. See, for example, George P. Rawick, ed., *The American Slave: A Composite Autobiography*, 19 vols. (Westport, Conn., 1972), *Georgia Narratives*, XII (1), 3; *South Carolina Narratives*, II (2), 70; *Mississippi Narratives*, VII (2), 4; H. C. Bruce, *The New Man: Twenty-Nine Years a Free Man* (York, Pa., 1895), 30.

Especially in the Hill Country, Hundley added disconcertedly, "you will frequently see black and white, slave and freeman, camping out together, living sometimes in the same tent or temporary pine-pole cabin . . . [with the slaves calling farmers] by Christian names."[47] The racial demography and exigencies of family farming in regions like the Georgia Upcountry encouraged a more casual approach to slave discipline and promoted forms of racial interaction distinct from those of the Black Belt. But these conditions hardly signaled an emerging interracial egalitarianism. When settlers proclaimed the "Free State of Carroll" in the 1830s, they did so with an eye toward maintaining a predominantly "white man's country." In general, these farmers saw the legal subordination of black people as a safeguard for their way of life.[48]

While becoming a force in their own right, the racial attitudes of Upcountry yeomen constituted a historically specific variant of broader class attitudes: those of small property holders toward the propertyless poor. The fear and contempt that seventeenth- and eighteenth-century republicanism, and its American disciples, reserved for those individuals who depended on the whims of the market or the wills of other men for their livelihoods struck early and deep roots, North and South. It was no coincidence that the pejorative racial attributes ascribed to the Afro-American character were often identical to the pejorative ethnic attributes ascribed to the Irish-American character. Irish immigrants composed the bulk of the unskilled labor force in many antebellum Northern cities. Nor was it any coincidence that yeoman farmers, who claimed a precarious independence, could share a racist outlook with planters, just as native artisans, who faced the prospect of proletarianization, could share an antiforeign, anti-Catholic outlook with Northern elites.[49] Whatever else they were, blacks were laborers devoid of means and subject to the dictates of their white owners—the very status that most terrified smallholders. And, by conventional

47. Daniel Robinson Hundley, *Social Relations in Our Southern States* (New York, 1860), 193–94.

48. James C. Bonner, *Georgia's Last Frontier: The Development of Carroll County* (Athens, 1971), 22.

49. Edmund S. Morgan, *American Slavery, American Freedom: The Ordeal of Colonial Virginia* (New York, 1975), 319–26, 369–87; David Montgomery, "The Shuttle and the Cross: Weavers and Artisans in the Kensington Riots of 1844," *Journal of Social History*, VI (Summer 1972), 411–46; Bruce Laurie, "Nothing on Compulsion: Lifestyles of Philadelphia Artisans, 1820–1850," *Labor History*, XV (Summer 1974), 354–66.

wisdom, the slaves had a thorough disregard for property rights, making them an actual, as well as symbolic, threat to the basis of yeoman independence. The petty pilfering widely viewed as a natural disposition among blacks may have had a logic and morality of its own and may have entertained the planters and confirmed their own sense of superiority; it could not be taken lightly by farmers who had a difficult enough time managing from year to year.[50]

The class dimensions of these attitudes are brought into sharper relief by the vigilante actions waged by small farmers in some sections of the Georgia Upcountry during the early nineteenth century against roving bands of landless whites, Indians, and runaway slaves who lived by hunting and preying upon homesteads—actions which had precedents in the western Carolinas of the late eighteenth century, if not before.[51] During the 1850s, of course, a sizable portion of the Upcountry's white population owned no land. But this was not a floating group that rejected the cultural predicates of the yeoman community. Rather, these individuals frequently had ties to landowning farmers through kinship and a life cycle which normally made landlessness and youthfulness synonymous. In the antebellum period, social and cultural divisions among nonelite Southerners largely fell along racial lines.

Linking race and class, such attitudes could have nurtured anti-slavery sentiments, as they did in the Midwest; with isolated exceptions, they did not. Residing in a society that sanctioned racial bondage and yet included diverse geographic and economic regions, Upcountry yeomen could sensibly view slavery both as a bulwark of social order and as a means for preserving a white majority in their locales. Governor Joseph Brown seemed to recognize as much when, in mobilizing support for secession, he chose to describe the special consequences of Emancipation: "So soon as the slaves were at liberty thousands of them would leave the cotton and rice fields . . . and make their way to the mountain region [where] we should have them plundering and stealing, robbing and killing." The abolition of slavery, thereby, would strike "at the very foundation of society, and if carried out, would destroy all property and all protection to life, liberty, and happiness." Only in remote areas of northernmost Georgia, where the

50. Eugene D. Genovese, *Roll, Jordan, Roll: The World the Slaves Made* (New York, 1974), 599–612.

51. Bonner, *Georgia's Last Frontier*, 33–34; Rachel Klein, "Ordering the Backcountry: The South Carolina Regulation," *WMQ*, 3rd ser., XXXVIII (October 1981), 661–80.

chattel institution had virtually no presence, would there be expressions, as one of Brown's lieutenants put it, of "anti-nigger slavery."[52]

Those who blame the failure of Southern antislavery on elite repression or the nonslaveholders' ignorance would do well to reflect on the nature of the antislavery argument and on the character of the common folk it intended to stir to action. Men like Hinton Rowan Helper, Cassius M. Clay, Daniel Reeves Goodloe, and Henry Ruffner railed against slavery, not out of sympathy for the travail of blacks, but out of concern for the institution's adverse impact on Southern economic development. Compiling a vast array of statistics on population, crop production, urbanization, and industry, they sought to demonstrate, with a polemical zeal, that the South lagged behind the North in every respect. And like their counterparts in the free states, these critics condemned slavery for the inefficiency of labor, the apparent degradation of the white lower classes, and the general retardation of education and culture in the South. Had their views been widely circulated, they might have fueled class antagonisms. But we may ask what the antislavery writers had to offer the majority of Southern whites who lived outside the Plantation Belt, engaged in semisubsistence agriculture, confined trading relations primarily to their own locales, and evinced little desire to exchange their way of life for the uncertain benefits of "progress." If anything, the Helpers and the Clays wished to expand the very marketplace that Upcountry yeomen saw as a threat to their independence. Not by accident did the handful of Southern warriors against slavery hail from the Upper South and embrace Whiggish politics; they spoke for the interests of Southern industrialists and commercial farmers who did not depend on slave labor and whose economic horizons extended north of the Mason-Dixon line.[53]

An acceptance of slavery by yeomen in nonplantation areas of the Lower South did not, however, smooth the road to Southern unity. A

52. Milledgeville *Federal Union*, December 11, 1860; W. A. Campbell to Governor Joseph E. Brown, Fannin County, February 23, 1861, Executive Dept., Incoming Corresp., 1861–1865, Letters, Box 5. Also see Johnson, *Patriarchal Republic*, 30, 50; Thornton, *Politics and Power*, 205–9; William L. Barney, *The Secessionist Impulse: Alabama and Mississippi in 1860* (Princeton, 1974), 225–30; Eugene H. Berwanger, *The Frontier Against Slavery: Western Anti-Negro Prejudice and the Slavery Extension Controversy* (Urbana, Ill., 1971).

53. Hinton Rowan Helper, *The Impending Crisis of the South: How to Meet It* (New York, 1860), 17–100; Hugh C. Bailey, *Hinton Rowan Helper: Abolitionist Racist* (Tuscaloosa, Ala., 1965), 19–40; David L. Smiley, *The Lion of Whitehall: The Life of Cassius M. Clay* (Madison, Wis., 1962); Carl N. Degler, *The Other South: Southern Dissenters in the Nineteenth Century* (New York, 1974), 47–96.

tradition of political independence in the Upcountry, if not a healthy contempt for planter pretensions, was an ever present feature of antebellum politics and proved a nagging concern for the elite as it became increasingly apparent that an ultimate test of faith might be in the offing. While partisan loyalties helped integrate diverse regions and social groups into a political system, those loyalties reflected, rather than fully absorbed, class interests and tensions, as the conflict over banking and the discord within the Democratic party plainly indicated. And as the two-party structure collapsed in the 1850s, warring factions pressed their claims, at times in ways that offended the sensibilities of yeomen who had a strong sense of their rights and little taste for bullying. Witness the stinging protest of a Floyd County farmer against the manipulative tactics of local secessionists:

> I am a plain farmer, but I hope I am nevertheless a freeman. I have to work hard for my living, and make my bread by the sweat of my brow. I was warned to appear in town last Saturday to muster. When we were dismissed we were notified that Mr. [Walter T.] Colquitt would speak in the afternoon. This set me thinking and I found others thinking too. How, thinks I to myself, does it happen that we are called out, when we are all busy gathering our little crop . . . and compelled to come to Rome through the heat and dust to muster! I then recollected that our general was a fire-eater . . . and that they were anxious to make everyone like themselves, and if the people wouldn't come to town and hear without, they would get up a sham muster and make them come and hear anyhow. This sorter raised me that I should be compelled to have the same politics as my general, and I and some of my neighbors are determined more than ever, that we will go for the [Unionists]. . . . The next attempt, I fear, if the secessionists get into office, will be to march us poor working people to the polls, with their swords swinging over our heads, make us vote for who they please. . . . I should like to know whether this is a free country, or whether we are to be dragged out from our business to gratify the military men and the political demogogues.[54]

Others scoffed at "the dream of a cotton Republic." The fiery Thomas R. R. Cobb thus urgently summoned the services of his moderate-turned-secessionist brother Howell in December 1860: "By all means come *directly to Athens* or else send me a list of appointments for you to speak in the following counties—*Franklin, Banks, Habersham, Union,*

54. Rome *Weekly Courier*, September 25, 1851.

Lumpkin, Forsyth, Hall, and Gwinnett. We have trouble above here and *no one* but *yourself* can quell it."[55]

Wary of class and regional frictions and fearing the worst, some planters and their political representatives moved to strengthen ties to the slave regime: attempts to reopen the African slave trade and exempt slave property from levy for debt were largely designed to broaden the base of slaveownership.[56] For other members of the ruling class, the social and political turmoil testified to the unavoidable excesses of democracy. Indeed, the antidemocratic impulse commonly associated with the postbellum era had its origins here. "[W]herever ignorance abounds Democracy flourishes," the conservative Athens *Southern Watchman* asserted in 1857. A wealthy planter, who had previously waxed effusive over the Southern *Herrenvolk*, voiced similar sentiments a year later: "Thanks to Mr. Jefferson we have made a mistake . . . and pushed the love of democracy too far. . . . [A] vulgar democracy and licentious 'freedom' is rapidly supplanting all the principles of constitutional 'liberty'! When shall the American people perceive that all our difficulties arise from the absurdities of deciding that the 'pauper' and the 'landholder' are alike competent to manage the affairs of a Country, or alike entitled to vote for those who shall?"[57]

Agitation in Georgia for measures to reduce the size of the legislature, extend the term of the governor, and make judgeships appointive, some of which found their way into the new constitution of 1861, signaled the appearance of latent elite disenchantment with political democracy. One Augusta paper went so far as to advocate "an Executive for life, a vastly restricted suffrage, Senators elected for life . . . and the most popular branch of the Assembly elected for seven years, the Judiciary absolutely independent and for life, or good behavior."[58] A gnawing

55. Columbus Morrison Papers, November 20, 1860, Vol. 3, SHC; T. R. R. Cobb to Howell Cobb, Athens, December 15, 1860, in Phillips, ed., *Correspondence*, 522.

56. *Southern Cultivator*, XVII (March 1859), 83–84; Augusta *Dispatch*, quoted in Cassville *Standard*, February 3, 1859; Athens *Southern Watchman*, February 12, 1857; Cassville *Standard*, January 22, 1857, February 19, 1857.

57. Athens *Southern Watchman*, January 29, 1857; Alfred M. Huger to Mr. Wickham, June 1, 1858, quoted in Roark, *Masters Without Slaves*, 27, 93.

58. Macon *Telegraph*, quoted in Athens *Southern Watchman*, January 13, 1859. On agitation to reduce the size of the legislature, see Athens *Southern Watchman*, May 19, 1858, December 1, 1859, December 8, 1859; Rome *Weekly Courier*, March 30, 1859, November 9, 1859. On general antidemocratic sentiment, see Augusta *Chronicle and Sentinel*, December 8, 1860, quoted in Johnson, *Patriarchal Republic*, 100–101; Carrollton *Advocate*, December 14, 1860.

belief that numerous Southern whites might sympathize with an "Abolition Government," that a Republican president might use his patronage to build an antislavery party in the South, that "the contest for slavery [might] no longer be between North and South . . . [but] between the people of the South," led hesitant planters down the secessionist road. The slaveholders' struggle for home rule received enormous reinforcement from the need to solidify their rule at home.[59]

The secession crisis revealed the dimensions of the planters' political hegemony. When Georgians marched to the polls on January 2, 1861, to select delegates to the convention that would decide the state's future course, they chose between immediate secessionist and cooperationist candidates, neither of whom questioned the right of disunion, the sanctity of slavery, or the peril posed by a Republican in the White House. And by that time, South Carolina had already severed its ties with the Union, thus strengthening the hand of the radicals. Counseling against internal strife, urging that the "best men" be selected to deliberate on a matter of such gravity, and insisting that disunion would not mean war, the secessionists, whose ranks now included virtually all of Georgia's prominent political leaders, pushed for a popular mandate. Since they had previously enlisted the powerful voice of Joseph Brown, who had the trust of many Upcountry yeomen, their victory seemed, to numerous observers, assured.[60]

The results of the election, therefore, must have offered them only small comfort. According to the most careful estimate, the secessionists received, at best, a narrow majority of the popular vote, although it translated into a decisive edge in the convention. Strongest support for immediate secessionist candidates came from town counties and large slaveholding counties that normally voted Democratic. Whiggish counties in the Black Belt generally favored immediate secession as well, but by slimmer margins. The cooperationists, on the other hand, mustered much of their strength in the predominantly white counties of the Pine Barrens, Wiregrass, and Upcountry. As a whole, the Upcountry gave the secessionists a slight advantage, yet fully half of

59. Candler, ed., *Confederate Records*, I, 47; Charleston *Mercury*, quoted in Johnson, *Patriarchal Republic*, 50; Alexander Stephens to A Friend in the North, November 25, 1860, in Phillips, ed., *Correspondence*, 504–5.

60. Milledgeville *Federal Union*, November 27, 1860, December 11, 1860; Newnan *Independent Blade*, November 30, 1860; Candler, ed., *Confederate Records*, I, 51; L. S. D'Lyon to William H. Stiles, Savannah, January 9, 1861, C. William Henry Stiles Papers, Folder 74, SHC.

the counties, including Carroll, which had thrown its weight behind the Southern Rights party earlier in the decade, opted for cooperationist delegates. In the Mountains, cooperationism, if not outright Unionism, held sway.[61]

Given the ability of the planters to define the issue as one of means rather than ends, one must interpret these voting results with great caution. An easy equation of cooperationism with staunch opposition to secession would be just as misleading as would an easy depiction of cooperationism as a mere variant of secessionist sentiment. Among the elite, and in all likelihood within the Black Belt at large, the question came down to one of strategy based on a fundmental commitment to the protection of slavery. Fearing that upon secession "all the bad and destructive elements of the South will be unbridled and turned loose among us," planter cooperationists wished to stall summary action. The most conservative expressed willingness to accept a Republican president if strict constitutional guarantees could be exacted; others, having abandoned any real hope of sectional reconciliation, desired a unified Southern response to smooth the process of disunion. In neither camp were loyalties in doubt.[62]

Matters were far more complicated in nonplantation areas, particularly in the Upcountry. The relatively low voter turnout in an election of such importance can probably be attributed as much to popular confusion, if not to a rejection of the alternatives, as to the rains which soaked Georgia's soil on election day. And the returns provided less than a clear-cut verdict on either side. A vote for secession could have been an expression of support for state rights and local autonomy as well as an expression of support for a slaveholders' republic; a vote for cooperationism could have represented any one of several positions. When a resident of Hall County told Howell Cobb that "there seems to be still some among us disposed to act with the Black Republican party," he pointed to the most extreme possibility. Others displaying a profound localism asked "the Confederacy on the one hand and the Union on the other, to leave us alone, unmolested, that we may work out our political and financial destiny here in the hills. . . ." Perhaps a majority subscribed to the spirit of a resolution offered by James P.

61. Michael P. Johnson, "A New Look at the Popular Vote for Delegates to the Georgia Secession Convention," *GHQ*, LVI (Summer 1972), 268–70; Johnson, *Patriarchal Republic*, 63–78.

62. Rome *Weekly Courier*, January 8, 1861, quoted in Johnson, *Patriarchal Republic*, 54–55; Potter, *Impending Crisis*, 494–95, 546–47.

Simmons, Gwinnett County's dissenting delegate at the secession convention: "While we solemnly protest against the action of . . . adopting an ordinance for the immediate and separate secession of this State, and would have preferred a policy of cooperation with our Southern sister States, yet as good citizens we yield to the will of the majority . . . and we hereby pledge 'our lives, our fortunes, and our sacred honor' to the defense of Georgia, if necessary from any source whatever." In the uncertain months of late winter and early spring, as North and South perched on the threshold of conflagration, Upcountry Georgians could only watch and wait. Yet, as the cannons boomed in Charleston harbor, a Union flag waving defiantly in northern Pickens County served as a sobering reminder of the proud Southern Confederacy's fragile foundation.[63]

IV

War tests the fabric of a social order as does nothing else, taxing social and political ties as much as human and material resources. In a desperate quest for home rule, the slaveholders staked their survival as a class on valor in battle, on the power of "King Cotton" in the international market, and on the loyalties of the slaves and the white lower classes. The cause of the Confederacy would bring rich and poor into closer quarters than ever before, demand an unprecedented level of discipline and sacrifice on the part of each, and exact devastating tolls on the battlefields and home front.

The social fabric could not meet the test; under these strains it began to unravel, and in so doing lay bare its complex and contradictory textures. For just as the enthusiastic response of the slaves to the invading armies and to Emancipation exposed a face partially obscured by decades of bondage and the planters' self-serving rhetoric, the behavior of yeomen, especially those from the Upcountry, displayed their values and priorities in ways that partisan conflicts only hinted at

---

63. Ibid., 500; A. M. Evans to Howell Cobb, Hall County, March 20, 1861, in Phillips, ed., *Correspondence*, 551–52; James P. Simmons, quoted in J. C. Flanigan, *History of Gwinnett County*, 2 vols. (Hapeville, Ga., 1943), I, 189. The request that the people of the Hill Country be left alone by both sides comes from Winston County, Alabama. But the recollection of Judge William Alonzo Covington of Cherokee County, Georgia, suggests similar sentiments in the Georgia Upcountry. See Wesley S. Thompson, *The Free State of Winston: A History of Winston County, Alabama* (Winfield, Ala., 1968), 4; Rev. Lloyd G. Marlin, *History of Cherokee County* (Atlanta, 1932), 73.

and in ways that frequently confirmed some of the planters' deepest apprehensions. It was, in the fullest sense, a "moment of truth" for the master class and the society over which it ruled.[64]

However ambivalent the attitude of yeoman farmers toward secession, the aftermath of Fort Sumter brought a groundswell of support for the nascent Confederacy. Lincoln's call for troops not only pushed several wavering states in the Upper South to repudiate their ties to the Union, but seemed to validate the secessionists' claims that "Black Republicans" wished to lord over the South, by force if need be. So many Southerners volunteered for military service that sufficient weapons had not been stockpiled to supply them all, and President Jefferson Davis, along with the war governors, had little alternative to rejecting numerous applications. The enthusiasm for war, to be sure, was not unanimous. Rebecca Carter of Jackson County found it necessary, when presenting the flag to a local volunteer company, to pair her effusions "over the long catalogue of grievances which we as Southern people have suffered from the North" with the irritated complaint that "some of you do not feel the interest which you should, and were it not you were rather compelled you would stay at home." At the earliest stages, however, this apparent lack of concern was more than compensated for by a widespread desire to have a crack at the Yankees.[65]

The initial effervescence was based, in large part, on the belief that hostilities would not be of long duration. Who could doubt that men priding themselves on the ability to "bark off" a squirrel at a hundred paces would be more than a match for any foe? The first major encounter at Manassas seemed to bear this out. The Confederates won a stunning victory that left the Union army beating a hasty retreat toward Washington. Much to the chagrin of Confederate leaders, not to say sympathetic military historians of a later day, the Southern command failed to pursue and, perhaps, lost an opportunity to bring the war to a speedy and favorable conclusion. They probably had little choice: hundreds of their troops reacted to the feat with great jubilation

64. Raimondo Luraghi, *The Rise and Fall of the Plantation South* (New York, 1978), 5; Genovese, *Roll, Jordan, Roll*, 97–112.

65. Athens *Southern Banner*, July 17, 1861; W. B. Jennings Memoirs, Floyd County Confederate and U.D.C. Collection, 23, GDAH; John B. Gordon, *Reminiscences of the Civil War* (New York, 1904), 3–9; Charles W. Ramsdell, *Behind the Lines in the Southern Confederacy* (Baton Rouge, 1944), 6–7; T. Conn Bryan, *Confederate Georgia* (Athens, 1953), 18–26.

and then promptly departed for home. They had whipped the Yankees, had they not? The war was over, was it not?[66]

Such a disregard for military discipline, which led observers to call the Confederates "the best of fighters and the worst of soldiers," was a product of the type of people Southern whites were and of the society in which they lived; it foreshadowed trouble despite early success in the field. Both planters and plain folk were touchy and proud. They had no patience for taking orders either from those whom they looked upon as social inferiors or from those whom they did not know and whose authority they were reluctant to recognize. The mere distinction of uniform could make little difference, as General Wigfall discovered when he accosted a common soldier taking guard duty casually and showing no humility when confronted with the officer's inquiries. "Do you know who I am sir?" the general abruptly asked. "Wall, now 'pears like I know your face, but I cant jes' call your name," the private ingenuously replied, "who is you?" "I'm General Wigfall," the officer shot back. "General, I'm pleased to meet you," the soldier genially responded, extending his hand in greeting, "my name's Jones." Others more bitterly rejected the deference that military protocol demanded. "[W]e have tite Rools over us," Henry Robinson, a Gwinnett County blacksmith wrote his wife, "the order was Red out in dress parade the other day that we all have to pull off our hats when we go to the coln or generel." "You know that is one thing I wont do," he railed. "I would rather see in hell before I will pull off my hat to any man and tha Jest as well shoot me at the start. . . ." Small wonder that Jones's and Robinson's peers might be less than courteous when faced with what they thought to be arbitrary and unreasonable orders, as was the case with one artilleryman who felt no compunction about inviting a bothersome sergeant to kiss his posterior. Exasperated as they were by this blatant disrespect for military, not to mention social, station and discipline, the well-to-do had little right to complain. When one young worthy resigned his "position" as private because he was not permitted to take "a dozen face and a smaller number of foot and bath towels" on campaign, he hardly set a sterling example of sacrifice for the cause.[67]

66. Gordon, *Reminiscences*, 37–46; Joseph E. Johnston, *Narrative of Military Operations During the Late War Between the States* (New York, 1874), 60; Clement Eaton, *A History of the Southern Confederacy* (New York, 1954), 151–53.

67. Jennings Memoirs, 10; Henry W. Robinson to Wife, Granger, Tennessee, July 25, 1862, Henry Robinson Letters, EU; Bell I. Wiley, *The Life of Johnny Reb: The Common Soldier of the Confederacy* (New York, 1943), 229–30, 234–35, 240; David Donald, "The Confederate as Fighting Man," *JSH*, XXV (May 1959), 188.

More than a pervasive independent spirit or general social tensions, the disciplinary problems reflected an ongoing conflict between the exigencies of a major war effort and the fundamental commitments of many of its participants. Consider the matter of military organization. Volunteers usually insisted upon joining companies raised in their own counties and, especially, upon electing their officers. By and large, following a pattern of antebellum politics, they chose men of standing in the community, men who, in all likelihood, had commanded the local militia and earned their trust, though politicking for military preferment did take place and occasionally stirred dissension among the troops. Professional military men, along with officials of the Confederate government, found these procedures a detriment to combat efficiency, but any attempt to withdraw the privilege—the "right," as the soldiers would have it—met with instantaneous resistance, if not mutiny or desertion. What is more, volunteers often refused to have their companies sent out of the state. After all, the war was being fought to defend Georgia and their locales from the invading Yankees. Thus the protest of F. M. Johnson, a private from Cass County. Not only had the officers "prevented us from having elections . . . [but] we have been transferred from one company to another without our consent or knowledge and against our wills as if we were so many hogs or cows driven from one pen to another," he charged. "I have been separated from friends who served with me last year in the Etowah Infantry . . . friends who was near and dear to me who I expected to serve through the war with." No longer would Johnson be so treated by "petty tyrants." "I expected to fight through this war as a Georgian not as a Mississippian Louisiannan Tennessean nor any other state," he cried, "and if I canot fight in the name of my own state I dont want to fight at all."[68]

These sentiments brewed widely. Indeed, the issue of authority over state troops generated one of the many confrontations between Georgia's Governor Brown and Jefferson Davis. But the problems of discipline and commitment were specially troublesome among Upcountry recruits. Owning few or no slaves, their families depended

68. F. M. Johnson to Governor Brown, Kingston, November 13, 1862, Exec. Dept., Incoming Corresp., Letters, Box 15; S. S. Campbell to Governor Brown, Camp Stephens, Pensacola, Florida, December 19, 1861, ibid., Box 5; J. Donaldson to Governor Brown, Canton, February 3, 1862, ibid., Box 8; John B. Beall, *In Barrack and Field, Poems and Sketches of Army Life* (Nashville, 1906), 296–97; Candler, ed., *Confederate Records*, II, 335–36, 343; David Donald, "Died of Democracy," in David Donald, ed., *Why the North Won the Civil War* (Baton Rouge, 1960), 82.

on their labor. When these men enlisted for either six- or twelve-month service in 1861, they fully anticipated returning home thereafter. Some figured to make short work of the Yankees and be back on the farm in time for harvest or certainly for spring planting. "[P]lease inform me at your earliest convenience if I can be received with a company of men for six months and furnish us with arms, to serve in the state or if strictly necessary, by your order I would leave the state," a Haralson County officer could request of Governor Brown, "my company will be made up of Farmers who are anxious to serve their country, though [they] want to come home in time to make a crop." Hence the impatience with prolonged drilling and the reluctance to sign on for extended tours of duty. When the captain of an Upcountry unit heard news of the fighting at Fort Pickens in the spring of 1861, he could only express relief: "I hope the report is true, for the longer we delay the greater the diversion, which seems to be increasing among the people in this section, will grow and I am in the hopes that a brush or two will set them on a proper basis. . . ."[69]

Yet, as the months passed, word of problems in raising sufficient volunteers began filtering in. "Backing out," a Hall County correspondent wrote as early as the fall of 1861, "has become so prevalent in this county that it is difficult to get off with a company." Two years later the captains of a Floyd County regiment spoke of a similar dilemma in mustering troops for purely local service. "[W]e were made to believe . . . that we were to be used only in emergencies, that when the soil of the state of Georgia was invaded, our homes threatened by a ruthless invader, that we were to suspend business seize our arms, drive back the invader, and return to our avocations," they reasoned. But while such a requisition ordered by "the President of the Confederate States" initially elicited a "great response," the "men have now been away from their homes over a month and their crops are ready for gathering and they made no preparation for planting a wheat crop." "[S]urely it is not wisdom on the part of the government to act in bad faith toward her people," the captains remonstrated. "If there exists . . . any emergency demanding that we should . . . stand sentinel around the city of Rome or meet the enemy in the mountain passes of Upper Georgia . . . then we are willing to forget home and our

---

69. T. Sanford Garner to Governor Brown, Haralson County, October 18, 1861, Exec. Dept., Incoming Corresp., Letters, Box 10; A. J. Hutchinson to Fitz, Alpharetta, April 9, 1861, Nathan L. Hutchins Papers, Box 2, Folder 3, DU.

agriculture and other interests for the time and do our duty." Otherwise, they asked that the men be temporarily discharged. Another officer made much the same point: "Most of our men are farmers, many of them small farmers whose families are entirely dependent upon their presence at home . . . [or] the ensuing year would find their families in want. . . . But trusting to the good faith of the Confederate Government in the promise it made through you [the governor] as agent, they patriotically and promptly volunteered in over double the number called for." "Is it [then] in accordance with the terms of our enlistment," he queried, "that we should have been kept in camp ever since, waiting for something to turn up which could be construed into an emergency requiring us to be called from our home?"[70]

By the winter of 1861–1862 the Confederacy began to face its first problems of manpower. The wave of enlistments that had followed the outbreak of hostilities gradually ebbed to a trickle, and the twelve-month volunteers, who constituted between one-third and two-thirds of the troops in the field, neared the end of their term of service. Many, contemplating a short war, had rushed off without making adequate provision for their families and now looked forward to taking their leave or were home on furlough. That December, Governor Brown arranged for re-enlistments, and in February, threatening a draft if not enough came forward, he appealed for more volunteers to fill Confederate requisitions. As if to single out a particular audience, Brown coupled his pleas with warnings of the dire consequences that would attend a Union victory—warnings he had blared in his efforts to mobilize support for secession. "The Lincoln Congress has passed laws confiscating a very large property of the Southern people," the governor declared, "and a bill is now pending before that body . . . to assess an exceedingly burdensome tax against the lands of every man in the South. . . . The object of this Act is the general confiscation of all lands of the South." Pointing to the boasts of one Northern general that it was settled policy to use Southern lands as colonies for blacks "under the supervision of Northern appointed masters," Brown maintained that "To accomplish this, it is proposed to arm the negroes and incite them to destroy our

70. Dr. M. P. Alexander to Governor Brown, Hall County, September 16, 1861, September 19, 1861, Exec. Dept., Incoming Corresp., Letters, Box 1; Captains Floyd County Cavalry Regiment, Georgia State Guard, to Governor Brown, Camp, October 13, 1863, Exec. Dept., Incoming Corresp., Letters, Box 5; Lt. Col. M. W. Lewis to Governor Brown, November 12, 1863, Candler, ed., *Confederate Records*, III, 435–36.

wives and children." "I warn you of the danger which surrounds you, my countrymen and . . . summon you immediately to arms," he exclaimed. "Strike before it is too late, for your liberties, your families, your homes, and your altars." Two months later, nevertheless, after much of the Mississippi Valley and New Orleans in the west and Roanoke Island in the east had fallen into Northern hands, and as the Union armies pressed into the valleys of the Cumberland and the Tennessee, the Confederate Congress enacted the first conscription law in American history.[71]

While Brown may have accepted the need for and the legitimacy of a state-controlled draft, he and others in Georgia and elsewhere—notably North Carolina's Governor Zebulon Vance—took a rather different view of such action on the part of the Confederate government. Conscription under centralized authority, Brown cried, trampled on individual rights, subverted the sovereignty of the states, and smacked of military despotism.[72] Perhaps no issue more deeply divided the Southern leadership, and the heated diatribes that blistered through personal correspondence and the press only served to fuel already smoldering resentments among the common soldiers. Designed to compel twelve-month troops to re-enlist as well as to coerce the recalcitrant to enter the service, conscription seemed a tyrannical exercise of power and a threat to the very independence that yeomen and poorer whites believed they were fighting to preserve. Growing disaffection was the price of maintaining adequate strength in the field. "I am comin when my time is out," the Cass County volunteer William Hood brashly informed his kinfolk upon learning of the impending draft. "I volunteered for six months and I am perfectly willing to serve my time out, and come home and stay a while and go again, but I dont want to be forced to go." Hundreds of soldiers, fearful that the stern new measure would place their families in jeopardy of starvation, expressed similar sentiments with their feet, taking unauthorized leaves or

71. "Executive Proclamation," February 11, 1862, Candler, ed., *Confederate Records*, II, 188–89, 195; J. W. Goldsmith to Governor Brown, Cartersville, February 10, 1862, Exec. Dept., Incoming Corresp., Letters, Box 10; Albert B. Moore, *Conscription and Conflict in the Confederacy* (New York, 1924), 9–13; Louise B. Hill, *Joseph E. Brown and the Confederacy* (Chapel Hill, 1939), 55–60.

72. "Special Message to the General Assembly," November 6, 1862, Candler, ed., *Confederate Records*, II, 284–85, 299–300, 305–8; Joseph Brown to Jefferson Davis, April 22, 1862, June 21, 1862, October 18, 1862, ibid., III, 192–98, 251–81, 294–301; Frank L. Owsley, *State Rights in the Confederacy* (Gloucester, Mass., 1961), 204.

outright deserting. As a Heard County farmer complained, "I am liable at any time to be taken from my little crop leaving my family almost without provisions and no hope of making any crop atal." On the home front, men who had avoided enlistment from the first, for reasons of principle or cowardice, went into hiding, at times forming bands with fellow resisters. The Upcountry, in particular, began to fill with fugitives from the conscription officers. And with the establishment, in October 1862, of military exemptions for planters or overseers supervising at least twenty slaves—the despised "twenty nigger" law—the cry of "rich man's war and poor man's fight" could be heard in the ranks and through the hills.[73]

Morale sustained a further blow from deteriorating conditions within the army itself. Beginning in 1862, owing to food deficits, the government cut back on rations. Additional curtailments took effect in 1863 and 1864, as the destruction of transportation facilities stalled the flow of supplies. Cornbread and meat, if that, became the mainstays of the Rebel diet. Shortages of clothing, and especially of shoes and blankets, also plagued the ranks by the third year of the war, bringing great hardship during the winter months. Describing the snow, cold, and meager rations in Tennessee in December 1862, a Gwinnett County soldier told his wife that "there is a heep of gorgia boys a deserting and going home. . . ." To make matters worse, disease ran rampant in the camps. The lack of proper sanitation among men sharing such close quarters bred infection, and the troops from the rural districts proved highly susceptible. "This company was from the hill country," a Carroll County officer explained, citing the large numbers who had taken sick. "It was not so bad with those gathered from the cities and towns . . . [for they] were, generally, less affected by the exposure incident to camp life. . . ." An Upcountry recruit made the same point: "The town boys as a general thing stand camp life better than the country boys." Without adequate medical treatment, measles, dysentry, malaria, typhoid, pneumonia, smallpox, scurvy, and tuber-

73. William Hood to Father and Mother, Savannah, February 22, 1862, Rebecca Hood Papers, EU; Harlan Fuller to Governor Brown, Heard County, May 1, 1864, Exec. Dept., Incoming Corresp., Letters, Box 9; William Bowen to Governor Brown, Rome, May 15, 1863, ibid., Box 3; Beall, *In Barrack and Field*, 296–97; Athens *Southern Watchman*, June 24, 1863, September 30, 1863; Ella Lonn, *Desertion During the Civil War* (Gloucester, Mass., 1966), 14–15; Bell I. Wiley, *The Plain People of the Confederacy* (Baton Rouge, 1944), 65.

culosis, not to mention complications arising from battle wounds, claimed countless lives.[74]

Yet, perhaps nothing struck the Confederacy as deep an internal wound, or provoked such social tension, or revealed as much about the values and priorities of the common people, as did developments on the home front. Although the war effort brought privation throughout the South, nowhere did the repercussions hit more severely than in nonplantation areas. Unable to depend on slave labor, many families faced great difficulties when husbands and sons marched off with the army. As early as the spring and summer of 1861, county officials, recognizing what prolonged fighting might hold in store for soldiers' dependents, took steps to raise funds for those in need. A meeting in Jackson County passed resolutions instructing the Inferior Court to levy a tax for the support of "destitute families of volunteers" and to borrow money from individuals, issuing county bonds as security. But within a year, as a devastating drought turned the exertions of women, children, and the elderly to naught, the problem of relief overwhelmed local resources. "We are grieved and appalled at the distress which threatens our people especially the widows and orphans and wives and children of our poor soldiers," the Jackson County grand jury declared in August 1862, and similar reports sounded elsewhere in the Upcountry. In response, the state legislature, acting upon the recommendations of Governor Brown, allocated $2,500,000 for the indigent in December 1862. When the funds were distributed among the counties the following spring, the ten leading recipients were in northern Georgia. Gwinnett, Cherokee, Carroll, Bartow, Floyd, and Cobb counties all listed more than 1,500 beneficiaries.[75]

The home folk wasted little time sending word of the profound hardships to their husbands and kin, with the expected consequences. "Desertion from the army is primarily caused by letters from home," an

---

74. Henry Robinson to Wife, Midel Tenn [sic], December 9, 1862, Robinson Letters; Beall, *In Barrack and Field*, 307; William Dobbins to Mother, Western Virginia, October 18, 1861, John S. Dobbins Papers, Reel 2, EU; Wiley, *Plain People*, 4–12.

75. Athens *Southern Banner*, June 12, 1861; Grand Jury Presentments, Jackson County, August 1862, Superior Court Minutes, 1860–1876, GDAH; Candler, ed., *Confederate Records*, II, 262–66, 399–406; Athens *Southern Watchman*, March 18, 1863, September 23, 1863. The legislative relief appropriation rose to $6,000,000 for 1864 and to $8,000,000 for 1865. See Peter R. Wallenstein, "From Slave South to New South: Taxes and Spending in Georgia From 1850 Through Reconstruction" (Ph.D. diss., Johns Hopkins University, 1973), 196–97.

Upcountry correspondent to the Columbus *Enquirer* observed. "The husband receives a letter from his wife detailing her trials and suffering her children's cries for bread when there is not a handful of meal. . . . They are continually writing to their sons, husbands, and brothers to come home; if they cannot obtain a furlough then runaway and come at all hazards." Charging that "Deserters from the Army have become so frequent," officers moved to tighten discipline and surveillance and "to have arrested and returned to their commands all who are absent without leave." Such measures never effectively plugged the sieve, though in preventing numerous soldiers from responding to their families' pleas, they created increased rancor. "[I]t is no use fur you . . . to depend on us," Henry Robinson of Gwinnett County told his wife with bitter resignation, "we are all in fur the ware and this damd old Jinrel woant give you a furlow or a discharge til you are dead ten dayes and then you have to prove it tha all hate him as bad as the devel he keepes a gard all the time and it is a fine thing fur he would be very apt to come up mising. . . ." Facing the same dilemma, a Franklin County farmer passionately wrote, "Frankey I hade rather sea you than to have the Sothern Confedracy." Wives therefore often turned their appeals to Governor Brown, as did Salley Batchelor of Jackson County: "Thay have taken my husban into what tha call the home gard leveing seven children and no one to provide for them but my self which is impossible fo mee to doo without his help. . . . I want you pleas to discharge him I believe you are a friend to the poore and distressed. . . ."[76]

Soaring prices—a product of real shortages, rapidly inflating currency, and the designs of speculators—placed needed goods well beyond the means of most Upcountry families and exacerbated their predicament.[77] But it was the Confederate tax-in-kind and policy of impressing supplies, coming on the heels of conscription and suspension of the writ of habeas corpus, that began turning disenchantment with

76. Columbus *Enquirer*, quoted in Athens *Southern Banner*, May 18, 1864; Maj. Gen. S. B. Buckner to Governor Brown, Knoxville, Tenn., June 9, 1863, Exec. Dept., Incoming Corresp., Letters, Box 4; Henry Robinson to Elizabeth, Cumberland Gap, Tenn., May 25, 1862, Robinson Letters; James Wadkins to Frankey, Campbell County, June 28, 1864, James W. Wadkins Confederate Letters, EU; Salley Batchelor to Governor Brown, Jackson County, October 9, 1864, Exec. Dept., Incoming Corresp., Letters, Box 2.

77. Mrs. Jett to R. B. Jett, North Fulton County, December 12, 1864, Richard B. Jett Papers, EU; Ramsdell, *Behind the Lines*, 43–44; Eaton, *History of Confederacy*, 230–31; Wiley, *Plain People*, 41.

the course of events into growing opposition to the slaveholders' republic itself. Both measures unquestionably were necessary to the prosecution of the war; but in commonly amounting to a wholesale appropriation of property as well as to outside intervention in the marketplace, they represented an attack on the rights that plain folk claimed for their own and a betrayal of the trust conferred upon Confederate leaders to defend those rights.

According to the law passed in the spring of 1863, the tax-in-kind was on one-tenth of the annual agricultural production over an allowance made for subsistence. Stinging protests against the tithe, however, suggested that tax collectors rarely took much care in seeing that subsistence requirements were met, and that even when they did, the tithe was widely viewed as an extraordinary burden at a time of general privation. Urging the secretary of war to suspend the levy, John Beall of Carroll County explained that "The county never produces a large surplus for market. This year [1864] it made none. . . ." And Beall was joined by a large number of fellow residents who expressed the "opinion [that] there are certain portions of said county that should be exempt from the late act of the legislature which should it be enforced to any considerable extent we would have three-fourths of the families embraced in the western portion of said county in a deplorable condition indeed."[78] Aware that much of the Upcountry "is well-nigh eaten out," Governor Brown recommended "the propriety of declaring all North Georgia impracticable, i.e., unable to furnish the tax-in-kind, or any other supplies, without distressing the inhabitants." A Floyd County farmer had a different solution, which would have entertained neither Brown nor the planter class. "Is it right that the poor man should be taxed for the support of the war, when the war was brought about on the slave question, and the slave at home accumulating for the benefit of his master, and the poor man's farm left uncultivated, a chance for his wife to be a widow, and his children orphans?" he asked. "Now, in justice, would it not be right to levy a direct tax on that species of property that brought about the war to support it?"[79]

78. Beall, *In Barrack and Field*, 398; Petition From Carroll County to Governor Brown, n.d., Exec. Dept., Incoming Corresp., Petitions, Box 1; Wallenstein, "Slave South to New South," 240.

79. Candler, ed., *Confederate Records*, II, 505, 515–16; Maj. J. F. Cummings to Col. L. B. Northrop, Atlanta, February 3, 1864, ibid., III, 469; Rome *Weekly Courier*, quoted in Paul D. Escott, "Joseph Brown, Jefferson Davis, and the Problem of Poverty in the Confederacy," *GHQ*, LXI (Spring 1977), 63.

Impressment, like the tithe, was to apply solely to surplus produce and was enacted as a means of stabilizing the market price for goods purchased by the Confederacy. The law established a procedure whereby the terms of trade would emerge from a bargain struck between the commissary agent and the producer, aided perhaps by a "loyal and disinterested citizen." Yet matters were far different in practice. When agents bothered to reimburse farmers for their foodstuffs, they often did so with piddling sums. Indeed, by 1865, government prices ranged from 50 to 90 percent below market values. Little wonder that yeomen, paying far more for their·own provisions, began to avoid the impressment officers like the plague.[80]

For the most part, such niceties as payment, however minimal, were dispensed with entirely. At times with the approval of the Confederate command, impressment became nothing better than a euphemism for plunder. Rebel troops and men posing as agents roamed the country-side appropriating crops and livestock at will. "[T]he army waggons and parts of command of cavalry of our army is taking our produce our horses cattle sheep and hogs and very seldom pay anything when they do it," a north Georgian groaned, " . . . they go into the cornfields and load their wagons and goes off and dont let a person know anything about it. . . ." A Paulding County farmer reported that "there is a man going through this section pressing the wheat imposing upon the Soldiers wifes and widows taking their wheat away from them . . . he says he is the Government Agent . . . [but] the people think he is an imposition [sic]." Similarly, petitioners from Floyd County told of "armed men [with pretended authority] traversing our 'neighbor-hoods' taking, in many instances, the last animal fit for beef, and insulting all who dare to claim their right to food. . . ." "These seizures are not impressments," they roared, "[these seizures] are robbery." Prompted by Governor Brown, who pointed to Confederate abuses in "the northeastern section of the state," the Georgia legislature in November 1863 set stiff penalties for violation of the impressment law. But the action did little to stem the tide of depredations and less to mitigate an increasingly "profound sense of injustice and injury."[81]

80. Rebecca Christian, "Georgia and the Confederate Policy of Impressing Supplies" (M.A. thesis, Emory University, 1939), 30–32; Stephen E. Ambrose, "Yeomen Discontent in the Confederacy," *Civil War History*, VIII (September 1962), 259–61; Owsley, *State Rights*, 222; E. Merton Coulter, *The Confederate States of America, 1861–1865* (Baton Rouge, 1950), 226.

81. John W. Cains to Governor Brown, Whitfield County, September 28, 1863, Exec.

That "profound sense of injustice and injury," largely an expression of growing class antagonisms, soon manifested itself in swift, direct retaliation. With no alternative to hunger, poor families in rural districts "turned to stealing" and often selected as targets wealthy neighbors who hoarded provisions. Bands of deserters, infesting the Upcountry by 1864 and causing widespread havoc, relished the opportunity to ransack the property of the well-to-do. When Sherman's army marched through Cobb County in June 1864, one resident noted that "every one of the houses of the respectable settlers of Roswell had been broken open and plundered and everything of value had either been taken away or destroyed," but added significantly that the damage was "done almost entirely by the operatives [from the Roswell factories]."[82]

As early as the spring of 1863, moreover, a wave of provision riots, usually initiated by soldiers' wives, swept the South. Angered by a spiraling market over which they had no control, by the engrossments of impressment officers, and by the greed of "speculators," they sought to appropriate needed goods and to settle some scores. Parading a banner inscribed "Bread or Blood," women raided dry-goods concerns in Mobile, Alabama; in Milledgeville, Georgia, according to a local observer, "a lawless mob . . . engaged in pillaging the stores of merchants"; and in Richmond, "some whair between 800 and a thousand . . . soldiers' wives" marched to provision stores and shoe shops, "broak down window frames broak out glass and went in at the windows [and] got large quantities of shoes callicoes shales . . . bacon flower candles soap Brooms beef lard butter and evry thing they could get" for three hours, before none other than Jefferson Davis quelled them with the assurance "that any thing he had they was welcome to if they needed it. . . ." Such explosions of popular wrath also occurred in Atlanta, Columbus, and Augusta and in Salisbury, North Carolina. And a short distance from Marietta, "28 women, drawn up across the

Dept., Incoming Corresp., Letters, Box 5; Joseph C. Harris to Governor Brown, Paulding County, August 10, 1863, ibid., Box 12; Citizens of Floyd County to Gen. Bragg, n.d., Simpson Fouche Papers, SHC; Candler, ed., *Confederate Records*, II, 505, 515–16; Christian, "Georgia and Confederate Policy," 62.

82. W. S. Shockley to Wife, Petersburg, Va., June 15, 1863, W. S. Shockley Papers and Letters, DU; Elisha Lowrey to John Dobbins, Gordon County, March 19, 1865, Dobbins Papers, Reel 2; William R. King Diary, Cobb County, July 9, 1864, William R. King Papers, SHC.

road—most of them armed with knives and pistols," ambushed a Confederate supply wagon.[83]

According to the Atlanta *Southern Confederacy*, "These 'women seizures' [were] . . . a preconcerted movement among very wicked and ignorant women, generally instigated thereto and led by rascally individuals who aim at plunder and robbery." Conceding that "These bad men and women received their first lessons from those high officials who set the example of lawlessness by appropriating what did not belong to them without any necessity for it," the paper nonetheless insisted that "decent, respectable, and sensible ladies, no matter what may be their circumstances . . . will never unsex and disgrace themselves by joining in such forays. . . ." The Athens *Southern Watchman* reminded its readers, more ominously, that "The French Revolution . . . was inaugurated by women and men dressed in women's clothes," and called "upon those hoarding provisions and refusing to sell to change their policy," while prescribing severe punishments for rioters. In response, Upcountry leaders called numerous meetings in 1864 for the purpose of fixing prices on produce.[84]

Disloyalty to the Confederacy was evident from the first. Areas such as eastern Tennessee, western Virginia, and much of Arkansas and Missouri not only opposed secession but rendered substantial numbers of recruits to the Union army. Nonplantation districts of the Lower South also occasionally displayed strong Unionist sentiments, although they normally took the form of refusing to join the Confederate army, lending assistance to deserters, or, in rare cases, organizing peace societies. A handful of counties in northern Georgia, Alabama, and Louisiana and in southeastern Mississippi defiantly hoisted the Union flag, made plain to Rebel conscript officers that they would enter at the risk of their lives, and allegedly threatened to "secede" from the Confederacy.[85] Other Union sympathizers scattered through the

83. Bessie Martin, *The Desertion of Alabama Troops from the Confederate Army* (New York, 1932), 132–33; Henry C. Wayne to Commander of 33rd Regiment, Milledgeville, April 10, 1863, Candler, ed., *Confederate Records*, II, 440; H. W. Winn to Sister, Richmond, Va., April 2, 1863, H. W. Winn Personal Narrative, GDAH; Atlanta *Southern Confederacy*, April 16, 1863, April 24, 1863; Athens *Southern Watchman*, April 8, 1863.

84. Atlanta *Southern Confederacy*, April 16, 1863, April 24, 1863; Athens *Southern Watchman*, April 8, 1863, February 24, 1863; Athens *Southern Banner*, February 10, 1864.

85. Georgia L. Tatum, *Disloyalty in the Confederacy* (Chapel Hill, 1934); Thomas W. Hume, *The Loyal Mountaineers of Tennessee* (Knoxville, Tenn., 1888); Walter L. Fleming, *The Civil War and Reconstruction in Alabama* (Gloucester, Mass., 1949), 108–47; Bryan, *Confederate Georgia*, 139–40, 144–47.

Upcountry, who, according to the records of the Southern Claims
Commission, were overwhelmingly small farmers and artisans, did their
best to adhere to their principles, frequently at grave personal danger.[86]

Yet, by 1864, amid mounting casualties, tightening discipline, and
pervasive suffering, Upcountry disaffection spread dramatically. The
gubernatorial election of the previous October had given some
premonition of shifting sentiments. Brown ran for an unprecedented
fourth term after having swept to victory in 1857, 1859, and 1861 with
the aid of massive support in north Georgia. As wartime governor,
staunchly upholding state rights, he came to blows with the Davis
administration time and again, but never wavered in his commitment
to resisting Northern aggression. His opponents in 1863 included
Timothy Furlow, a Black Belt planter and Davis backer, and Joshua
Hill, a former congressman who had opposed secession and been
accused of sympathizing with north Georgia Unionists. When the
ballots were counted, Brown won a clear victory, amassing 56 percent of
the vote statewide. But the Upcountry tallies told a different story: there
he obtained only 48 percent of the vote, a far cry from his earlier
performances, and failed to attain majorities in more than half of the
counties. Hill ran virtually even with Brown, winning outright in eight
counties, while a smattering of votes for Furlow tipped the balance
against the incumbent. In an interesting switch, Brown triumphed in
those Upcountry locales bordering the Black Belt and having large
commercial centers, precisely where he had had his least success
earlier.[87]

Within months, opposition to the war became even more apparent.

---

86. Testimony of Allen D. Sims, Carroll County, December 1874, Southern Claims
Commission, Record Group 217, General Accounting Office, 1871–1876, Claim Number
36524/Settlement Number 9298, Box 2, NA; Testimony of John Addington, Bartow
County, March 4, 1878, ibid., 1877–1883, 51795/3710, Box 21; Testimony of Harriet
Lewis, Heard County, August 20, 1872, ibid., 1871–1876, 1580, Box 10. Of seventy
Upcountry residents filing claims with the Southern Claims Commission during the 1870s
for whom I could obtain information about property holdings, 54 (77%) farmed fewer
than 200 acres, 8 (11%) rented land, 3 (4%) were landless artisans, and 1 (1%) was a
landless farmer. These data pertain to the Civil War period. Some of the individuals
made their way to Union lines when it was opportune and on occasion joined regiments.

87. Athens *Southern Watchman*, October 21, 1863; Parks, *Brown of Georgia*, 251–52; Bryan,
Confederate Georgia, 45–46. The vote in the Upcountry was as follows: Brown—4,343;
Hill—3,809; Furlow—900. Hill won in Bartow (formerly Cass), Clayton, Carroll,
Cherokee, Forsyth, Heard, Paulding, and Hall counties, while with the votes of Furlow
the opposition also carried Gwinnett, Jackson, and Polk.

One correspondent, "mingling freely with the common people," found "with much regret that among that class generally there is a strong Union feeling . . . [a belief] that the people could not fare any worse under Lincoln than [they] are fairing under Jeff [Davis]. . . ." John Beall of Carroll County made a similar observation when he returned home around the same time: "I found the masses weary of war and much discouraged. There had grown up, especially in the counties of Paulding and Haralson, a strong sentiment in favor of reconstruction." A group of petitioners called Governor Brown's attention to "the existence of a number of loyal men" in Polk, Paulding, Haralson, Floyd, and Bartow counties who "are not in any organization whatever—and are achieving nothing for our cause."[88] Meetings in several Upcountry counties, including Jackson, resolved to "sustain the Government in its most vigorous efforts" to drive out the Northern invaders, while vowing a readiness "to make honorable peace with Northern conservatives." As Sherman's army began to scorch the Upcountry, letters pleading for an unequivocal end to the war poured into the state capital. "Can nothing be done to bring a cessation of hostilities!" a resident of Forsyth County desperately asked the governor. "[S]top the effusion of innocent blood . . . open the way to negociation and expedite peace." So, too, implored an anonymous writer "in favor of peace": "Do for God's sake put an end to this unrighteous war! We shall be eaten up by Confederate officeholders and speculators. You are the representative of the Yeomanry of the land—who are now helpless. Provoque the legislature and let us hear from the people again."[89]

Along with the swelling exodus of slaves from the plantations, which made Emancipation a fait accompli, the disaffection of Upcountry yeomen pushed the Confederacy to the edge of internal collapse as the Yankees pressed to victory on the battlefield. Indeed, the growing internal crisis served to deepen the military predicament. Faced with superior manpower and armaments, the South found its prospects dimming after the summer of 1863, when the Union won decisive

88. Samuel D. Knight to Governor Brown, Pine Mountain, February 22, 1864, Exec. Dept., Incoming Corresp., Letters, Box 16; Beall, *In Barrack and Field*, 391–92; Petition From Polk County to Governor Brown, September 5, 1864, Exec. Dept., Incoming Corresp., Petitions, Box 2.

89. Athens *Southern Watchman*, March 9, 1864, January 18, 1865; Athens *Southern Banner*, March 16, 1864; F. M. Hawkins to Governor Brown, Cumming, December 16, 1864, Joseph E. Brown Papers, Box 1, Folder 24, UGa; Anonymous in Favor of Peace to Governor Brown, n.d., Exec. Dept., Incoming Corresp., Letters, Box 1.

battles at Gettysburg and Vicksburg. The only hope of avoiding defeat lay in an effective strategy of defense tailored to prolong the war, exacerbate an already declining Northern morale, and thus force the federal government to seek peace. But such a strategy demanded armed and determined popular resistance along with military engagement on favorable terrain, and here the Confederacy came up against its most profound dilemma. For, on the one hand, the Confederates would have had to enlist the slaves, thereby effectively abolishing slavery, while, on the other, they would have had to rely on strong support in the Hill Country, where such tactics would be most feasible. The Southern leadership refused to arm the slaves until the final months, and by 1864, if not well before, they could no longer count on a loyal Hill Country.[90] The Confederacy "died" largely under the weight of inherent contradictions and class conflict.

Still, the Confederate nation managed to command sufficient social unity to struggle on for four years. And it was precisely those backwoods farmers, sacrificing their lives in great numbers, who formed the backbone of the war effort and enabled the Southern armies to remain in the field as long as they did. The casualty lists are staggering reminders of the price these men were willing to pay: among twelve Floyd County companies, the death toll reached at least 25 percent; among six Jackson County units, it reached at least 40 percent. Yet, the very perseverance of these small farmers may have expressed distinctive class feelings in no less compelling a way than did the desertions of many of their counterparts. James Barrow, a Carroll County yeoman and Baptist preacher, who had sent his sons off to war with the ringing motto "liberty or death" and who maintained his allegiance to the cause despite losing four of his kin and seeing one come home a cripple, probably shared the sentiments of a Hall County farmer who "volentarily Entered the Service" while insisting that "Mr. Davis and me does not put the same construction" on things.[91] They fought for a "liberty and independence" not beholden to slaveownership but rooted in

90. Raimondo Luraghi, "The Civil War and the Modernization of American Society," *Civil War History*, XVIII (September 1972), 230–50; Robert F. Durden, *The Gray and the Black: The Confederate Debate on Emancipation* (Baton Rouge, 1972).

91. Willis N. Harden, *Roster of Confederate Soldiers, Jackson County*, (JCC); Floyd County Muster Rolls, Floyd County Confederate and U.D.C. Collection; James Barrow to Governor Brown, Carroll County, November 25, 1863, Exec. Dept., Incoming Corresp., Letters, Box 2; L. H. Hall to Col. Pope, Gainesville, July 1, 1867, BCA, Record Group 393/Entry 5782, Box 2, NA.

communities of petty producers. In the wake of Appomattox, neither of these proud and determined men could know that this struggle, which consumed their lives and those of their families for several bloody years, would enter a new and in many ways more bitter and protracted phase.

PART TWO
The Vortex of the Cotton Economy

4

The Transformation of the Countryside

I

In the late spring of 1865, John B. Marable, who farmed seventy-five acres in Paulding County, looked out upon a grim landscape that all but typified the Georgia Upcountry. His fields, once thick with growing crops, showed only ravaged earth and sprouting weeds; what was left of his rail fencing lay in ruins; his supplies of corn, wheat, and bacon along with most of his livestock had fallen prey to marauding soldiers; and his house had suffered two ransackings. It had been, for Marable and countless others like him, a scissor-play of destruction: what the depredations of Confederate cavalry, stragglers, and deserters failed to accomplish, those of General William Tecumseh Sherman's troops did. Sweeping southeastward from Chattanooga, Sherman cut a wide swath of destruction across much of the western and central Upcountry before he tore through the older cotton counties on his way to Savannah.[1] As

1. Testimony of John B. Marable, Paulding County, December 5, 1877, Southern Claims Commission, Record Group 217, General Accounting Office, 1877–83, Claim No. 48295/ Settlement No. 4989, Box 32, NA. Also see Mary Noble to Lelia Montan, Rome, November 20, 1864, Noble-Attaway Papers, Folder 1, SHC; James M. Carr Diary, Kingston, August 14, 1864, SHC; William R. King Diary, Cobb County, July 1864, SHC; and generally the Southern Claims Commission, 1871–1876, Boxes 1–20, and 1877–1883, Boxes 24–27.

the general had written his wife from Big Shanty in Cobb County, "The country is stripped of cattle, horses, hogs, and grain, but there are . . . prime fields of growing oats . . . which our horses and mules devour as we advance." "We passed through a country which shows the effects of war," another federal officer observed near Atlanta in November 1864. "No houses—no fences and the road side strewn with dead mules and broken wagons." Even the eastern Upcountry, skirted by Sherman's main path, felt the scourge of his flank. "The Yankees came through Franklin and Hart counties, and just tore up everything as they came along," a resident later recalled. "They took all the cows, horses, and mules. They killed the hogs in the pens, and carried them off for their own food. They went through the houses and took whatever they wanted. . . ."[2] Sections of the western Upcountry bordering Alabama managed to escape Sherman's wrath only to be victimized by the raids of Stoneman's and Rousseau's cavalry. As late as 1867, a Freedmen's Bureau agent in Carroll County, distributing rations among "The extreme destitute of this poor poverty stricken and God forsaken country," could travel for miles without seeing "a cleared field or a fence rail." "[N]othing plentiful here except pine trees flint rocks and reconstructionists," he recorded.[3]

Wartime devastation and wrenching hardships visited Southerners in plantation as well as nonplantation districts. Large estates much as small farms had their fields trampled, livestock slaughtered, and dwellings plundered. Emancipation, a now worthless currency, and disrupted lines of credit and trade led to the virtual overnight collapse of many proud fortunes. The abolition of slavery, if nothing else, immediately eliminated the most highly valued assets the planters possessed. In Georgia alone the loss amounted to roughly $275,000,000. Land values also plummeted, the decline ranging from 55 percent in Georgia to 70 percent in Louisiana. Hundreds of miles of rail lines lay worn out or destroyed, especially in Georgia, where Sherman's ability to cut his army loose from Northern supply lines made possible a policy of wholesale demolition. In the ports, many factorage houses closed their doors or struggled only briefly to revitalize familiar operations

2. William T. Sherman to Ellen, Big Shanty, June 12, 1864, William Tecumseh Sherman Letters, UGa; Lt. C. C. Platter Civil War Diary, November 12, 1864, UGa; Federal Writers' Project, Life Histories, Georgia, Box 12, Folder 154, 3–4, SHC.

3. J. D. Harris to W. O. Bannon, Carrollton, May 29, 1867 (courtesy of Mrs. Edna Lackey, GDAH); James C. Bonner, *Georgia's Last Frontier: The Development of Carroll County* (Athens, 1971), 85–86.

before they did.[4] The fate of individual planters varied considerably; the fate of the planters as a class ultimately rested on the actions the national government would take and on their own success in re-establishing control over the newly liberated black labor force. The unfolding of that process and the new aspect it lent to the structure of agriculture would have far-reaching consequences for the social, economic, and political life of the entire region.

Yet, it was a cruel irony that saw areas of the South least receptive to secession as the primary fields of battle. Save for the lower Mississippi Valley and the South Carolina coast, fighting centered in the Upper South until the latter stages of the war, and even then the Hill Country of Louisiana, Mississippi, Alabama, and Georgia was often hard hit. In the short run, Union military forays exacerbated the difficulties already created by labor shortages, crop failures, and Confederate pillaging. In the long run, coupled with significant alterations in social relations and networks of trade, they helped usher in a new era—an era of expanding staple agriculture, increasing economic dislocation, and growing white landlessness. Linked dynamically to developments in the plantation sector and the nation as a whole, these transformations in the Upcountry economy and in the lives of Upcountry yeomen thus elucidate the larger meaning of the Civil War itself.[5]

II

The problems of destitution and relief remained chronic in the Upcountry through the 1860s, compounded as they were by adverse weather and increasingly widespread indebtedness. The serious droughts that plagued the area, and much of the South, during the sectional conflagration persisted into the immediate postwar years, worsening the travails of recovering from war-related destruction. "[I]t

4. Donald B. Dodd and Wynelle S. Dodd, *Historical Statistics of the South, 1790–1970* (Tuscaloosa, Ala., 1973), 18–21; Roger L. Ransom and Richard Sutch, *One Kind of Freedom: The Economic Consequences of Emancipation* (Cambridge, 1977), 51, 107–9; John F. Stover, *The Railroads of the South, 1865–1900: A Study in Finance and Control* (Chapel Hill, 1955), 20–22.

5. For the main lines of recent historiographical debate, see Harold D. Woodman, "Sequel to Slavery: The New History Views the Postbellum South," *JSH*, XLII (November 1977), 523–54; Jonathan M. Wiener, "Class Structure and Economic Development in the American South, 1865–1955," *AHR*, LXXXIV (October 1979), 970–92, and the comments that follow by Robert Higgs and Harold Woodman.

would be hard to exaggerate the disaster, or the suffering and distress which result [from the drought]," the ex-governor Joseph Brown wrote in September 1866, "the corn crop is almost an utter failure in a large part of the state embracing the upper section." One month later, citing "the short crops made in our county and the distressed condition of our people and the uncertainty of future prospects," the Carroll County grand jury urged that "our next legislature . . . use all the power with the Constitution for the relief of our people especially for the widows and orp[h]ans and the maimed and distressed souldiers. . . ."[6] Such reports continued to flow out of the Upcountry the next year. "[F]ur the two last years the drought has been very fatal and cut the crops very short and . . . there is a lurg number of widows and orphans entirely out of Bread," a Gwinnett County resident informed the local Freedmen's Bureau agent in April 1867. An inhabitant of Cherokee County similarly told of "Extreme want and destitution" and of "Hundreds of Widows and orphans on the verge of starvation," as did correspondents from Bartow, Hall, and Forsyth counties. Around the same time, a federal army officer noted that "The people of Carroll, Haralson, Polk, Paulding, Campbell, Coweta, and Heard . . . are represented to me as not having provisions to last them [a month]. . . ."[7]

Heading relief efforts, the Freedmen's Bureau listed nearly 10,000 destitute persons in the eleven Upcountry counties composing its Atlanta district alone in the spring of 1867, roughly two-thirds of whom were white. When distributing foodstuffs donated by several charitable organizations shortly thereafter, the bureau allocated more than one-third of the supply for the entire state to those and other counties in the region.[8] Upcountry blacks, to be sure, also suffered considerably during

6. Joseph E. Brown to Rev. N. M. Crawford, Atlanta, September 18, 1866, Joseph E. Brown Papers, Box 1, Folder 37a, UGa; Grand Jury Presentments, October 1866, Superior Court Minutes, Carroll County, 1857–1869, GDAH.

7. John Mills to Col. C. C. Sibley, Lawrenceville, April 5, 1867, BRFAL, Record Group 105, Records of the Assistant Commissioner, Reel 15, NA; W. J. Bryan to Col. C. C. Sibley, Canton, May 16, 1867, ibid., Reel 14; William T. Wofford to Col. C. C. Sibley, Cartersville, May 15, 1867, ibid., Reel 16; C. H. Sutton to Maj. J. J. Knox, Clarksville, April 5, 1867, ibid., Reel 15; W. J. Bryan to Maj. J. R. Lewis, Atlanta, October 23, 1867, BRFAL, Record Group 105, Vol. 230, NA; William Chunn to Elizabeth Chunn, Cassville, July 7, 1867, Chunn-Land Papers, Box 1, Folder 2, GDAH; Atlanta *Daily Intelligencer*, April 9, 1867, in Ulrich B. Phillips Collection, Box 39, Folder—Fortunes in War, YU.

8. Lt. Col. John Leonard to Col. C. C. Sibley, Atlanta, April 9, 1867, BRFAL, Asst.

this period, particularly those "who are old and infirm," though observers often claimed that the freedmen "are doing as well and [perhaps] even better than the poorer class of Whites." While receiving low wages and frequently being cheated out of their just remuneration—if not outright turned off without payment after harvest—the blacks reaped at least some benefit from a pervasive labor shortage in the form of daily rations. Because little currency was in circulation and provision prices were high, small farmers whose crops withered in the dry soil and blistering heat found themselves in dire straits. As late as 1869 a visitor to Jackson County could write that the "farmers are very despondent and assure me that the drouth will cut down the yield . . . to about one-third of a crop. I learn that a movement is on foot to organize an association to buy Western corn before it gets beyond their reach."[9]

Statistics from the 1870 federal census, despite their shortcomings, bear striking testimony to the magnitude of economic tribulation. Upcountry farm values had declined by more than 25 percent from their 1860 levels, and although the population had grown by about 5 percent during this ten-year period, farmers raised 40 percent fewer bushels of corn, 45 percent fewer bales of cotton, and 35 percent fewer head of livestock. Indeed, per capita grain production dropped by almost 40 percent between 1860 and 1870. Small wonder that newspapers could express the fear that "Cherokee Georgia" might soon find "many of her valuable citizens" emigrating west to more promising locales.[10]

As census officials tabulated their figures, however, a significant development in Upcountry agriculture was already becoming apparent. "[W]e learn that a considerable revolution has taken place in the last year or two in the productions of Carroll," the Carroll County *Times* observed in 1872. "Cotton, formerly cultivated on a very limited extent, has increased rapidly . . . so that if the ratio continues, the

Comm., Reel 15; Col. C. C. Sibley to Gen. O. O. Howard, Macon, May 23, 1867, ibid., Reel 32.

9. A. A. Buck to Capt. Eugene Pickett, Calhoun, May 24, 1867, BRFAL, Asst. Comm., Reel 14; James Steele to Elizabeth Brown, Cherokee County, February 8, 1866, Brown Papers, Box 1, Folder 37; Athens *Southern Banner*, September 3, 1869.

10. *Eighth Census of the United States, 1860* (Washington 1864), Agriculture 22–29; *Ninth Census of the United States, 1870 (Washington, 1872)*, Agriculture, 120–27; Cartersville *Express*, March 17, 1871.

county will, ere long, take rank among the foremost cotton producing counties of the state." The Columbus *Sun* reported a similar trend throughout the area a year later: "We took occasion in the spring . . . to direct attention to the rapid increase in cotton planting in the counties of upper Georgia. All the statistics and newspaper accounts received from the region confirm . . . the extensive planting of cotton. . . ."[11]

There was much to recommend the new orientation. With short crops and generally depleted resources, farmers faced a difficult enough road to recovery. But that road had also become ridden with debts— debts contracted during those dim and desperate years of war and Reconstruction (often at much inflated prices) as the purchasing of provisions, seed, and implements grew more necessary and extensive. Although grain crops could bring attractive returns and thus help families regain a stable economic footing, the advantage was undercut by the cost of hauling them to market. Cotton, on the other hand, not only brought a relatively high price in the late 1860s and early 1870s but, according to the Cartersville *Standard and Express*, did "not cost one half [of what corn costs] to carry. . . ." As a Jackson County paper put it, "The majority of the farmers are going to plant largely of cotton, as most of them are in debt, and cotton is the only thing raised on the farm that will command ready money in the fall."[12]

Growing a cash crop traditionally had been part of the general farming practiced by Upcountry yeoman households. The need for money to pay state and local taxes, for goods that could not be made at home, and for additional productive property to maintain the independence of the family led these farmers into the market. Like peasantries in much of the world, they could respond to commercial incentives, could evince an acquisitive disposition. Yet such acquisitiveness fell within a larger "security first" framework, and even under the trying conditions that followed the war they made no radical departure from familiar patterns, as a Black Belt newspaper took care to note: "While many of our south Georgia planters have . . . failed to plant sufficient corn or raise their own meat, but have devoted most of their labor to cotton, the farmers of upper Georgia have first made sure of their grain, provender,

11. Carroll County *Times*, February 2, 1872; Columbus *Sun*, quoted in ibid., September 12, 1873.

12. Cartersville *Standard and Express*, February 29, 1872; Jefferson *Forest News*, March 23, 1878. On cotton prices, see Ransom and Sutch, *One Kind of Freedom*, 191–92.

and provisions, and then bestowed their surplus labor on cotton."[13] Nevertheless, a survey issued by the state commissioner of agriculture in 1875 gave unmistakable evidence of cotton's burgeoning importance in the Upcountry. Of the total acreage planted in the five major crops on white-operated farms, cotton accounted for more than one-quarter, stood only second in size to corn, and nearly amounted to the acreage sown in wheat, oats, and sweet potatoes combined (see Table 4.1).

The expansion of cotton culture was sustained and accelerated by the construction of rail lines into the Upcountry and by the increasing use of commercial fertilizers. Railroad promoters, stymied during the 1850s by capital shortages, skepticism about profitability, and popular opposition, renewed their efforts within a short time after the war's end. Meetings in numerous Upcountry counties during the late 1860s and early 1870s, convened at the behest of commercially minded interests situated in or near the small market towns, pressed for the revitalization of formerly chartered projects or the establishment of new companies. Spurred by local merchants and substantial farmers, a gathering at the Jackson County seat of Jefferson urged completion of the Northeastern Railroad. The line, designed to connect Athens and Clayton, near the North Carolina border, promised to be routed through the town. Similar groups in Franklin and Hart counties passed a series of resolutions emphasizing a need for the rapid construction of the Air

Table 4.1 Crop Acreage in the Upcountry, 1875 (White-Operated Farms)

Crop	Acres	Percentage
Corn	316,002	43.2
Cotton	199,486	27.2
Wheat	133,578	18.2
Oats	76,339	10.4
Sweet Potatoes	6,693	1.0
Total	732,098	100.0

Cotton/Corn Ratio—63%

Source: Thomas P. Janes, *Annual Report of the Commissioner of Agriculture for the State of Georgia, for the Year 1875* (Atlanta, 1875), 146–57.

13. Columbus *Sun*, quoted in Carroll County *Times*, October 10, 1873.

Line Railroad, linking Atlanta and Charlotte, and announcing "a willingness to contribute liberally" to the cause.[14] Citizens of Carrollton impatiently watched the progress of the Savannah, Griffin, and North Alabama Railroad, which had absorbed the abortive Carrollton Railroad Company, as it inched up from Newnan. They hoped the road would make their town "one of the best markets in all western Georgia." A meeting in Forsyth County, conceding the inability to raise sufficient local capital, pledged "to tender right of way to the first company that will build a road through the county," and recommended contacting the president of the Macon and Knoxville Railroad for such purposes.[15]

As in the 1850s, promoters faced an uphill battle. The Civil War hardly remedied the dearth of available capital, and the war's physical repercussions did not quite make the Upcountry alluring economically. "[T]imes hard, money scarce, [and] trade dull," a supporter of the Cartersville and Van Wert sighed in 1868, explaining the lack of interest in the enterprise. Competition among towns over routing and among local worthies over, as one official said, "whether [the road] is going through Col. Turk's land or whether Judge Candler is going to have a depot," did not make matters any easier.[16] Furthermore, the postwar years witnessed no dramatic turnabout in the attitudes of yeoman farmers. While they confronted hardship, required more supplies from the outside, and began planting greater quantities of cotton, many retained their misgivings about the railroad and the changes it might bring. Thus, when the chief engineer of the Air Line Railroad received a letter from several Banks County residents advocating the speedy completion of the line, he apprised them of a major obstacle: "[T]he men are studying about and trying to make up their minds what sort of thing a Rail Road is, and how many . . . Cows . . . Horses . . . and Hogs will be killed."[17]

It should be of little surprise, therefore, that Upcountry railroad

14. Athens *Southern Banner*, December 4, 1868, January 1, 1869, January 22, 1869, June 17, 1870, November 25, 1870; Grand Jury Presentments, April 1869, Superior Court Minutes, Franklin County, 273–74, GDAH; Henry V. Poor, *Manual of the Railroads of the United States, 1869–1870* (New York, 1870), 274; *Poor's Manual, 1877–1878* (New York, 1878), 512.

15. Carroll County *Times*, January 12, 1872; Newnan *Herald*, quoted in ibid., April 19, 1872; Gwinnett *Herald*, April 10, 1872; *Poor's Manual, 1871–1872* (New York, 1872), 453.

16. Cartersville *Express*, July 10, 1868, July 17, 1868.

17. Athens *Southern Banner*, May 21, 1869.

development progressed only gradually during the 1870s, particularly since the Panic of 1873 erected yet another roadblock. No more than two major projects, the Air Line and Northeastern, began service before the late 1870s. Both had been chartered before the war, both received state aid from the Reconstruction government in the form of bond endorsements, and one—the Air Line—benefited from outside backing and its position as a vital nexus in what would become the Piedmont Air Line stretching between Atlanta and Richmond. In the western Upcountry, the Savannah, Griffin, and North Alabama reached Carrollton in 1872 but failed to attain its goal of Guntersville, Alabama, by the end of the decade. Several other roads, mostly short branch lines, were also incorporated during this period, though as a result of financial stringencies they did not open until the late 1870s and early 1880s.[18] Slow and halting as the process was, however, the ramifications would be far-reaching. Railroads in the antebellum South ran from the coast into the Black Belt, intensifying plantation agriculture and strengthening the factorage system. Postbellum roads, by contrast, extended into nonplantation areas and linked the interior directly to Northern markets, thereby enlarging the sphere of commercial agriculture, laying the faltering factors to rest, and thrusting the furnishing merchant into a new and powerful place in the countryside.[19]

The extension of rail lines coupled with falling international guano prices led to the greater availability of commercial fertilizers, which played a key role in propelling the expansion of Upcountry cotton production. Aside from a widespread penchant for general farming,

18. *Poor's Manual, 1869–1870*, 264; *Poor's Manual, 1875–1876*, 435–36; *Poor's Manual, 1877–1878*, xxiv, 580; *Poor's Manual, 1871–1872*, 453; *Poor's Manual, 1881*, 404; *Poor's Manual, 1885*, 437, 441–43, 445; Thomas C. Hardman, *History of Harmony Grove—Commerce* (Commerce, Ga., 1949), 64; Peter S. McGuire, "The Railroads of Georgia, 1860–1880," *GHQ*, XVI (September 1932), 194–95. The board of directors for the Air Line Railroad included the president of the Richmond and Danville Railroad and two New Yorkers. Before the war, Southern railroads had been indigenously owned and controlled. While Reconstruction saw the influx of Northern capital as the roads were rebuilt, Northern investments were not substantial. Only with the Panic of 1873, which threw many Southern lines into receivership, did the process of consolidation under the auspices of Northern finance truly begin, but it did not reach fruition until the 1890s. By 1915 all important railroads in Georgia had been incorporated into one of four great rail systems dominating the South.

19. Stover, *Railroads of the South*, 186–209; Ransom and Sutch, *One Kind of Freedom*, 106–25; Harold D. Woodman, *King Cotton and His Retainers: Financing and Marketing the Cotton Crop of the South, 1800–1925* (Lexington, Ky., 1968), 279–82.

north Georgia cotton cultivation was limited by late-spring and early-autumn frosts which shortened the growing season. Fertilizers not only enriched the soil and increased yields but also enabled farmers to plant "their cotton a month later than they could formerly, and have it mature fully as soon, if not sooner than it did under the old system." The new method did not receive an unequivocal welcome. Indeed, as an observer from one section of Gwinnett County remarked, "There is but little demand for guano . . . [for] as a general thing our farmers pronounce it a humbug."[20] And many who began purchasing the composts did so out of necessity rather than by choice, as the credit structure increasingly locked them into the cotton market. But, especially in areas with ready access to the railroad, the trend was clear. "The farmers of this and adjoining counties, are buying large amounts of Guano this season," a Carroll County *Times* correspondent asserted in 1873, "and nearly every day for the last week, there have been from 75 to 100 wagons here [small town of Whitesburg] after Guano." John H. Dent, the agricultural reformer, said much the same for Floyd County: "The amount of fertilizers purchased this season throughout the South have been enormous even in the up counties it has been large—the sales have been more than double any previous year. . . . The agents in Cave Spring have sold $10,000 . . . [and] this means . . . a large cotton crop will be planted." Between the 1874–1875 and the 1880–1881 seasons, the quantity of fertilizer inspected for the entire state rose more than threefold and much of it was destined for the Upcountry, with, as one fertilizer manufacturer made plain, significant consequences. "In the region above Atlanta, prior to the introduction of commercial fertilizers, little or no cotton was raised, from the fact that the seasons were too short," he maintained, "but since the introduction of commercial fertilizers the production of cotton in this section of the state has been greatly increased. In fact, it has come to be a very considerable item of production there."[21]

A very considerable item of production to be sure. In 1880, Upcountry counties grew roughly 180,000 bales of cotton, an almost 200-percent increase over the harvest in 1860 and a more than 200-

20. Gwinnett *Herald*, February 11, 1874.

21. Carroll County *Times*, March 14, 1873; Cottage Home Farm Journal, Floyd County, April 10, 1873, John H. Dent Papers, GDAH; Testimony of M. A. Stovall, *Report of the Committee of the Senate Upon the Relations Between Labor and Capital*, Committee on Education and Labor, 5 vols. (Washington, 1885), IV, 765–66.

percent increase over the harvest in 1870. Per capita cotton production doubled during the same period. Perhaps of greater importance, the place of the Upcountry in Georgia's staple agriculture changed dramatically. Whereas in 1860 the region grew less than 10 percent of the total cotton raised in the state, by 1880 it grew close to 25 percent. This shift was reflected in the composition of the overall crop mix. During the antebellum era, corn was the Upcountry's major crop. Yet, within two decades following the Civil War, corn's status relative to cotton's declined substantially. A 22-percent increase in corn production between 1860 and 1880 paled when compared with that of cotton. No figures on crop acreage are available until the mid-1870s, but the change in the five years preceding 1880 was itself highly suggestive. In 1875, cotton acreage was about two-thirds the size of the acreage planted in corn; in 1879, it was about nine-tenths. And as per capita cotton production rose by 100 percent between 1860 and 1880, per capita corn production dropped by 20 percent. These patterns were evident in Jackson and Carroll counties, as well as in the Upcountry at large (see Table 4.2).[22]

The transformation did not escape the attention of local observers. "[W]e cannot help feeling a little proud of the position our country

Table 4.2 Cotton and Corn in the Upcountry, 1860–1880

Item	Upcountry		Jackson County		Carroll County	
	1860	1880	1860	1880	1860	1880
Cotton (Bales)	63,094	179,892	1,594	9,482	3,982	9,300
Corn (Bushels)	5,009,639	6,122,449	290,684	295,641	331,692	370,892
Per Capita Cotton Production (Bales)	0.3	0.6	0.2	0.6	0.3	0.6
Per Capita Corn Production (Bushels)	26.0	20.9	27.4	19.6	27.6	21.9

Sources: *Eighth Census*, Agriculture, 22–29; *Tenth Census*, Report on Productions of Agriculture, 183–84.

22. *Eighth Census*, Agriculture, 22–29; *Ninth Census*, Agriculture, 120–27; *Tenth Census of the United States, 1880* (Washington, 1883), Report on the Productions of Agriculture, 183–84, 262–65; Robert P. Brooks, *The Agrarian Revolution in Georgia, 1865–1912* (Madison, Wis., 1914), 79–80.

occupies as a cotton producer," the Jackson *Herald* boasted in 1881, ". . . . only twenty-five counties made more cotton than ours [in 1879] . . . [and the] result is not peculiar to this county, but is found to be true of most of the counties in Northeastern Georgia." Others noted the same phenomenon but saw less to prate about. John Dent of Floyd County wrote in 1879 that "the area planted in cotton is at least 20 percent more than last year and the area in corn is 20 percent less," and found that farmers "have bought largely of fertilizers and [are] buying corn and bacon more extensively than they have for the last three years." According to another Upcountry Georgian, "the farmers are not in so good a condition as they were before the war." "It would surprise anyone who knew the country 25 years ago," he exclaimed, "to witness the large amount of (?) and Bacon sold here and at other points in the county now when formerly the county supplied itself with everything. . . ." The Gwinnett *Herald* pointed to a similar transition: "From all sections of the county comes almost a universal complaint of scarcity of corn, fodder, wheat, and in fact nearly everything that is necessary to sustain man and beast. For the first time in several years the farmers of Gwinnett will have to look to the West for corn, flour, and meat. . . . Gwinnett has always been known as a grain growing county . . . but within the last few years nearly everybody has abandoned the ways of their fathers . . . and caught the cotton planting mania."[23] Over the short span of fifteen years, the Upcountry moved from the periphery into the vortex of the market economy.[24]

Luke Wadkins of Jackson County did not need to consult the statistics compiled by the State Department of Agriculture or the Federal Census Bureau to comprehend the meaning of social change. He experienced it directly. In 1860 he had farmed 40 of his 190 acres with the assistance of only his wife and children, raising well over 200 bushels of corn, 20 bushels of oats, 32 bushels of wheat, 100 pounds of tobacco, 40 bushels of

23. Jackson *Herald*, August 5, 1881; Cottage Home Farm Journal, Floyd County, May 1, 1879, Dent Papers; W. J. Rusk to John S. Dobbins, Clarksville, August 10, 1875, John S. Dobbins Papers, Reel 2, EU; Gwinnett *Herald*, February 23, 1881.

24. The integration of Georgia's Upcountry into the cotton market after the Civil War had parallels in other nonplantation areas of the Lower South. See Anthony Tang, *Economic Development in the Southern Piedmont, 1860–1950* (Chapel Hill, 1958), 35–36; Roger W. Shugg, *Origins of Class Struggle in Louisiana: A Social History of White Farmers and Laborers During Slavery and After, 1840–1875* (Baton Rouge, 1939), 272; Stanley L. Engerman, "The Legacy of Slavery" (Paper presented to the Duke University Symposium on *One Kind of Freedom*, February 1978), 16–17.

sweet potatoes, and one bale of cotton, a pattern of general farming he had followed for at least ten years. Taking into account the grain required for seed, livestock feed, and household subsistence, he nonetheless was left with a small surplus that could be stored, traded for cash, or bartered for necessary goods. Two decades later Wadkins still resided in Jackson County, yet much in his economic life had been altered. He cultivated about 60 acres of what was now a 90-acre farm, where he grew only 150 bushels of corn, 20 bushels of wheat, 60 bushels of oats, and 25 bushels of sweet potatoes in addition to nine bales of cotton. Indeed, he devoted fully one-third of his cropland to the staple, and at no inconsiderable expense. His fertilizer purchases for the year amounted to $131, hardly a mean sum for a man whose farm was worth a scant $400 and whose annual produce was valued at $369. At year's end he would have to buy provisions for his family, doubtless at inflated credit prices, for his grain supply no longer sufficed to meet the nutritional demands of his household.[25]

All too many yeoman farmers shared Wadkins's predicament. Between 1860 and 1880 a sharp decline in the number of unimproved acres, head of livestock, and production of foodstuffs, together with a striking rise in cotton production, was common to many white-owned farms embracing fewer than 200 improved acres (see Table 4.3). The change was particularly dramatic in Jackson County, where, as in other parts of the eastern Upcountry, cotton culture had been very limited before the Civil War; it was less dramatic in Carroll County, where, as in other counties of the western Upcountry, a surge of cotton production had occurred during the 1850s. But the trends were impressive everywhere, especially the falling harvest of grain. And the smallest farms in both counties tended to experience the greatest slide.[26]

Cotton became, at once, an almost universal as well as a substantial crop on Upcountry yeoman farms. By 1880, 90 percent of the farmers in Jackson and Carroll counties grew the fiber for sale, and the proportion was even higher among those having between 25 and 199 improved acres. Increased cotton production, moreover, came largely as the

25. Manuscript Census, Georgia, Jackson County, Schedule II, 1850, 1860, 1880. In 1860 Wadkins raised a surplus of 22.7 bushels of grain per household member after necessary deductions for seed and livestock feed were made. Ten years earlier he had had an even larger grain surplus, for he had grown no cotton. In 1880, however, Wadkins had a grain deficit of 8 bushels per household member. For the method of determining this "self-sufficiency index," see Appendix.

26. Appendix, Tables V–VI.

Table 4.3 Acreage, Livestock, and Crop Production on Yeoman Farms, Jackson and Carroll Counties 1860–1880 (Mean Values)

Item	Farm Size (Improved Acres)							
	1–24		25–49		50–99		100–199	
	1860	1880	1860	1880	1860	1880	1860	1880
Jackson County:								
Unimproved Acres	89	46	111	71	238	146	294	247
Livestock[1]	17	8	20	13	32	22	44	35
Foodstuffs[2]	147	74	264	199	489	279	717	713
Cotton (Bales)	0.5	2.0	0.8	4.5	1.7	6.8	3.8	13.4
Cotton/Imp. Acres[3]	—	47%	—	40%	—	27%	—	31%
Cotton/Corn Acres[4]	—	92%	—	100%	—	89%	—	81%
Number of Farms	20	22	79	39	85	38	47	17
Carroll County:								
Unimproved Acres	92	64	110	109	141	143	293	135
Livestock[1]	17	14	27	22	42	29	55	21
Foodstuffs[2]	240	153	307	338	459	363	745	476
Cotton (Bales)	2.8	2.6	2.4	4.1	3.6	5.4	7.9	6.4
Cotton/Imp. Acres[3]	—	39%	—	30%	—	20%	—	15%
Cotton/Corn Acres[4]	—	75%	—	70%	—	65%	—	71%
Number of Farms	76	42	69	57	54	40	30	19

[1] Head of horses, mules, milch cows, other cattle, oxen, sheep, and swine.

[2] Bushes of corn, rye, oats, wheat, peas and beans, Irish and sweet potatoes.

[3] Ratio of acres in cotton to total improved acres.

[4] Ratio of acres in cotton to acres in corn.

Source: Manuscript Census, Georgia, Jackson and Carroll Counties, Schedule II, 1860, 1880.

result of expanded acreage rather than augmented yields, to which the drop in corn production can in good measure be attributed. Cotton acreage on yeoman farms ranged from 15 to about 50 percent of the total cropland, averaging out at something over 30 percent. Compared to corn acreage alone, cotton acreage constituted between two-thirds and fully the equivalent (Table 4.3). Farmers with 200 or more acres in crops also enlarged their cotton planting, though proportionately less than did smallholders.[27]

A sign both of Upcountry farmers' efforts to feed themselves and their families and of cotton's new importance in the economy emerges from

27. Also see Appendix, Tables II, V–VII.

another shift in production patterns. For as corn output declined precipitously between 1860 and 1880, wheat and oat production increased by as much as fivefold in some yeoman-farm categories.[28] Neither of these small grains, it should be said, nearly matched the favor of corn in the Southern diet. Oats, in fact, served primarily as feed for work animals. But cotton and corn had overlapping growing seasons, and unless a farmer had an extensive tract of land and a large labor force, the time and acreage allotted to cotton normally came at the expense of corn. Wheat and oats, on the other hand, could be planted and harvested at points during the year when there was less conflict with labor requirements for corn or cotton, winter wheat being the most popular variety.[29] That yeomen made such adjustments in their farming practices suggests an ongoing attempt to maintain the independence that only a relative degree of self-sufficiency could bring; that the adjustments had to be made at all indicates that cotton was rapidly extending its kingdom.

Yet for all the changes that took place after the Civil War, the late 1870s and early 1880s still represented a transitional phase in the rise of Upcountry staple agriculture. Throughout the region, grain continued as the most important crop, in acreage if not in value, on small and large farms alike, and the progress of commercial farming itself had an uneven quality. The slow pace of railroad construction left many sections of the Upcountry as isolated as they had been in the antebellum period. So a market-conscious Cherokee County inhabitant complained, emphasizing the need for transport facilities: "Here lie beautiful fertile valleys, scarcely semi-cultivated . . . [and with the county's] present insulation . . . agriculture is thriftless because of the expense of marketing." Even within developing counties, certain districts resisted what seemed to be the inexorable thrust of cotton culture, and smallholders in some parts of the Upcountry had more success at withstanding the most adverse consequences of extensive cotton planting. The greater soil fertility in Carroll County compared with that in long-settled Jackson, for instance, enabled its farmers to obtain higher yields and thereby larger grain crops. And while yeoman farmers raised similar quantities of cotton in both counties, those in

28. Appendix, Tables V–VI.

29. U. S. Patent Office, *Report to the Commissioner of Patents for the Year 1851* (Washington, 1852), Pt. II, 318–19; Sam B. Hilliard, *Hogmeat and Hoecake: Food Supply in the Old South, 1840–1860* (Carbondale, Ill., 1972), 152, 163–64, 168–69.

Carroll spent less on fertilizers and sowed fewer acres. Thus, a considerable number of Carroll County yeomen raised at least marginal grain surpluses. In Jackson County, grain shortages were widespread.[30]

By the end of the century, if not by 1890, however, yeoman farmers in Carroll County would face the same plight their counterparts in Jackson did in 1880, and cotton would reign as king in the Upcountry. But the staple's protracted ascendancy suggested that the majority of its subjects did not easily submit to its rule. Indeed, however much the initial growth of cotton production came as a response to the hardships of the immediate postwar years, Upcountry yeomen did not relinquish their proud independence simply by choice. The Civil War altered more than the region's crop mix: a new and exploitative credit system linked to the changing structure of local, national, and international markets—the subjects of the next chapter—decisively transformed the relations of production and exchange, tied smallholders firmly to staple agriculture, and pushed them to the wall. The dynamics of that experience would stir political turbulence in the Upcountry during the 1880s and fuel the fires of Southern Populism.

III

The Upcountry had never been dominated by plantations. During the antebellum period, yeoman farms composed the overwhelming majority of agricultural units and embraced most of the land under cultivation. By 1880, large farms and plantations were even fewer in number and had even less economic importance. They constituted under 5 percent of all agricultural units and embraced under 15 percent of the cropland. Yet the further predominance of small farms did not reflect a redistribution of wealth. As before the war, substantial landowners held a disproportionate share of Upcountry real estate. In 1870 the richest tenth of real-property holders in Jackson and Carroll counties owned 37 percent and 45 percent of the real wealth respectively, much the same proportions as had prevailed ten years earlier.[31] While the 1880 census did not record the value of individual

30. Cartersville *Express*, February 10, 1876. Carroll County yeomen spent no more than two-thirds of what Jackson County yeomen did on fertilizers. For the percentage of yeomen farms raising grain surpluses in both counties, see Appendix, Tables V–VI.

31. Manuscript Census, Georgia, Jackson and Carroll Counties, Schedule I and II, 1860, 1870, 1880. For a complete presentation of relevant statistics on the changing distribution of farm land and real wealth, see my doctoral dissertation, "The Roots of

real-estate holdings, there is no reason to believe that the structure of wealth became less concentrated during the 1870s. If anything, the expansion of commercial agriculture, the construction of railroads, and the attendant rise in land values led to greater concentrations.

The paradox of proliferating small farms and persisting, if not increasing, concentrations of agricultural wealth was common to the Black Belt as well as to the Upcountry, and resulted from both the failure of land reform and the reorganization of labor during Reconstruction. Although the abolition of slavery struck the planting elite a telling blow, in a rural society control of land as much as control of labor defined the boundaries of social relations. Had the federal government embarked upon a policy of confiscating large plantations and dividing them among the ex-slaves—a policy anticipated by wartime military exigencies and supported by a handful of Radical Republicans—the postwar South would have been very different. The decision of President Andrew Johnson to restore confiscated property to its former owners and the commitment of most Republicans to the sanctity of private property and the revitalization of the cotton economy, however, combined to doom the federal initiative.[32]

The defeat of confiscation in the White House and Congress did not lay the issue entirely to rest; it continued to influence politics and race relations in the South. But the eclipse of land reform as an element of national Reconstruction policy left intact one of the vital foundations of the planter class. It is true that land titles changed hands as the result of death, tribulation, and geographical mobility, though, significantly, at a rate no higher than during the 1850s and certainly not in a manner that broke up large holdings. Indeed, in some areas, planters not only persevered in considerable numbers but actually enlarged their share of real wealth.[33] Whatever their trials, they were in a far better position to

Southern Populism: Yeoman Farmers and the Transformation of Georgia's Upper Piedmont, 1850–1890" (Ph.D. diss., Yale University, 1979), 429, 434.

32. C. Vann Woodward, *Origins of the New South, 1877–1913* (Baton Rouge, 1951), 178–79; Ransom and Sutch, *One Kind of Freedom*, 78–80; Eric Foner, *Politics and Ideology in the Age of the Civil War* (New York, 1980), 128–49; William S. McFeely, *Yankee Stepfather: General O. O. Howard and the Freedmen* (New York, 1970), 92–97, 211–14; Willie Lee Rose, *Rehearsal for Reconstruction: The Port Royal Experiment* (New York, 1964), 320–28.

33. Jonathan M. Wiener, "Planter Persistence and Social Change: Alabama, 1850–1870," *Journal of Interdisciplinary History*, VII (Fall 1976), 235–60; Michael Wayne, *The Reshaping of Plantation Society: The Natchez District, 1860–1880* (Baton Rouge, 1983), chap. 3; Kenneth S. Greenberg, "The Civil War and the Redistribution of Land: Adams County, Mississippi, 1860–1870," *AH*, LII (April 1978), 292–307.

withstand the economic woes of the immediate postwar years than were their poorer neighbors. In the Upcountry, too, the richest farmers and planters—as a group—had more success in weathering the storm than did smallholders and often found themselves more powerfully situated in 1870 than in 1860. If, for example, we consider the distribution of real wealth among all white household heads rather than simply among all white landowners, the top tenth and top quarter in Carroll and Jackson counties claimed more than 55 percent and 80 percent respectively in 1870, sizable jumps over the course of the decade. Once again, middling and lesser yeomen stood as the relative losers.[34]

If the failure of land reform along with economic dislocations facilitated a greater concentration of agricultural wealth, the growing number of small farm units represented the outcome of the planters' efforts to reestablish authority over the liberated black labor force. Insisting that the freedmen were inherently lazy, indolent, and unreliable and would not work unless compelled, former slaveholders, while reluctantly accepting Emancipation, hoped to maintain plantation organization and supervision. And for the first year or two following the war they did just that. Blacks continued to live in the old slave quarters, continued to receive rations and clothing from the landowners, and continued to cultivate the land in gangs, although now they were entitled to a low wage or a small share of the crop as further remuneration. The freedmen had other ideas, however. They wished to escape from the rigors of plantation life, farm their own land, and provide for themselves. Having meager resources and facing the fierce opposition of the landed elite, few attained the goal of independent proprietorship. But the ex-slaves did their best to force something of a labor market on planters who preferred "some species of serfdom or peonage, or . . . other form of compulsory labor," and thereby struck better bargains than white landowners had originally intended to offer. By resisting gang labor in a variety of ways, moreover, the freedmen helped bring about a major reorganization in the system of production. Gradual though the process was, as early as 1870 many plantations were being divided into small parcels farmed by black tenant and sharecrop-

---

34. In Jackson County, the top decile of white household heads claimed 59.9 percent of the real wealth in 1870, almost 12 percent more than in 1860; the top quarter claimed 89 percent, almost 15 percent more than in 1860. In Carroll County, the top decile and top quarter claimed 56.8 percent and 80.9 percent of the real wealth respectively in 1870, each about 5 percent more than in 1860. For a full statistical breakdown, see Hahn, "Roots of Southern Populism," 430.

per families having a greater measure of personal autonomy. With few alternative employment opportunities, the freedmen remained tied to the land and subject to the exploitation of landlords and merchants, but the struggle for control of production and exchange was a persistent feature of economic and political life.[35]

In the Upcountry neither plantations nor black labor had the social and economic significance they did in the Black Belt. Joseph Brown's warning notwithstanding, Emancipation did not prompt an extensive migration of freedmen from the cotton counties to the hills. The racial demography of the Upcountry remained remarkably stable: blacks would never represent more than one-quarter of the region's total population.[36] As in the Black Belt, however, the first years after abolition saw the continuation of former patterns of labor organization. Immediately following the war, one large landowner from Jackson County could recall, he had "conducted the plantation wholly with hired labor." The method of payment might vary considerably, from shares of the crop—anywhere between one-eighth and one–half—to monthly or yearly cash wages, but for the most part blacks also received "quarters and rations." Of over 100 labor contracts filed with the Freedmen's Bureau in Floyd County in 1867, fully three-quarters stipulated housing, food, and wages, the latter ranging from $5 to $15 per month.[37] Work routines also appear to have been maintained. Thus, when Quill Gober and his family signed on with C. H. Little in Franklin County that same year, they agreed to "do all and every kind of work, which is necessary to be done, on [Little's] plantation or elsewhere if so ordered." For this the Gobers would receive "one hundred dollars [for the year] to be paid in money or provisions at customary prices," though they were required to "feed, clothe, and board themselves and to pay medical costs." Another landowner made

35. *Southern Cultivator*, quoted in Paul S. Taylor, "Slave to Freedman," *Southern Economic History Project*, VII (Berkeley, 1970), 27; James L. Roark, *Masters Without Slaves: Southern Planters in the Civil War and Reconstruction* (New York, 1977), 157–69; Leon F. Litwack, *Been in the Storm So Long: The Aftermath of Slavery* (New York, 1979), 292–335.

36. *Ninth Census*, Population, 21–22; *Tenth Census*, Compendium, 341–43.

37. Testimony of Luther Elrod, Jackson County, in Robert P. Brooks, Inquiries Concerning Georgia Farms, I, UGa; Labor Contracts, Floyd County, 1866, BRFAL, Record Group 105/Entry 998, Vol. 345, NA; Labor Contracts, Franklin County, 1867, BRFAL, 105/822, Subordinate Field Office, Contracts and Monthly Reports, Box 13, NA; John J. Knox, "Monthly Report on Contracts," Athens, March 1867, BRFAL, 105/727, Sub. Field Off., Box 6, Letters Received, NA; ibid., December 1867, January 1868, February 1868.

similar arrangements with a black family for one-sixth of the crop.[38]

By the late 1860s and early 1870s, sharecropping—which had the landowner furnish the laborer with a tract of land, farming implements, work animals, and seed, and pay him, perhaps, one-half of the crop— had become somewhat more common. The share might have been larger if the cropper owned livestock; in either case he had to purchase his own provisions. Renting farms to freedmen, on the other hand— when the landlord received a share of the crop as payment and allowed the tenant freedom from close supervision—was quite rare.[39] But it appears that surprisingly few Upcountry blacks became even share-croppers. In Jackson County, which boasted one of the region's largest black populations, almost nine of ten freedmen engaged in agriculture were reported as "farm laborers" in 1880. Only a handful cropped or rented; proportionately more, in fact, owned farms than worked on shares. In Carroll County, which had one of the region's smallest black populations, a larger percentage of sharecroppers could be found. Nonetheless, about half of the black agriculturists were farm laborers, a situation which seems to have prevailed elsewhere. While often living in scattered one-family houses, as did croppers, these blacks worked the land collectively. Tenancy and sharecropping in the Upcountry would be predominantly white institutions.[40]

White landlessness, by no means inconsequential during the antebel-lum period, became more extensive after the Civil War. Though economic hardship affected both rich and poor, small farmers had a particularly difficult time of it. Generally in debt and left with depleted resources during the 1860s, they faced growing pressure from creditors who responded to the financial havoc and political uncertainties of Reconstruction by attempting to clear their balance sheets as quickly as possible. And they showed little reluctance to resort to the auction block if necessary. "I have now a large amount of executions in my hand for collection," the Franklin County sheriff told General John Pope,

38. Labor Contract: C. H. Little and Quill Gober, Franklin County, January 1, 1867, BRFAL, 105/822, Sub. Field Off., Contracts and Monthly Reports, Box 13; Labor Contract: Perlina Atkinson and Beveley Stobull, Franklin County, February 10, 1868, ibid.

39. On the distinctions between sharecropping and share renting, see Harold D. Woodman, "Post–Civil War Southern Agriculture and the Law," *AH*, LIII (January 1979), 324–27; Brooks, *Agrarian Revolution*, 48–54.

40. Appendix, Tables I, IX; Testimony of L. G. Hardman, Jackson County, 1910, in Robert P. Brooks, Economic Conditions on Georgia Plantations, I, UGa.

commander of the Third Military District, "which if done will cause a great sacrifice of property there being but little money in the country." Old political feuds also came into play. Complaining that the "Shirriff of this Co[unty] is a Strong Reb and all connected with the office is," a Jackson County Unionist advised federal officials that the "Secessionists have oppressed [my husband] ever since Georgia seceeded. They are as venomous now as they were then. . . . [H]e went Securrity for some of them during the war who have proved insolvent, now his little remaining Property is taken to pay other debts." She joined what had become a resounding chorus in asking that "the Sales of property [be stopped] untill the people can make money to pay creditors with. . . ."[41] Three-quarters of the state's citizens were debtors, W. L. Goodwin, an Upcountry delegate, apprised the Republican-dominated constitutional convention of 1868, and if judgments were pressed to the limit "the entire landed estates of Georgia will pass into the hands of a few extremely wealthy men." "This is a strife between capital and labor; between the wealthy aristocrats and the great mass of the people," Goodwin proclaimed. "Let me appeal to you . . . stretch forth your helping hands, give the desired relief to the debt-ridden and over burthened people. . . ."[42]

Responding to the pleas of men like Goodwin and hoping to court the favor of north Georgia yeomen, the convention effectively abolished debts contracted prior to June 1, 1865, and recommended substantial homestead exemptions on real and personal property, which the legislature promptly enacted into law.[43] For many farmers, however, such relief measures came too late. Fewer Upcountry whites owned land in 1870 than in 1860, and the trend only worsened thereafter. An upswing in land values during the 1870s coupled with declining prices for agricultural commodities—especially cotton—placed real property increasingly beyond the reach of whites who began their adult lives in a condition of landlessness. As numerous participants in a survey conducted early in the twentieth century remarked, the "small white

41. Thomas W. Neal to Gen. Pope, Franklin County, May 22, 1867, BCA, Record Group 393/Entry 5782, Box 1, NA; Carrie Hays to Gen. Pope, Jefferson, September 9, 1867, BCA, 393/5782, Box 4.

42. W. L. Goodwin, quoted in Henri H. Freeman, "Some Aspects of Debtor Relief in Georgia During Reconstruction" (M.A. thesis, Emory University, 1951), 33.

43. Freeman, "Aspects of Debtor Relief," 28–35, 50–51; Elizabeth Studley Nathans, *Losing the Peace: Georgia Republicans and Reconstruction, 1865–1871* (Baton Rouge, 1968), 60–64.

farmer did not find it easier to secure a farm after the war than before."[44]

Upcountry farm tenancy had antebellum precedents, but it changed in extent and character as the region moved into the staple economy. During the 1850s nearly nine of ten farm operators owned the land they cultivated; by 1880, among whites, only between six and eight of ten did. While these figures underestimate the full range of landlessness (and perhaps of tenancy) in both periods, they indicate important differences in the ownership structure of individual farm units.[45] At the same time, the landlord-tenant relationship underwent a significant transformation. In the prewar era, when the Georgia Upcountry was still thinly settled and on the periphery of the market economy, white tenants were renters: that is, they leased a tract of land in lieu of certain obligations, which could include cash payments, a share of the produce, or labor services. Under these circumstances the tenant had considerable freedom in his agricultural operations and retained legal control over the crop. The terms of contract normally did not specify patterns of cultivation and the lessees generally made their own arrangements for the purchase of supplies and the sale of surpluses. While many renters raised cotton, doubtless in part to accumulate resources sufficient to become freeholders, their farming practices closely paralleled those of yeoman neighbors. These relations began to change after the war, as farm renting increasingly gave way to sharecropping, a system in which the landlord held legal rights to the crop, exercised extensive supervision, and paid out rather than received a share of the harvest.[46]

A dearth of material possessions among landless whites and blacks contributed to the rise of sharecropping, for under such arrangements landowners commonly furnished draft animals and farm tools in

44. Testimony of H. J. McCormick, Bartow County, 1912, in Brooks, Inquiries Concerning Georgia Farms, I. In 1860 between 65 and 70 percent of the white household heads in Jackson and Carroll counties owned real estate. In 1870 between 55 and 60 percent did. The 1880 census did not record the value of real-estate holdings, but the tax digests show that the percentage of landowners continued to drop to as low as 50 percent by that year. See Manuscript Census, Georgia, Jackson and Carroll Counties, Schedule I, 1860, 1870; Jackson County Tax Digest, 1880; Carroll County Tax Digest, 1880.

45. See below Table 4.4. These figures do not include farm laborers or other landless farmers who did not appear on the agricultural schedule as farm operators.

46. Enoch Banks, *The Economics of Land Tenure in Georgia* (New York, 1905), 82; Oscar Zeichner, "The Legal Status of the Agricultural Laborer in the South," *Political Science Quarterly*, LV (September 1940), 412–28. On the prewar period, see above, Chapter Two.

addition to a piece of land. As a Floyd County landlord put it, "all the hands I employ come to me poverty stricken and have to be found in all supplies—I never yet, since the negroes were freed, had a negro or white man I employed that ever came to me with anything but the cloths they had on their back. . . . " This may be something of an exaggeration, for the tax rolls from Carroll and Jackson counties demonstrate that almost all whites and blacks owned at least a small amount of personal property. But it suggests a condition of widespread economic dependency.[47]

More centrally, the growth of sharecropping reflected the expansion of staple agriculture, for a hallmark of contracts was a detailed delineation of the crop mix—a provision rarely found in antebellum agreements. Thus, when Lucius H. Featherston "allow[ed] . . . Moses Moreland to cultivate during the year 1870 fifty acres more or less, of his farm near Franklin [Heard county]," he supplied Moreland with "stock and farming tools necessary to cultivate said land in good farmer like stile," and directed Moreland to sow "30 acres in cotton and the balance in corn." "[A]fter all advances of money, forage, provision, and other things" were repaid, Moreland would have "one half of the crop." John H. Dent and Harvey Lemmings reached similar terms in Floyd County three years later. Dent was "to furnish a horse or mule, all implements and feed [for the animals]"; Lemmings was "to cultivate and harvest 15 acres of corn and . . . 5 acres of cotton," and "receive 1/2 corn and fodder and . . . 1/2 cotton" out of which he would pay for any provisions supplied by Dent.[48]

Both Featherston and Dent plainly stipulated that "the title and possession of the entire crop is to remain in . . . [their hands] until said advances and debts are settled." As of 1872, such an inclusion was no longer necessary. In that year the Georgia Supreme Court issued a ruling that acknowledged the new aspects of the staple economy and bolstered the power of landlords by distinguishing the rights of sharecroppers and tenants. The tenant "has a possession of the

47. Cottage Home Farm Journal, Floyd County, January 1, 1886, Dent Papers. For property ownership among landless whites and blacks, see Jackson County Tax Digests, 1880–1890; Carroll County Tax Digests, 1880–1890. In Jackson and Carroll counties for the year 1890, between 80 and 90 percent of the blacks owned at least some property. Around 60 percent had livestock, and around 30 percent had farm tools.

48. Labor Contract: Lucius H. Featherston and Moses Moreland, Heard County, 1869, Featherston Papers, Box 1, Folder 5; Labor Contract: John H. Dent and Harvey Lemmings, Floyd County, December 1873, Dent Papers.

premises, exclusive of the Landlord, [the cropper] has not," the court announced. "The one has a right for a fixed time, the other has a right only to go on the land to plant, work, and gather the crop. The possession of the land is with the owner against the cropper." In the eyes of the law, the cropper was no more than a wage laborer or, as men like Dent and Featherston would have it, a "hand."[49]

It is impossible to determine the precise statistical breakdown of various forms of labor organization during this period, for the census made a distinction only between "share tenants" and "cash tenants," the latter of whom usually did not pay cash but rather "fixed" or "standing rent." The cash tenants would be renters in the fullest sense, and it is telling that there were relatively few. Most of the landless whites who operated farms came under the rubric of "share tenants." While it is likely that fewer than half were sharecroppers by 1880, cropping was clearly on the rise.[50] And over time, whatever may have been true in legal theory, the differences between share renting and sharecropping seemed to dissolve in practice. Scattered contracts demonstrate that share-renters, like croppers, generally agreed to plant specifically designated acreage in specifically designated crops and to accept the landlord's direct supervision. When Paschal Wood "rented" 100 acres in Heard County, for example, he consented to "cultivate [75 acres] in cotton and the ballance or remainder in corn" and "to pay over" one-fourth of the cotton and one-third of the corn. With the emergence of the crop lien, moreover, landlords and merchants could lay claim to the renter's crop. In 1880, the vast majority of Upcountry whites who worked tracts of land they did not own entered into such arrangements (see Table 4.4).[51]

49. Appling v. Odom, 46 *Georgia Reports* 583.

50. According to labor statistics compiled by the Georgia Commissioner of Agriculture in 1875, which are not distinguished by race, 11,607 (44.4%) of the "hands" in the Upcountry rented, 9,223 (35.3%) cropped, and 5,292 (20.3%) worked for wages. Excluding the wageworkers, 56 percent rented and 44 percent cropped. If the figures included only whites, it is probable that the proportion of croppers would be somewhat lower. But it is an indication of the growing incidence of white sharecropping that by 1929 some 54 percent of the white tenants were croppers and only 46 percent were renters. See Georgia Department of Agriculture, *Report of the Commissioner of Agriculture for the State of Georgia, 1875* (Atlanta, 1876), 159–70; *Fifteenth Census of the United States, 1930* (Washington, 1932), Agriculture, Vol. II, Pt. 2, 524–35.

51. Labor Contract: Lucius H. Featherston and Paschal Wood, Heard County, September 21, 1872, Featherston Papers, Box 1, Folder 7; Banks, *Economics of Land Tenure*, 78–116.

Table 4.4   White Farm Tenancy in Jackson and Carroll Counties, 1880

	Jackson County		Carroll County	
Category	Number	Percentage	Number	Percentage
Owner-Operator	119	78.3 %	168	67.7 %
Share-Tenant	23	15.1	73	29.4
Cash Tenant	10	6.6	7	2.9
Total	152	100.0 %	248	100.0 %
	Jackson County		Carroll County	
Category	Number	Percentage	Number	Percentage
Share-Tenant	23	69.7 %	73	91.3 %
Cash Tenant	10	30.3	7	8.7
Total	33	100.0 %	80	100.0 %

Source: Manuscript Census, Jackson and Carroll Counties, Schedule II, 1880.

Landlord-tenant relations common to the antebellum Upcountry did not entirely disappear after the Civil War. As late as 1885, W. R. Ward of Heard County "acknowledg[ed] that I have cleared six or seven acres of land and built a house and made improvements . . . and have had the cultivation and use of said six or seven acres of land and use of said house for the last six or seven years as [a] tenant," and contracted "to pay . . . the sum of $10 as Rent for said cleared land for the year 1885." But the patterns of production on both rented and cropped farms showed the decisive imprint of staple agriculture. For one thing, farms tended to be very small: almost nine of ten included fewer than fifty acres and only a handful had any unimproved land. And, on average, cotton took up about half of their fields, with the remainder devoted primarily to corn. It is, indeed, a sign of market orientation, that renters and croppers raised far fewer bushels of wheat, oats, and sweet potatoes than did comparable yeomen—a situation that could also be found on units farmed by black tenants. "[The poor whites] work for shares . . . under the general direction of landowners . . . [and] produce cotton almost exclusively," a Polk County observer noted. "Families who in the antebellum days only produced from 2–3 bales of cotton now produce from 5–20." Left with little in the way of foodstuffs, they drifted into debt for "everything they needed, except bread, [and] some even buy that."[52]

While some renters and croppers hired a white or black hand for specific tasks or perhaps for steady help, the overwhelming majority cultivated their tracts entirely with household labor. In either case, they could not have felt terribly independent. Along with instructions about the crop mix, they had to contend with the meddling of a landlord or his manager. As J. W. Daniel, a Heard County plantation owner later recalled, he gave "close supervision to tenants on the share system." Furthermore, contractual obligations often extended beyond the bounds of the small units, especially when a landlord had several tenants on his place. Harvey Lemmings, the Floyd County cropper, agreed not only to work the twenty acres he resided on but also "to assist in feeding and watering [the landowner's] stock and to assist in repairing lot fencing, keeping [the landowner] in firewood and putting fencing around the field he cultivates." Too, men and women like Lemmings occasionally performed day labor at a small wage for their landlords or for neighboring farmers when odd jobs had to be done or crops harvested. Jim Holcomb and his sons, Cherokee County tenants who "cultivated about twenty acres of cotton and twenty acres of corn," had "to work all the time." "During the winter and between the laying-by of the crops and fodder-pulling time," according to a local resident, "Jim worked as a section hand on the railroad ten hours a day for ninety cents. During moving time in the fall he and his neighbor Gordon Covington moved families in their two horse wagons from one farm to another." Jasper Hendrix, also of Cherokee County, "traveled all over the settlement cutting wheat with a cradle for a dollar a day." As prospects for escape narrowed, cotton tenancy proved to be a path of proletarianization for many Upcountry whites.[53]

Not a smooth path, however, as landlords perpetually complained. Men who prized personal, as well as economic, independence had little taste for living under the thumb of a well-to-do landowner, and they did

52. Labor Contract: Lucius H. Featherston and W. R. Ward, Heard County, 1885, Featherston Papers, Box 1, Folder 17; *Report on Cotton Production in the United States*, 2 vols. (Washington, 1884), II, 173; Appendix, Tables VII–VIII.

53. Testimony of J. W. Daniel, Heard County, 1912, in Brooks, Inquiries Concerning Georgia Farms, I; Labor Contract: John H. Dent and Harvey Lemmings, Floyd County, December 1873, Dent Papers; Cottage Home Farm Journal, Floyd County, February 23, 1872, ibid.; Floyd C. Watkins and Charles H. Watkins, *Yesterday in the Hills* (Chicago, 1963), 59, 65.

not capitulate easily. So John Dent, the Floyd County planter and agricultural reformer, discovered. "Heretofore I have been advocating white labor as the most reliable, believing it was impossible for the white man to be worse than a negro in point of morals, his reliability, and industry," he declared, but a year's experience convinced him otherwise. Having hired "white and black laborers on the same terms and conditions," he found that while the blacks had few wants, "the wants of the white men were insatiable, their discontent . . . and their efforts to take advantage of every circumstance that would pay them for so doing . . . constant." "In a word," Dent scoffed, "the white man was selfish and avaricious whilst the negro was far more accommodating." A Gwinnett County landlord put it more succinctly: "White tenants . . . don't take kindly to advice."[54]

The tensions between landlords and laborers did not simply reflect the inequitable distribution of land; they also reflected qualitative changes in the class relation and a struggle for control—control over time and work rhythms, over subsistence, over the market crop. Whatever the law may have dictated, these matters were hammered out in daily and yearly confrontations. When, for instance, landlords railed about their tenants' unreliability, lack of industry, absence of discipline, and insubordination, they implicitly acknowledged the points of contention at the heart of the labor system. Thus John Dent engaged in a protracted wrestling match with his croppers. "This letting hands have [garden] patches . . . is not a good plan and don't work well," he grumbled in 1876, "they neglect their crops for their patches and the proprietor is the loser." On a different occasion, field work was interrupted because "my farm hands white and black are making fish traps." "The whole creek [is] dammed up with fish traps," he fretted, "fish is the paramount idea with them." And then there was old Harvey Lemmings, who had the audacity to bring his wheat crop to "a traveling thresher to do the work in preference to us[ing] my barn thresher" because Dent refused to contribute part of the toll. "[I]t is all pretense our hiring help or laborers," Dent groaned, "they are *punctual* and *faithful* but to *two things* and that is to get their *meals* and *money*." Or, as another Upcountry landlord admitted, tenants under the share system "generally want to farm independent of us. . . ."[55]

54. Cottage Home Farm Journal, Floyd County, August 15, 1872, Dent Papers; Testimony of Robert Craig, Gwinnett County, 1910, in Brooks, Economic Conditions on Georgia Plantations, I.

55. Cottage Home Farm Journal, Floyd County, July 6, 1872, April 4, 1872, April 19,

Sheer physical movement offers another measure of tenants' efforts to resist the landlord's exactions. Although numerous renters and croppers found themselves tied to particular farms because of their failure to settle debts, the extent of turnover is impressive. A study of Gwinnett County suggests that between one-half and two-thirds of the tenants shifted farms every year or two. "Tenants changing landlords; landlords changing tenants," the Jackson *Herald* observed. John Dent, who encountered the problem on his own plantation, also reported it to be widespread. "There has been considerable moving about for the last two or three weeks among the renters as well as croppers," he noted one January. "Several renters have moved from this neighborhood to Alabama and croppers have changed places considerable." Leaving for Alabama or other locales outside the county was, in fact, uncommon. For the most part, tenants traveled short distances, perhaps a few miles, rarely farther than ten. But the impact was felt in the way of an imposed labor shortage.[56]

The share system itself, in the Upcountry as in the Black Belt, represented a concession to landless whites and blacks within a context of unequal economic power. Finding "hired labor . . . sorry and unreliable" and fearing an "exodus of laboring men from North Georgia" due to dissatisfaction over wages and a desire to seek out land in "Arkansas and Texas," landlords hoped that share renting and cropping, which gave hands a stake in the crop along with somewhat more autonomy, would stabilize labor relations and provide a ready surplus. Rather than stability, however, the share system brought on a new stage in the struggle over the substance and meaning of class relations in the developing cotton economy—a struggle that quickly moved beyond the bounds of individual farms and plantations, divided whole communities, and left a decisive stamp on local and state politics for years to come.[57]

1872, July 1872, December 15, 1876, July 1, 1872, Dent Papers; Testimony of J. G. D. Erwin, Gordon County, 1912, in Brooks, Inquiries Concerning Georgia Farms, I.

56. Howard A. Turner and L. D. Howell, "Condition of Farmers in a White-Farmer Area of the Cotton Piedmont, 1924–1926," U.S. Department of Agriculture, Circular No. 78 (September 1929), 35–36; Jackson *Herald*, January 15, 1886; Cottage Home Farm Journal, Floyd County, January 3, 1891, Dent Papers. Also see Carroll *Free Press*, January 22, 1886.

57. Testimony of H. J. McCormick, Bartow County, 1912, in Brooks, Inquiries Concerning Georgia Farms, I; *The Plantation*, III (November 1872), 41. A number of

Yet, the emerging patterns of social differentiation among Upcountry whites, however much they involved new and exploitative relations, retained some important features from the previous era, muting their cultural and political ramifications. During the antebellum period, landlessness was widespread, but, as in many peasant communities, it was often "disguised" by ties of kinship and a life cycle that normally made freehold independence a relatively late acquisition. Ostensibly distinct social groups thereby maintained significant links. While the postwar years saw landlessness become a more pervasive as well as an increasingly permanent status, the broad structure of the traditional life cycle persisted. Moreover, evidence indicates that perhaps as many as one-quarter of the white renters and croppers worked land owned by relatives, a circumstance that complicated undeniably intensifying class antagonisms. Though the status of propertyless whites came to approximate that of black laborers according to economic criteria, it was the black population that composed, socially and culturally, the Upcountry's readily distinguishable rural proletariat.[58]

IV

"Hard times" was the cry in the Upcountry by 1890. Low cotton prices, short food crops, and indebtedness for supplies went into making of a vicious cycle that enveloped the lives of small farmers, white and black,

---

economic historians have recently argued that sharecropping evolved from the mutual agreement of landlord and laborer in the context of a free, though capital-short, market. While properly recognizing the dynamic character of postwar labor relations, this view overlooks the inequalities of power and resources, the coercion, and the absence of real alternative employment opportunities that defined the boundaries of such a marketplace. See, especially, Robert Higgs, *Competition and Coercion: Blacks in the American Economy, 1865–1914* (Cambridge, 1977); Joseph D. Reid, Jr., "Sharecropping as an Understandable Market Response: The Postbellum South," *Journal of Economic History*, XXXIII (March 1973), 106–30.

58. In 1880, white farm-owning household heads in Jackson and Carroll counties were, on average, forty-seven and forty-four years old respectively; white tenant household heads, on average, were in their thirties. See Manuscript Census, Georgia, Jackson and Carroll Counties, Schedule I and II, 1880. On kinship ties between tenants and landowners, see Turner and Howell, "Condition of Farmers," 11. For an important theoretical treatment of rural proletarianization, see Sidney Mintz, "The Rural Proletariat and the Problem of Rural Proletarian Consciousness," *Journal of Peasant Studies*. I (April 1974), 291–323.

owners and tenants, for during the 1880s staple agriculture fastened its grip on the region's economy. If the 1870s and early 1880s marked a transitional period, the direction of change was apparent, and as the last decade of the nineteenth century opened, the Upcountry stood fully transformed, wrenched from the margin into the mainstream of the cotton market.[59]

The pace of commercialization may well have quickened during the 1880s. Railroad construction, slowed through the 1870s by war-induced hardships and by the Panic of 1873, finally hit its stride. Between 1879 and 1886, six new lines embracing 252 miles of track came into operation, an almost 60-percent hike in mileage. Most were feeders, connecting small courthouse towns with major roads. The Gainesville and Jefferson, the Marietta and North Georgia, the Hartwell, and the Lawrenceville Branch railroads, among others, commenced service, often after long periods of incubation, and gave much of the Upcountry its first ready access to the outside world. Promoting the rise of land values and facilitating the flow of produce and fertilizers, the railroads also blazed the trail of King Cotton.[60]

Few observers could deny that cotton ruled the Upcountry in 1890. Certainly those who filled the newspapers and agricultural journals with lectures on the need for crop diversification and the importance of raising "meat and meal" at home, who urged a return to the "old times under which we prospered so greatly," could not. Neither could the mass of rural producers. Output of the staple continued to increase during the 1880s at a rate far outstripping that of other crops, including corn, and the expansion of cotton acreage was even more dramatic. While the total number of improved acres in the Upcountry grew by about 20 percent over the course of the decade, the acreage planted in cotton jumped by more than 70 percent. As a fraction of all cropland, acreage devoted to the staple rose considerably and, for the first time, surpassed corn. Carroll County's experience is a case in point. Between 1880 and 1890, local farmers expanded their cultivated land from 92,000 to 116,000 acres, an increase of roughly 25 percent. But during the same period, cotton acreage leaped from 22,000 to 39,000 acres, or

59. *Southern Cultivator*, quoted in Carroll *Free Press*, February 12, 1886.

60. *Poor's Manual, 1879*, 513–33; *Poor's Manual, 1881*, 395–414; *Poor's Manual, 1885*, 429–48. In 1879 the Upcountry had 444.8 miles of track. By the late 1880s the region boasted 696.8 miles, an increase of 57 percent. These mileage figures include small sections that extended into the Mountain region of the state, into the northern tier of the Black Belt, and into western Alabama.

by more than 70 percent. Although in 1880 corn could boast about 20 percent more acreage than cotton, a decade later the ratio had been entirely reversed.[61]

The manuscript census for 1890 no longer exists. Therefore, detailed information about individual farms is unavailable. Aggregate county-level figures from the published returns, however, tell enough of a story. Per capita cotton production remained relatively stable or increased during the 1880s; per capita corn production, on the other hand, continued to slide, further undercutting already dwindling food surpluses and driving farmers into deeper dependence on store purchases for necessary provisions. At the same time, the proportion of farm owners in the Upcountry dropped significantly. In 1880, proprietors worked almost 60 percent of all farm units; ten years later they worked fewer than half (see Table 4.5). Although these statistics are not

Table 4.5 Crops, Acreage, and Land Tenure in the Upcountry, 1880–1890

Item	Upcountry		Jackson County		Carroll County	
	1880	1890	1880	1890	1880	1890
Cotton (Bales)	179,892	215,500	9,482	16,490	9,300	17,635
Corn (Bushels)	6,122,499	6,349,307	295,641	347,524	370,890	450,769
Improved Acres	1,470,729	1,811,579	70,912	123,245	92,360	116,214
Unimproved Acres	2,547,990	2,096,638	140,914	84,176	162,617	119,771
Cotton Acres	348,921	596,947	24,874	41,278	22,593	39,072
Corn Acres	399,707	475,695	27,675	29,015	28,964	31,320
Cotton/Imp. Acres	24%	33%	35%	34%	25%	34%
Cotton/Corn Acres	87%	126%	90%	142%	78%	125%
Per Capita Cotton Prod.	0.6	0.6	0.6	0.9	0.6	0.8
Per Capita Corn Prod.	20.9	19.0	18.1	18.1	21.9	20.2
Total Farms	32,946	38,859	1,458	2,289	2,235	2,773
Owner Farms	19,672	18,768	1,129	1,068	1,425	1,529
% Owner Farms	60%	48%	77%	47%	61%	55%

Sources: *Tenth Census*, Report on Productions of Agriculture, 183–84, 40–45; *Eleventh Census*, Agriculture, 128–32, 202–4, 360–61, 393–94.

61. Carroll County *Times*, n. d.; *Tenth Census*, Agriculture, 40–45, 183–84; *Eleventh Census*, Agriculture, 202–4, 360–61, 393–94.

distinguished by race, the tax records demonstrate a steady decline in the number of white landowners. In Jackson County, about six of ten whites who appeared on the tax rolls in 1873 owned at least some real estate, and they constituted a majority in every district in the county. By 1890, fewer than five in ten owned real estate, and they constituted a majority in fewer than half of the districts. Once the domain of yeoman freeholders, the Upcountry was fast becoming a territory of the dispossessed.[62]

"Hard times," to be sure, proved ever present features of rural life in the Upcountry, and elsewhere, during the nineteenth century. The whims of nature and the fluctuations of the market placed farmers, especially family farmers, in a perpetually vulnerable position. There is no need to glorify the existences of yeomen, North or South, in early America, for whether or not they attained that fabled sturdy self-sufficiency, they labored long hours, had relatively few material comforts, and could never be certain that their efforts would be rewarded. Yet, the postwar years gave "hard times" a new and increasingly enduring aspect. Falling prices for agricultural produce on the international market, discriminatory freight rates, the erection of high protective tariffs, the demonetization of silver, and land policies that favored speculative engrossment combined to squeeze farmers throughout the United States as a national economy was consolidated under the auspices of industrial and financial capital. Supplying raw materials for Northern factories, the South in particular was relegated to junior partnership—if not colonial status—in a powerful industrializing society. Landlords, merchants, and petty cultivators alike groaned under the yoke of subordination fastened by "Wall Street" financiers.[63]

All did not suffer like fates, however. For if the national and international market conquered and absorbed the Upcountry in the

---

62. The precise figures for Jackson County real-estate owners are 57.2 percent in 1873 and 48.8 percent in 1890. Carroll County also saw a decline in the proportion of white real-estate owners during this period, although the decline was far less dramatic: from 61 percent to 59 percent. In both cases, however, the figures overstate the proportion of landowners, for the poorest whites do not appear in the tax records. See Jackson County Tax Digests, 1873, 1890; Carroll County Tax Digests, 1873, 1890.

63. Woodward, *Origins of the New South*, 175–204, 291–320; Fred A. Shannon, *The Farmers' Last Frontier: Agriculture, 1860–1890* (New York, 1945); Samuel P. Hays, *The Response to Industrialism, 1885–1914* (Chicago, 1957), 133–34. The subordination of agriculture to industry was an international phenomenon, as much of the world came under the hegemony of industrial capital. See Eric J. Hobsbawm, *The Age of Capital, 1848–1875* (New York, 1975), 173–92 and passim.

years after 1865, that conquest was not achieved by impersonal forces, by an "invisible hand," or by 'Wall Street" financiers. It was accomplished, in large part, by landlords and, especially, by merchants who sought to make the best of postwar conditions, to extend the realm of staple agriculture, and to reap its profits. If they remained junior partners in an emerging, though unquestionably tense, sectional reconciliation, they tended to fare considerably better than the small producers whose economic surpluses they appropriated for their own. No wonder that yeoman farmers and tenants soon turned their wrath, not simply on Northern capitalists, but on local storekeepers and landlords as well.

5
Merchants, Farmers, and the Marketplace

The residents of Faulkner's Frenchman's Bend were in for a rude shock when Flem Snopes assumed his duties as a clerk in Will Varner's store. Fittingly Varner himself, the largest landowner and "chief man of the country," was the first to taste of the new arrangements. Commanding Flem to fetch a plug of tobacco as he entered the store, Varner found a seat, cut off a chew, and struck up a conversation with some of the regulars when he suddenly noticed Flem standing expectantly at his elbow. "Hey?" Varner said. "What?" "You ain't paid for it," the clerk replied, ". . . the tobacco." Stunned, Varner could only fumble for a nickel, hand it over, and resume his chat. Soon Flem would be riding in Varner's buggy, living in Varner's house, owning Varner's land, controlling Varner's hamlet. Then on to the county seat of Jefferson, where he eventually became president of the local bank. And so the New South displaced the Old.[1]

Flem Snopes's rigid "cost accounting," his meticulous bookkeeping, and his reluctance "to credit anyone with anything" may have been

---

1. William Faulkner, *The Hamlet* (New York, 1956), 5, 53–54; William Faulkner, *The Town* (New York, 1957).

somewhat atypical of postbellum merchants. Surely his predilection for cash transactions was. Too, the fictionalized Frenchman's Bend lay cradled in the heart of the Cotton Belt, "the original grant and site of a tremendous pre–Civil War plantation," where the planters had presided over their extensive acres, black laborers, and white dependents. Thus, a transfer of long-held social and economic power, rather than its institutionalization, was effected. But as a metaphor for social change, the rise of Flem Snopes spoke to a phenomenon that soon touched all corners of the South. Indeed, the necessity of mortgaging crops, land, and other property in order to purchase provisions must have proved far more unnerving for backwoods yeomen than did the peculiarities of a stranger for the denizens of Frenchman's Bend. In areas like the Georgia Upcountry, the furnishing merchant, not simply the cotton plant, ushered in the new era.

Yet, to come full circle, the increasingly prominent role that merchants played in the postbellum Upcountry was inseparable from social and political developments in the Black Belt—inseparable, that is, from the efforts of former slaveholders to reestablish authority over the freedmen. Although the failure of Congress to enact a program of land reform left a foundation of the planters' power intact, that foundation would be of little value unless the newly liberated black labor force and the surpluses it produced could be controlled. The planters, therefore, had to struggle on several fronts: they had to limit the agricultural alternatives available to, as well as the geographical movement of, men and women who wished to farm their own land or at least escape the close supervision of their ex-masters; they had to prevent the implementation of any plan for industrialization that could lure the freedmen from the cotton fields; and, with the emergence of tenancy and sharecropping, they had to circumscribe the intrusion of merchants.[2]

Before the Civil War, planters normally furnished their slaves with provisions obtained through their factors. Country merchants in the cotton districts may have supplied the plantations with goods on occasion, but for the most part they traded with small farmers who had neither the collateral nor the productive capacity to enter the factorage system independently. The war dramatically altered the financial

---

2. Jonathan M. Wiener, *Social Origins of the New South: Alabama, 1860–1885* (Baton Rouge, 1978); Michael Schwartz, *Radical Protest and Social Structure: The Southern Farmers' Alliance and Cotton Tenancy, 1880–1890* (New York, 1976), 57–63, 284–85.

landscape, however. Factors sustained a devastating blow from the economic dislocations at war's end. While some had capitalized on high wartime cotton prices and, perhaps, less-than-patriotic dealings to reap windfalls, the collapse of Southern banks and cotton brokerages—the principal sources of credit—left most in trying circumstances. In Georgia, only three of forty-one state-chartered banks operating in 1860 opened their doors in 1865. For a time, factorage houses began a hoped-for recovery by renewing ties with old and reliable customers, and in the lower Mississippi Valley such relations persisted into the 1880s. But the credit squeeze generally got the best of the system. Now slaveless proprietors of land that had plummeted in value, planters were rather risky clients, all the more so after crop failures in 1866 and 1867. No longer could they make transactions on the favorable antebellum terms. Factors who had credit to extend made that credit costly and often demanded mortgages on the plantation as added security. Reluctant to pay the price, planters soon looked to other arrangements.[3]

Had Southern banking rejuvenated, some semblance of the factorage system might have been salvaged or, at minimum, a ready solution to the credit problem might have been found. But by the time Reconstruction commenced, major obstacles stood in the way. Under the leadership of Secretary of the Treasury Salmon P. Chase and Ohio Senator John Sherman, the Republican-dominated wartime Congress had enacted legislation creating a national currency and a national banking structure that severely disadvantaged rural areas, particularly the capital-scarce South. Banks were required to have no less than $50,000 in paid-in capital to obtain a charter; they faced restrictions on note issue and deposit formation; and they were prohibited from extending mortgages on real estate. State-chartered banks did not fall subject to these provisions, but in an effort to stem such potential competition, Congress also imposed a 10-percent tax on notes issued by non-national institutions, effectively limiting, if not entirely eliminating, their operations. Thus, the national and state banks that did emerge in the postwar South were few in number, largely confined to urban centers, and considerably smaller in terms of capital, note issue, and deposits than were their Northern counterparts. In time, banks

3. Roger L. Ransom and Richard Sutch, *One Kind of Freedom: The Economic Consequences of Emancipation* (Cambridge, 1977), 107–9; Harold D. Woodman, *King Cotton and His Retainers: Financing and Marketing the Cotton Crop of the South, 1800–1925* (Lexington, Ky., 1968), 199–294; Michael Wayne, *The Reshaping of Plantation Society: The Natchez District, 1860–1880* (Baton Rouge, 1983), chap. 5.

appeared in small country towns, though they were private concerns and often adjuncts to other businesses.[4]

Changes in the structure of staple agriculture, even more than economic stringency, contributed to the downfall of the antebellum system of marketing and supply. As plantation organization built upon gang labor gave way to tenancy and sharecropping, arrangements for food, clothing, seed, and farm implements no longer could be made for the blacks or for the plantation as a whole; they often had to be made with individual black families. Laborers, like planters, became credit risks. And if the factors made credit dear for landowners whose fortunes remained, at best, uncertain in the immediate postwar years, they surely were not about to take a chance on the freedmen who possessed little if any property and who, by reputation, would not work without compulsion. A first-hand knowledge of customers and the ability to supervise farming operations seemed prerequisites of financial transactions.

With new lines of transportation and communication rapidly linking Northern and Southern markets by rail and wire, with the existence of a national system of credit rating, and with the influx of Northern capital during the first years of Reconstruction, the country merchant stepped into the economic vacuum. Some were newcomers, Yankees or foreigners, who hoped to tap fresh sources of profit; others were natives who either had kept stores before the war and had credit accounts with Northern wholesalers or Southern commission merchants, or had moved into merchandising after 1865, anticipating that it might prove more rewarding than farming. Men of limited means, few initially owned real estate or had goods worth more than $5,000, and they set up their concerns in towns and crossroads hamlets proliferating through the countryside.[5]

Obtaining their stocks on consignment, merchants passed the credit charges on to customers by instituting a two-price system—one for cash and one for time payments—the latter being considerably higher. Markups could, in fact, range from 40 to 70 percent, an exorbitant rate of interest even with the risk of potential defaulters. To buttress their finances further, storekeepers demanded security. Since the freedmen

4. Robert P. Sharkey, *Money, Class, and Party: An Economic Study of the Civil War and Reconstruction* (Baltimore, 1959), 221–37; Ransom and Sutch, *One Kind of Freedom*, 110–16.

5. Ransom and Sutch, *One Kind of Freedom*, 117–20; Woodman, *King Cotton*, 295–314; Thomas D. Clark, *Pills, Petticoats, and Plows: The Southern Country Store, 1865–1900* (Norman, Okla., 1944), 28–33.

had scarce resources to serve as collateral, mortgages or liens were taken on the growing crop. During the late winter and spring, black tenants would purchase various supplies on credit, turning over lien rights to what they cultivated. Following the harvest, merchants would then lay claim to the crop and use it to defray the debts owed them, whereupon the remainder would be returned to the freedmen. Not surprisingly, storekeepers frequently took advantage of the blacks' illiteracy and inexperience in the marketplace to cheat them out of their just shares and maintain them in a state of dependency.[6]

Yet, while merchants played a critical role in the recovery of the staple economy, their new presence manifested a challenge to the planting elite. Though most planters initially evinced reluctance to take on the duties of merchandising, they did not welcome the intrusion of outsiders who offered the freedmen at least a measure of independence from their authority. Much as the slaveholders scorned itinerant peddlers who, on occasion, conducted illicit trade with the slaves, postbellum landowners decried "a low and unprincipled class of traders, keepers of small shops," who, "by a little flattery and poisonous whiskey, easily cheat [the freedman] out of the little his bad management and indolence permit him to make." It was a situation that did not comport well with notions, as one planter put it, of an "organic society."[7] Self-serving rhetoric to be sure, but rhetoric that spoke to a deeper dilemma. For as tenancy and sharecropping became widespread, the planters' economic well being hinged on their ability to extract surpluses from their laborers—that is, on their ability to control the crop. Should merchants have the right to execute liens freely, or better, to have the superior lien, that control would be partly, if not entirely, undermined. Seeking to eliminate such a threat, the landowning elite flexed their political muscle.

As early as 1866, before the advent of Radical Reconstruction, the planter-dominated Georgia Assembly enacted a lien law that gave them the upper hand in the struggle. Accordingly, the statute entitled

6. C. Vann Woodward, *Origins of the New South, 1877–1913* (Baton Rouge, 1951), 180–81; Ransom and Sutch, *One Kind of Freedom*, 120–23; Harold D. Woodman, "Post-Civil War Southern Agriculture and the Law," *AH*, LIII (January 1979), 327–29. For a dissenting point of view on the exorbitance of credit rates, see Claudia Goldin, "'N' Kinds of Freedom," *Explorations in Economic History*, XVI (January 1979), 18–29.

7. Wiener, *Social Origins*, 85–86; Joseph P. Reidy, "The Agrarian Revolution in Georgia, 1865–1910: Planters and Freedmen in the New South" (Paper, University of Maryland, 1978), 9.

landlords alone to obtain liens on the crops of tenants for livestock, farming implements, and provisions furnished. Factors and merchants, on the other hand, could execute liens for supplies on the crops of farmers, but "farmers" were defined specifically as proprietors. Remaining on the books throughout Reconstruction, the statute did not resolve the conflict between planters and merchants, however. During the 1870s the statehouse provided the arena for a series of skirmishes. In 1873, for example, merchandising interests acquired sufficient legislative support to win lien rights commensurate with those of landlords for provisioning tenants, though the landlord's lien for rent was deemed superior. Undaunted, the planters quickly fought back and the next year, once again, successfully deprived merchants of leverage over tenants. Finally, in 1875, contending parties struck a compromise which nonetheless favored landowners: landlords retained the exclusive privilege of taking supply liens from tenants, but they could transfer the liens to merchants if they so chose. On the legal terrain, planters in the Black Belt emerged triumphant.[8]

The law embodies and legitimizes relations of power; it does not neatly determine day-to-day social reality. While the lien laws circumscribed the inroads of merchants in plantation districts, they did not uniformly reduce merchants to minor functionaries. Especially in areas in which the planters suffered severe financial setbacks, the law was ignored in practice by virtue of necessity if nothing else. Furthermore, storekeepers could take liens on the crops of white farmers and planters and, thereby, establish a foothold by servicing smallholders or furnishing tenants indirectly through the landlord. And by the process of debt defaulting, some managed to accumulate real estate and become landlords in their own right. But for the most part, the planting elite reasserted their economic authority. It was not long before landlords moved into the merchandising business themselves, operating stores and effectively curtailing the merchants' claims to the crop. Hence, V. D. Gresham, "a solid planter . . . worth 6–8 [thousand dollars]" in Greene County, Georgia, began "selling goods" in 1872. Other planters became involved as "silent partners" in mercantile concerns, some of which were run by friends or relatives; and for large landowners who did not find their way into provisioning, first lien on

8. Robert P. Brooks, *The Agrarian Revolution in Georgia, 1865–1912* (Madison, Wis., 1914), 32–33; Enoch Banks, *The Economics of Land Tenure in Georgia* (New York, 1905), 47; David Irwin, *The Code of the State of Georgia* (Macon, 1873), 344; Lewis N. Wynne, "Planter Politics in Georgia: 1860–1890" (Ph.D. diss., University of Georgia, 1980), 276–78.

the crop for rent gave them their returns even if the merchant furnished their laborers. By the late 1870s and early 1880s, the planters' economic and political adversaries were freedmen, industrialists, and increasingly yeomen and landless whites, not merchants.[9]

If the struggle between planters and merchants helped shape social and political developments in the Black Belt during the decade after the Civil War, its outcome held significant consequences for the Upcountry as well. The planting elite did not simply push landless merchants out of their domain. But in legally limiting storekeepers' levers to relations with farm proprietors, they, at least inadvertently, made nonplantation areas alluring while providing merchants in those areas with new means of economic power. As an Upcountry planter recalled, "When the lien law was passed the town merchant became an important factor in farming."[10]

II

The speculators, adventurers, and agents of Northern wholesalers who followed fast on the heels of the Union army or swarmed into the South at war's end did not confine themselves to plantation districts. Travelers and other contemporary observers remarked on their ubiquity. Sidney Andrews, the Northern journalist, for one, noted the multitude of "runners" from Cincinnati and Louisville who could be found in northern and western Georgia in late 1865. And with good reason, according to William S. Thomson, a western Virginian who had relocated in Marietta. "This is a place to obtain success if a man is deserving of it," he wrote his father in October 1865, "the judicial district embraces some of the wealthiest and most populous counties in Geo . . . [and] when RRs are completed which are now in progress, there will be an interminable amount of business carried on here. . . . I see the most brilliant prospects for enterprising and business men."[11]

9. R. G. Dun and Company, Credit Reporting Ledgers of the Mercantile Agency, Georgia, XV, 78L, Baker Library, Harvard University; Wayne, *Reshaping*, chap. 5; Woodward, *Origins of the New South*, 184.

10. Testimony of H. J. McCormick, Bartow County, 1912, in Robert P. Brooks, Inquiries Concerning Georgia Farms, I, UGa. Also see Testimony of J. W. Daniel, Heard County, 1912, and Testimony of Unidentified Planter, Gwinnett County, 1912, in ibid.

11. Sidney Andrews, *The South Since the War: As Shown by Fourteen Weeks of Travel and Observation in Georgia and the Carolinas*, intro. by David Donald (Boston, 1971), 365–66; William S. Thomson to W. A. Thomson, Marietta, October 10, 1865, William S. Thomson Papers, Box 1, Folder 8, EU.

It took a spirit of unbridled optimism coupled with a faith in the irresistible exploitability of resources to issue such a forecast. For the hint of brighter horizons which may have shone in Marietta stood in great contrast to the gloom that had fallen on the countryside. Ransacked homes and barns, barren fields, and widespread destitution could offer little encouragement even to the Yankee eye. Surely, local merchants would have had difficulty sharing Thomson's enthusiasm. While some had managed to profit from inflated food prices, most had serious troubles. Of storekeepers operating in 1860, a considerable number either failed to reopen in 1865 or survived for only a short time thereafter. A Carroll County mercantile firm established in 1857, for example, was "in debt, being sued, poor, and out of business" by 1866. William Awtrey, who ran a dry-goods concern during the 1850s, had "gone into farming" that same year, as had Charles Kingsbury. J. L. Cheney, another antebellum merchant, went "out of business" within a year after the war and "moved to Chattooga county," while N. R. Sheats, still merchandising in 1866, planned to "move to Paulding county." As an inhabitant of Rome glumly recorded, "Our own merchants are exhausted of all ready means upon which to do business."[12]

Prospects seemed hardly more propitious for the remainder of the decade. Crop failures in 1866 and 1867 exacerbated already straitened conditions. "[T]imes hard, money scarce . . . [and] trade dull" became all too familiar a complaint in the late 1860s. Small wonder that country merchants found it difficult to keep their heads above water. If Jackson and Carroll counties are representative of experiences throughout the Upcountry, no more than one-quarter of the mercantile establishments doing business at the outset of the Civil War lasted until 1870. The period, in fact, saw an absolute decline in the number of Upcountry stores. The R. G. Dun and Company reported fourteen concerns in Jackson County in 1860; in 1870 it reported only ten. Carroll County had just over twenty general stores and groceries in the last antebellum year; a decade later the county had a mere thirteen.[13]

During the 1870s, however, a significant turnabout occurred. As railroads began pushing their way through the hilly terrain of the

12. Dun and Company, Credit Ledgers, Georgia, V, 113, 115, 116, 119; Dr. Robert Battey to Mary Halsey, Rome, July 19, 1865, Robert Battey Papers, Folder 6, EU.

13. Cartersville *Express*, July 10, 1868; Dun and Company, Credit Ledgers, Georgia, V, XVIII.

Upcountry, small towns and villages dotted the countryside in growing numbers. In 1860 the federal census enumerated six towns other than Atlanta for the entire region. By 1880 it enumerated fifty. Local observers marveled at the appearance virtually overnight of places like Whitesburg, Mulberry, Harmony Grove, Norcross, Suwanee, Flowery Branch, and Victory. Located along the rail lines or at junctures of other thoroughfares, these were hardly rising urban centers. Northerners would probably have laughed at their being dignified as "towns." Fewer than ten had over 1,000 inhabitants in 1880; thirty-five had under 500. Lacking an industrial base or diversified commercial enterprises, these towns depended on agriculture and, increasingly, staple agriculture for their existence. Bowdon, in Carroll County, proved typical. In 1878 it had a population of between 300 and 400 along with six stores, two blacksmith shops, two doctors, two lawyers, two preachers, and "a half dozen good mechanics."[14]

The multiplication of Upcountry towns and hamlets both reflected and encouraged an influx of merchants. In the years after 1870, mercantile establishments sprang up at an ever quickening pace. Carroll County was a case in point. In 1870 a scant thirteen concerns serviced the county, eight of which had begun operations since 1865. By 1875 the number had risen to thirty-six, by 1880 to forty-nine, and by 1885 the county could boast of seventy. Following a similar pattern, Jackson County's ten stores in 1870 had grown to fifteen by 1875, to twenty-seven by 1880, and to sixty-seven by 1885. Unlike some Black Belt areas, very few Upcountry merchants came from the North or Europe; most were native Georgians with little capital and small inventories. According to the records of the R. G. Dun and Company, upwards of 80 percent were worth less than $5,000, while almost half were worth less than $2,000.[15] In Maysville, Jackson County, for instance, one storekeeper who began business in 1875 kept "a respectable little stock of goods" and owned "no property only paying

14. *Eighth Census of the United States, 1860* (Washington, 1864), Population, 74; *Eleventh Census of the United States, 1890* (Washington, 1894), Compendium, 92–105; Carroll County *Times*, March 15, 1878; J. C. Flanigan, *History of Gwinnett County, Georgia*, 2 vols. (Hapeville, Ga., 1943), I, 247–48.

15. R. G. Dun and Company, *The Mercantile Agency Reference Book (and Key) Containing Ratings on Merchants, Manufacturers, and Traders Generally, Throughout the United States and Canada, 1870* (New York, 1870); Dun and Company, *Reference Book, 1875* (New York, 1875); *Reference Book, 1880* (New York, 1880); *Reference Book, 1885* (New York, 1885). The Dun and Company *Reference Books* do not contain page numbers but are organized by state and county within each volume.

poll tax." In Carrollton, a grocer opened his doors in 1879 with a mere $300 in capital. Indeed, whereas antebellum merchants had commonly owned land and combined trade with farming, many of their postbellum counterparts at least started out possessing little if any real estate. In 1860 landownership was characteristic of perhaps eight merchants in ten; in 1880 only three in ten reported acreage (see Table 5.1).[16]

Table 5.1   Merchants and Merchandising in Jackson and Carroll Counties, 1860–1880

A.   Growth of Merchandising

Number of Firms

County	1860	1870	1875	1880	1885
Jackson	15	10	15	27	67
Carroll	21	13	36	49	70

B.   Capitalization of Mercantile Firms

Number of Firms, 1880

County	Under $2,000	$2,000– 4,999	$5,000– 9,999	$10,000 +	Not Reported
Jackson	8	5	1	3	10
Carroll	19	16	3	3	8

C.   Merchant Landownership

Number of Merchants[1]

County	Own Land		Own No Land		Not Reported	
	1860	1880	1860	1880	1860	1880
Jackson	16	9	4	19	3	1
Carroll	17	16	2	38	12	1

[1] Includes all those named by the R. G. Dun and Company as partners in mercantile firms. Those recorded as "Owning No Land" reported either no real-estate holdings or only "town property" but no acreage.

Sources: Dun and Company, Credit Ledgers, Georgia, V, XVIII; Dun and Company, *Mercantile Reference Books, 1870–1885*; Jackson County Tax Digest, 1880; Carroll County Tax Digest, 1880; Manuscript Census, Georgia, Jackson and Carroll Counties, Schedule I, 1860.

16. Dun and Company, Credit Ledgers, Georgia, XVIII, 37; V, 107; Manuscript Census, Georgia, Jackson and Carroll Counties, Schedule I, 1860; Dun and Company, *Reference Book, 1880*; Jackson County Tax Digest, 1880, GDAH; Carroll County Tax Digest, 1880, GDAH.

Railroad development alone did not make the Upcountry enticing for merchandisers. It was no accident that the growth of the merchant class coincided with the passage of the lien laws and their resolution in favor of landlords in the Black Belt. On the one hand, the lien system gave storekeepers new leverage in exchange relations with farmers while, on the other, it limited their prospects in plantation areas where the majority of customers were tenants or croppers. To be sure, a handful of Upcountry merchants, especially the better situated, had antebellum experience in the trade; by and large, they seemed new to the business and frequently came from outside the region. Thus, B. F. Bass and W. K. Curtis moved from West Point, in Georgia's western Black Belt, to Carrollton in 1873, where they opened a dry-goods store. G. W. Camp also apparently found the old Cotton Belt less than promising, for he traveled from Coweta to Carroll County at roughly the same time to establish a general store, as did W. J. Wood. For William H. Rust, Carrollton represented a stop along an unsuccessful trail that included Griffin, Georgia, and Statesville, North Carolina. In Jackson County, W. B. Stockton, a "native Georgian" who "was formerly engaged in planting and has no commercial experience," started "a small business" in 1875. Others were local farmers or their kin who tried a hand at merchandising. N. W. and J. L. Montgomery of Franklin County, "sons of Capt. Montgomery a farmer of thereby," for example, began operations in 1878.[17]

The lien laws would have been of little consequence in the Upcountry had antebellum conditions persisted. Farmers had normally raised sufficient foodstuffs to feed their families and perhaps to trade for additional supplies; they had cows, cattle, sheep, and large numbers of hogs to furnish dairy, meat, and wool; and their sizable grain crops left them with seed for the next year's planting. Dependence on merchants for necessary goods, therefore, was limited. The physical destruction, economic hardship, short crops, and dramatic decline in livestock brought about by the war and its aftermath, however, undermined the general self-sufficiency of many yeoman households. And neighboring farmers, who had customarily exchanged their surplus produce with those failing to make ends meet, were in no position to lend assistance. The efforts of the Freedmen's Bureau and charitable organizations provided some measure of relief for the extremely destitute, but

17. Dun and Company, Credit Ledgers, Georgia, V, 116L, 133; XVIII, 35; XII, 273.

provisions increasingly came from the West and were obtained through local storekeepers.[18]

Farmers did not simply rely more heavily upon merchants for supplies. They encountered a rather new system of exchange relations. Credit had always been a central feature of trade in the Georgia Upcountry. With little specie or other currency in circulation, goods could rarely be paid for at the time of purchase. Indeed, the rhythms of agriculture governed transactions. Farmers expected to acquire items as needed over the course of a year and to settle accounts after harvest either by means of cash or barter. Interest that may have been charged began to accrue only if debts were not squared at year's end. Yet, by the early 1870s the rules of the merchandising game had been transformed. Receiving their stocks directly from Northern wholesalers or from drummers or commission houses in Southern market towns, Upcountry merchants, like their Black Belt counterparts, sought to protect their own finances, and then some, by establishing cash and credit prices for provisions.[19] Although the differential varied from place to place, from year to year, and from crop to crop, a survey conducted by the Georgia Department of Agriculture for the northern section of the state during the 1880s showed markups ranging between 25 and 35 percent on corn and bacon. And this was solely for six months credit. If accounts remained open longer, additional interest was assessed When James Hay of Carroll County purchased $61.60 worth of goods from the merchant Appleton Mandeville in 1884, for example, he "promise[d] to pay A. Mandeville or bearer [said sum by November 1] with 12% interest from date." Elsewhere, farmers buying on a year's credit could pay even more over the cash price.[20]

The viability of such a system, which by the standards of the day made essential credit extraordinarily costly, hinged on the ability of merchants to shift the energies of yeomen into producing for the market—that is, into producing much larger quantities of cotton. The crop lien served as a ready device. By demanding a lien as a prerequisite

18. Athens *Southern Banner*, September 3, 1869; Ransom and Sutch, *One Kind of Freedom*, 156–59.

19. Dun and Company, Credit Ledgers, Georgia, VI, 56; Jackson *Herald*, November 4, 1887.

20. *Publications of the Georgia Department of Agriculture, 1883* (Atlanta, 1883), IX, 350; *Supplemental Report of the Georgia Department of Agriculture, 1882* (Atlanta, 1882), 10–11; Ordinary Estate Records, Annual Returns, Carroll County, January 3, 1884, Vol. I, 133, GDAH. Also see Ransom and Sutch, *One Kind of Freedom*, 128–31, 237–43.

for credit, storekeepers not only received collateral to buffer the risk of default; they also gained a foothold in the productive process itself. Unlike sharecropping agreements, liens did not specify the acreage to be planted in particular crops. Nevertheless, merchants plainly indicated their preference for the staple. One simply does not find liens executed on grain crops alone. At times, only the cotton crop was claimed as security. Thus, C. C. Jones of Carroll County mortgaged "his cotton crop which consists of 5 acres in the Lowell district" to J. M. Fields and Company "for value received in provisions" worth $58.65. More commonly, the entire growing crop, including cotton, fell under lien. The transaction between J. O. Blair, owner of fifty acres in Carroll County, and the merchant L. C. Mandeville was typical. During the late winter, Blair purchased provisions valued at $85.79, which he promised to pay by October 15. To secure the debt, he mortgaged "all growing crops of corn, cotton, wheat, and oats" to Mandeville. The very expense of credit, moreover, clearly encouraged farmers to raise the staple without the storekeepers' proddings. Though the prices of various food crops may have been favorable on occasion, their bulk and perishability made shipment difficult and often unprofitable. Cotton stood as the most readily marketable agricultural commodity, in short, as the crop most likely to bring returns.[21]

Many Upcountry farmers, of course, turned to cotton on their own account. With relatively high prices in the immediate postwar years, the staple offered a means of recouping war-related losses if nothing else. But the significant expansion of cotton culture, which drew the attention of local observers, began during the 1870s, at precisely the time when merchants, strengthened by the lien law, appeared in growing numbers. They turned cotton from one item in a crop mix, from a market-oriented expedient in a system of general farming, into an enduring and, indeed, defining feature of the Upcountry economy. When a group of Gwinnett County farmers petitioned the state legislature in 1875 for repeal of the lien laws, they demonstrated that social consensus did not pave the road to the new order.[22]

Although the developing lien system favored landlords over merchants, the absence of a substantial planter element in the Upcountry enabled storekeepers to become more directly involved in supplying

21. Mortgage: C. C. Jones to J. M. Fields and Co., Carroll County, May 3, 1882, Mortgage Book, 1881–1883, 110–11, CCC; Mortgage: J. O. Blair to L. C. Mandeville, Carroll County, January 15, 1885, Mortgage Book, Vol. B, 346–47.

22. Gwinnett *Herald*, February 10, 1875.

tenants and croppers than was true in the Black Belt. Some large land and slaveholders, of course, had active interests in merchandising which they maintained after Emancipation in an effort to secure greater control over their laborers. Jackson County's Dylmus R. Lyle, owner of 700 acres and well over twenty slaves, was also a prominent merchant during the 1850s. He abandoned neither pursuit in 1865, and as late as 1890 he was one of the county's wealthiest landlord-merchants. Other antebellum planters opened stores following the war or served as intermediaries in the furnishing business. John Dent of Floyd County took the latter route. Dealing with several mercantile concerns in Rome, he purchased supplies for and marketed the cotton crop produced by the sharecroppers on his plantation. Hence, in January 1875 Dent "sent up 2 Bales Cotton . . . to Berry's and Co by Isaac Newton and 2 Bales Cotton . . . by Jim Hamilton," while three months later he "Received 4 sacks guano [from] Daniels and Rowland . . . [and] turned it over to Ike for his use." Similarly, Lucius H. Featherston of Heard County obtained $164.23 worth of flour, molasses, corn, and bacon in 1872 from the Atlanta firm of West and Edwards for the tenants on his place.[23]

Most of the tenants, white and black, lived on smaller units where landowners had neither the means, nor the connections, nor the wherewithal to challenge the merchants' inroads. Occasionally poor farmers themselves who had lost sons during the war or faced an economic squeeze, these landlords rented out parcels of land to a tenant or two in order to make ends meet. Holding first lien for rent and probably reluctant to assume the responsibilities and risks of furnishing supplies, they permitted their tenants to trade directly with the merchants. In 1884, for example, William Wilson, a freedman, bought $30 of provisions from the establishment of Chunn and Gilbert in Bartow County, for which he gave "a mortgage on any crops now growing on Miles Dobbins' place near Crow Springs consisting of corn, cotton, fodder, peas and c." J. W. Thigpen, a white man in Carroll County, worked land owned by J. Malley and T. D. Beck but was supplied by the storekeeper J. A. Rhudy in lieu of a mortgage on Thigpen's "entire crop consisting of sixteen acres about one acre of which is planted in corn ballance in cotton." Another Carroll County

23. Manuscript Census, Georgia, Jackson County, Schedules I–III, 1850, 1860; Dun and Company, *Reference Book, 1890*; Jackson County Tax Digests, 1880, 1885; Cottage Home Farm Journal, Floyd County, January 14, 1875, April 12, 1875, John H. Dent Papers, GDAH; Lucius H. Featherston Papers, 1882, Box 1, Folder 16, EU.

mercantile firm, J. M. Fields and Company, furnished J. D. Lyle with $7.43 of goods in 1881, Lyle creating "a lien and mortgage . . . [on the] cotton crop growing at this time on James Martins lands."[24]

To some extent, the merchants' power over tenants and croppers, as well as over farmers, derived from a "territorial monopoly" which prevented competition in the extension of credit. With liens providing prior claims to the crop and with generally poor means of transportation throughout the region, a crossroads merchant could procure a clientele within a limited geographical area that would be difficult to challenge.[25] However, mercantile establishments tended to concentrate in and around the few county towns having railroad depots for shipment. Of forty-nine concerns in Carroll County in 1880, for instance, forty-six were located at or near one of four such towns. Farmers and tenants, furthermore, did not always trade with one merchant exclusively. James Hay, who had accounts with at least two Carrollton dry-goods stores, was not altogether atypical. The Carroll *Free Press* decried the practices of what it called "gypsy renters" who "pitch their tents or log huts on some farmers land and trade at first [with] one country store and then another, on the strength of a transferred lien, until the credit is gone and then shift their carcasses to new fields of swindling." As a consequence, numerous firms failed to remain viable for long. One storekeeper in Jefferson, Jackson County, who opened in 1874 was "out of business—broke" a year later. Another had a similar experience with his venture at Chambley Mills, going in and "out of business" between 1873 and 1874.[26] For every Flem Snopes there were several of these men.

The power of Upcountry merchants as a class, nonetheless, did stem from a monopoly—a monopoly over the sources of necessary credit in a system increasingly dominated by staple agriculture. Whether or not a

24. Lien: William Wilson to Chunn and Gilbert, Cassville, June 2, 1884, Chunn-Land Family Papers, Box 2, Folder 18, GDAH; Mortgage: J. W. Thigpen to J. A. Rhudy, Carroll County, April 30, 1890, Mortgage Book, Vol. F, 166–67; Mortgage: J. D. Lyle to J. M. Fields and Co., Carroll County, May 25, 1881, Mortgage Book, 1881–1883, 24. Although these supply liens are stated to cover the "entire crop," this probably means the entire crop less the amount owed for rent, since all landlords had first lien for rent unless they chose to transfer it. I am indebted to Harold D. Woodman for this suggestion.

25. Ransom and Sutch, *One Kind of Freedom*, 146–48.

26. Dun and Company, *Reference Book, 1880*; Ord. Est. Recs., Annual Returns, Carroll County, January 3, 1884, Vol. I, 133, 138; Dun and Company, Credit Ledgers, Georgia, XVIII, 23, 33; Carroll *Free Press*, January 22, 1886.

farmer dealt with more than one merchant, he had little alternative to the country store for advances, and thereby entered what rapidly became a vicious cycle of involvement in the export market. The acquisition of credit demanded an expansion of cotton production, an expansion of cotton production meant proportionately shorter food crops, and shorter food crops sent the farmer back to the merchant's door for provisions. Jephta Dickson of Jackson County, who in 1884 purchased $53.37 worth of flour, meal, peas, meat, corn, and syrup from Austin and Company along with $2.53 worth of potatoes, peas, and sugar from the firm of Stanley and Lyle, would have been an exceptional case during the antebellum period. By the 1880s his was no longer the exception but the rule.[27]

Trading with more than one merchant or moving about from farm to farm may have enabled yeomen and tenants to avoid abject dependency. Indeed, what spokesmen for the elite saw as "swindling" and "insubordination" represented the efforts of small producers to limit exploitation and maintain some semblance of independence. Yet, owing to minimal employment opportunities outside of agriculture, such forms of resistance, while squeezing an occasional merchant or landlord, could not effectively challenge the structure as a whole. There were, in short, few feasible means of escape from the rule of King Cotton and his new Upcountry retainers.[28]

Cotton made the fortunes of the Old South. Despite periodic downswings in price, the burgeoning industrial revolution generated a tremendous demand for the fiber which the South virtually alone supplied, creating highly favorable conditions on the international market. Had these circumstances persisted, some Upcountry yeomen and tenants might have found a measure of prosperity in the staple; many, at least, would have been able to keep their heads above water even with an exploitative credit system. But during the postwar era, conditions on the world market underwent important and, for the South, detrimental changes. The seemingly insatiable demand for cotton began to plateau at precisely the time when new sources of supply—most notably in Egypt and India—became available. While prices maintained their prewar levels through the 1870s, the postbellum

27. Court of Ordinary, Inventories and Appraisements, Jackson County, May 23, 1885, Vol. H, 260–61, 264–65, GDAH. Also see ibid., 279.

28. Jay R. Mandle, *The Roots of Black Poverty: The Southern Plantation Economy After the Civil War* (Durham, N.C., 1978), 16.

years saw, not occasional fluctuations, but rather a steady downward trend, following a pattern common to other major agricultural commodities. A pound of cotton commanded about eleven cents in 1875, around nine cents in 1885, and less than five cents in 1894, well below the cost of production. "At the close of the war a 500 lb bale of cotton would bring $100," a Cherokee County tenant exclaimed in 1891, "and today it will bring $32.50." The South found itself in a prolonged depression and as the servant of Northern industrial might; petty producers, white and black, landed and landless, in the Upcountry and Black Belt, found themselves increasingly mired in a position tantamount to debt peonage.[29]

III

Few Upcountry farmers had direct contact with an international market that was turning small-scale staple agriculture into a losing enterprise. Even in the 1880s, the railroad seemed the most visible manifestation of an industrial capitalism shaping the world in its own image. But these farmers did not have to travel to Wall Street, or to Atlanta for that matter, to feel the pulse and impact of forces simultaneously creating a national and world economic system. Those forces became apparent daily in the Georgia hills. For as agents and beneficiaries of the new order, postbellum merchants did not simply give commercial agriculture a firm foothold in a region previously devoted to general farming; they helped transform the structure and workings of the local marketplace itself.

The growing dependence of yeomen and tenants on storekeepers for foodstuffs was only one sign of changing patterns of exchange. The erosion of household self-sufficiency extended beyond nutritional requisites. Although the census ceased recording relevant statistics, probated inventories from Carroll and Jackson counties show a dramatic drop in the capacity for home manufactures: whereas seven households in ten had spinning wheels and looms in the 1850s, only two households in ten did by the 1880s. Among those farmers who continued to engage in home industry, moreover, the declining number of sheep raised along with the market orientation of cotton production doubtless

---

29. Gavin Wright, *The Political Economy of the Cotton South: Households, Markets, and Wealth in the Nineteenth Century* (New York, 1978), 158–59, 182–83; Woodward, *Origins of the New South*, 185–86; Cherokee *Advance*, December 11, 1891.

cut into the available supplies of farm-grown raw materials.[30]

Major alterations in the network of trade accompanied the erosion of self-sufficiency. Local demand for food, clothing, and other goods, of course, was not purely a postbellum phenomenon. Short crops, natural calamities, and the basic exigencies of agricultural production and processing had traditionally left farmers in need of various supplies and services. But whereas these needs had been met primarily through transactions with other petty producers before the Civil War, merchants increasingly dominated exchange relations thereafter. Access to newly constructed railroads and arrangements with wholesalers enabled them to obtain a greater variety of goods at lower costs. Wealthier storekeepers, in fact, soon stocked extensive assortments. In addition to meat, meal, flour, coffee, sugar, lard, salt, molasses, and other edibles, they carried farming tools, kerosene, cloth, ribbons, medicines, and finished apparel such as shoes, trousers, shirts, socks, hats, and suspenders, not to mention that favored extract of corn, whiskey. As one firm put it, "We deal in Genl Mdse, consisting in part D.G. [dry goods], B & S [boots and shoes], Hats, Notions, Clothing, Hardware, Bagging, and a genl stock of groc & c." Thus, when Jackson County's seat of Jefferson saw a rail line enter its limits for the first time in 1883, the fortunes of its merchants brightened considerably. In 1882 about $40,000 of "general merchandise" had been sold in the town; in 1885 the figure approached $300,000 annually.[31]

Once established in a viable business, merchants often extended their operations. For one thing, they played a critical role in marketing the staple. Storekeepers purchased cotton from local producers or acquired it by virtue of a crop lien and then either resold it directly to manufacturers or sent it to large commission houses, which, in turn, shipped the fiber to be processed. "The cotton trade has been brisk [in Harmony Grove]," the Jefferson *Forest News* declared in 1878. "Before

30. Of 257 inventories probated in Jackson and Carroll counties during the 1880s, only 52 (20.2 %) reported spinning wheels and looms. See Ord. Est. Recs., Inv. and App., Carroll County, Vol. A; Court of Ord., Appraisements, Administrators, Guardians, and Executors, Jackson County, Book A, JCC. On the declining number of sheep, see Appendix, Tables V–VI. In laying claim to the cotton crop, the lien system made it more difficult for farmers to use cotton to fill home needs.

31. Jackson *Herald*, June 12, 1885; Dun and Company, Credit Ledgers, Georgia, V, 116L; Frary Elrod, *Historical Notes on Jackson County* (Jefferson, Ga., 1967), 130; Thomas C. Hardman, *History of Harmony Grove—Commerce* (Commerce, Ga., 1949), 64; Clark, *Pills, Petticoats, and Plows*, 41–42.

the last days of April the merchants of [the] town will have bought four thousand bales of cotton. Up to the first of the present month 3852 bales have been purchased—Hood and Co. buying 2200; Harbor and Bros. and Co. 926; S. M. Shankle 560; and five or six other merchants ranging from 60 bales downward." Buying cheaply and selling for a higher price proved to be a profitable route, as Carrollton's L. J. Smith and Company discovered when they "made $500 . . . in the fall of 1871."[32]

To strengthen their position and bolster surpluses, many merchants also moved directly into ginning. Indeed, one of the key new features of postwar agriculture, in the Upcountry and Black Belt, was the shift of ginning facilities from the countryside to the towns and the merchants' involvement in preparing cotton for shipment. Especially in nonplantation areas, where landlords and small farmers alike were frequently men of limited means, prospering storekeepers with ready lines of credit were best able to afford costly steam gins. And once they had the gins, they could enlarge their clienteles by insisting that customers sell the cotton to them as well. Furthermore, some merchandisers found their way into the guano business, acting as retailers or agents for outside fertilizer companies. "Extensively engaged in buying cotton and selling guano" in 1879, Carroll County's Ernest G. Kramer, among others, was fast becoming more than "tolerably successful."[33]

With capital accumulated from the trade, merchants not only bought land; they invested in a variety of local enterprises. Jasper N. Thompson of Jackson County did "a large and profitable business in farming, milling, wool carding, and merchandising" during the 1870s. G. A. McDaniel, a large landholding merchant in Carroll County, also owned a mill in the hamlet he controlled much as did Will Varner and later Flem Snopes. A few miles away, W. C. Branan operated a shingle machine, a sawmill, and a cotton gin in addition to a dry-goods store, prompting one observer to reckon that he "has too many irons in the fire." That observer might have said the same of the Jackson County mercantile firm of Smith and Carithers. Along with running a general store in the village of Jug Tavern, they bought cotton, sold guano, and had "livery, feed, and sales stables." Eventually, merchant capital

32. Jefferson *Forest News*, April 1878; Dun and Company, Credit Ledgers, Georgia, V, 116A, 119; Woodman, *King Cotton*, 301–3.

33. Dun and Company, Credit Ledgers, Georgia, V, 116E, 139; Woodman, *King Cotton*, 301–2. Also see Dun and Company, Credit Ledgers, Georgia, V, 118, 134; Jackson *Herald*, June 3, 1887; *Report on Cotton Production in the United States*, 2 vols. (Washington, 1884), II, 170.

would be channeled into Upcountry banking and manufacturing.[34]

The merchants' growing control over the Upcountry marketplace came particularly at the expense of local artisans. Confirming fears that surfaced as early as the 1850s, the railroads, in facilitating the influx of finished goods at lower costs, struck hard at producers doing custom work for their neighborhoods. In 1860, about 10 percent of the white household heads in Jackson and Carroll counties listed craft occupations, and these ranged over a considerable spectrum. Besides blacksmiths, millers, and carpenters, there were boot and shoemakers, tanners, saddlers, bricklayers, hatters, weavers, tailors, potters, tinners, wagonmakers, cabinetmakers, wheelwrights, stone cutters, and chairmakers. Thereafter, the artisan presence declined both in number and variety. By 1880, fewer than 5 percent of the white household heads in the two sample counties listed trades (see Table 5.2), and it is telling that they were overwhelmingly blacksmiths, millers, and carpenters—occupations that simply could not be replaced in an agricultural economy with proliferating small towns. Horses had to be shod, farm tools repaired, grain processed, and buildings constructed. Other skilled workers who made clothing, furniture, farm equipment, and sundry goods were less fortunate. They were the first victims of mass production and distribution.[35]

Table 5.2 Artisans in Jackson and Carroll Counties, 1860–1880

County	% of White Household Heads	
	1860	1880
Jackson	11.0	3.3
Carroll	11.4	4.6
Combined	11.2	3.9

Source: Manuscript Census, Georgia, Jackson and Carroll Counties, Schedule I, 1860, 1880.

34. Dun and Company, Credit Ledgers, Georgia, XVIII, 31; V, 116, 121, 138; Jackson *Herald*, June 3, 1887; Jefferson *Forest News*, August 7, 1875; Carroll County *Times*, August 3, 1888; Carroll *Free Press*, April 26, 1889, May 24, 1889.

35. In 1860, for example, millers, blacksmiths, and carpenters composed 51 percent and 41 percent of all craft occupations in Carroll and Jackson counties respectively. In 1880, they composed 65 percent and 66 percent respectively. See Manuscript Census, Georgia, Jackson and Carroll Counties, Schedule I, 1860, 1880.

The changing structure of debt further highlights the new dimensions of the Upcountry marketplace and the merchants' power within it. For the grid of indebtedness common to the antebellum era, linking farmers, craftsmen, and laborers in an extensive network of exchange, gave way to one of strikingly different character in the years following the Civil War. G. P. Driskell, who owned forty-six acres in Carroll County, had twenty-three notes totaling $310.91 owed to his estate when he died, in 1872.[36] In the 1850s, seven of ten inventories probated in Carroll and Jackson counties showed the same form of asset, though generally for lesser sums. Yet among his contemporaries, Driskell was increasingly unusual. By the 1880s only half of the inventories showed debts. What is more, control of debts became highly concentrated. If, for example, we rank individuals by the value of debts owed to their estate, we find that the top 10 percent increased their share of the value of total debts from around 50 percent to well over 70 percent during this period (see Table 5.3). And the most substantial creditors were merchandisers like J. W. Adamson of Bowdon in Carroll County, who held notes and accounts amounting to $9,254.65 in 1888, or S. M. Shankle of Harmony Grove in Jackson County, who claimed notes worth $17,505.92 in 1885.[37] The Adamsons and the Shankles, not the Driskells—merchants, not producers—dominated postbellum exchange.

With far-reaching consequences. By tying Upcountry farmers to staple agriculture and by enlarging their sphere of enterprise, merchants not only assumed a commanding role in local trade. They also transformed the very terms of trade. When, during the antebellum period, Upcountry residents faced each other in the marketplace, they usually did so as independent producers for whom exchange supplemented a general household self-sufficiency. Raising primarily food crops and having little currency at their disposal, they often entered into transactions involving payments in kind or labor. While prices attached to various goods and services were influenced by external markets, trade was regulated by specific use-values and by custom. Corn, wheat, shoes, and clothing, rarely shipped out of the region but rather produced, consumed, and sold locally, could all serve as "money." These practices were accepted by country storekeepers and they did

36. Ord. Est. Recs., Inv. and App., Carroll County, February 7, 1872, Vol. G, 289–90.
37. Ord. Est. Recs., Inv. and App., Carroll County, Vol. A, 1888; Court of Ord., App., Jackson County, Book A, 1885.

Table 5.3 Distribution of Debts Owed to Estates, Jackson and Carroll Counties, 1850s–1880s (By Decile of Debt Value)

| | Percentage Total Debts | | | | | |
| | Jackson County | | | Carroll County | | |
Rank	% 1850s	% 1880s	% Change 1850s–80s	% 1850s	% 1880s	% Change 1850s–80s
Top Decile	52.7	73.1	+20.4	50.1	72.7	+22.6
Second Decile	23.8	15.4	−8.4	24.5	17.6	−6.9
Third Decile	12.3	6.8	−5.5	11.9	6.0	−5.9
Fourth Decile	6.1	3.3	−2.8	5.7	2.8	−2.9
Fifth Decile	3.5	1.3	−2.2	4.2	0.9	−3.3
Sixth Decile	1.3	0.1	−1.2	2.6	0.0	−2.6
Seventh Decile	0.3	0.0	−0.3	0.8	0.0	−0.8
Eighth Decile	0.0	0.0	0.0	0.2	0.0	−0.2
Ninth Decile	0.0	0.0	0.0	0.0	0.0	0.0
Tenth Decile	0.0	0.0	0.0	0.0	0.0	0.0
Total	100.0	100.0		100.0	100.0	
Total Value of Debts	$48,830.03	$74,646.45		$15,662.24	$91,685.05	

Sources: Ordinary Estate Records, Inventories and Appraisements, Carroll County, Vols. C–D, 1850s, GDAH; Court of Ordinary, Inventories and Appraisements, Jackson County, Vol. A, 1850s, GDAH; Ord. Est. Recs., Inv. and App., Carroll Country, Vol. A, 1880s, GDAH; Court of Ord., Appraisements, Administrators, Guardians, and Executors, Jackson County, Book A, 1880s, JCC.

persist into the postbellum era. As late as 1878, James Hunt could settle an account with the Carroll County merchant William Beall Candler with nails, eggs, corn, hides, and a small amount of cash. Two years earlier a Gwinnett County general store could announce that "all kinds of country produce" would be taken as barter.[38]

But important changes occurred as commercial agriculture took hold. It was not that the currency supply expanded, for with virtually no banking facilities in the Upcountry and monetary contraction nationwide, the shortage remained chronic. It was, instead, that cotton became the predominant money commodity. Storekeepers advertising goods for "all kinds of country produce" came to be the exception rather than the rule. By the late 1870s, and certainly by the 1880s,

38. William Beall Candler Ledger, Carroll County, 1878, DU; Gwinnett *Herald*, November 8, 1876. Also see above, Chapter Two.

mercantile concerns bothering to specify asserted that they sold for "cash or cotton." Even William Beall Candler, who might agree to barter, dealt primarily in cotton. One of his customers, F. M. Fielder, for example, squared a debt of $47.70 by giving Candler "491 lbs of cotton . . . [and] $1.60 in cash." Another paid most of his $229.50 bill with "2068 lbs cotton," adding some "wood, calf skins . . . and bark."[39] Fertilizer companies followed suit. T. H. Wilson, a Jackson County farmer, purchased guano from W. J. Edwards, "agent for Geo J. Howard and Bros.," in May 1880. He gave Edwards a note for $6.75, accepting the option to pay by November 1 either "in middling cotton at 15c per lb" or "in U.S. currency." John Bryant of Carroll County agreed to similar terms when he bought about $60 worth of fertilizer from four different concerns in the town of Whitesburg.[40]

When Upcountry farmers engaged in semisubsistence agriculture and when "all kinds of country produce" or labor services constituted the medium of exchange, notions of a "just price" could define the boundaries of the marketplace. When farmers became enmeshed in staple agriculture, when they became more dependent on the merchant for supplies, and when cotton emerged as the basic medium of exchange, however, the terms of trade were regulated by a market over which they had little or no control, a market subordinating countryside to town, agriculture to industry. The antebellum Upcountry was haunted by the specter of a bad harvest and possible starvation; the postbellum Upcountry was haunted by the fluctuations of worldwide supply and demand, the problem of overproduction, and collapsing prices. The hard-money men of the Jacksonian era spoke for petty producers who feared the market's encroachments; the soft-money men of the Populist era spoke for petty producers who lived under the market's hegemony.[41]

39. Dun and Company, Credit Ledgers, Georgia, V, 107, 116D, 116P, 123, 125, 136–37; VI, 56, 65; Gwinnett *Herald*, November 8, 1876.

40. Court of Ord., Inv. and App., Jackson County, November 11, 1885, Vol. H, 295–96; Ord. Est. Recs., Inv. and App., Carroll County, Vol. A, 163–66. Also see Court of Ord., Inv. and App., Jackson County, Vols. F–G, 20; Featherston Papers, April 30, 1873, Box 1, Folder 7.

41. For a comparative perspective, see Eric J. Hobsbawm, *The Age of Capital, 1848–1875* (New York, 1975), 176–77; Edward Whiting Fox, *History in Geographic Perspective: The Other France* (New York, 1971), 19–32 and passim.

IV

The transformation of the Upcountry economy and local marketplace under merchant auspices was made possible by a lien system that encouraged the spread of cotton culture; it was accelerated by a process of dispossession that turned independent proprietors into tenants and farm laborers and supply merchants into agricultural employers. Beginning as an effort to safeguard their furnishing businesses against the risk of defaulting customers, merchandisers were able to lay claim to the real and personal property, as well as to the crops, of their yeoman clientele by taking advantage of legal "reforms" and their growing command over credit and exchange. As a consequence, they assumed increasingly direct control, if not outright ownership, of the means of production and thereby made themselves into an agrarian-commercial bourgeoisie, further reshaping Upcountry class relations.

In spite of, and to some extent because of, ongoing class and regional tensions during the antebellum period, the productive property of smallholders received a strong measure of protection from the slave regime. Having an enslaved black labor force and needing the loyalty of yeoman whites, the planters supported legislation exempting a considerable amount of land, livestock, farm equipment, and other household property from levy for debt. What was known as the "homestead exemption" did not, to be sure, conflict with the interests of an elite for whom the contraction of sizable debts was a matter of course. But it offered special benefits to small farmers whose financial dealings were not extensive. Few yeomen were indebted for sums that would not be covered by the homestead. Mortgaging for supplies or other advances, therefore, was unusual, limiting the potential power of merchants and creditors.[42]

Save for the lien law, Reconstruction saw no departure from antebellum policy in this regard. Indeed, Georgia Republicans, hoping to build a constituency among petty property owners in nonplantation areas, took care to recommend a substantial homestead exemption at the state constitutional convention of 1868. Although the Moderate wing of the party scaled down the Radicals' initial proposal, the final measure—soon enacted by the legislature—protected $2,000 of real and $1,000 of personal property for each family head from attach-

---

42. T. R. R. Cobb, *A Digest of the Statute Laws of the State of Georgia* (Athens, 1851), 389–90; R. H. Clark, T. R. R. Cobb, and David Irwin, *The Code of the State of Georgia* (Atlanta, 1861), 398–99. Also see above, Chapter Two.

ment.[43] But in the 1870s, as staple agriculture expanded in the Upcountry, dissident rumblings could be heard from the towns and the merchants. Newspapers, normally advancing the views of commercial interests, complained that the homestead exemption embodied "loose ideals of legal obligations," drew "capital from the state," and "embarrassed enterprise." While storekeepers could secure a lien on the farmer's crop, they argued that it alone provided little recourse should the proceeds of the harvest fail to settle the account. The homestead exemption offered "no assurance that any creditor can ever collect one cent," a Carroll County resident charged at a meeting chaired by three prominent Carrollton merchants, adding that under the statute "every free man is deprived of the right of managing his own property, not allowed to sell it or bind it away." Another proponent of reform contended that the homestead contradicted notions of "the inviolability of contracts."[44]

The homestead issue by no means unified Georgia elites. If anything, it exposed serious divisions that found their way into all questions bearing on the nature of social relations in the postwar South. Traditionalist planters, whose vision was informed by the organic relationship of slavery and who faced difficult problems of adjustment after Emancipation, had scant taste for strict market values and little desire to facilitate further mercantile inroads. Thus, they shared oppositional ground with yeomen who hardly considered the merchants' definition of "every free man's right" attractive. In pursuing their own interests, however, conservative planters gave merchandisers and their allies an opening. Following the demise of Reconstruction, the landed elite pressed to dismantle the Republican-inspired constitutional edifice of 1868. Most particularly, planters sought to reverse a trend toward centralization of power, reduce the cost of government, cut taxes generally, and circumscribe industrial development. The state Republican leader John L. Conley was quite right when he warned that "If [a constitutional] convention is called, it will be done through the efforts of the Bourbon element of the Democratic party."[45]

---

43. Elizabeth Studley Nathans, *Losing the Peace: Georgia Republicans and Reconstruction, 1865–1871* (Baton Rouge, 1968), 60–64; Henri H. Freeman, "Some Aspects of Debtor Relief in Georgia During Reconstruction" (M.A. thesis, Emory University, 1951), 35, 50–51.

44. Cartersville *Express*, April 14, 1870; Carroll County *Times*, August 3, 1877; Gwinnett *Herald*, July 16, 1873.

45. Carroll County *Times*, June 1, 1877; William P. Brandon, "Calling the Georgia

Commercially minded Upcountry forces backed the planters' call for a convention and most of the measures they proposed, with the exception of the one to return the state capitol to Milledgeville from Atlanta. Yet they evinced special concern for the homestead exemption. J. L. Cobb, a wealthy landowner from the Carrollton district, among others, favored the abolition or substantial reduction of the homestead exemption. "We see our agricultural interests waning every year . . . why is this?" the Cartersville *Express* asked. "One of the reasons is the large homestead exemption which begets extravagance because there are many who will go into debt as long as they can find credit, knowing that the homestead will save them for $3,000 if worst comes to worst."[46] Many Black Belt planters accepted a different explanation for the plight of agriculture. "The experience of the past ten years in Georgia . . . proves that farming on credit don't pay," a delegate from Muscogee County declared. "[A] waiver of the homestead means the payment to the Shylocks of trade over cash prices of 50 to 100 per cent." Led in the convention by Robert Toombs, they sought to block attacks on the homestead exemption much as they sought to wrest control of the lien system, precipitating a wrangle which eventually resulted in compromise. Defeating efforts to abrogate the exemption entirely, the convention nonetheless sliced it by almost half and, more significantly, permitted debtors to waive its protection.[47]

The Carroll County *Times* joined other Upcountry town spokesmen in applauding the convention's work, while local merchants wasted no time in seizing their opportunity. Beginning in the late 1870s, waiving the homestead exemption and mortgaging property in addition to crops became conditions for obtaining credit. When B. S. Brown of Carroll County purchased $50 of provisions from the storekeeper E. S. Roberts in 1881, for example, he surrendered his rights to the homestead and "mortgage[d] all [his] corn and cotton crop along with all horses, mules, cattle, wagons, and farming utensils." Similarly, W. C. Adams waived the homestead and "mortgaged all crops and 50

Constitutional Convention of 1877," *GHQ*, XVII (September 1933), 189–90; Judson C. Ward, "Georgia Under the Bourbon Democrats, 1872–1890" (Ph.D. diss., University of North Carolina, 1948).

46. Carroll County *Times*, April 6, 1877; Cartersville *Express*, January 3, 1876; Rome *Courier*, quoted in Carroll County *Times*, April 13, 1877.

47. *Proceedings of the Constitutional Convention Held in Atlanta, Georgia, 1877* (Atlanta, 1877), 463–64, 451; Freeman, "Aspects of Debtor Relief," 63–64.

acres of land" upon receiving $100 of supplies from Appleton Mandeville four years later. F. H. Wilson and J. S. Freeman of Jackson County made the same concessions when they conducted business with the Harmony Grove storekeeper C. W. Hood in 1885 and 1886 respectively. According to a disgruntled Bartow County farmer, "merchants now demand that the homestead be waived if a farmer wants to buy $20 worth of supplies."[48]

Before the Civil War, property mortgaging was an infrequent recourse when transactions involved large sums of money. With the demise of the homestead exemption, it became the usual procedure regardless of how much was expended. Mortgages, as the Bartow County farmer scowled, were taken even if the account totaled a few dollars. And as the years passed, the amount of property under mortgage grew dramatically. Carroll County's records are most complete, and though they may underestimate its extent, they make the trend quite apparent. In 1875, prior to constitutional revision, the county court listed 18 individual mortgages. By 1882 the annual number had exceeded 150, and by 1885 it had surpassed 900, a staggering 5,000-percent increase within the span of a decade. The situation in Jackson County was no less striking. Twenty-three mortgages were recorded in 1875, 87 in 1880, and while concrete evidence does not exist for the 1880s, the county clerk said enough when noting that he recorded more mortgages in 1891 than during a previous ten-year term.[49]

Mortgages on personal property far outnumbered those on real estate. Farmers who viewed landownership as the foundation of their independence were understandably reluctant to risk it. Tenants and sharecroppers of both races, furthermore, often owned a few head of livestock, some farming tools, or household furniture which merchants claimed as security in addition to the crop. Of 153 mortgages recorded

48. Cartersville *Express*, May 4, 1876; Mortgage Book, Carroll County, July 11, 1881, 28; ibid., December 3, 1885, Vol. C, 267–68; Court of Ord., Inv. and App., Jackson County, November 11, 1885, May 25, 1886, Vol. H, 280, 299. Also see Mortgage Book, Carroll County, Vol. B, 331, 346–47, 355, 362, and passim; Court of Ord., Inv. and App., Jackson County, Vol. H, 39; Ord. Est. Recs., Annual Returns, Carroll County, Vol. I, 133, 138, 268, 325–27.

49. Superior Court Deeds and Mortgages, Carroll County, 1875, GDAH; Mortgage Book, Carroll County, 1882; ibid., 1885, Vols. B–C; Superior Court Deeds and Mortgages, Jackson County, 1875, Vol. N, GDAH; ibid., 1880, Vol. T; Jackson *Herald*, April 10, 1891.

in Carroll County in 1882, for instance, only 16 covered real estate. Three years later, only 131 of 916 mortgages involved real property. Still, the amount of land coming under mortgage in the Upcountry was not inconsiderable. In 1885 alone, Carroll County farmers mortgaged almost 8,000 acres. Along with their growing crops, T. M. West, J. D. Story, and J. M. Robinson mortgaged twenty-five, fifty, and twenty-five acres of land to the mercantile concerns of H. O. Roop, L. C. Mandeville, and Askew, Bradley, and Company that year. The agricultural reformer John Dent observed a similar tendency in Floyd County. "Went to Cave Spring this morning," he wrote in February 1881. "Farmers contracting with merchants to run them on credit for supplies this year by giving them mortgages on their farms." "[B]ad business," he added.[50]

The expansion of various forms of farm tenancy throughout the Upcountry during the 1880s came largely as a product of such credit arrangements. As yeomen turned their energies to cotton production and were confronted with both exorbitant credit rates and declining prices, the auction block increasingly became the resort for the hopelessly indebted. "Sheriffs advertisements," in the words of the Gwinnett County paper, were "as long as your arm," and as the Jackson *Herald* indicated, "sale day" brought heavy trafficking in real estate. "Last Tuesday was a red letter day in the annals of Jackson county landed interests . . . when we take into consideration the amount of land that changed hands," it reported in November 1883. "The whole number of acres sold was 2,297 1/2. . . ." Only one of many subsequent "red letter days," however, for in the fall of 1891 the *Herald* claimed that so much land was on the market "that it is doubtful whether [the sale] can be finished before night." With over 3,000 acres sold, the paper reckoned "it . . . to be one of the biggest sale days in the history of Jackson county."[51]

By virtue of mortgage foreclosures or bidding at public auction, merchants availed themselves of the opportunity to accumulate land.

50. Mortgage Book, Carroll County, 1882; ibid., 1885, Vols. B–C; ibid., Vol. B, 331, 355, 362; Cottage Home Farm Journal, Floyd County, February 15, 1881, Dent Papers. The annual acreage mortgaged underrepresents the total county acreage under mortgage at any given time, for mortgages were often carried from one year to the next when debts remained outstanding. See *Eleventh Census, 1890*, Report on Real Estate Mortgages, 373, 380, and passim.

51. Gwinnett *Herald*, n.d.; Jackson *Herald*, November 9, 1883, October 30, 1891, November 6, 1891.

While the wealthiest merchandisers frequently had antebellum roots in the Upcountry or had acquired real estate early on in the postwar era, it is clear that they capitalized on the woes of their landholding customers. L. C. Mandeville was the son of a substantial farmer who also had mercantile interests, but in 1880 he owned only a town lot in Carrollton where he conducted a dry-goods business. During the 1880s he carried on an extensive credit trade and, thereby, soon held a great number of mortgages. Just in the year 1885, for instance, Mandeville obtained thirteen real and seventy-nine personal-property mortgages. And he apparently had limited tolerance for wayward debtors, for by the end of the decade he owned more than 3,000 acres of land. The Bowdon storekeeper John H. Word also had decidedly good fortunes in the 1880s. Beginning with $500 worth of town property, he possessed over 500 acres ten years later. Other merchants who already had land in 1880 enlarged their holdings during the same period. Thus, G. A. McDaniel added 700 acres to his 1,400-acre estate.[52]

Prospects for merchants were no less encouraging in Jackson County. W. T. and George Harbor opened a general store in Harmony Grove during the 1870s. In 1880 they owned no more than the lot their establishment occupied. Within five years, however, they had accumulated 400 acres and by 1890 they had acquired an additional 200. Jefferson's W. P. De Lapierre, on the other hand, had engaged exclusively in farming before the early 1880s, when he entered the furnishing trade. It proved to be a wise choice, for the 250 acres he owned in 1880 had become 1,630 acres by the decade's end. L. G. Hardman of Harmony Grove experienced a similar boom: between 1885 and 1890 alone, he came into possession of about 700 acres, as did the neighboring storeowner, W. L. Williamson. Indeed, during those five years a group of twelve Jackson County and Carroll County landowning merchants engrossed nearly 8,000 acres between them (see Table 5.4).[53]

The merchants' accumulation of Upcountry land did not lead to the emergence of antebellum-style plantations. Although some did own large tracts of land, their holdings consisted, for the most part, of

52. Dun and Company, *Reference Book, 1880*; Carroll County Tax Digests, 1880, 1890; Mortgage Book, Carroll County, 1885, Vols. B–C.

53. Dun and Company, *Reference Book, 1880*; *Reference Book, 1885*; *Reference Book, 1890*; Jackson County Tax Digests, 1880, 1885, 1890; James A. Furgeson, "Power Politics and Populism: Jackson County, Georgia, as a Case Study" (M.A. thesis, University of Georgia, 1975), 39–40.

Table 5.4   Land Accumulation Among Selected Merchants, Jackson and
Carroll Counties, 1885–1890

Merchant	County	Acres—1885	Acres—1890
W. P. De Lapierre	Jackson	545	1,630
W. T. and Geo. Harbor	Jackson	404	590
C. W. Hood	Jackson	1,200	1,575
S. M. Shankle	Jackson	765	891
Elbert Askew	Jackson	200	565
W. L. Williamson	Jackson	6	735
L. G. Hardman	Jackson	425	1,100
G. A. McDaniel	Carroll	1,164	2,160
L. C. Mandeville	Carroll	163	3,159
C. B. Simonton	Carroll	50	258
E. G. Kramer	Carroll	25	100
J. P. Griffin	Carroll	270	327
Total		5,217	13,090

Sources: Jackson County Tax Digests, 1885, 1890; Carroll County Tax Digests, 1885, 1890; Dun and Company, *Reference Books, 1880–1885*; James A. Furgeson, "Power Politics and Populism: Jackson County as a Case Study" (M. A. thesis, University of Georgia, 1975), 39–40.

relatively small units scattered over a district or two or, perhaps, over the entire county and farmed by tenants and croppers. William Gilley, a Carrollton merchandiser, for example, owned 2,200 acres of land during the 1880s. Two hundred sixty were located in the Sixth District of Carroll County on three separate land lots; 186 acres were on a lot in the Ninth District; 43 acres were on a Seventh District lot; and the remaining 1,700 acres were on nine additional lots in the Fifth District. Some of these units were adjacent and could have formed discrete plantations. But Gilley did not reside in a "Big House" on the estate. Rather, he had a "dwelling house" as well as a "store house" in town. And Gilley was by no means atypical. The tax digests, which list landholdings according to lot number, show similar patterns for other substantial landowning merchants.[54]

Yet, whatever their success in accumulating land, Upcountry merchants did not appear to foreclose mortgages indiscriminately or

54. Ord. Est. Recs., Inv. and App., Carroll County, July 7, 1886, Vol. A, 511–13. See, for example, the landholdings for the merchants L. C. Mandeville, E. S. Roberts, John H. Word, W. S. Tweedle, G. A. McDaniel, and John K. Roop in Carroll County Tax Digest, 1890.

buy up as many acres as they could. They tended to go after only better-quality land. Compared with mean county valuations, the holdings of merchandisers normally merited higher assessments. In 1890, Jackson County farmland averaged $5.80 per acre. The Jefferson merchant I. T. Austin's real estate, however, was valued at over $8 per acre; L. G. Hardman's at more than $7; the Harbor brothers' and S. M. Shankle's lands at over $6.[55] And with good reason did they favor richer soils. The supply of labor in the Upcountry, white or black, was never abundant. Landlords perpetually complained about the difficulty of attracting hands. Should a merchant hold a mortgage on a farm containing at least some reasonably fertile acreage, it might pay him to foreclose if the proprietor failed to settle debts. In such a case it would be less problematic to find a willing tenant, and even if the landowner chose to stay on, the merchant could secure greater returns by receiving rent and directly controlling production. Should the mortgaged farm embrace rocky, sandy soil with little promise of decent yields, as many Upcountry units did, foreclosure would be a riskier undertaking. Nothing would be gained by acquiring land that remained unoccupied for a stretch of time, and there were no guarantees that a new tenant would be more successful than the hapless yeoman. Better to run the debt and maintain some flow of surplus than chance an extended search for a replacement. "Carrying" a farmer for years, according to one merchant, was not at all uncommon.[56]

Thus, landownership did not measure the full extent of the merchants' power, nor did tenancy measure the full extent of changing social relations. Ernest G. Kramer, a Carrollton merchant, owned a mere 100 acres in 1890. But he could be counted among the two or three wealthiest retailers in the county. His personal-property holdings came to thousands of dollars, he owned railroad stock and shares in a cotton factory, and he soon took charge of the newly established Carrollton bank. The locals surely must have been impressed by his extended trip to Europe around that time, to which the Carroll *Free Press* gave much publicity. Kramer apparently felt that railroads and banking offered more lucrative rewards than did land for the profits from his large furnishing business. In any event, mortgages on real estate, crops, livestock, and farming implements, which protected his operations, made him a virtual, if not an actual, landlord.[57]

55. Jackson County Tax Digest, 1890; Furgeson, "Power Politics," 40.

56. Quoted in Schwartz, *Radical Protest*, 65.

57. Carroll County Tax Digest, 1890; Mortgage Book, Carroll County, 1890, Vols. E–F; Carroll *Free Press*, April 26, 1889, May 24, 1889.

Yeoman farmers trading with Kramer or other Upcountry merchants during the 1880s may have retained formal title to their property— retained, that is, the legal status of independent producers. Yet the structure and dynamic of their household economy had been recast. Having once embraced the dominant social relations by virtue of its own division of labor, control of productive resources, and orientation to self-sufficiency, the yeoman household remained the basic unit of production while at the same time moving toward specialization as a whole through its growing dependence on a market mediated by merchant capital. With the decline of home manufactures, with the heavy mortgages on land, tools, and work animals, and with the influence of the credit system on the crop mix, the range of household economic activity narrowed and the total labor time devoted to staple cultivation increased. Household production fell subject to the logic of commercial agriculture and to an ever widening social division of labor. Exploitation within the household was intensified by exploitation of the entire household in the new market economy. Self-exploitation at the point of production was now burdened by outside exploitation in the sphere of exchange.[58]

Complicated as this transition was from a theoretical standpoint, it had a palpability that Upcountry yeomen could articulate quite plainly. Will Carleton, a Cherokee County farmer, told the story in bitter verse:

> We worked through spring and summer,
> through winter and through fall;
> But the mortgage worked the hardest and
> the steadiest of them all;
> It worked on night and Sunday, it worked
> each holiday;
> It settled down among us and it never went away.

58. Useful comparisons might be drawn with the transition from peasant to "proto-industrial" households in Europe, whereby individual functions of production within the family eroded while the family itself became a "structural unit of work." See Hans Medick, "The Proto-Industrial Family Economy: The Structural Function of Household and Family During the Transition From Peasant Society to Industrial Capitalism," *Social History*, III (October 1976), 291–315. We need to know much more about the changing division of labor within Southern rural households, but some evidence suggests that after the war white female household members began devoting more of their energies to field work. See, for example, Margaret Jarman Hagood, *Mothers of the South: Portraiture of the White Tenant Farm Woman* (New York, 1977; orig. pub., 1939), 14–15, 77, 86–9; Anne Firor Scott, *The Southern Lady: From Pedestal to Politics, 1830–1930* (Chicago, 1970), 107–9.

Whatever we kept from it seemed almost
as bad as theft;
It watched us every minute and ruled us
right and left
The rust and blight was with us sometimes, and
sometimes not;
The dark brown scowling mortgage was
forever on the spot.

The weevil and the cut worm, they went as
well as came;
The mortgage stayed forever, eating hearty
all the same
It nailed up every window, stood guard
at every door;
And happiness and sunshine made their
place with us no more.

John F. Armstrong, a cotton-growing landowner in Jackson County, put it in a more succinct, but no less compelling, way. Suffering under the burdens of debt and encumbrance to the Jefferson firm of A. H. Brock and Company, Armstrong fled to Alabama in desperation, leaving his wife with the crop to settle the account. When the proceeds failed to cover the debt, Brock and Company sued, and managed to have Armstrong captured and returned to the county. "I just got tired of working for the other fellow," he grimly explained, "I worked and toiled from year to year and all the fruits of my labor went to the man who never struck a lick. . . . I never made anything, and I determined to go to a grain country and quit cotton." For Carleton, Armstrong, and their counterparts, the mortgage system amounted to "slavery."[59]

Relatively few Upcountry merchants wielded the power of an Ernest Kramer, an L. C. Mandeville, or an L. G. Hardman. Most remained petty suppliers whose total assets consisted of a small stock of goods and, perhaps, a parcel of land in town or in the countryside on which they erected a store. Having a marginal clientele in a depressed economy and squeezed by Northern creditors, not to mention the railroads, they often found themselves in a predicament similar to that of their debt-ridden customers. "Closed out," "insolvent," "bursted to atoms," as

59. Cherokee *Advance*, December 5, 1890; Jackson *Herald*, February 26, 1892. Also see Schwartz, *Radical Protest*, 65; Rupert P. Vance, *Human Geography of the South: A Study in Regional Resources and Human Adequacy* (Chapel Hill, 1932), 190.

the R. G. Dun and Company put it. But those who survived, enlarged their businesses, and wrested control of productive resources signified more than the sum of their numbers. They represented the leading edge of a new order of class relations. If their road to power created frictions with substantial local landowners, those frictions eased over time as merchants accumulated real estate—or at least claims to real and personal property—became landlords, and shared an interest in the "labor question," which they also helped resolve. By the 1880s, an elite deriving surpluses from both land and commerce held the economic reins in the Upcountry.

Command of the productive process, as postbellum landlords and merchants alike well knew, is inseparable from command of the political process. The struggle over the lien laws and the homestead exemption made the connection quite apparent and lent new meaning and urgency to the attainment of political influence in the state. But power in the statehouse ultimately hinged on power in the county. While men of "property and standing" had long played a considerable role in local affairs, the transformation of the Upcountry economy and social relations after the Civil War redefined the stakes of politics. County offices, and control of the county government in general, carried leverage stretching beyond the realm of personal or community prestige as political and economic issues became increasingly intertwined. Landlords, merchants, and other town-associated interests actively sought to dominate local governing bodies and the local Democratic party.

Not without opposition, however. For the elites' political offensive affronted popular sensibilities no less than did their economic offensive. Although complicated by race, it exacerbated divisions between rich and poor, town and countryside, and provided a focus for developing resistance. If the efforts of small farmers and tenants to combat exploitation found expression in daily, monthly, and yearly conflicts over credit and labor arrangements, those efforts tended to be atomized and of limited effect. Instead, these producers would meet the social, economic, and cultural challenge of the new order on the terrain of politics.

6

Power and Politics

I

Jesse Wade, a white tenant farmer from Cobb County, who "was a Union man . . . like my daddy befo'e me" and suffered more than his share of abuse during the war, believed that justice demanded a far-reaching policy of Reconstruction. "We should tuk the land, as we did the niggers, and split it, and gin part to the niggers and part to me and t'other Union fellers," he told the English traveler J. T. Trowbridge in late 1865, feeling confident that "they'd have to submit to it, as they did to the niggers." And, according to Trowbridge, a number of freedmen listening in on the conversation "were unanimously of this opinion."[1] To Southern planters, Wade's sentiments and the enthusiastic response they elicited from the blacks nurtured their deepest fears that Emancipation began rather than concluded a convulsive era of social change. One wealthy landowner fretted that there was "bound to be another revolution of some sort" for "seven tenths of the people of the South would vote for . . . confiscation of Southern property." "Every negro would vote for such a proposition," he insisted, "and a vast

1. J. T. Trowbridge, *The South: A Tour of Its Battlefields and Ruined Cities* (Hartford, Conn., 1866), 456–58.

number of the whites." Another planter envisioned a similar nightmare: "Negroes and Tories will form a government for us [and bring about] Repudiation—abolition of poll tax division of land disfranchisement of Rebels regulation of the price of labor and rent of land—all to the benefit of the negro and the poor."[2]

The specter of a biracial coalition of poor Southerners long weighed ominously on the mind of the planter class. The proslavery argument, in its appeal for the allegiance of the white lower classes, tacitly acknowledged the planters' uneasiness. Social tensions during the secession crisis and, especially, during the war hardly offered solace. But Reconstruction held out dramatic new possibilities. The prospect of extensive land reform, anticipated by General Sherman's field order reserving much abandoned coastal land in Georgia and South Carolina for exclusive black settlement, suggested that a truly revolutionary transformation might be the price of sectional reconciliation.[3] Although Southerners acquainted with the temper of national politics, like Alexander Stephens, could rest assured that conservative instincts would circumscribe congressional policy, others saw in the radical stances of Charles Sumner, Thaddeus Stevens, and George Julian the mainstream of "Black Republicanism."[4] If radical measures did indeed falter in the halls of Congress, the creation of a Republican party in the South shifted the arena of political contention and gave added dimensions and vitality to major social questions. This potential challenge to the very fabric of Southern society fueled the political turbulence of the postwar years.[5]

From the first, Republican efforts to forge an electoral majority in the South threatened a new political departure. Whether or not they shared a commitment to radical reforms, Republicans recognized that the

2. Quoted in James L. Roark, *Masters Without Slaves: Southern Planters in the Civil War and Reconstruction* (New York, 1977), 193; C. H. Sutton to John S. Dobbins, Clarksville, June 1, 1867, John S. Dobbins Papers, Reel 2, EU.

3. Willie Lee Rose, *Rehearsal for Reconstruction: The Port Royal Experiment* (New York, 1964), 320–31; William S. McFeely, *Yankee Stepfather: General O. O. Howard and the Freedmen* (New York, 1970), 97, 219.

4. Alexander H. Stephens to J. Barrett Cohen, Crawfordsville, July 15, 1867, in Ulrich B. Phillips, ed., *The Correspondence of Robert Toombs, Alexander Stephens, and Howell Cobb* (Washington, 1913), 687. On perceptions of the Radicals and Northern policy, see Cartersville *Express*, January 24, 1868.

5. W. R. Brock, *An American Crisis: Congress and Reconstruction, 1865–1867* (New York, 1966), 284–304; Manuel Gottlieb, "The Land Question in Georgia During Reconstruction," *Science and Society*, III (Summer 1939), 356–88.

freedmen would constitute a significant element in a nascent Southern wing. Yet only in South Carolina and Louisiana were blacks likely to account for more than half of the eligible voters. Success, thereby, hinged on the ability to attract a considerable number of native whites, and the Upcountry seemed to hold special promise for such an undertaking. There, a long-standing distaste for planter prerogatives saw expression in Unionism, if not outright hostility to the Confederacy; there, the largest concentration of whites loyal to the federal government might be found at war's end. The counties of north Georgia "were all strongly opposed to secession in 1860–61, and this Congressional district furnished several hundred soldiers to our armies," Sidney Andrews observed from Atlanta in November 1865. "Its disposition toward the government is now, as a whole, probably better than that of any district in the state." Numerous witnesses before Congress's Joint Committee on Reconstruction the next year issued similar reports.[6]

Republicans faced a formidable task in cementing the coalition. The Upcountry in Georgia, as well as in other states of the Lower South, had been antebellum strongholds of the Democratic party. Partisan loyalties had deep generational roots. There was, furthermore, little love lost between resident yeomen and blacks. As one federal officer noted in 1866, "The poorer classes of white people . . . have a most intense hatred of the negro, and swear he shall never be reckoned as part of the population."[7] Developments during the immediate postwar years served only to exacerbate animosities, for if abolition itself did not shake smallholders severely, its consequences quickly did. As an initial response to liberation, many Upcountry blacks, like their counterparts in the Black Belt, left the plantations and farms and wandered through the countryside. Those finding employment were frequently dismissed without pay after harvest. Hunger often drove them to kill hogs foraging in the woods and, at times, to steal from white homesteads. Complaints of such offenses poured into the local offices of the Freedmen's Bureau. While the planters may have viewed this petty thievery simply as a

6. Sidney Andrews, *The South Since the War: As Shown by Fourteen Weeks of Travel and Observation in Georgia and the Carolinas*, intro. by David Donald (Boston, 1971), 342; *Report of the Joint Committee on Reconstruction*, 39th Cong., 1st Sess. (Washington, 1866), Pt. III, 6, 61; Elizabeth Studley Nathans, *Losing the Peace: Georgia Republicans and Reconstruction, 1865–1871* (Baton Rouge, 1968), 40–45; Armstead L. Robinson, "Beyond the Realm of Social Consensus: New Meanings of Reconstruction for American History," *JAH*, LXVIII (September 1981), 278–80.

7. *Joint Committee on Reconstruction*, 6.

manifestation of the freedmen's "natural disposition," yeomen desperately struggling to feed themselves and their families were not
entertained. The "depredations" committed by the blacks seemed to
offer hard evidence for the warnings of proslavery theorists that
Emancipation would cast the property of all white Southerners in
jeopardy. Small farmers, therefore, occasionally joined vigilante bands
organized by members of the local elite, who were primarily concerned
with reestablishing labor controls, in an effort to discipline the
freedmen. It was a lesson neither white nor black would easily forget.[8]

The dire straits that many Upcountry yeomen found themselves in
did provide an opening for the Republicans, however. Cries for debtor
relief sounded throughout the region within a short time after the
surrender, and little satisfaction came from the planter-dominated state
legislature of 1866. Governor Charles Jenkins, a Whig turned
Democrat, vetoed the one measure designed to alleviate distress—the
stay law, which would have postponed the settlement of private debts—
charging that "no state shall pass any law impairing the obligation of
contracts." When the assembly enacted a second stay law later that
year, this time over Jenkins's veto, the State Supreme Court, presided
over by Chief Justice Hiram Warner, a Democrat, struck it down as
unconstitutional.[9] Thus, a meeting in Jackson County, viewing efforts
"by the last legislature [as] insufficient," demanded "relief according to
what the people estimate and value," and called upon recalcitrant
assemblymen to "resign their position that representative men may
be . . . sent to serve the people." Should the legislature balk, the
meeting warned, "the people know their rights . . . and will take up
their own work, and in convention do it . . . effectually." Another
Jackson County resident went so far as to predict mob violence if action
was not taken.[10]

8. Lt. D. C. Poole to E. L. Jackson, Atlanta, February 12, 1866, BRFAL, Record Group
105/Entry 729, Subordinate Field Office, Vol. 98, 59, NA; Nathan W. Carithers to
General Pope, Jefferson, November 20, 1867, BCA, Record Group 393/Entry 5785, Box
4, NA; Fred Mosebach to Bvt. Brig. Gen. C. C. Sibley, Atlanta, April 9, 1868, BRFAL,
105/729, Sub. Field Off., Vol. 99, 203; Andrews, *The South Since the War*, 382.

9. Allen D. Candler, ed., *The Confederate Records of the State of Georgia*, 6 vols. (Atlanta,
1909), IV, 499–511; Henri H. Freeman, "Some Aspects of Debtor Relief in Georgia
During Reconstruction" (M.A. thesis, Emory University, 1951), 4–5, 12–14, 17–20.

10. Athens *Southern Watchman*, August 15, 1866; N. W. Carithers to Editor, Athens
Southern Watchman, Jefferson, October 26, 1866, BCA, 393/5782, Box 1. Also see Petition
Regarding Debtor Relief, Jackson County, May 29, 1867, BCA, 393/5782, Box 2; Robert
White to Maj. Gen. Pope, Jackson County, June 8, 1867, in ibid.

Propelled by the Reconstruction Acts of 1867, which enfranchised the ex-slaves, and by growing resentment toward planter conservatives, Republicans seized their opportunity. The Georgia party's Radical wing, based in Augusta and guided by John E. Bryant, Foster Blodgett, Rufus Bullock, and Benjamin F. Conley, had already spurred the formation of the Georgia Equal Rights Association, a politically inspired organization of freedmen. Now, anticipating the upcoming elections for a state constitutional convention, they spelled out a program tailored to attract disaffected yeomen. At an Atlanta gathering in July dominated by the Radicals, the party approved the congressional plan of Reconstruction, assured "equal rights" for all citizens, and pledged support for relief, homestead laws, and free schools.[11]

As early as the summer of 1866, Loyal Leagues—the organizational predecessors of the Republican party—had established a foothold in north Georgia, and by the winter of 1867 a conservative inhabitant of Marietta could groan that "Leagues are being formed all over the country. . . ." A few months thereafter, a Freedmen's Bureau agent in Carroll County announced that "The different Loyal Leagues of this county held a very large meeting" attended by "over one thousand of the loyal voters of the county."[12] But the new registration laws and the campaign for constitutional reform gave the movement added momentum. Rallies in Cobb, Clayton, Campbell, Bartow, and Cherokee counties that August brought out voters of both races and ratified the Republican planks.[13] As the editor of the Democratic Cartersville *Express* sneered, "Early Saturday morning last, our streets were alive with sable citizens—male and female—of African descent, and now and then a sprinkling of whites [for the Republican mass meeting]." Henry P. Farrow, a party leader from the Upcountry, felt "exceedingly encouraged by the reports of progress made in organizing the Union Republican party in North Georgia" and proclaimed that "the

11. Nathans, *Losing the Peace*, 41; Circular, quoted in C. Mildred Thompson, *Reconstruction in Georgia: Economic, Social, and Political, 1865–1872* (Gloucester, Mass., 1964), 194.

12. William S. Thomson to W. A. Thomson, Marietta, February 12, 1867, William S. Thomson Papers, Box 2, Folder 1, EU; J. O. Harris to William Markham, Carrollton, May 8, 1867, BCA, 393/5782, Box 1. Also see Emanuel B. Martin to Maj. Gen. Pope, Carrollton, May 7, 1867, in ibid.; Roberta F. Carson, "The Loyal League in Georgia," *GHQ*, XX (June 1936), 125–53.

13. Atlanta *Daily Opinion*, August 7, 1867, August 11, 1867, August 16, 1867, August 21, 1867; Cherokee *Georgian*, August 23, 1867, all in Henry P. Farrow Papers, Scrapbook II, UGa; Henry P. Farrow to Gen. Pope, Cartersville, August 1867, BCA, 393/5782, Box 3.

question of convention will carry by an overwhelming majority. . . ."[14]

The November election bore out Farrow's assessment. A landslide of voters cast ballots in favor of the convention. But the turnout statewide amounted to just a hair over the requisite 50 percent of those eligible: many Democrats, particularly in the Black Belt, voiced their dissatisfaction with congressional Reconstruction simply by refusing to participate. And while native Republicans clearly commanded the ensuing convention, serious divisions within their own ranks soon came to the surface. The well-organized Radicals, standing squarely on the platform drawn up the previous summer and committed to black suffrage and officeholding, encountered resistance from a loose, though sizable, Moderate faction. With politics and political alignments in flux, many of the Moderates had joined the Republican party intending to exercise a conservative influence; others merely had axes to grind with the Augusta leadership. In the convention, they opposed debtor relief and homestead exemptions while expressing grave doubts about the extension of full political rights to blacks. Although the Radicals, with the aid of Democratic defectors from the Upcountry, managed to push through the relief and homestead measures, Moderates whittled down the homestead's coverage and then succeeded in blocking efforts to disfranchise former Confederates and to guarantee black officeholding. In this, the Moderates won the support of north Georgia delegates. Recognizing that a fight on the question of political participation would cost Upcountry votes, the Radicals gave in.[15]

The dissension among Georgia Republicans had close parallels in other Southern states and, in an important sense, reflected a national party debacle. Sharing a commitment to the resurrection of a Union based on equality of opportunity under law, congressional Republicans nonetheless divided over how that vision should unfold and what its meaning should be. The Radical-Moderate schism emerged in debates over Southern policy as well as over issues of money, banking, and tariffs.[16] Racism and a complementary concern about broadening party appeal did not alone shape the terrain of discussion; divergent notions about the dimensions of freedom and Union loomed throughout. The

14. Cartersville *Express*, August 23, 1867; Atlanta *Daily Opinion*, August 27, 1867, both in Farrow Papers, Scrapbook II.

15. Candler, ed., *Confederate Records*, VI, 306–8, 367–75, 453–55, 597–99, 699–722; Nathans, *Losing the Peace*, 60–67; Freeman, "Aspects of Debtor Relief," 28–35.

16. Robert P. Sharkey, *Money, Class, and Party: An Economic Study of the Civil War and Reconstruction* (Baltimore, 1959); Brock, *An American Crisis*, 95–211.

most far-reaching proposals for Reconstruction equated freedom with
control over productive resources and saw economic independence as a
prerequisite of political democarcy in a smallholders' republic. Thus,
the preoccupation of some Radicals with breaking the back of the
planter class and initiating land reform. Congressional Moderates, on
the other hand, who increasingly held ideological sway, viewed
freedom of contract in the marketplace as the foundation of a national
economic system in which a revitalized cotton South would be a
significant component. Linking moral and material progress, and
convinced—by direct and indirect evidence—that the freedmen
favored subsistence farming, they believed that black economic power
could threaten national development. Hence they grew committed to
the encouragement of entrepreneurial elements in rural and urban
areas and gradually abandoned the party's Radical Southern wing.[17]

If the split between Radicals and Moderates in Georgia had
somewhat different features from the one in Congress, it also highlighted
internal social tensions. The Radicals may have welcomed the accession
of men like the former governor Joseph E. Brown, especially because of
his Upcountry following, but Brown had his own ideas about party
goals. Despite solemn pronouncements in support of the Republican
platform, he, along with a handful of industrial promoters and a larger
contingent of ex-Whigs who together formed the core of the Moderate
faction, had greater interest in smooth reconciliation and economic
growth than in social and political reform. Wishing to attract outside
capital and diversify the economy, they pressed for a broader constituency than one of freedmen or poor Southerners generally.[18] At the

17. Eric Foner, *Politics and Ideology in the Age of the Civil War* (New York, 1980), 108–12,
128–49; Lawrence N. Powell, *New Masters: Northern Planters During the Civil War and
Reconstruction* (New Haven, 1980); Michael Perman, *Reunion Without Compromise: The South
and Reconstruction* (Cambridge, 1973), 6–11 and passim; David Montgomery, *Beyond
Equality: Labor and the Radical Republicans, 1862–1872* (New York, 1967). This sketch
somewhat overdraws distinctions between congressional Radicals and Moderates. Many
of the Radicals shared the Moderate outlook on the future course of American economic
development. But the vision of men who favored confiscation, like Thaddeus Stevens,
George Julian, and Wendell Phillips, was indeed different. Their defeat not only ended
the land issue in Congress; it also ended the progressive thrust of the Northern bourgeoisie
and paved the way for the consolidation of industrial and financial capital, with
antidemocratic repercussions. Stevens died in 1868, but, significantly, Julian and Phillips
found their way into the labor movement.

18. Herbert Fielder, *A Sketch of the Life and Times and Speeches of Joseph E. Brown*
(Springfield, Mass., 1883), 428–31; Joseph H. Parks, *Joseph E. Brown of Georgia* (Baton
Rouge, 1978), 364–72; Nathans, *Losing the Peace*, 39–41.

same time, the task of maintaining a coalition which included yeomen and blacks presented the Radicals with delicate problems that the constitutional convention did little to resolve.

The campaigns for ratification of the newly drawn constitution and for state and congressional offices, which occurred simultaneously during the late winter and early spring of 1868, displayed a clever short-run strategy that could promise only disastrous long-term consequences. Taking the support of blacks for granted and focusing their energies on the Upcountry, Republicans hoped to court yeomen by playing, at once, to class and racial resentments.[19] An "Appeal by Republicans to the Poor White Men of Georgia," for example, proclaimed, "Be a man! Let the Slaveholding aristocracy no longer rule you," and counseled a vote "for a constitution which educates your children free of charge; relieves the poor debtor from his rich creditor; allows a liberal homestead for your families; and more than all, places you on a level with those who used to boast that for every slave they were entitled to three-fifths of a vote in congressional representation." The Republican Atlanta *New Era* similarly urged "poor men" to cast their ballots for the party promising "Relief, Homesteads, and Schools for the people," while the gubernatorial aspirant Rufus Bullock publicly styled himself the "workingman's candidate."[20]

Coupled with this emphasis on the economic benefits of a Republican victory came assurances that "negro rule" was not in the offing. Party faithfuls had long admonished "the negroes to banish from their minds the idea of Confiscation," but spokesmen touring the Upcountry in 1868 took special care in raising the matter of the freedmen's potential political power. While Black Belt Republican leaders insisted that the new constitution protected the freedmen's right to hold office, their counterparts in the Upcountry issued a rather different message. Joseph Brown, in particular, who appeared at several north Georgia rallies, claimed that although the blacks were legally enfranchised, nowhere was their access to officeholding guaranteed.[21]

Yet, however much such appeals to racism may have eased yeoman

19. Atlanta *Daily Opinion*, January 30, 1868, February 19, 1868; Atlanta *Intelligencer*, February 13, 1868; Griffin *Union*, February 7, 1868, all in Farrow Papers, Scrapbook II; Cartersville *Express*, February 21, 1868.

20. "Appeal" quoted in Thompson, *Reconstruction in Georgia*, 204; Atlanta *New Era*, March 22, 1868, quoted in Nathans, *Losing the Peace*, 89.

21. Atlanta *Daily Opinion*, August 21, 1867, in Farrow Papers, Scrapbook II; Parks, *Brown of Georgia*, 408–10.

acceptance of the Republican program, they ultimately weakened the party's prospects by shattering the foundation of the very coalition that could make the program viable. The Republicans had a difficult enough row to hoe in creating a durable organizational structure. Accommodating as the Moderates might have been, the party retained its image as the agent of disruptive social change. If not in Georgia, then in Virginia, the Carolinas, and Maryland, "confiscation radicals"—overwhelmingly black—maintained a significant bearing and forced conservative elements to make good on the issue of civil and political rights for the freedmen. "By the presence of armed soldiers and continued threats of confiscation and the halter," the Cartersville *Express* warned in 1868, the Republicans "design to awe us into submission." It was "the Radical party," the paper reminded its readers, "which associates the negro and the poor white man together as a class in common . . . break[ing] down all distinction between white and black . . . mingl[ing] the two together on terms of equality."[22] For the Southern elite, "Black Republicanism" symbolized more than a new system of race relations; it symbolized a new system of class relations.

And so commenced the "reign of terror." Georgia Democrats were in disarray, unable to formulate a strategy capable of unifying their forces. But local leaders played a hand in enforcing a special kind of discipline. Vigilante violence, employed since the war in an effort to control black laborers and to even scores with white Unionists, took on new political dimensions. It was no accident that the Ku Klux Klan spread through much of the South in the spring of 1868, after a series of Republican victories the preceding November, and in Georgia the Klan's reputed leader was none other than John B. Gordon, the Democratic gubernatorial hopeful. Reports of the Klan's social composition varied, but few doubted that men of "property and standing" associated with Democratic or "Conservative" clubs figured prominently. As one Upcountry Republican asserted, "the order was gotten up and is kept up, as a rule, by the men who are disfranchised."[23]

With the Reconstruction Acts stacking the electoral cards against them, Democrats launched a campaign of intimidation. "I learn that a

22. Cartersville *Express*, January 24, 1868; F. B. Morris to Brother, Dalton, March 30, 1867, Franklin County Papers, Box 1, Folder 6, DU; Foner, *Politics and Ideology*, 145–47.

23. Senate Reports of Committees, *Report of the Joint Select Committee to Inquire Into the Affairs of the Late Insurrectionary States*, 42nd Cong., 2nd Sess., (Washington, 1872), Georgia, I, 23, 50, 74, 395–400, 417–24, 548–52.

secret Democratic meeting held . . . at [Cartersville] . . . resolved that there should be no more than one ballot box opened," a Freedmen's Bureau agent complained shortly before the national election of 1868, "and that every colored voter shall be challenged if he has not paid all his taxes his vote shall not be taken and that the white man shall not be challenged. . . ." In Jackson County another bureau agent found "that large bodyes of armed men are roving through the districts . . . halting and hailing all col'd men they see and compelling them [with] threats of violence . . . to sign . . . an oath that they will vote the democratic ticket in November 1868." "[N]o white radical or col'd man will be allowed to vote in the next president elections unless he vote the democratic ticket," the agent added.[24]

Indeed, local Republican leaders and sympathizers of both races faced constant harassment, if not narrow brushes with death. "[T]he Rebs is working hard against the Rads in this place troping letter saying to leve or tak 300 Lashes on the Bare Back," one white Madison County denizen told the governor. "I received 2 to that effect sum time agow. . . ." Joseph Addison, a small white farmer from western Haralson County, suffered similar treatment from the "Ku Klux," being ordered to leave the area under threat of death. "I just think it was on account of politics—that it was because I was radical," he reckoned. J. R. Holliday of Jackson County, a self-proclaimed Union man, was administered a beating; Cherokee County's James McCoy saw his house burned to the ground. "[F]or some weeks previous to the election the leading members of the democratic party . . . resorted to every imaginable means to intimidate the poor white man, as well as the colored man," the Hart County craftsman J. A. Bowers testified in 1868. "These threats so much intimidated both white and colored voters that many republicans did not go out to the election."[25]

That much of the politically inspired violence was directed against Upcountry blacks suggests the extent of the freedmen's response to the promise of Reconstruction. And, in an important way, their very self-activity and enthusiasm for politics, coinciding with the Republicans'

24. C. B. Blacker to Governor R. B. Bullock, Cartersville, October 30, 1868, BRFAL, 105/824, Sub. Field Off., Letters Sent, Vol. 215, 65; Howell C. Flournoy to Brig. Gen. C. C. Sibley, Athens, October 5, 1868, BRFAL, 105/725, Sub. Field Off., Letters Sent, Vol. 173, 32–33.

25. N. L. Collins to Governor Rufus B. Bullock, Madison County, November 1, 1870, Reconstruction File, Folder 16, GDAH; *Affairs of the Late Insurrectionary States*, Georgia, I 63–64, 395–400, 417–24, 545–48.

racist appeal to white yeomen, created further obstacles to the establishment of an organized party. As early as 1865, J. T. Trowbridge found a large number of ex-slaves in Atlanta assembled, dressed in their "Sunday clothes," and engaged in an "animated discussion of their political rights." For Trowbridge the gathering seemed an "outdoor convention of the freed people." When the Reconstruction Acts extended the franchise to blacks, those in the Upcountry registered in large numbers and wasted little time in displaying their partisanship.[26] The Cartersville *Express* could note derisively that at a local Republican meeting "about two hundred negroes formed themselves in a line—*à la militaire*—marched through [the streets]—up and down and back and forth during the whole evening . . . and filled the air almost incessantly with yells and screams without significance, to the annoyance of all quiet population." Henry P. Farrow could feel relief when party rallies began drawing more than a smattering of whites. Twenty-four freedmen could send written protest of Klan abuse as members of the "Union Republican Party."[27] In many Upcountry counties, blacks constituted the most significant Republican element.

Attracted to the Republican program of debtor relief yet circumscribed in their partisanship by deeply rooted political loyalties, the threat of physical retribution, and black assertiveness, yeoman whites seemed of divided minds. The results of the spring 1868 elections bore ample testimony to this condition. The Upcountry provided much needed support for the new constitution, which won ratification by a margin of about 18,000 votes; it provided somewhat less support for the gubernatorial candidate Rufus Bullock, who eked out a victory despite the disadvantages hampering Democrats; and it sent only a small delegation of Republicans to the state legislature.[28] By a very conservative estimate, the Republican party could expect to receive the votes of between 15 and 25 percent of the eligible whites regionwide, and perhaps near majorities in counties with the fewest blacks or in

26. Trowbridge, *The South*, 458; "Registered Voters," 1867, BCA, 393/5782, Box 5; "Registered Voters," 1868, Farrow Papers, Scrapbook III.

27. Cartersville *Express*, August 23, 1867, in Farrow Papers, Scrapbook II; Farrow to Gen. John Pope, Cartersville, August 1867, BCA, 393/5782, Box 3; Twenty-four Freedmen to Bvt. Maj. Gen. John Pope, Calhoun, August 25, 1867, BRFAL, Records of the Assistant Commissioner, Georgia, Reel 17, NA.

28. Athens *Southern Banner*, April 29, 1868; Athens *Southern Watchman*, May 29, 1868, June 3, 1868.

relatively poor, almost exclusively white county districts.[29] For this, party leaders might have felt some satisfaction. While these areas had been strongholds of the Democracy, economic issues appeared capable of cutting them loose from their political moorings. So, at least, the conservative Athens *Southern Watchman* surmised in explaining the Republican vote in northeastern Georgia: "[I]t was not Radicalism, but relief, that played mischief there. . . . Thousands of our people who, on a square fight between Democracy and Radicalism, would always vote the Democratic ticket, were induced to vote for the constitution on account of relief, and also for the Radical candidates."[30]

Had the Georgia Republicans pressed forward with their social and economic program, they might have been able to hold on to their new Upcountry yeoman adherents and then win new ones. They also might have begun to build some bridges across racial lines. But this did not come to pass. Propped by an unwieldy coalition of groups with divergent interests and expectations, Republicans quickly found themselves embroiled in heated squabbles over patronage, black officeholding, and economic reforms. Though achieving some success, the party never fully delivered on its promises, and by the presidential contest in the fall of 1868, under added strains of violence and intimidation, its electoral strength had eroded substantially. Ulysses S. Grant mustered a scant 32 percent of the ballots cast in the state and fared even more poorly in the Upcountry, as the white vote shrank to a trickle.[31] Some Upcountry counties occasionally favored a Republican for the legislature through the early 1870s. Carroll County elected the Republican

29. This estimate is based on the vote for the new state constitution and for Rufus Bullock. It compares the vote for each, less the total of registered black voters, with the total of registered white voters, thus assuming that all registered black voters turned out and cast ballots for the constitution and for Bullock. Since this is unlikely and since numerous white Republican sympathizers might have stayed away from the polls or voted Democratic under threat of violence, the figure is probably a considerable underestimate. Nonetheless, the projected white vote for the constitution was between 20 and 25 percent, and for Bullock between 15 and 20 percent, of those eligible. The highest individual county projections, ranging between 30 and 50 percent, came in counties like Banks, Paulding, and Haralson, with the most overwhelming white majorities. For election returns and registered voters, see Farrow Papers, Box 1, Folder 6, and Scrapbook III; Athens *Southern Banner*, April 29, 1868.

30. Athens *Southern Watchman*, May 6, 1868.

31. Atlanta *Constitution*, November 13, 1868; Farrow Papers, Box 1, Folder 6. The Upcountry counties for which returns are available gave Grant just under 30 percent of their votes, but the projected white vote slipped to under 10 percent of those registered.

Benjamin M. Long in 1872, although it appears that his personal popularity in the traditionally Democratic Carrollton district proved decisive. As a political alternative capable of vying for or maintaining state power in Georgia, however, the Republican party was dead.[32]

In 1869, a Cobb County Republican bitterly assailed the emergence of "jo Brown and his Satillites . . . in the first rank as leaders" of the party, branding them as "traitors."[33] His stinging rebuke captured the disenchantment of Upcountry supporters who found the party's conservative drift and the growing influence of industrial promoters hard to swallow. For other yeoman whites, aversion to the Republican standard reflected different social antagonisms. Whatever their economic tribulations and resentments toward Black Belt planters, they were small property holders who feared that Republican political power might pose a threat to their way of life. That Upcountry blacks quickly aligned with the party of Emancipation only made that threat seem more immediate. Planter concerns notwithstanding, the Jesse Wades, who hoped for radical land reform, had a decidedly limited presence. The new political departure held out by Reconstruction thus foundered on the rocks of class and racial tensions. It would have another day as the Upcountry was swept into the vortex of the cotton economy.

II

When, in early 1868, an effort to defeat the Republican state constitution and gubernatorial candidate spawned the formation of a "Conservative party" in Jackson County, members of the local elite played a leading role. Especially prominent in the movement for "white unity" were James E. Randolph, J. B. Silman, W. B. J. Hardman, W. C. Howard, J. D. Long, W. I. Pike, W. F. Stark, J. H. Rhinehardt, and W. J. Colquitt. What distinguished these men were their residences and occupations: Randolph was a merchant living in the county seat of Jefferson; Silman an attorney; Hardman a merchant and doctor in the town of Harmony Grove; Howard a Jefferson lawyer; Long a Jefferson physician; Pike a Jefferson attorney; and Colquitt a planter closely

32. Nathans, *Losing the Peace*, 129–30, 144–45; James C. Bonner, *Georgia's Last Frontier: The Development of Carroll County* (Athens, 1971), 90.

33. ? to Henry Farrow, Marietta, April 18, 1869, Farrow Papers, Box 1.

linked to Jefferson.³⁴ Similar profiles could be claimed by a number of Carroll County inhabitants actively organizing to meet the Republican challenge in their locale. Joining R. L. Richards and Oscar Reese, two attorneys from the town of Carrollton, were the Carrollton merchants J. Y. Blalock and J. W. Merrill, the Bowdon merchant J. W. Adamson, the Villa Rica merchandiser S. C. Candler, the editor of the Carrollton-based weekly newspaper E. R. Sharp, and two large landowners living within the Carrollton district, M. R. Russell and J. L. Cobb.³⁵

The influence of town-associated interests on Upcountry politics was not entirely new. Because poor means of transportation and the demands of family farming limited regular mobility, the inhabitants of and around the small antebellum towns and villages had more immediate access to county government and sundry political activities. The county seat served, at once, as the meeting place of the court and local officialdom, as the marketplace, and as the staging ground for partisan assemblies, rallies, and conventions. The handful of professionals and storekeepers often appeared on party executive committees and grand juries. But during the prewar period the farming population held sway. Most county officeholders made their homes in the rural districts, and while substantial farmers and planters figured large in the political process, yeomen filled county posts in considerable numbers. If indicative of the relative unimportance of towns and commerce, this pattern also reflected a specific set of social relations.³⁶

The war and Emancipation began to change the local political landscape much as it did the social and economic. Although slavery did not have the significance in the Upcountry that it had in the Black Belt, its demise disrupted the region's economy and seemed to create widespread chaos nonetheless. Freedmen leaving the farms and plantations not only wandered in the countryside; they frequently headed to the towns, which at least offered some refuge from the

34. James A. Furgeson, "Power Politics and Populism: Jackson County, Georgia, as a Case Study" (M.A. thesis, University of Georgia, 1975), 20–21; Athens *Southern Banner*, September 23, 1870; Southern Historical Association, *Memoirs of Georgia; Containing Historical Accounts of the State's Civil, Military, Industrial, and Professional Interests, and Personal Sketches of Many of Its People*, 2 vols. (Atlanta, 1895), II, 431.

35. Carroll County *Times*, July 7, 1872, July 19, 1872; R. G. Dun and Company, *The Mercantile Agency Reference Book (and Key) Containing Ratings on Merchants, Manufacturers, and Traders Generally, Throughout the United States and Canada, 1870* (New York, 1870).

36. For a discussion of county politics during the antebellum era, see above, Chapter Three.

drudgeries and close supervision of farm labor. Village residents complained of "unruly" blacks congregating in the streets and "grog shops" and disturbing the peace. Dr. Robert Battey of Rome bemoaned the influx of "idle negroes . . . lounging in town . . . in the prime of their manhood," who, he believed, sustained themselves by stealing. "[M]y dogs keep me awake at night running persons out of my garden and orchard," he grumbled. To men like Battey, the Republican party, greeted with unmistakable enthusiasm by the blacks, must have appeared an ominous threat. Small wonder that white townspeople joined with wealthy landowners to "redeem" their counties. The "Conservative party" in Jackson County, and similarly designated organizations elsewhere in the Upcountry, constituted bridges to a revitalized Democratic party; cries for "white unity" expressed the desire to stabilize social relations along broadly traditional lines.[37]

Other war-related dislocations, coupled with methods of decision making, further contributed to the towns' growing influence in the Democratic party. Residents of rural districts, who normally had a difficult time attending to political affairs, faced even greater obstacles as hardships on the home front turned their energies to the matter of basic subsistence as never before. And the system of candidate selection, involving a day-long meeting at the county seat rather than a primary, limited their impact on the party slate. But postwar economic developments proved perhaps the greatest spur, for they lent the towns a new importance and vitality. Railroad construction and the extension of commercial agriculture activated once sleepy villages and nurtured an elevated civic awareness among dwellers whose well-being increasingly depended on the cotton plant. In Carrollton, for example, storekeepers and professionals organized a Masonic lodge, a debating club, and an "Industrial, Scientific, and General Improvement Society," where they hoped "to foster honest and manly pride in the growth and prosperity of the entire county."[38]

A greater town voice in party circles soon had more concrete manifestations. With Republican voting strength largely confined to blacks by the early 1870s, Democratic candidates for county office had a relatively easy time, and those candidates came increasingly from the

37. Dr. Robert Battey to Mary Halsey, Rome, July 19, 1865, Robert Battey Papers, Folder 6, EU; Nathan W. Carithers to Gen. Pope, Jefferson, November 20, 1867, BCA, 393/5785, Box 4; Cartersville *Express*, January 17, 1868.

38. Carroll County *Times*, January 19, 1872, August 16, 1872, December 13, 1872, April 4, 1873.

town districts. Thus in 1873 almost half of the elected officials in Jackson County hailed from Jefferson alone, and by the end of the decade the county seat could boast a decided majority. When officeholders from Harmony Grove and the wealthiest rural district which bordered Jefferson are added, the proportion climbed from 50 per cent in 1873 to 63 percent in 1875, to 70 percent in 1877, to 85 percent in 1879, and finally to 100 percent in 1881.[39] The trend was even more pronounced in Carroll County, where citizens of Carrollton saw a railroad arrive in 1872, after several years of eager promotion. The next year, seven of eight county officials came from the town's district, the remaining officer being an inhabitant of the wealthiest rural precinct. While an exception to the pattern appeared occasionally, town dominance of the county government continued through the 1870s and into the 1880s. In 1877, representatives from Carrollton occupied every county post, and it was a rare year when more than one official could claim a different residency (see Table 6.1).[40]

The emergence of the towns as a political force in the Upcountry symbolized changing dimensions of power wider in scope. Town districts embraced not only urban incorporations but the immediately surrounding countryside as well, which often included some of the

Table 6.1 Residences of County Officers, Jackson and Carroll Counties, 1873–1881

	Jackson County		Carroll County	
	No.	Percentage	No.	Percentage
Town District	13	44.8%	36	87.8%
Wealthiest Rural District	7	24.1	1	2.4
Other Rural Districts	9	31.1	4	9.8
Total	29	100.0%	41	100.0%

Sources: Executive Department, County Officers, Jackson and Carroll Counties, 1873–1881, GDAH; Tax Digests, Jackson and Carroll Counties, 1873–1881, GDAH.

39. Executive Department County Officers, Jackson County, 1873–1881, GDAH; Jackson County Tax Digests, 1873–1881, GDAH. The tax digests list eligible taxpayers by their district of residence.

40. Executive Department County Officers, Carroll County, 1873–1881, GDAH; Carroll County Tax Digests, 1873–1881, GDAH; Carroll County *Times*, January 12, 1872; Bonner, *Georgia's Last Frontier*, 97.

choicest, most highly improved land in the county. Real-estate values normally exceeded those for any other district. The local Democratic leadership mirrored the growing links between landed and commercial wealth. Consider an aggregation of prominent Jackson County Democrats listed by the Jefferson *Forest News* in 1876. Of thirty individuals, fully one-third were professionals, merchants, or members of families engaged in merchandising; the other two-thirds were large landowners, almost all of whom employed white or black farm hands. Indeed, their landholdings averaged nearly 450 acres. Some, like W. B. J. Hardman, combined occupations. Hardman sold goods in Harmony Grove while owning 950 acres close by. Leading Democrats from Carroll County had similar backgrounds.[41]

Wealth had long commanded political power in the Upcountry, much as it had in the Black Belt. But the meaning of political power altered significantly as the region was absorbed into the cotton economy. If, during the antebellum period, small farmers had direct voices in local affairs, they usually did so by virtue of elite backing, and the more prestigious offices such as ordinary, sheriff, state representative, and state senator generally fell to the well-to-do. This democratically sanctioned structure of patronage and deference was made possible by a wide, though unequal, distribution of property and by the relative unimportance of exploitative relations between different groups of whites. Whatever their political muscle, substantial farmers and planters simply did not hold much economic leverage over their poorer white neighbors. And their political success, aside from enhancing personal followings, served the interests of their settlements, districts, and counties.

As the expansion of commercial agriculture began to rupture white class relations, politics took on a new aspect. No easy road welcomed the system of credit and labor relations upon which postwar cotton culture boomed. State law and local custom protected the productive property of smallholders, limited the repercussions of debt, and often subordinated the will of the marketplace to the larger concerns of the community. Local officials and county courts played key roles in legitimizing and enforcing the "rules of the game." They adjudicated contracts and other financial obligations, assessed taxes for county services and projects, administered mortgaging, and carried out foreclosures and public sales. Postbellum landlords, merchants, and

41. Jefferson *Forest News*, July 22, 1876; Jackson County Tax Digest, 1876.

town professionals, whose livelihoods came to rest on the institutionalization of market relations, thus saw political preferment as a springboard
to reshaping Upcountry society. It was not merely a self-conscious
process of manipulation; they believed the commercialization of
agriculture a vital stepping-stone to economic and moral progress. The
town boosterism of the 1870s, seeking to promote railroad development
and attract other capital, gave vivid expression to these sentiments.
That "progress" increasingly jeopardized the welfare and independence of a growing segment of the white population turned political
contention into far more than a matter of personal and local pride.[42]

The political alliance of large landowners and merchants was neither
tension free nor complete. Social and economic changes that drew
elements of the elite together also generated conflicts. The lien system
fostered competition over control of the cotton crop and, thereby, over
the surpluses produced by tenants and sharecroppers. Rich and poor
farmers alike felt squeezed by the combination of inflated credit and
declining commodity prices. If the burdens fell most heavily on yeomen
and the landless, landlords were by no means immune from "financial
distress."[43] Appeals for the establishment of county agricultural
societies, which resounded through the Upcountry during the late
1860s and early 1870s, cited the need for "cooperation among farmers"
to defend their interests and blamed economic woes on the designs of
"middlemen." "It was the duty [of farmers] to act in concert for their
own protection," the president of the Gwinnett County Agricultural
Society declared in 1873, reminding his audience that the "planters
were the only class of laborers in the country who allowed purchasers to
fix the price of their productions." Only "by such cooperation," a Floyd
County landowner proclaimed, can we "protect ourselves against the
exactions and speculations of middle men in commercial relations."[44]

The Grange, which spread across the South beginning in 1872, gave
these efforts their widest organizational expression. It planted its firmest
foothold in the Black Belt, where the struggle between planters and

42. Cartersville *Express*, January 28, 1869; Heard County *News*, quoted in Carroll
County *Times*, January 12, 1872; Carroll County *Times*, August 30, 1872, June 13, 1873,
February 15, 1878.

43. Edward King, *The Great South: A Record of Journeys* (Hartford, Conn., 1875), 348;
Carroll County *Times*, November 14, 1873.

44. Gwinnett *Herald*, August 6, 1873; *The Plantation*, III (November 1872), 7–8. Also see
Athens *Southern Banner*, September 16, 1870; Jefferson *Forest News*, March 9, 1878, June
13, 1879.

merchants was most intense. Indeed, despite the accession of many small farmers, large landowners clearly dominated the order. Interest in cooperative purchasing and the "labor question," along with advocacy of a deflationary monetary policy, "pay as you go" buying, and habits of thrift and industry reflected the outlook of a landed elite hoping to stabilize labor relations and curtail the inroads of merchandisers. Connections between the Grangers and conservative Democrats became apparent, if not openly admitted, and facilitated the passage of measures prohibiting traffic in produce at night and providing for more stringent enforcement of contracts.[45]

Granges sprouted in the Upcountry within a short time after their appearance in the Black Belt. Floyd and Gwinnett counties saw initial gatherings in 1873, Bartow County did in 1874, and by 1875, organizations could be found throughout the region.[46] Although yeomen were more conspicuous here, wealthy landowners again played the major role. "The new order called the Patrons of Husbandry have established a Grange . . . [and] among its members are found some of our best citizens," the Cartersville *Standard and Express* reported. The Gwinnett *Herald* also noted that the local Grange "is composed of many of our leading farmers. . . ."[47] While railing against "speculators," "monopolists," and "all combinations operating against the farmers," Grangers insisted that they "make no war upon any body or class." Anticipating later activities of the Southern Farmers' Alliance, some Granges made trading arrangements with receptive mercantile firms. But for the most part, meetings involved little more than debates over various methods of agricultural improvement and speeches on the necessity of "raising supplies at home," leading small farmers to wonder whose interests were being served. One Carroll County yeoman interrupted a discussion on the "merits of guano" with the blast that "he didn't want any guano and while it might pay to use it, it wouldn't

45. Alex M. Arnett, *The Populist Movement in Georgia* (New York, 1922), 36–37; William Warren Rogers, *The One-Gallused Rebellion: Agrarianism in Alabama, 1865–1896* (Baton Rouge, 1970), 67–73; Roger L. Hart, *Redeemers, Bourbons, and Populists: Tennessee, 1870–1896* (Baton Rouge, 1975), 13; Solon J. Buck, *The Granger Movement: A Study of Agricultural Organization and Its Political, Economic, and Social Manifestations* (Cambridge, Mass., 1913), 102, 107–8.

46. Cottage Home Farm Journal, Floyd County, July 1873, John H. Dent Papers, GDAH; Gwinnett *Herald*, November 26, 1873; Cartersville *Standard and Express*, April 1, 1874; Jefferson *Forest News*, August 7, 1875.

47. Cartersville *Standard and Express*, April 1, 1874; Gwinnett *Herald*, August 25, 1875.

pay to buy it, and it caused production of too much surplus."[48] The only
extensive campaign waged by the Grange took on, not the local
merchant, but "manufacturers and general agents of commercial
fertilizers [who] have combined together in fixing the price . . . beyond
remunerative value to the planter." Thus, the Jefferson *Forest
News* could applaud the "wisdom . . . [of] the Grange movement,"
which it once feared would be controlled by "communistic
influences."[49]

Town elements continued to express concern that organizations like
the Grange did, in fact, array "farmers against all other non-
agricultural occupations, especially merchants," while numerous planters remained steadfast in their suspicion of all "middlemen," particularly as declining cotton prices made trying circumstances chronic.[50]
Yet, tensions eased over time as broader class interests began to mitigate
the divisions and nagging quarrels among the Upcountry elites.
Prosperous merchants amassed real estate and became landlords; large
landowners employing tenants and croppers occassionally moved into
the supply business. And whether or not such a "merger" was effected,
both groups faced common problems of labor discipline and surplus
extraction in a society in which social relations were increasingly
mediated by the marketplace. If unity was never fully achieved, the rise
of the towns as the leading force in the region's Democratic party
symbolized the social and cultural metamorphosis of the newly
aggressive ruling class.

Other developments made the association of political and economic
power clearer for Upcountry Georgians by the mid-1870s. Leading
Democrats, enlisting the aid of county newspapers which sprang up
over the region during the decade, agitated for the abolition of usury
laws and for a state constitutional convention primarily to reform the
homestead statute. "[A] man has the same right to put a price upon his
money that he has to price his horse or his lands," they charged; the

48. Gwinnett *Herald*, February 25, 1874; Cottage Home Farm Journal, Floyd County,
July 1873, September 17, 1876, Dent Papers; Jefferson *Forest News*, September 18, 1875;
Carroll County *Times*, March 17, 1877. According to John Dent, many Southern farmers
"looked upon [the Grange] with distrust from the first. Those who joined it entered with
zeal and entertained great hopes of its accomplishing much good . . . but the spirit soon
languished. . . ."

49. Carroll County *Times*, February 14, 1879, March 7, 1879; Jefferson *Forest News*,
August 4, 1877.

50. Gwinnett *Herald*, March 4, 1874.

"inviolability of contracts" must be assured, they announced.[51] Little wonder that disaffection from the Democratic party focused, in part, on such issues. As one independently inclined Floyd County inhabitant warned, if the usury laws and homestead exemption were repealed, "the producing classes" would be "shaved." "The producing classes must have their work tools; they must have something of real and personal property to produce," he cried. "Their wives and children must know in the future, as they have in the past, what 'home' means."[52]

Local issues also began to heighten awareness of the dimensions of political power. In 1878 the Jackson County grand jury recommended construction of a new courthouse in Jefferson to be funded by a bond issue. The Jefferson *Forest News* and other town interests threw their weight behind the proposal, only to be greeted by staunch popular resistance. Some objected to the method of finance, others to the location, but most questioned the entire undertaking. "We have been taught that the people were their own rulers . . . but [the Jefferson ring] has dictated contrary to the wishes of 2/3 of the people, or perhaps more, that we shall build a new courthouse," one opponent protested, adding that "the people of Jackson do not wish to be taxed . . . for the benefit of Jefferson." Another like-minded spokesman claimed that "the people do not, as a mass, like the way they were forced into the matter, altogether against their wishes; so they feel hurt and that their rights have been invaded and trampled upon."[53] At a time when farmers increasingly fell under the burden of debt and encumbrance and increasingly faced the specter of the auction block, the courthouse seemed to embody the very forces of distress, and they joined to hand the project a stiff rebuke when it came to a vote. Only the Jefferson district cast a majority of favorable ballots. Most Upcountry counties witnessed a similar contest on various occasions during the next decade.[54]

51. Ibid., February 26, 1873, July 16, 1873; Cartersville *Express*, June 1, 1877; Carroll County *Times*, April 6, 1877, March 9, 1877.

52. Augusta *Chronicle and Sentinel*, quoted in Cartersville *Express*, April 27, 1876.

53. Jefferson *Forest News*, May 11, 1878, September 5, 1879, September 26, 1879.

54. Ibid., May 11, 1878, April 18, 1879, September 26, 1879; Gwinnett *Herald*, January 1, 1884, February 19, 1884. Voting on the courthouse issue in Jackson County was technically on the method of finance rather than on whether the courthouse would be built, since its construction was mandated by the grand jury. Voters chose "bonds" or "no bonds," but most seemed to view the latter as a rejection of the entire project. This was

The charge of "ring rule" was familiar to the region's politics. Antebellum Democrats, chafing under the Black Belt's dominance in party circles, had blamed the intrigues of, say, the Athens "clique." But in the 1870s the cry had a new immediacy and reflected new conditions. No longer was an abstract principle—fear of the potential consequences of excessive influence and power brought home by the institution of slavery—at issue. No longer were social tensions and political battles drawn primarily along regional lines. Emancipation, the expansion of commercial agriculture, and the development of market relations of production and exchange in the postwar Upcountry transformed the nature and reality of power and conflict: they became more localized, more direct, and arrayed different social groups. The rumblings of discontent, signaled by complaints of "ring rule," gave notice that "white unity" and the "solid South" would be long in coming.

III

The failure of the Southern Republican party to marshal a constituency sufficiently large to vie for political power without the assistance of federal authorities left a vacuum that Democrats could fill only with difficulty. The Republicans, of course, maintained a distinct presence well after Reconstruction, as freedmen and Mountain whites helped the party muster a substantial percentage of the vote in many states.[55] Hopes of attracting former Whigs on a program of economic development, though, proved at best short-lived. Scattered Republican support among wealthy planters faded as freedmen and yeoman whites pressed for political and economic reforms with the sympathies and aid of congressional Radicals. By the time that a "union of the propertied" became national Republican policy, most of these Whiggish elements had left the fold. Yet the Democracy did not afford them the most comfortable of homes. Partisan loyalties died hard, and while the threat of radical social change encouraged ex-Whigs to unite with their old

---

brought home by one particular election when the format was changed to "bonds" or "direct tax." Few voters turned out. The courthouse was ultimately built, but widespread opposition considerably delayed completion.

55. J. Morgan Kousser, *The Shaping of Southern Politics: Suffrage Restriction and the Establishment of the One-Party South, 1880–1910* (New Haven, 1974), 11–44; Gordon B. McKinney, *Southern Mountain Republicans, 1865–1900: Politics and the Appalachian Community* (Chapel Hill, 1978).

adversaries under the Democratic banner and to reap more than their share of political offices, the coalition was uneasy.[56]

Democratic troubles were caused by more than the Whig accession. Real divisions among Southern elites over what the postwar world would be like and who would command it also provoked party tensions. Black Belt landlords and merchants battled for control of the black labor force; aspiring industrialists struggled with planters over the issues of economic diversification and agricultural reform—and all the jousting took place, virtually by necessity, within Democratic ranks.[57] To these conflicts can be added the long-standing animosities between plantation and non-plantation regions that often factionalized the Democracy of the antebellum era. The Southern version of the "Great Barbecue" only made matters worse. If Redemption toppled the Radical regimes, it did not end the most egregious features of financial corruption—however exaggerated by Southern apologists—that marred Republican rule. Joseph Brown, who returned to the Democrats, along with John B. Gordon and Alfred H. Colquitt, together composing Georgia's "Bourbon Triumvirate," found healthy profits in political machinations. Conservatives like Robert Toombs could but reel in disgust at men seeking to live off rather than for politics. "There is no principle involved in politics since the war," a planter of similar instincts wrote. "It is only a contest between the *ins* and the *outs* for place and power for the privilege and opportunity to rob the U.S. treasury." And so it was for those who found principle less imposing and grew frustrated when unable to share the spoils.[58]

By the early 1870s, these varied strands of discontent saw political manifestation in a loosely coordinated challenge of Independents. Complaining, in particular, of "packed" nominating conventions which excluded the public and concentrated power in the hands of a few "professional politicians," candidates in several congressional districts bolted the Democratic party and ran independently. Perhaps most prominent among them was William H. Felton, a well-to-do

56. C. Vann Woodward, *Origins of the New South, 1877–1913* (Baton Rouge, 1951), 1–22; idem, *Tom Watson: Agrarian Rebel* (New York, 1938), 52–72.

57. Lewis N. Wynne, "Planter Politics in Georgia: 1860–1890" (Ph.D. diss., University of Georgia, 1980), 199–312; Jonathan M. Wiener, *Social Origins of the New South: Alabama, 1860–1885* (Baton Rouge, 1978), 77–221.

58. Cottage Home Farm Journal, Floyd County, August 12, 1882, Dent Papers; Woodward, *Origins of the New South*, 66–74; Woodward, *Tom Watson*, 56–66; Parks, *Brown of Georgia*, 475–533.

farmer and Methodist minister residing in Bartow County, who had previously aligned with the Whigs. Following a heated six-way battle for the northwestern Seventh District congressional nomination in 1874, he struck off on his own, even declining the promise of a second contest if he would remain faithful. Three years later the northeastern Ninth District witnessed a similar showdown when Emory Speer took on the Democratic nominee Hiram W. Bell for the congressional seat vacated by Benjamin H. Hill. Speer, much like Felton, cited "the so-called Congressional conventions" as "unjust and unfair . . . a fraud on [the people's] rights—which cheats them of their preference and serves, year to year, to perpetuate the political power of the district in the hands of a ring of politicians."[59]

Felton and Speer, among others, availed themselves of an Independentism that first emerged in local politics. No clear regional lines defined its impact, but the Upcountry seemed especially active.[60] When, in 1872, the Democratic convention in Jackson County selected T. C. Williams for the state legislature, a disappointed Green R. Duke bolted. A candidate for ordinary in Cherokee County followed a similar tack that same year when informed that the party nomination "was a family concern." In Bartow County, another aspiring ordinary charted an Independent route, calling the local convention "anti-Democratic." "I concluded to submit my case to the Democracy of the people rather than the oligarchy of sixty men," he explained. A former Republican in Carroll County, proclaiming that he had "lived in Carroll 54 years and [was] fully identified with the people of the county," sought a legislative seat as an Independent in 1876.[61]

Self-righteousness and political purity, to be sure, were often the garbs of self-aggrandizement. For men facing bleak prospects on the farm, political preferment at least offered a steady income, if not more lucrative rewards. A veritable flood of office-seekers appeared in the years after Reconstruction. "It has been said that Carroll has no less than a dozen candidates for the [legislative] nomination," one resident

59. Atlanta *Constitution*, September 3, 1874; Athens *Southern Watchman*, quoted in Jefferson *Forest News*, February 17, 1877; George L. Jones, "William H. Felton and the Independent Democratic Movement" (Ph.D. diss., University of Georgia, 1971), 5, 37–44; Furgeson, "Power Politics," 24.

60. Jones, "Felton and Independent Movement," 5–8.

61. Furgeson, "Power Politics," 23; Cartersville *Standard and Express*, July 11, 1872, September 26, 1872; Carroll County *Times*, August 25, 1876.

moaned in 1872, "each one feeling called not by his fellow citizens, but by himself. . . ." The Cartersville *Standard and Express* found that local elections in neighboring Cherokee County caused a great "state of excitation" because of the "many candidates in the field." "The county is overrun with candidates, some 12 or 14 for the legislature, 8 or 10 for sheriff, 6 or 8 for tax collector, all trying to reach soft places," Floyd County's John Dent scowled.[62]

Yet, if mere office seeking or factional disputes initially led aspiring politicians down the Independent road, their candidacies soon tapped developing social antagonisms and growing resentments of the country-side toward the towns. One Felton supporter explained his preference by noting that all members of Georgia's congressional delegation were lawyers while Felton stood "as an admirable representative of the farmers." Charging that "After the war a set of cunning politicians got into power when honest men's hands were tied," another north Georgian proclaimed that Felton "does not belong to the legal fraternity . . . [but] stands by the farmer, the producer."[63] An independently oriented Carroll County denizen attributed the Democratic congressional nomination in the Fourth District to "a few little plug hat fellows [who] got together in the towns and manipulated the thing. The great mass of the people, the wool hat boys had nothing to do with it." "This was not democracy but aristocracy," he thundered. In Bartow County, the Democratic Cartersville *Express* bore the accusation of being the "organ of the cotton ring," while in Floyd County a disgruntled resident later declared that "by heavy taxation" and other "unjust burdens . . . Rome rule[d] the county."[64]

Conservative ex-Whigs of the Toombs-Stephens ilk may have looked favorably upon Independentism as the true representative of "Democratic principles" and "local government" against centralizing tendencies and the power of "gigantic corporations." They spoke for planters who feared the designs of the Democratic party's industrial wing and saw the decentralization of wealth and authority as their best

62. Carroll County *Times*, August 30, 1872; Cartersville *Standard and Express*, July 18, 1872; Cottage Home Farm Journal, Floyd County, August 25, 1876, September 2, 1876, Dent Papers.

63. Cartersville *Express*, November 2, 1876; Countryman, "To the Farmers of Gordon County," n.d. (1876), Rebecca Latimer Felton Collection, Scrapbook I, Box 8, UGa.

64. Carroll *Free Press*, October 17, 1884; Cartersville *Express*, December 2, 1875, April 30, 1876; Cottage Home Farm Journal, Floyd County, March 15, 1887, Dent Papers.

means for securing control of the black labor force.[65] Indeed, numerous Independents took occasion to announce their ultimate fealty to what they believed proper Democratic doctrine. But in the Upcountry, at least, an emerging constituency of small producers disenchanted with the social relations and economic consequences of commercial agriculture pushed party bolters leftward.

The Independent career of Willian Felton, who represented a large section of Georgia's Upcountry, is a case in point. Striking out in opposition to the nominating process controlled by the "Atlanta ring," Felton initially evinced a clear conservatism. In a speech before the Cartersville Grange, he bemoaned "the senseless requirements of [Northern] Trades' Unions" in "demanding of the national and municipal governments 'work or bread'" and in "asserting their right to reduce their hours of labor without a corresponding reduction of wages." "It is the old leaven of Red Republicanism and Constitutionalism; of Internationalism," he cried, praising instead the farmers as the vanguard "of the conservative and Christian hosts." Yet, once in public office, he responded to popular sentiment by pressing for currency and banking reform, railroad regulation, an end to the poll tax, and the abolition of the convict-lease system. Corresponding with the Georgia Greenbacker Ben E. Green, Felton denounced a "privileged class of creditors" and maintained that "Congress shall provide . . . money adequate to the full employment of labor, the equitable distribution of its produce, and the requirements of business, fixing a minimum amount per capita."[66]

Local Independents also sought to ride a growing tide of popular unrest. One aspirant for county office, accusing the incumbent of financial mismanagement, blamed the situation on "a class of men, mostly in town," and pledged "to be economical with the people's money . . . [and] to do exact justice to all without regard to riches or poverty, race or color. . . ." A Floyd County Independent urged limitations on the public debt and on state liability for corporations, while railing against efforts to abolish usury laws and the homestead. And in Carroll County, a candidate for the legislature exclaimed that

65. Phillips, ed., *Correspondence*, 729–30, 738; Rebecca L. Felton, *My Memoirs of Georgia Politics* (Atlanta, 1911), 254, 397.

66. Cartersville *Standard and Express*, February 5, 1874, in Felton Collection, Scrapbook I, Box 8; *Congressional Globe*, 45th Cong., 1st Sess. (Washington, 1878), 403–4; Cartersville *Express*, January 24, 1878; Felton, *Memoirs of Georgia Politics*, 436–37, 446; Fletcher M. Green, "Ben E. Green and Greenbackism in Georgia," *GHQ*, XXX (March 1946), 9.

"there are little if any differences between the two national parties on major issues," and favored "correcting the abuses existing in the state government like exempting a large amount of property over $100,000 from taxation while taxing the poor heavily."[67]

Yet for Democrats, this issue orientation proved perhaps less disconcerting than did other potential ramifications of the Independent challenge. Loyal partisans occasionally admitted that "the Democratic party in the state has grown too big to accommodate all the aspirants for office," that "there are real grievances," and that reform in nominating procedures was necessary. But they counseled fidelity to the party standard for fear that a divided vote would permit a Republican victory. "There is an apprehension, founded upon what appears to be sound reason and common sense," the Jefferson *Forest News* warned, "that the hope of the Republican party . . . lies in what is called the Independent movement." The chairman of the Democratic executive committee in the northeastern Ninth Congressional District fretfully issued a similar forecast: "Our enemies are organizing. . . . The Radical party [intends] . . . to support Independent candidates . . . with a view of dividing the solid South, increasing their numbers in Congress and thus controlling the General Government." "Independent Democracy in the South must inevitably lead to Republicanism," the fiery Benjamin Hill declared. As he saw it, "no Independent can get the Republican support . . . without giving himself over absolutely, definitely, and finally to that party." Independentism, in short, marked "an attempt to Africanize the South. . . ."[68]

Both the Republican party's stance toward the Independents and the Independents' stance toward the Republicans remained ambiguous for much of the 1870s. Still hopeful of maintaining at least a share of political power in the state, many Republicans were reluctant to jettison their own ticket in favor of Independent candidates whose loyalties were often unclear. And numerous Independents, either serious in styling themselves true Democrats or fearful that a coalition with Republicans would cost votes, approached the matter with great

---

67. Carroll County *Times*, November 5, 1880, December 17, 1880; Augusta *Chronicle and Sentinel*, quoted in Cartersville *Express*, April 27, 1876; Carroll County *Times*, August 25, 1876.

68. Jackson *Herald*, February 3, 1882; Jefferson *Forest News*, June 29, 1878, May 25, 1878; Carroll County *Times*, February 3, 1882.

caution, if at all.[69] After suffering a sound beating in the elections of
1876, the Republican state leadership recommended "support for
Independent candidates . . . in those districts in which it is thought
best," but not until 1881 were formal steps taken. In a confidential
letter to William Felton, Henry P. Farrow suggested "getting up a
political combination in Georgia to run through 1884" with the objects
of securing "the recognition of the right element of Republicanism in
Georgia by the powers that be in Washington . . . [and] the recognition of the Independents," and of promoting Felton's "interests as the
leader of the Independents to whom we must look for success." Shortly
thereafter, Farrow, Felton, and a small group of other Republicans and
Independents met in Atlanta and drew up an agreement based on a
platform calling for "a free ballot and a fair count," repeal of internal-
revenue laws, internal improvements, redemption of silver and green-
backs, state-supported free public schools, and an end to "monopolies"
and the convict-lease system.[70]

On the local level, however, Republicans and Independents often
made a separate peace earlier on. While denying "private" arrangements with the powerful Atlanta faction, Felton hoped to attract
Republican votes from the first—and with obvious success. One Floyd
County Democrat sneered in 1876 that "the Radical of the District,
Major Zack Hargrove of Rome made a political speech at Cave
Spring—his audience was composed of 30 niggers and all the Feltonites
of the village. To the Niggers he extrolled Grant and his administration to the skies . . . and to his white audience he remarked
[that] . . . Felton was his man." Indeed, this Democrat blamed
Felton's initial victory in 1874 on the support "of the Radicals and
niggers."[71] Elsewhere in the Upcountry similar, though perhaps more
tentative, developments unfolded. In the Ninth Congressional District
race for a vacated seat in 1877, a Democrat, a Republican, and an

69. Olive H. Shadgett, *The Republican Party in Georgia: From Reconstruction Through 1900*
(Athens, 1964), 62–63; Judson C. Ward, "The Republican Party in Bourbon Georgia,
1872–1890," *JSH*, IX (May 1943), 199; Jones, "Felton and Independent Movement,"
76–77, 173–85.

70. Jefferson *Forest News*, June 29, 1878; Henry P. Farrow to William H. Felton,
December 3, 1881, Farrow Papers, Letterbook II, 639–40; Felton, *Memoirs of Georgia
Politics*, 340–44; Shadgett, *Republican Party in Georgia*, 68–70.

71. Samuel E. Crawford to William H. Felton, Bartow County, September 18, 1874,
Felton Collection, Box 1; Cottage Home Farm Journal, Floyd County, August 30, 1876,
September 29, 1876, Dent Papers.

Independent entered the field, with success falling to the Democrat by a small margin. The next year, district Republicans chose not to put up a candidate, and the Independent emerged triumphant. In Carroll County a Republican ran for the state legislature under the banner of Independentism.[72]

Men like Felton may have dismissed the charge that their Independent political course threatened to "Africanize" the state, but courting Republicans in the Upcountry, much as in the Black Belt, meant repudiating the plea for "white unity." For while the Republicans retained a small white constituency, by the mid-1870s the party's rank and file was overwhelmingly black. Independent overtures testified to the persistence of black political participation and mobilization. Even under intimidation, the region's blacks continued to go to the polls. As one Floyd County landlord could grumble in 1876, "all business suspended for the election today, a full nigger vote cast in the county. . . ."[73] Such resolve emanated from developing Afro-American communities that provided networks for mutual interaction, organization, and protection. Building upon customs and institutions forged under slavery, Upcountry blacks strengthened bonds among themselves and, in so doing, became a force to be reckoned with, however outnumbered they were in the population as a whole.

It was an impressive achievement and one that renders inappropriate the categorical dualities of "accommodation" or "resistance," "integration" or "racial solidarity," political or apolitical. The most common manifestations of community life did, to be sure, seem to mark a turn inward, a defensiveness, a shift away from political confrontation to the cultivation of racial pride and self-help after Reconstruction: social gatherings and celebrations, religious meetings, musical groups, fire companies, and educational associations. But these were never fully divorced from, and were often thoroughly infused with, politics. When, for example, Paulding County blacks "enjoyed a grand festival" one May, they not only feasted and heard two brass bands; they also listened to "plenty of speeches." A large camp meeting of Floyd County blacks in 1873 served, according to the landlord John Dent, as both a spiritual convocation and a forum to discuss "getting higher wages—more privileges—and greater liberties." Blacks in Jackson County es-

72. Furgeson, "Power Politics," 24–26; Carroll County *Times*, August 25, 1876.

73. Cottage Home Farm Journal, Floyd County, November 7, 1876, Dent Papers.

tablished seventeen schools for their children during the 1870s while pressing the state government for increased funding.[74]

Such activities were the foundation of a more formal political structure which sought to link racial improvement with the acquisition of full citizenship rights. Despite the violence of Redemption and the ascendancy of the "lily-white" faction in what was left of the state Republican party, Upcountry blacks kept local Republican organization alive. Under the direction of their own county executive committees, they held meetings, sent delegates to state party conventions, and occasionally ran black candidates for local office.[75] In this way, black leaders mitigated political demoralization, drew black voters to the polls, and rallied opposition to white discrimination and injustice. Thus, "a large crowd of colored citizens of [Jackson] county" could gather at the courthouse one afternoon to protest their exclusion from grand juries. "Their intention," the local paper reported, "was to ask humbly and respectfully for the right which they thought they were entitled to enjoy as much as any other privilege of citizenship." Elsewhere blacks called for reform of the convict-lease system, more effective support for black education, and elimination of the new poll tax.[76]

The Independents did little to address the specific concerns and grievances of the black community. They hardly spoke for equality between the races, nor did they pledge many political favors. Yet, with the fortunes of Upcountry Republicans in unmistakable decline and with state patronage in the hands of the "lily-white" faction, the Independent offer of a "free ballot and a fair count" served as an attractive alternative to Democratic attacks on black political rights. Felton's initial campaign, in fact, drew an enthusiastic response. "The negroes assembled [in Cartersville] today," the Atlanta *Daily Herald* reported. "The notorious negro Crumley . . . made a bitter speech against [Felton's Democratic opponent], denouncing him as the candidate of an odious party of outrages and Ku Kluxism . . . [and]

---

74. Paulding *New Era*, May 17, 1883; Cottage Home Farm Journal, Floyd County, September 1873, Dent Papers; Jefferson *Forest News*, July 17, 1875, October 30, 1875, December 12, 1879; Jackson *Herald*, November 9, 1883; Carroll *Free Press*, July 9, 1883.

75. Jackson *Herald*, July 7, 1882; Cottage Home Farm Journal, Floyd County, October 6, 1880, Dent Papers; Cherokee *Advance*, December 24, 1886.

76. Jackson *Herald*, March 18, 1881; Olin B. Adams, "The Negro and the Agrarian Movement in Georgia, 1874–1908" (Ph.D. diss., Florida State University, 1973), 42–44, 79.

spoke strongly in favor of Dr. Felton." Two years later, a disconcerted Floyd County Democrat found that local blacks cast ballots in large numbers "for Hays, Wheeler, and Felton." In 1878, the Gwinnett *Herald* attributed the defeat of the Democratic nominee in the Ninth Congressional District to "overconfidence," lack of "organization," and "underrating the strength of the opposition." "We did not count on the negro vote going solid," the paper explained, "but . . . nine-tenths of them voted the Independent ticket."[77]

Black support for Independent candidates formed part of a developing political alignment that Radical Republicans hoped to forge for their own benefit and that would become more apparent in the 1880s and 1890s. The Upcountry long displayed an independent spirit in state politics, whether in the antebellum Democratic party, in the secession crisis, or during the Civil War. Thus, it is not surprising that the region proved receptive to Democratic bolters thereafter. William Felton fared well from the beginning, winning a narrow victory in 1874, when he carried six of eight Upcountry counties by overwhelming majorities.[78] Reelection came more easily in 1876, and in 1878 he won in every Upcountry county in the district, as well as in two Mountain counties previously in the Democratic camp.[79] The Independent Emory Speer got off to a slower start in the northeastern Ninth District, losing to the Democrat in a three-way race for a vacated congressional seat in 1877. But the next year, when the Republican dropped out, Speer turned the tables in a closely fought contest.[80]

Election returns from districts within Upcountry counties, however, reveal emerging divisions between town and countryside and between

77. Atlanta *Daily Herald*, October 31, 1874, in Felton Collection, Scrapbook I, Box 8; Cottage Home Farm Journal, Floyd County, November 7, 1876, Dent Papers; Gwinnett *Herald*, November 13, 1878.

78. Jones, "Felton and Independent Movement," 52. Felton defeated the Democratic candidate 7,587 to 7,505, the Republican receiving a mere 197 votes. In Upcountry counties that he carried, Felton obtained 73 percent of the vote, while in all Upcountry counties in the district, he obtained 63 percent. The Democrat won in all the Mountain counties.

79. Cartersville *Express*, November 9, 1876, November 14, 1878. Felton won by 13,274 to 10,807 in 1876, carrying six of fourteen counties in the district. In 1878 he won by 14,315 to 12,963, carrying nine of the fourteen counties.

80. Jefferson *Forest News*, March 31, 1877; Jones, "Felton and Independent Movement," 125. The Democrat won in 1877 by 5,173 to 3,734 with 1,614 votes going to the Republican. In 1878, Speer won by 10,897 to 10,675, carrying seven of twenty counties in the district.

rich and poor farmers. In Gwinnett County, for example, the Democratic congressional candidate rolled up sizable majorities in the three town districts and in two of the wealthier rural districts in 1878; the Independent, on the other hand, swept six of the nine remaining rural districts, including most of the poorest by measure of per capita wealth. A similar, though somewhat less distinct, trend was evident in Jackson County that same year. The Democrat carried the town and five of the rural districts, including the more well-to-do. The Independent won three rural districts, two of which were among the poorest in the county (see Table 6.2). In Carroll County, the Independent candidate for the Fourth Congressional District received

Table 6.2 District Voting Returns in Congressional Races, Gwinnett and Jackson Counties, 1878

	Gwinnett County				Jackson County		
District	Per Capita* Wealth	Dem.	Ind.	District	Per Capita* Wealth	Dem.	Ind.
Town Dist.:				*Town Dist.:*			
Lawrenceville	$1,436	401	364	Jefferson	$977	464	404
Duluth	973	101	52	Harmony Grove	1,090	183	147
Norcross	?	103	33	Maysville	619	67	20
Rural Dist.:				*Rural Dist.:*			
Hog Mountain	649	14	25	Clarksboro	557	86	48
Bay Creek	792	24	21	Newtown	622	150	149
Cates	692	17	49	Miller	640	50	0
Martins	779	27	54	Cunningham	497	37	14
Rockbridge	653	51	33	Randolph	661	83	117
Harbins	614	23	0	House	646	83	82
Ben Smith	522	81	55	Chandler	530	51	71
Berkshire	774	81	9	Santafe	397	28	37
Buford	?	114	128	Total		1,282	1,088
Cains	545	36	38				
Suwanee	?	31	85				
Total		1,104	946				

* Total wealth divided by total number of persons on tax rolls.

Sources: Gwinnett *Herald*, November 13, 1878; Jefferson *Forest News*, November 9, 1878; Gwinnett County Tax Digest, 1880; Jackson County Tax Digest, 1880.

the support of four relatively poor rural districts while sustaining a sound defeat elsewhere.[81]

These results, to be sure, failed to demonstrate a clear-cut convergence of social and political antagonisms. Some poor rural precincts remained within the Democratic fold, while wealthier counterparts occasionally threw their support to Independents. Partisan loyalties did not unravel easily; small farmers, tenants, and croppers of both races might face the coercion of merchants and landlords; and many voters continued to follow the lead of well-known political figures. Still, Democratic hegemony appeared to be shaken in the countryside. In 1878 roughly half of the voters in all rural districts cast ballots for Independent congressional candidates in Gwinnett and Jackson counties. In 1880 well over half chose the Independent alternative.[82] As poor white farmers increasingly joined blacks in protest at the ballot box, a new political day seemed to be dawning in Georgia and other Southern states.[83]

The Democrats recognized as much, resorting to the tactics of fraud and intimidation that proved successful during Reconstruction. If men like Felton came under fierce verbal assault, Independent constituents frequently encountered more trying episodes. One Feltonite complained of several forms of electoral corruption practiced by local Democrats: "whiskey brought in and distributed, illegal voting, closing polls early, and voting all the negroes." Carroll County denizens spoke of widespread "bulldozing," and in the eastern Upcountry, Democrats waged a multisided campaign to unseat Emory Speer. "Candler clubs [the Democratic candidate] were organized all over the district, nightly meetings were held, committeemen traveled through the country for weeks and money was spent freely," the Independent Gainesville *Southron* charged. "Banners were painted, voting places were hung with all sorts of devises, mottoes, and bulldozing insults. . . . Three clubs took possession of the polls here, at Athens, Madison, Jefferson, and

---

81. Carroll County *Times*, November 1878 (n.d.).

82. Jefferson *Forest News*, November 9, 1878; Jackson *Herald*, November 11, 1880; Gwinnett *Herald*, November 13, 1878, November 10, 1880. In 1878 rural districts in Jackson and Gwinnett counties delivered 47 percent and 50 percent of their respective votes to the Independent; in 1880 the proportions rose to 63 percent and 57 percent.

83. On Independentism elsewhere, see William Ivy Hair, *Bourbonism and Agrarian Protest: Louisiana Politics, 1877–1900* (Baton Rouge, 1972), 65–78; Rogers, *One-Gallused Rebellion*, 37, 50–55; Albert D. Kirwan, *Revolt of the Rednecks: Mississippi Politics, 1876–1925* (New York, 1965), 18–39; Woodward, *Origins of the New South*, 76–106.

Toccoa . . . and every Speer man knows it was difficult to get to the polls and back without being insulted. . . . "[84] For other Democrats, electoral "reform" promised the best solution to political unrest. It was no accident that the new state constitution, written under Democratic auspices in 1877, included a retroactive poll tax and stiffer residency requirements for voting; Felton, along with numerous local Independents, had already triumphed over Democratic "rings." And additional measures soon merited consideration. "There is a good deal of talk among some of the papers about a general registration law . . . [which] would undoubtedly have a good effect towards purifying the ballot box," the Carroll County *Times* sympathetically reported.[85]

The Democratic counterattack wore heavily on the Independents, who never developed an organized party or coherent program to unify and discipline favorably inclined voters. This failure, in part, attested to the divergent motivations of Independent politicians, many of whom expected to return to the Democratic house. Attempting to lure Alexander Stephens into the gubernatorial race in 1882 hardly represented a radical initiative, and even the formal Independent-Republican coalition of 1881, which issued a platform, came from the efforts of a handful of political leaders unable to command the clear loyalties of a mass following. Furthermore, those Independents hoping to forge a new party faced a formidable task in organizing small farmers, whose collective experiences within settlements fostered a profound localism and whose racism continued to hamper an essential political alliance. Thus, by the early 1880s, Democrats had recaptured the two Upcountry congressional seats and the Independents were generally in disarray.[86]

Yet the spirit of Independentism lived on in the Upcountry. Democratic congressional nominees still had to weather challenges capable of amassing substantial votes, and numerous counties, including Jackson, Carroll, Heard, Bartow, Cherokee, and Campbell, sent an

---

84. R. S. Church to William H. Felton, Graysville, November 8, 1878, Felton Collection, Box 1; Carroll County *Times*, June 30, 1882; Gainesville *Southron*, quoted in Jackson *Herald*, January 11, 1884.

85. Carroll County *Times*, June 21, 1881; Kousser, *Shaping of Southern Politics*, 209–10; Walter McElreath, *A Treatise on the Constitution of Georgia* (Atlanta, 1912), 501.

86. Jones, "Felton and Independent Movement," 231–43; Woodward, *Tom Watson*, 73–95.

occasional Independent to the state legislature.[87] More than this, the Independent upsurge, whatever its origins, began to offer a political focus for rising social antagonisms; divisions within the postbellum elite created a significant opening for movements from below. Though it may not have been of the radical, biracial brand that the tenant farmer Jesse Wade espoused, political insurgency expressed developing class conflicts which threatened to bridge the racial chasm. Trapped in a cycle of indebtedness and ultimate dispossession, yeoman landholders increasingly shared the fate of the region's blacks. Joseph Brown could only agree with his fellow Democrat L. N. Trammell's bleak assessment "of the condition of popular sentiment." "There is a growing feeling among our people of opposition to all accumulation of capital," Brown answered him in 1883. "There is an agrarian tendency among our people."[88] Events of the 1880s in the Georgia Upcountry would give ample credence to Brown's forecast.

87. Cherokee *Advance*, October 5, 1888, November 9, 1888; Gwinnett *Herald*, November 13, 1888; Jones, "Felton and Independent Movement," 269, 296, 308.

88. Joseph E. Brown to L. N. Trammell, Washington, D.C., May 23, 1883, L. N. Trammell Papers, Folder 3, EU.

7

Common Right and Commonwealth

I

"The stock law is the topic in this part of the county now. I want to say to the voters of Carroll county, that we as poor men and negroes do not need the law, but we need a democratic government and independence, that will do the common people good." So thundered the white dirt farmer L. J. Jones in an 1885 letter to the local newspaper.[1] Jones was not alone in viewing the stock law as an instrument of class oppression or as an issue that transcended purely economic concerns. Nor was he alone in challenging the tenets of white supremacy and racial solidarity. Nor, indeed, did he articulate strictly regional sensibilities. Hundreds of small farmers and laborers of both races in the Georgia Upcountry rallied with Jones to protect the grazing rights that the stock law threatened to abridge. For them, the law was the starkest instance of efforts by the emerging postbellum elite to cast petty producers into a state of dependency. And in associating social and economic dislocation with new expressions of political power, they joined industrial workers in Northern cities and farmers in the Midwestern countryside who assailed the corruption of the democratic process in Gilded Age

1. Carroll *Free Press*, May 15, 1885.

America, in a campaign to defend their own version of the Revolutionary republican heritage.[2]

It has been customary to portray the 1880s in the South as a political hiatus, a period of relative quiescence between the turbulent eras of Reconstruction and Populism. With the end of military rule, it is argued, the Bourbon Democrats crushed indigenous Independent movements, consolidated their hold on the political system, and reigned virtually unopposed until the advent of the Southern Farmers' Alliance.[3] Such a picture does have some plausibility if we focus on the Black Belt or the statehouses, though recent studies suggest persisting contests.[4] But in the Upcountry the 1880s saw the intensification of social and political conflicts that had begun to surface in the years after 1865. A variety of issues stirred local politics and sharpened divisions created by the developing staple economy, none more so than the stock, or fence, law.[5] Bitterly fought out over the course of the decade, the fencing controversy galvanized budding antagonisms that the Independents initially tapped, it revealed the cultural, as well as economic, dimensions of political struggles, and it paved the road to Populism.

Efforts to reform fencing statutes which provided for common or "open-range" grazing had been made during the antebellum era. Concerted agitation, however, began only after the Civil War, as part of

2. For a pioneering study of the political response of industrial workers to American capitalism during the Gilded Age, see Leon Fink, *Workingmen's Democracy: The Knights of Labor and American Politics* (Urbana, Ill., 1983). Also see David Montgomery, *Beyond Equality: Labor and the Radical Republicans, 1862–1872* (New York, 1967).

3. See, for example, Allen J. Going, *Bourbon Democracy in Alabama, 1874–1890* (Tuscaloosa, Ala., 1951); William J. Cooper, *The Conservative Regime: South Carolina, 1877–1890* (Baltimore, 1968); William Ivy Hair, *Bourbonism and Agrarian Protest: Louisiana Politics, 1877–1900* (Baton Rouge, 1972), 107–41; Alex M. Arnett, *The Populist Movement in Georgia* (New York, 1922), 45–48. C. Vann Woodward essentially takes this view, arguing that after the collapse of Independentism "insurgency was almost unheard of in the South" and that the "region lapsed into a period of political torpor more stultifying, perhaps, than any in its long history." But he also notes the emergence of divisive local issues. See *Origins of the New South, 1877–1913* (Baton Rouge, 1951), 85, 103–6 and *Tom Watson: Agrarian Rebel* (New York, 1938), 84–95.

4. J. Morgan Kousser, *The Shaping of Southern Politics: Suffrage Restriction and the Establishment of the One-Party South, 1880–1910* (New Haven, 1974), 11–44; William W. Rogers and Robert David Ward, *August Reckoning: Jack Turner and Racism in Alabama* (Baton Rouge, 1973), 83–179; James T. Moore, *Two Paths to the New South: The Virginia Debt Controversy, 1870–1883* (Lexington, Ky., 1974).

5. *Atlanta Constitution*, November 11, 1883; Woodward, *Origins of the New South*, 85.

a series of skirmishes over social relations and property rights. The impetus came from the Black Belt, where the "labor question" first surfaced after Emancipation. Believing black dependency to be the handmaiden of work discipline, the planters moved to circumscribe the freedmen's mobility and access to the means of production and subsistence. The legal and extra-legal actions taken by the planting elite to prevent blacks from owning land, to tie them to the plantation sector, and, with the rise of tenancy, to control their crops were products of such an offensive—one waged by large landowners throughout the Western Hemisphere and continental Europe in response to the liberation of slaves and peasants.[6] Day-to-day matters of work rhythms, provisioning, and leisure also proved to be bones of contention. Complaining of the freedmen's "lack of forethought," their failure to "appreciate the importance of making hay while the sun shines," and their generally "lazy disposition," and attributing these "habits" to innate racial characteristics, the planters nonetheless acknowledged conflicting sets of priorities.[7]

This confrontation was not peculiar to the postbellum period, but it became more salient when the prerogatives of slaveownership and the old plantation forms of management dissolved. By seizing upon privileges they had transformed into rights as slaves, the freedmen tried to stake out spheres of autonomy within a system of unequal economic power. Securing family sustenance was an important one of them. Freedmen, the traveler Edward King observed during his tour through the South in 1874, "are fond of the same pleasures which their late masters gave them so freely—hunting, fishing, and lounging; pastimes which the superb forests, the noble streams, the charming climate minister to very strongly." These "pleasures" may have been viewed as paternal indulgences by wealthy slaveholders; following abolition, they amounted to direct challenges to the planters' authority and claims on the freedmen's labor time.[8]

6. C. Vann Woodward, "The Price of Freedom," in David Sansing, ed., *What Was Freedom's Price?* (Jackson, Miss., 1978), 93–113; Wilhemina Kloosterboer, *Involuntary Labour Since the Abolition of Slavery* (Leiden, 1960); Jerome Blum, *The End of the Old Order in Rural Europe* (Princeton, 1978), 357–441.

7. *The Plantation*, II (August 1871), 487; Hinds County (Mississippi) *Gazette*, November 1, 1867; Howell Cobb to Wife, Sumter County, December 1866, in Ulrich B. Phillips, ed., *The Correspondence of Robert Toombs, Alexander Stephens, and Howell Cobb* (Washington, 1913), 684.

8. Edward King, *The Great South: A Record of Journeys* (Hartford, Conn., 1875), 274, 371;

Hence, when Georgia's landed elite regained political power after Reconstruction, they set their sights on remedying the problem. Commencing in 1872, a series of game laws, localized in nature, fanned out over the Black Belt. Three counties enacted statutes in that year, fourteen did so in 1874, and twenty-four followed suit in 1876. By 1880, fishing and hunting had come under regulation in most of the plantation districts.[9] The laws covered three main areas: they established hunting seasons for a considerable assortment of animals and fowl, prohibited certain methods of trapping, and restricted access to game on unenclosed private land. An act passed for Burke, Taylor, and Jefferson counties in 1875, for example, prescribed it a misdemeanor to "kill or destroy" deer and partridges between April and October, to "trap, snare, or net" partridges, to catch fish by means of drugs or poison, and to "hunt, trap, or fish" on an individual's land without permission. At times these measures were passed separately, and strictures against trespass might encompass no more than specific districts or plantations within a county.[10]

Proponents of game laws cited a "wholesale and ill-seasoned destruction of deer, partridges, and wild turkeys by shooting, hunting, trapping, and other means," and there is no doubt that some planters, relishing the hunt, feared a gross depletion in the supply of game. Yet, if bans on hunting between April and October or November corresponded to the seasons when animals raised their young, they also corresponded closely to the seasons of agricultural labor. Prohibitions against specific fishing practices, moreover, were plainly targeted: poisoning of fish and several other forms of trapping outlawed in the 1870s had long been used by Southern blacks and appear to have had West African roots.[11]

The trespassing ordinances require little explanation, but their

---

Eugene D. Genovese, *Roll, Jordan, Roll: The World the Slaves Made* (New York, 1974), 97–112, 486–90. I have discussed this issue at some length in "Hunting, Fishing, and Foraging: Common Rights and Class Relations in the Postbellum South," *RHR*, XXVI (1982).

9. *Acts and Resolutions of the General Assembly of the State of Georgia, 1872* (Atlanta, 1872), 469; *Acts and Resolutions, 1874* (Atlanta, 1874), 389–401; *Acts and Resolutions, 1876* (Atlanta, 1876), 315–52.

10. *Acts and Resolutions, 1875* (Atlanta, 1875), 296–303. Also see *Acts and Resolutions, 1874*, 389–401; *Acts and Resolutions, 1876*, 315–52.

11. *Acts and Resolutions, 1873* (Atlanta, 1873), 235; Peter Wood, *Black Majority: Negroes in Colonial South Carolina From 1670 to the Stono Rebellion* (New York, 1974), 122–23.

implications were the most far-reaching. For by restricting entrance to unenclosed lands, the planters did not simply limit the freedmen's ability to hunt and fish, to obtain a portion of their subsistence independently; they also began a process of redefining use rights, a process of enlarging absolute and exclusive property. While fee simple landownership had always been the abiding principle, pre–Civil War custom and law turned unimproved acreage into "commons." The slaves could not, of course, freely use the forests as hunting and fishing grounds, though individual planters often permitted it. But blacks understood local custom and expected that it would continue to govern social relations, if the liberties they took upon Emancipation are any indication. Poorer whites in the Black Belt also held to their hunting privileges with great tenacity.[12] In response to the new conditions of the postwar era, however, the elite subjected such common rights to an increasingly withering attack.

The fencing issue, which emerged as a central feature of this attack, also saw conservation, as well as agricultural improvement, serve as justifications for curtailing use rights. The antebellum practice of enclosing crops and turning livestock out to forage long commanded widespread support and worked to the special advantage of small-holders, tenants, and laborers. Only in the Upper South did attempts at reform make any headway prior to the war, and limited headway at that.[13] After 1865, though, agitation won a closer hearing and soon a larger following. In Georgia and other states of the Lower South, planter organizations, such as local and state agricultural societies and the Grange, took the lead. Arguing that the "old habits" threatened the supply of timber, exacted undue expense, and encouraged theft, they called for new laws requiring the fencing of stock rather than crops.[14] And they received eager assistance from railroad companies liable for damages if locomotives struck animals straying on the tracks. According to the presidents of several Georgia railways, these disbursements

12. William Elliott, *Carolina Sports by Land and Water Including Incidents of Devil-Fishing, Wild-Cat, Deer, and Bear Hunting, etc.* (New York, 1859), 254–60; Genovese, *Roll, Jordan, Roll*, 486–90; Guion Griffis Johnson, *Antebellum North Carolina: A Social History* (Chapel Hill, 1937), 555–56.

13. See above, Chapter 2.

14. *The Plantation*, II (June 1871), 323–24; II (July 1871), 355; Memorial of the State Grange, February 4, 1874, Legislative Department, Petitions, Record Group 37/Series 12, GDAH; Hahn, "Hunting, Fishing, and Foraging."

amounted to $70,000 annually, and as one agricultural reformer put it, the open range "impede[d] business" by slowing rail traffic.[15]

The planter class did not close ranks on the fencing question. As with other matters bearing on social relations in the postwar South, some planters clung to the traditional ways. Representatives from many nonplantation counties, particularly in the cattle-raising Wiregrass region, also balked. Consequently, a blanket statewide law failed to pass the assembly. But advocates mustered sufficient strength to see local-option legislation through, and "An Act Relating to Fences and Stock and for the Protection of Crops" obtained approval in 1872. It provided for a county election when fifty freeholders submitted a petition to the county ordinary. All eligible voters, whether they owned property or not, were entitled to cast ballots. If a majority favored the initiative, the law, which forced farmers to enclose their livestock and deemed land boundaries legal fences for crops, would take effect within six months.[16]

Traditionalist planters were not alone in opposing the new fence law in the Black Belt. Small-landholding and landless whites, along with the freedmen, accurately saw the measure as a threat to their ownership of livestock, and in some counties succeeded in defeating, or at least postponing, implementation. As an index of their growing power in the area, however, promoters of the law achieved notable results in relatively short order. By the early 1880s much of the central Plantation Belt had the statute in operation, and it was being pressed vigorously in the southwestern section of the state.[17] While sharing with traditional planters the desire to keep the South a "cotton country," these "reformers" inspired a significant metamorphosis in the character of their class as a whole. For by accepting abolition and searching for new means of labor control, they enabled the landowning elite to withstand the demise of slavery and reassert their authority in the realm of production. In so doing, they contributed to a wider process through which the planters gradually transformed themselves into a type of agrarian bourgeoisie and market relations in agriculture took hold.[18]

15. Carroll County *Times*, January 10, 1873; James C. Bonner, *Georgia's Last Frontier: The Development of Carroll County* (Athens, 1971), 140.

16. *Acts and Resolutions, 1872*, 34–35.

17. Atlanta *Constitution*, November 11, 1883.

18. The recent debate over the character of the postwar South and of its ruling class would be enhanced by further consideration of changing property relations. For an excellent survey and critique of the main points of contention, see Harold D. Woodman,

II

Even before the enactment of local-option legislation, the fencing question drew the attention of Upcountry Georgians. The prominent agricultural writer John Dent, who had spent his antebellum years on a plantation in the Alabama Black Belt before moving to Floyd County, took up the cudgels of agitation in 1871. Directing his "remarks . . . chiefly to the up counties," he nonetheless expressed the sentiments of planter proponents in viewing the issue as a means of squaring Emancipation with commercial agriculture. "Our greatest trouble," Dent declared, "is Labor and Fencing." Shortly thereafter, as the state assembly provided for county-level reform, others in the region added their voices. A correspondent to the Cartersville *Standard and Express* in 1874, emphasizing the "burden" imposed upon farmers by the necessity of fencing their crops, believed the stock law to be the "most important issue occupying the public mind."[19]

That correspondent exaggerated. For if the problem of fencing prompted the energies of men like Dent, who shared the concerns and immediate dilemmas of the planter class, it did not stir the "public mind" in the Upcountry through the mid-1870s. With market relations of production only taking shape and political alignments being refashioned in the region, reformers still lacked the economic and political muscle to mount an assault on customary property rights. Local papers occasionally carried an article urging consideration of the stock law or reporting news of its progress elsewhere. Editors, who generally spoke for commercial interests, rarely made an effort to agitate on the law's behalf, however, questioning instead its suitability to the Upcountry.[20]

Indeed, not before the late 1870s and early 1880s, when the threshold of the new order had been crossed and Independentism had gone into eclipse, was a compaign launched. Spurred, in part, by the deliberations of the state agricultural society, Upcountry landlords and

"Sequel to Slavery: The New History Views the Postbellum South," *JSH*, XLIII (November 1977), 523–54. Also see idem, "Post–Civil War Southern Agriculture and the Law," *AH*, LIII (January 1979), 319–37.

19. *The Plantation*, II (December 1871), 755; Cartersville *Standard and Express*, June 24, 1874.

20. Carroll County *Times*, January 10, 1873, February 22, 1878, June 21, 1878; Cartersville *Standard and Express*, June 24, 1874; Jefferson *Forest News*, September 19, 1879; Gwinnett *Herald*, March 12, 1879.

merchants assumed the mantle of reform, hoping to consolidate their control over the region's economy. Through county newspapers, farmers' clubs, and associations linked to town and commercial elements, they made the stock law a subject of public discussion and, increasingly, acrimonious debate. Following the course charted by the General Assembly, they also provoked heated electoral contests.[21]

Upcountry supporters of the stock law trumpeted the refrains of their counterparts in the Black Belt. "There is considerable interest manifested over the effort now being made in some sections of the South, to abolish the old, unjust laws whereby each farmer is compelled to fence his fields; and to compel instead, the owners of stock to confine them," the Jefferson *Forest News* reported in 1880, adding that "wherever intelligence becomes widely disseminated, the injustice and folly of the present law is recognized." Pointing to the high cost and strenuous labor involved in fencing, the paper believed it "sad evidence of old fogyism, general ignorance, and backwardness of agriculture . . . that such a law as that now in force can exist." Other proponents similarly styled the stock law a means of conservation and a requisite for agricultural "progress." They felt it "absolutely necessary . . . to have such a law . . . from the fact that timber is becoming scarce" and the country overrun "with useless, scrubby stock." Sound reason demanded fencing reform, they maintained, "for we have found that it takes less labor and less expense to fence our stock than it does our crops. . . ." Insisting that the "law would greatly improve both stock and land," they proclaimed that "we must learn to give way to the fittest, for by so doing we will keep prospering."[22]

European agricultural reformers said much the same in favor of enclosures and the abolition of common rights to forage, woodlands, and waste; in America the arguments melded comfortably with the dominant bourgeois currents of the late nineteenth century. But such logic failed to win more than a scattering of acceptance among either the peasantries of Europe or the farming population of Georgia's Upcountry.[23] However much stock-law promoters claimed to speak for

21. Carroll County *Times*, February 22, 1878, March 3, 1882; Jackson *Herald*, September 25, 1885; Agricultural Club of Bartow County, No. 3, Minutes, 1883, GDAH.

22. Jefferson *Forest News*, April 23, 1880; Cherokee *Advance*, April 21, 1880; Carroll County *Times*, September 1, 1882. Also see Jackson *Herald*, March 20, 1885; Carroll County *Times*, September 8, 1882, August 4, 1882; Cottage Home Farm Journal, Floyd County, January 14, 1878, John H. Dent Papers, GDAH.

23. Blum, *End of the Old Order*, 262–71; Marc Bloch, *French Rural History: An Essay on Its Basic Characteristics* (Berkeley, 1966), 197–213.

the interests of Southern agriculturalists in general, their effusions on the benefits of "progress" fell on many deaf, if not hostile, ears. One Paulding County advocate admitted this when he grumbled that "for some reason most men will not take the time to study the advantages in many new, important, and advantageous ideas."[24] Those who took the time to study the matter often found the "new, important ideas" less than "advantageous." They ridiculed the alleged timber shortage as mere fabrication, denied that it was more costly to fence crops than stock, and even questioned the desirability of improved animal husbandry. A Bartow County cultivator said that there was a "great deal of timber . . . on land which can be used for nothing else," while a Carroll County farmer exclaimed that he and others "would be deprived of . . . thousands of acres of land that give our stock pasture . . . if the fence law was passed." T. Ramsden of Gwinnett County, challenging the notion "that it is cheaper to fence in stock than crops," charged that in states like South Carolina, which had the law in effect, "very few tenants, small landowners, and 'poor' people generally own milch cows and hogs," and that "pasturing runs down land much faster than cropping." Another stock-law opponent held that raising better breeds would quickly place livestock beyond the financial reach of the less fortunate.[25]

The fencing debate, as these spokesmen made plain, reflected more than a minor quarrel over the merits of agricultural innovation. Opponents of the stock law did not reject farm improvement per se; rather, they branded the statute a direct attack on the rights and economic welfare of small producers. "[T]he law would benefit the extensive land owners," a disgruntled Gwinnett County denizen wrote, and as one of his neighbors warned, it "would be the greatest curse to the poor laboring men that ever befell them."[26] Petty proprietors rarely had much besides cropland, they argued, for "it requires perhaps all of [their] land to make a support for . . . [their] family," while many whose farms included unimproved acreage "have not a drop of water on it." "What will they do for water for their stock?" they asked. Ramsden suggested that these farmers might be forced to sell out: "A

24. Paulding *New Era*, April 19, 1883.

25. Cartersville *Express*, June 21, 1880; Carroll County *Times*, June 7, 1878, September 8, 1882; Gwinnett *Herald*, October 18, 1882. Also see Carroll *Free Press*, May 1, 1885; Gwinnett *Herald*, June 29, 1885.

26. Gwinnett *Herald*, September 20, 1882, June 29, 1885. Also see Carroll *Free Press*, June 19, 1885, June 26, 1885; Jackson *Herald*, June 17, 1881; Carroll County *Times*, May 17, 1878; Cartersville *Express*, June 21, 1880.

man owning 65 acres in a stock law county rented a three-horse crop in this county . . . because he had not enough land to tend and pasture both." The measure threatened to divest yeoman freeholders of the means of production and subsistence and, therefore, undermine their "independence." "The stock law will divide the people . . . into classes similar to the patricians and plebeians of ancient Rome," a man who farmed 125 acres in Carroll County grimly predicted, while James W. Andrews of Gwinnett County concluded that "it would be proof of insanity for a poor man that don't own as much as 100 acres of land to vote for [the stock law]."[27]

Tenants and laborers seemed even clearer losers should fencing reform be effected. "We have yet to find a poor man of much intelligence who advocates 'no fence,'" a Jackson County correspondent reported, "while it is justly regarded by tenants, or non-landowners, as a measure calculated seriously to injure their rights and privileges." Access to forage enabled landless whites and blacks to raise work animals and other livestock of their own. With a horse or mule, a cow and some hogs, a tenant could strike a better contract and meet part of his family's basic needs. The stock law, then, spelled nothing but trouble. In the opinion of one Carroll County inhabitant, "no fence in this county is ultimately going to be the ruin of the people and most especially the poor people that have no where to keep their stock [and] . . . are entirely dependent on the landowners for pasture." He did not stand alone in forecasting that if the new statute became operative "not one man out of ten will let them have pasture room free of rent," and in all likelihood landlords would "charge them more than double what their milk and cow is worth." Few laborers could absorb the expense, and they would soon be dispossessed.[28]

A Jackson County defender of the open range detailed another possible scenario. "You just let the stock law pass," he explained,

> and in five years the landowners will say to the renters, "Well, I would like to rent you land, but I am tired of keeping other people's stock in my pasture, and if I rent you must sell your stock, or cut and

27. Gwinnett *Herald*, June 29, 1885, October 18, 1882, September 20, 1882; Carroll County *Times*, August 25, 1882.

28. Jackson *Herald*, June 17, 1881; Carroll *Free Press*, June 19, 1885. Also see Gwinnett *Herald*, June 29, 1885; Carroll County *Times*, May 17, 1878. The term *no fence* also refers to the stock law, reflecting the wording in the 1872 local-option statute. When the term *fence* is used, it refers to customary methods of enclosure.

split rails and make a pasture for them." Well, by next year his pasture fence wants repairing. "Well, now I will rent to you again if you will cut and split rails and reset the fence around my pasture." Well, he wants to rent again. "Well, you must sell your stock. I have two pastures now, but I want to change my stock from one to the other. In fact I don't want any other man's stock on my place. I will give you five dollars for that old cow, and three for that sow and six or seven pigs, and that old horse or mule of yours I don't want, but I will give you fifteen dollars for him. Well, as long as you are here and have been with me for two years, I'll do a little better—I'll give you twenty. Now I have gotten you; I can pull the rope. If you want a horse to go after the doctor, or to the mill, or anywhere, you must pay fifty cents for him. And if you want any milk, just pay me ten cents per quart. And if you want any butter . . . I will let you have 4 or 5 lbs at say fifty cents per lb." Well, Mr. Renter wants some pork. "Well, I'll let you have one of those shoats for three dollars that I bought from you last fall!"

Thus, he and others believed that "should such a law be adopted . . . in ten years not one tenant in twenty would own any stock."[29]

Stock-law advocates readily conceded that the issue divided Upcountry Georgian along class lines, but argued that the split stemmed from misapprehensions. "Three classes" opposed fencing reform, a Gwinnett County proponent complained: blacks; tenants and croppers who "from some conjectured up falacy of reason will vote with Africa"; and "men that have land" but "were 'born under a fence' [and] can't rise above their raising no matter how things and circumstances have changed." Scoffing at the idea that "the stock law would benefit the rich and oppress the poor," promoters insisted that the statute required landowners to provide pasture, that only minimal fees would be charged for its use, and, indeed, that tenants would be the beneficiaries.[30] Jackson County's "Progress," convinced that what was good for landlords was good for laborers, found it difficult to believe that poor whites and blacks risked victimization. "The income of tenants and wages of hirelings will be regulated by the profits of the land owners," wrote this devotee of liberal economics.[31]

29. Jefferson *Forest News*, January 14, 1881; Jackson *Herald*, August 21, 1883; Gwinnett *Herald*, September 20, 1882.

30. Gwinnett *Herald*, August 18, 1885, April 12, 1882; Cartersville *Express*, June 29, 1876; Carroll *Free Press*, May 1, 1885; Carroll County *Times*, September 1, 1882.

31. Jackson *Herald*, June 24, 1881.

Although an occasional tenant voiced agreement, even to the point of suggesting that fencing reform would extend landownership,[32] most had nothing but contempt for such reasoning. It is said "there never was anything that brought more relief to the tenant and laborer than the stock law," one noted sarcastically. "We agree with him there, as they are relieved of the privileges our fathers established. They will be relieved of the care and use of the cow, the hog, and in short, all the necessities, only as they are furnished by the landholders." John Stogner of Carroll County put in historical perspective what he, too, saw as a ploy:

> We were told in 1859 [sic] that secession was the greatest thing that the South could do, so it was to lead her to destruction. It was a rich man's war and a poor man's fight, so will the stock law be a benefit to a few landlords who have plenty of water on their lands, while nine-tenths of the people will be in a deplorable condition.

"God makes the grass[,] the mountains crown[,] and corn in the valleys grow," he concluded, "so let's not try to deprive our poor neighbors from receiving his blessing. . . ."[33]

Stogner's use of religious injunction as a counterpoint to political deception was not simply a polemical device. It bespoke a significant line of controversy running through the fencing debate. For if adversaries crossed swords over what appeared to be purely economic concerns, they imbued those concerns with deeper cultural and ideological meaning. What underlay contention over the material consequences of the stock law were considerably different, and increasingly antagonistic, ideas about social relations and property rights.

Thus, after parading the inconveniences he attributed to the traditional system of grazing, a contributor to the Jefferson *Forest News* set forth a maxim eagerly embraced by the supporters of reform: "The land outside a farm is as much the property of the farmer as that he may cultivate, and truly in essential justice no stock of other's has any right thereon without express permission." Other stock-law proponents similarly lectured that "a farmer's corn is just as much his property as his timber, and as his neighbor is prohibited from entering on the land and cutting down his trees, so he should be required to prevent his stock

32. Cherokee *Advance*, July 1, 1882; Jackson *Herald*, June 17, 1881, August 3, 1883; Carroll *Free Press*, May 15, 1881.

33. Carroll County *Times*, September 8, 1882; Carroll *Free Press*, June 26, 1885.

straying to devour and trample down the corn." These spokesmen found the open range a manifestation of "custom" rather than "law." They acknowledged that "when the land belonged to the government it was right for all to pasture" it, but once "the government transferred those lands to different individuals," no one had the "right to trespass on another man's land." "Before a man buys a horse, cow, or hog," a Jackson County advocate prescribed, "he should have something to feed them on."[34]

Regarding timeworn grazing practices as a custom dignified by little more than peculiar circumstances and hardheadedness, supporters of the stock law elevated absolute property to a moral, if not a natural, right. One contemptuously dismissed common foraging as a "privilege" or "favor" bordering upon theft. "My neighbor has (legally) as much right to pasture my enclosed land as he has my unenclosed, as his stock . . . robs it of its vegetable matter . . . making it poorer every day." J. M. Green of Carroll County held that the "idea of fencing a man's possessions against a neighbor's stock is a creation of local statute, and contrary to natural rights, nature, and common sense," adding that the "border of a man's possession is the supposed wall that protects them, and nobody has the right by himself or his cattle to trespass upon them." Rejecting any obligation to "feed another man's stock," the reformers bluntly proclaimed that "what is mine I have a right to do as I please with and no man has a right to graze my land whether enclosed or not."[35] Property, in short, was absolute in the individual, its ownership mediated solely by the market.

Stock-law men may have considered these arguments to be self-evident; others did not. As a Paulding County reformer grudgingly observed, "It is true that it is unlawful for the stock of one man to trespass upon the domain of another, still the privilege has been in vogue so long . . . that to most men it would seem to be a species of tyranny to suddenly enforce the restraints of law." Indeed, opponents of "no fence" reserved their deepest indignation for the legal and moral side of the question. Unfurling the banner of "equal rights, equal liberty, and equal privileges," of "equal rights to all and special

34. Jefferson *Forest News*, April 23, 1880; *The Plantation*, II (July 1871), 388; Jackson *Herald*, April 3, 1885.

35. Jackson *Herald*, May 27, 1881; Carroll County *Times*, January 6, 1882; Carroll *Free Press*, May 8, 1885. Also see Jackson *Herald*, June 17, 1881; Gwinnett *Herald*, August 30, 1882; Carroll County *Times*, June 7, 1878.

privileges to none," they elaborated a vision of the cooperative commonwealth and defended the claims of the community of producers.[36]

Stock-law opponents viewed local custom, not as an aberration, but as an expression of natural right. "The woods . . . were put here by our Creator for a benefit to his people," W. D. Lovvorn of Carroll County declared, "and I don't think it right to deprive a large majority to please a minority." Abner Nixon, another Carroll County farmer, also invoked higher authority in defense of traditional grazing practices: "The citizens of this county have and always have had the legal, moral, and Bible right to let their stock . . . run at large. We all knew this when we purchased our lands."[37] A Gwinnett County spokesman, questioning whether "a man has . . . [a] moral right to feed his stock on other's land," nonetheless accepted that "he has . . . a legal right derived from custom to the range." Echoing these sentiments, "Fairplay" of Jackson County reckoned that "our present system is an old one—so old that it would seem cruel to attempt an innovation upon it. From long usage our people have become accustomed to it, and any change in or abridgment of it will unquestionably work serious injury to a large number of our citizens."[38]

The force of custom stemmed from its connection with an array of social relations and cultural norms that the open range epitomized in a particularly compelling way. Common grazing was more than an expedient of frontier life: long before the 1880s the frontier passed well beyond the Georgia Upcountry. Common grazing embodied distinct ideas about labor, community, independence, and the role of the state—about commonwealth. A Jackson County correspondent, therefore, could say that advocates of the stock law were "men who never split but very few, if any, rails," and that he did not "call a man a farmer until he does keep his fields fenced, and well fenced at that." Such a distinction, based upon the performance of manual labor, served as a key element of nineteenth-century producer ideology, and its meaning was deepened by a cooperative principle that challenged the tenets of bourgeois individualism and property, that challenged the hegemony of the marketplace. "L.F.L." of Carroll County made that clear in tersely expressing what he saw as the abiding logic of the open range: "While

36. Paulding *New Era*, April 19, 1883; Carroll County *Times*, June 21, 1878.

37. Carroll *Free Press*, June 5, 1885, June 26, 1885.

38. Gwinnett *Herald*, October 18, 1882; Jackson *Herald*, June 17, 1881.

my cow is on my neighbor's land, eating grass, his is on mine, that makes it all right."³⁹

Looking to the state government as the protector of the public good, these rural folk had no doubt that common grazing rights received more than local sanction. A Carroll County yeoman farmer, wishing to "controvert [the] proposition [that] 'What is mine I have a right to do as I please with,'" explained the fundamental principles. "No man can deny that all the land of this country was once common property, belonged to all the people of Georgia in common as public domain," he confidently stated, "all once had a perfect right to graze it in common." "How or when did any of them loose [sic] that right?" he asked rhetorically, finding less than persuasive the argument "that they lost it in that game of chance called a lottery, when the drawee became the owner . . . to do as he pleased with." "[T]he fence law was in force at that time and each drawee, if he raises crops on his land, was required to enclose it," the farmer reminded his audience. He believed this to be unmistakable proof that "it was understood that all citizens of this country still retained the rights to let their stock run at large on all lands not so enclosed." And, in his eyes, "as citizens of this grand old commonwealth . . . they still . . . have that RIGHT."⁴⁰

One landlord and stock-law supporter fitfully ascribed to such attitudes "the spirit of communism fully displayed." Yet, opponents of the law hardly favored the abolition of private property. Like small producers elsewhere in the South and throughout the United States, they deemed property ownership the basis of freedom and independence and assailed fencing reform precisely because it threatened expropriation. The fiery L. J. Jones knew what he was about when he urged "every man [to] come and vote for fence if he wishes to be a free man."⁴¹ From the vantage point of the late twentieth century, this defense of both private property and common rights may appear peculiar if not contradictory; in the Georgia Upcountry of the late nineteenth century, it was neither. Instead, it reflected a complex world view, rooted in persisting strains of preindustrial republicanism, that linked the individual and the collective through the medium of *productive* labor and *productive* property. The freedom to which Jones and

39. Jefferson *Forest News*, January 14, 1881; Carroll *Free Press*, n.d.

40. Carroll *Free Press*, May 8, 1885.

41. Cottage Home Farm Journal, Floyd County, November 17, 1886, Dent Papers; Carroll *Free Press*, May 15, 1885.

others adhered was not merely that founded upon ownership of one's person and exchange in the marketplace, but that founded upon control over productive resources, labor time, and subsistence which, in turn, could be realized only through membership in the commonwealth of producers. The stock-law controversy set the republicanism of those producers against the values of the free market.[42]

III

The fencing issue ultimately came down to being a matter of politics and political power, and elections brought no less determined a response than did the debate ringing through the newspapers. During the weeks preceding an election, heated discussion spilled into public forums, political gatherings, and casual social meetings. Jackson County denizens assembled at the county seat of Jefferson one Saturday to hear "Mr. John N. Ross . . . [and] Capt. A. C. Thompson . . . give speech[es] on the stock law question . . . one for and the other against the fence." In Carroll County the grand jury shifted attention from the dockets in the fall of 1881 to deliberate on the issue.[43] Candidates for the state legislature in Cherokee County felt compelled to stake out a position during the course of the campaign.[44] The Gwinnett *Herald* believed the "fence law . . . of much more importance to the people of this county than [who] . . . shall be nominated for Governor." And, apparently, that opinion was shared widely. "The stock law is being fiercely discussed by the farmers," one Upcountry paper reported, while another noted that "the feeling is bitter between the two sides and the excitement is up to a white heat."[45]

Considering that the local-option statute of 1872 required only thirty

---

42. On the development and legacy of eighteenth-century republicanism, particularly as it regards petty producers and the sociopolitical struggles of the nineteenth century, see Eric Foner, *Tom Paine and Revolutionary America* (New York, 1976); Sean Wilentz, *Chants Democratic: New York City and the Rise of the American Working Class* (New York, 1984); Montgomery, *Beyond Equality*; Fink, *Workingmen's Democracy*. There has been growing attention to the impact of republicanism in the South, though largely as it shaped the world view of the planter class. But for a sweeping and provocative treatment, see J. Mills Thornton III, *Politics and Power in a Slave Society: Alabama, 1800–1860* (Baton Rouge, 1978).

43. Jackson *Herald*, September 22, 1882; Carroll County *Times*, October 14, 1881.

44. Cherokee *Advance*, July 10, 1884, September 4, 1884, September 18, 1884.

45. Gwinnett *Herald*, June 29, 1885, October 14, 1884; Cherokee *Advance*, November 24, 1883.

days notice before polling and that contests normally occurred in July before crops were "laid by," election day brought impressive turnouts. Beginning in the early 1880s, Upcountry Georgians, white and black, marched to the ballot box in numbers approaching 80 percent of those eligible to vote—and this several years after Georgia had instituted a retroactive poll tax. No other local issue, including prohibition, elicited such a response; it nearly matched that for national elections, which had the advantage of greater publicity and regular, post-harvest scheduling. In Jackson County, the vote in an 1881 stock-law election in fact exceeded the vote in a congressional race the preceding year when the controversial Independent Emory Speer had his hat in the ring.[46] Thus, the Atlanta *Constitution* observed that the "contests in the counties over fence and no fence have been as exciting as contests usually are in which the pockets and muscle of the voter is concerned," and a local paper could marvel that an election drew "perhaps one of the largest crowds ever seen."[47]

The voting returns gave stock-law advocates no cause to rejoice and indicated the extent of popular resistance. In county after county, the law met resounding defeat. About three-quarters of the voters in Carroll, Jackson, and Gwinnett counties rejected the measure during the early 1880s, and in Bartow County the opposition amassed 90 percent of the vote. Results from other Upcountry counties proved little different. Banks County saw "no fence defeated in 1882"; Forsyth County opposed it "by 1000 majority"; Hart County voters turned it down "by 500 majority"; in Floyd County it was "badly beaten in 1881"; and Franklin County set back "no fence . . . . by a 4 to 1 margin" the same year. Only in those counties bordering the Black Belt, such as Campbell, Clayton, and Rockdale, did the stock law obtain considerable support and occasionally manage to carry the day.[48]

Within most Upcountry counties, however, some militia districts showed the stock law more favor. These districts were not distinguished clearly by their racial composition or land-tenure arrangements: the racial mix changed relatively little from district to district and blacks

46. Jackson *Herald*, July 8, 1881; George L. Jones, "William H. Felton and the Independent Democratic Movement in Georgia" (Ph.D. diss., University of Georgia, 1974), 170 fn.

47. Atlanta *Constitution*, November 11, 1883; Jackson *Herald*, July 1, 1887.

48. Carroll County *Times*, January 11, 1882; Jackson *Herald*, July 8, 1881; Gwinnett *Herald*, July 14, 1883; Cartersville *Express*, July 15, 1880; Atlanta *Constitution*, November 11, 1883.

generally threw their weight against the law; the proportion of landholders varied throughout the counties in no readily discernible pattern.[49] Rather, the districts lending the stock law its substantial support tended to have the closest links to market centers, the highest real-estate assessments and per capita wealth, and the greatest concentrations of land held by large landowners. It was here that merchants, big landlords, and other commercial interests wielded most influence and authority. Poorer, rural districts having more evenly distributed landholdings, on the other hand, rejected the law overwhelmingly and at times almost unanimously. Here small farmers feeling the new strains of staple agriculture had their firmest cultural foothold.[50]

When, for example, Carroll County voters went to the polls in 1882, they defeated fencing reform by 1,616 to 620. Yet two districts turned majorities for it: the Tenth District, which included the largest town of Carrollton, and the Second District, which contained the town of Villa Rica. Indeed, over half of the countywide votes for the stock law came from these two districts alone. The law also obtained some backing in the town and village districts of Temple, Bowdon, Roopville, and Whitesburg. Together, these six districts provided the stock law with 80 percent of its votes. The eight remaining rural districts collectively spurned the statute by over six to one, with some delivering over 90 percent of their votes to the retention of common grazing rights (see Table 7.1). Another election several months later brought a larger turnout with much the same results.[51]

The fencing contest had similar dimensions in Jackson County. First casting ballots in 1881, voters defeated the law by the wide margin of 1,379 to 478. Unlike those in Carroll County, not one of the districts in Jackson County registered majorities in favor of reform, but it is telling

49. See Appendix, Tables XI–XII. Interestingly, while very few blacks owned land in the Upcountry, the proportion of black landowners tended to be higher in those districts most strongly opposed to the stock law. In Carroll County as a whole, for instance, not one black in ten owned land, but more than three in ten owned land in the rural districts of Kansas, Shiloh, and Flint Corner, where the stock law was defeated by about 90 percent of the votes.

50. See Appendix, Tables XI–XII, and above, Tables 7.1 and 7.2. Changes in militia district boundary lines as well as the carving out of new districts between 1860 and 1880 make precise calculations difficult, but there is good reason to believe that the militia districts most strongly opposed to the stock law experienced particularly large increases in cotton production during this period.

51. Carroll County *Times*, January 11, 1882, January 18, 1882, September 9, 1882.

Table 7.1 Militia Districts and the Stock Law, Carroll County

	Stock-Law[1] Districts	Anti-Stock-Law[2] Districts
Per Capita Wealth[3]	$1,129	$617
Percentage of Total Population White	81.4%	96.0%
Percentage of Landowners	61.3%	60.3%
Average Size of Landholdings (Acres)	144.2	125.4
Percentage of Land in Holdings of 500 or More Acres	17.9%	11.6%
Number of Holdings of 500 or More Acres	26	10
Number of Mercantile Firms	57	2

[1] Denotes districts most favorable to the stock law over several elections (over 40 percent of their votes for the law). Includes Carrollton, Villa Rica, Temple, and Roopville.

[2] Denotes districts most opposed to the stock law over several elections (under 20 percent of their votes for the law). Includes Smithfield, Kansas, New Mexico, Lowell, Turkey Creek, Flint Corner, and Shiloh.

[3] Total wealth divided by total number of persons on tax rolls.

Sources: Carroll County Tax Digest, 1890; Carroll County *Times*, January 11, 1882, September 9, 1882; Carroll *Free Press*, July 3, 1885, July 8, 1887.

that over 60 percent of the votes received by the stock law came from the three districts in which the towns of Jefferson, Harmony Grove, and Pendergrass were located. When the town and village districts of Wilson and House are added, the total climbs to over 80 percent. Excepting the wealthiest, the rural districts rendered only 12 percent of their votes to support the statute, and in the two districts previously strongholds of Independentism, the law failed to win even 10-percent approval. These districts had smaller farms and poorer farmers (see Table 7.2). Furthermore, they had undergone a dramatic shift since the war: while they had produced the fewest bales of cotton per farm in 1860, they produced among the most by 1880.[52] Symbolizing larger class and cultural divisions, the countryside rallied against the towns.

52. Jackson *Herald*, July 8, 1881. Again, changes in district lines complicate the picture, but a rough estimate suggests that those districts most strongly opposed to the stock law saw more than a fourfold increase in cotton production between 1860 and 1880, while those districts most favorable to the stock law saw only a bit over a twofold increase. See Manuscript Census, Georgia, Jackson County, Schedule II, 1860, 1880.

Table 7.2 Militia Districts and the Stock Law, Jackson County

	Stock-Law[1] Districts	Anti-Stock-Law[2] Districts
Per Capita Wealth[3]	$1,081	$646
Percentage of Total Population White	74.7%	70.7%
Percentage of Landowners	49.3%	49.0%
Average Size of Landholdings (Acres)	169.1	159.4
Percentage of Land in Holdings of 500 or More Acres	24.7%	15.5%
Number of Holdings of 500 or More Acres	35	19
Number of Mercantile Firms	47	8

[1] Denotes districts most favorable to the stock law over several elections (over 40 percent of their votes for the law). Includes Jefferson, Minishes, Wilson, Cunningham, and Harrisburg.

[2] Denotes districts most opposed to the stock law over several elections (under 20 percent of their votes for the law). Includes Clarksboro, Newtown, Chandlers, Santafe, and Randolph.

[3] Total wealth divided by total number of persons on tax rolls.

Sources: Jackson County Tax Digest, 1890; Jackson *Herald*, July 8, 1881, September 14, 1883.

Electoral returns from other Upcountry counties gave further evidence of this configuration. Bartow County voters flocked to the polls in 1880 and blasted the stock law by 2,086 to 223. Seventy percent of the ballots in the law's behalf, however, came from the four town districts of Cartersville, Euharlee, Kingston, and Adairsville. Four rural districts provided the remaining 30 percent, while two others voted unanimously against reform. Much the same story unfolded in Gwinnett County. Voters sent the stock law down to defeat 1,565 to 447 in an 1885 contest. Although support for reform was more evenly dispersed among the districts, those including the towns of Lawrenceville, Norcross, Buford, and Duluth delivered 40 percent of it. The nine rural districts lent the other 60 percent.[53]

Disappointed stock-law advocates did not need statistics to comprehend the parameters of their failure. Finding "it simply . . . a question of Labor vs Capital," the Floyd County landlord John Dent declared that "agrarianism rules[,] the Niggers and white trash voting against No Fence." Others reached the same conclusion with somewhat

53. Cartersville *Express*, July 15, 1880; Gwinnett *Herald*, July 14, 1885.

less passion and contempt. "Nonlandholders" in general and the "colored element" in particular stood "solid against the law," they insisted, believing "specious . . . the objection set forth" that, should the measure pass, landless whites and blacks could not "keep any stock on their own account."[54] Discouragement only steeled the reformers' determination, however, for the initial elections did not settle the issue. The 1872 statute made further contests possible, provided that the requisite number of signatures could be obtained, and proponents moved on several fronts to reverse their fortunes. They were, as the Jackson *Herald* observed after one abortive effort, "on the track again and thoroughly in earnest."[55]

This time, stock-law supporters launched a more organized drive. Utilizing the Democratic party, which they had come to dominate, and especially local agricultural clubs, they waged a campaign throughout the counties. One such club in Bartow County set the agitation of fencing reform as its first task when it formed during the early 1880s. The Norcross Agricultural Club of Gwinnett County, which had a longer history, resolved "to contribute articles on the advantages of the stock law" to the county newspaper, as did similar bodies elsewhere. Associations were founded, moreover, with the sole purpose of pressing for a popular mandate. Thus, the Apple Valley Stock Law Club in Jackson County, consisting primarily of prominent Democrats, county officials, merchants, and substantial farmers, met in the fall of 1885 and proceeded "to canvass the District in the interest of the" law.[56]

Electoral fraud and coercion, so familiar to postbellum Southern politics, also came into play. Neither camp could claim innocence, to be sure. As one paper put it, there was "some tail pulling on both sides."[57] But opponents of the stock law issued most of the complaints, citing cases of bribery, threats, ballot-box stuffing, and the tossing out of votes. Manipulating the choices on tickets in an effort to confuse the electorate proved a common method of deception. The local-option statute prescribed that voters favor either "Fence" or "No Fence," the latter

54. Cottage Home Farm Journal, Floyd County, December 15, 1881, October 24, 1883, Dent Papers; Carroll *Free Press*, September 10, 1886; Carroll County *Times*, September 1, 1882; Jackson *Herald*, June 10, 1881.

55. *Acts and Resolutions, 1872*, 36; Jackson *Herald*, July 20, 1883.

56. Agricultural Club of Bartow County, No. 3, Minutes, June 1884; Gwinnett *Herald*, August 9, 1882; Jackson *Herald*, September 25, 1885.

57. Jackson *Herald*, September 2, 1887.

meaning the stock law—a choice hardly designed to foster clarity in any event. Returns sent in by the districts, though, often included a considerable array of ballots. One Carroll County district reported: "For Stock Law 73," "For Fence 68," "Fence 30," "A Fence 2," "The Fence 2." On another occasion several districts sent in almost 200 ballots marked "more fence and better fence." In each instance the local official threw out a sizable number to the advantage of the stock-law forces.[58] Recognizing the impact of the black vote, reformers not infrequently "promised to pay [their taxes] if they would vote for no fence," while in one case promoters, attempting "to please the negroes," chartered them an excursion train to Atlanta—on the day of an election.[59]

These tactics brought only limited rewards. Despite drawing a greater percentage of the vote in countywide elections as the 1880s progressed, the stock law continued to meet defeat, as initial alignments broadly persisted. Carroll County deliberated five separate times between 1882 and 1890. Each time the measure was rejected, each time support for reform came primarily from the town districts, and each time the margin of difference narrowed. In 1882, 73 percent of the voters opposed the law; three years later the figure dropped to 67 percent; and in 1890 it declined to 61 percent. So, too, in Jackson County. In both 1881 and 1883, staunch resistance in the rural districts turned the stock law down, though reformers increased their share of the vote from 26 percent to 33 percent. And in neighboring Gwinnett County the years between 1885 and 1891 saw the vote against the law slide from 78 percent to 61 percent. It was a trend that held some promise for the elite, but one that certainly did not put victory close at hand.[60]

Indeed, frustrated stock-law advocates saw in these results the logic, in one man's words, of "pauper" democracy. As early as 1875, the state commissioner of agriculture, a leading fighter for reform, reasoned that "the present Act, which leaves the question of 'fencing stock' or 'fencing crops' to the *voters* of several counties is unjust, since it allows non-freeholders, who generally constitute a majority of voters in every

58. *Acts and Resolutions, 1872,* 36; Jefferson *Forest News,* November 19, 1880; Carroll *Free Press,* March 18, 1887; Carroll County *Times,* September 23, 1881, October 7, 1881.

59. Carroll County *Times,* September 23, 1881, October 7, 1881.

60. Ibid., January 13, 1882, September 9, 1882; Carroll *Free Press,* July 3, 1885, July 8, 1887, June 4, 1890; Jackson *Herald,* July 8, 1881, September 14, 1883; Gwinnett *Herald,* July 14, 1885, July 7, 1891.

county, to decide a question of policy and economy in which they have no direct interest." Hence, he explained that "the most equitable way of disposing of the question . . . is by legislative enactment leaving its decision to the *freeholders* of each county." A contributor to the *Dixie Farmer*, an agricultural journal, also believed that "in elections under the law . . . the voting should be restricted to the freeholders, as they are the class upon whom the entire expense of keeping up fences devolves, and whose rights alone are involved in the question."[61]

Upcountry reformers soon joined the chorus. "I could not find where a man has any right to vote in matters where he had no interest," a correspondent to the Jackson *Herald* announced in 1885, adding that "the man who has no land hasn't any interest in the matter and has no right to vote." A like-minded resident of Carroll County, acknowledging the opposition of "the non landholders and laboring class" to the stock law, bluntly stated that "none should be allowed to vote on this question except landholders." "[I]f the poor are going to hold this country back and be an impossible lump in the tube of progress," this spokesman scoffed, ". . . build a poor house like a palace . . . and send them there and feed them on cake and wine and let the country go on."[62]

Other members of the elite viewed the fencing conflict as a product of a more pervasive dilemma. Arguing that the stock law "would be our best plan" but that the votes of "two thirds of our population [who] own no land, but own on an average of one cow and two or three pigs" defeated it, John Dent drew a larger lesson. "Such show that capitalists and tax payers of the country are at the mercy of a class of men whose only capital are their votes," he exclaimed. "Such is the result of the Constitution and laws of this country, and ever will be so long as the pauper class are allowed a vote, and nothing but a restriction on the voters qualifications will ever protect capital from such injustice and wrongs. . . ." A Carroll County advocate also attributed the nation's problems to the fact "that the negroes and one fourth of the whites have been allowed the privilege of going to the ballot box," and hoped he would "see the day, when none will be allowed to vote, who do not own

61. Georgia Department of Agriculture, *Annual Report of Thomas P. Janes, Commissioner of Agriculture of the State of Georgia for the Year 1875* (Atlanta, 1876), 66; *Dixie Farmer*, quoted in Jefferson *Forest News*, September 10, 1880.

62. Jackson *Herald*, April 3, 1885, June 24, 1885; Carroll County *Times*, May 3, 1878.

so much property. . . ."[63] Although no movement to disfranchise the propertyless succeeded in this case, these sentiments help account for the antidemocratic tide that swept not only the South but the entire United States in the years after Reconstruction.[64]

For the mass of Upcountry yeomen, tenants, and laborers, these blasts against democratic rights confirmed fears that the stock law threatened more than their economic welfare. One compared the law's promoters "to the Breckinridge ring of Democrats that seceded from the Democratic convention at Charleston," and warned that unless "every man has the right to be his own judge about casting his vote," the "common farmer" would be led into the same "trouble as they were in 1860." The "monied men" wished to lord over the polity, another cried as he called upon "the poor people to open their eyes and come forward and stand up for their rights . . . and show [them] that they cannot have things their own way all the time." At stake was not merely economic independence but the very survival of the democratic commonwealth of producers.[65]

As the fencing conflict wore on, the weight of numbers proved an increasingly poor match for the weight of superior resources. Having the support of landlords, merchants, and business interests throughout the state, holding sway in the local Democratic party, and enlisting the aid of county newspaper editors and officeholders, stock-law advocates marshaled considerable political clout. And success eventually came their way when they availed themselves of an amendment to the 1872 local-option statute that permitted implementation at the district level. Through identical procedures of petition and election, one district alone within a county could enact the measure, and beginning in the

63. Cottage Home Farm Journal, Floyd County, January 14, 1878, Dent Papers; Carroll County *Times*, June 7, 1878.

64. The disfranchisement of Southern blacks in the late nineteenth and early twentieth centuries is quite familiar. But as J. Morgan Kousser has recently argued, suffrage restriction was directed against the poor of both races and stood as only the most flagrant manifestation of a national trend. See Kousser, *The Shaping of Southern Politics*, 52–53 and passim. We still know relatively little about developments in the North during the Gilded Age and Progressive era, but for some suggestive evidence see Walter Dean Burnham, *Critical Elections and the Mainsprings of American Politics* (New York, 1970), 11–90; Leon Fink, "Class Conflict in the Gilded Age: The Figure and the Phantom," *RHR*, III (Fall–Winter 1975), 56–73; and especially Michael McGerr, "The Decline of Popular Politics, 1876–1926" (Ph.D. diss., Yale University, 1984).

65. Carroll *Free Press*, June 5, 1885, June 19, 1885.

mid-1880s the districts became the centers of contention.[66] Not surprisingly, towns and wealthier districts stepped out front, but not without concerted effort. Other rural districts were far more troublesome, and adversaries locked horns in a struggle that could engender law suits and violence.

Thus, in 1884 fifty-three residents of Carroll County's Carrollton district signed a petition requesting a stock law election. Though they failed to achieve victory, two years later the town council passed an ordinance making it "unlawful for any cow, steer, bull, calf, heifer, hog, pig, sheep [etc.] to run at large within the corporate limits." The next year, by 353 to 251, voters extended the law's jurisdiction over the surrounding countryside.[67] The Villa Rica district had its first election in the fall of 1885. While returns had the stock law narrowly defeated, supporters charged irregularities and appealed to the county ordinary for a ruling. He found in the reformers' favor and awarded them the contest. By the end of 1887, Villa Rica and Carrollton had been joined by the town and village districts of Temple, Roopville, Whitesburg, and Bowdon.[68]

The rural districts of Carroll County offered greater resistance. Voters in Fairplay rejected the stock law in 1885 by a margin of 85 to 56, although the results were overturned after a legal battle. So, too, in the Kansas district, when local officials reversed an electoral majority against the law in 1887. The relatively well-to-do County Line district passed the measure that same year, but in poorer Cross Plains, Shiloh, and Lowell the stock law met defeat.[69] Gradually, however, even these areas of traditionally adamant opposition came into line: Shiloh approved the law in 1889, Cross Plains did so when it voted for a second time several months later, and in the next year Flint Corner and Smithfield followed, the latter only after an initially disputed election. By 1891 all except the Lowell and New Mexico districts had abandoned the open range.[70]

66. *Acts and Resolutions, 1880–1881*, 79–81.

67. Carroll *Free Press*, July 4, 1884, March 26, 1886, April 1, 1887.

68. Ibid., September 4, 1885, March 18, 1887, April 1, 1887, September 9, 1887, September 23, 1887. Also see Bonner, *Georgia's Last Frontier*, 141–42.

69. Carroll *Free Press*, September 4, 1885, April 1, 1887, April 15, 1887, June 3, 1887, June 24, 1887, December 16, 1887, September 10, 1889; Bonner, *Georgia's Last Frontier*, 141–42.

70. Carroll *Free Press*, March 1, 1889, August 2, 1889, July 18, 1890; Bonner, *Georgia's Last Frontier*, 142–43.

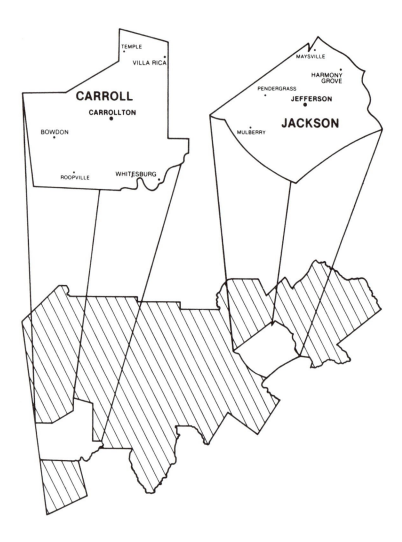

CARROLL AND JACKSON COUNTIES
1880'S

Similar developments unfolded in Jackson County. After voters turned down the stock law in countywide elections of 1881 and 1883, reform agitation looked to the districts. Complaining that he "can't keep stock off the courthouse grounds" and that "the county can't afford to make a public pasture of her property in this way," the sheriff, among others, sought to "improve" at least their own locales. By virtue of town ordinances or district balloting, Jefferson and Harmony Grove, along with three of the wealthier rural districts, put some form of the stock law into effect between 1885 and 1887.[71] Elsewhere in Jackson County, recalcitrance was the order of the day; fencing reform made no inroads. It took a special legislative act, later ruled unconstitutional, to bring the entire county to heel by the end of the decade.[72]

So it went throughout the Upcountry. The Gwinnett County electorate began casting ballots on district-level implementation a bit earlier than either Jackson County or Carroll County voters did. Yet until 1884, "in every instance 'fence' . . . carried." Thereafter the stock law made steady progress, and by 1887 the district embracing the county seat of Lawrenceville, in addition to six others, had adopted the statute.[73] Cherokee County took an even longer route to reform. Commencing in 1886, district voting initially gave stock-law advocates little cause for cheer, as most chose to retain the open range. Several districts stood firm enough to weather two or three elections.[74] But as the 1880s drew to a close, momentum gathered for reform. Wealthier districts south of the Etowah River slowly approved the law, and by the spring of 1891, gains had been made on the poorer north side. "It may take several trials to decide the question," the Cherokee *Advance* predicted, "but . . . it is quite probable that these districts [north of the Etowah] will also be forced to adopt the stock law." The years between 1885 and 1890 also saw districts in Paulding, Cobb, Floyd, Forsyth, Franklin, Milton, Hall, Douglas, Banks, and Heard counties accept the

71. Jackson *Herald*, March 27, 1885, July 1, 1887, September 2, 1887, November 11, 1887.

72. Ibid., March 12, 1886; *Publications of the Georgia Department of Agriculture*, XV (1889), 117–23.

73. Gwinnett *Herald*, October 17, 1883, September 23, 1884, October 14, 1884, September 27, 1887; *Publications of the Georgia Department of Agriculture*, XV, 117–23.

74. Cherokee *Advance*, April 16, 1886, October 15, 1886, October 22, 1886, November 4, 1887, November 30, 1888, August 8, 1890, August 29, 1890.

measure. Only in Madison, Haralson, and Polk counties did the open range prevail throughout.[75]

That contested elections and legal battles commonly accompanied the stock law's district-level triumphs suggests that reform was not simply a product of shifting voter sentiment. Sympathetic officials overturned adverse results in every county from which direct evidence is available. In some instances, returns changed so dramatically from one election to another that opponents of the stock law had little doubt that foul play was afoot. The Sugar Hill district of Gwinnett County, for example, defeated the law on two occasions by "good majorities," but a third contest brought it a narrow victory, prompting "great dissatisfaction . . . [on] the ground . . . that the election is illegally conducted and is therefore void."[76] When ballot-box tampering or official appeal proved ineffective, proponents of reform frequently petitioned the county to alter district boundaries in an effort to eliminate pockets of staunch resistance or attach pockets of strong support. In 1887 a group in Cherokee County asked for such a change in "the district lines between Bells and Sixes district . . . [so that] about 40 voters will be cut off of Bells into Sixes." "Although the petition did not state it," the local paper surmised "that the change is desired so that Sixes district may be able to adopt 'no fence.' " County officers acceded to the request and the Sixes district did enact the stock law by a small margin within six months.[77]

Advocates of fencing reform had other advantages. Public notification of impending elections rested in the hands of local officials and newspaper editors who recognized that large turnouts spelled defeat. It was no accident, then, that as the 1880s wore on, the papers gave district elections limited attention and sometimes failed to print the returns. As a result, the stock law's road to victory was often paved by declining voter participation. In Gwinnett County the number of ballots cast dropped by almost 60 percent between 1885 and 1891; in Carroll County it dropped by almost 65 percent during the same period. The

75. Ibid., May 31, 1887, July 15, 1887, September 23, 1887, November 11, 1887, April 3, 1891, February 27, 1891, August 21, 1891; Paulding *New Era*, August 30, 1889; Franklin County Records, Elections, 1889–1893, GDAH; *Publications of the Georgia Department of Agriculture*, XV, 117–23.

76. Gwinnett *Herald*, January 13, 1891, October 14, 1884, October 21, 1884; Carroll *Free Press*, n.d.

77. Cherokee *Advance*, August 26, 1887, November 11, 1887. Also see Carroll *Free Press*, October 31, 1890.

Gwinnett *Herald* could then note in 1890 that a contest in the Harbins district "passed off quietly," with the law winning by four votes.[78] Further, as more and more districts within a county adopted the law, it became increasingly difficult for holdouts, as inhabitants would be liable for damages should their livestock cross district lines and trespass in a stock-law district. One county newspaper, admitting that some "districts have good ranges and it would, perhaps, suit the people better to let the fences remain as they are," argued that "as the stock must be kept out of the no fence districts, it is quite probable each of these districts will be forced to adopt the stock law."[79]

The "wearing thin" of popular resistance reflected a larger and more chronic problem as well. Unlike their reform-minded counterparts, stock-law opponents never developed an organizational apparatus to mobilize their ranks and inspire confidence in their numerical strength. The problem had its origins less in a tradition of rugged individualism than in the social relations of Upcountry farming settlements, which fostered collective endeavor among neighboring families while nurturing a profound suspicion of outsiders. Although promoting a cooperative ethos, these relations circumscribed the development of extra-community ties and sustained political activity. Yeomen and tenants could rise to defend customary rights but make no move toward organizing their forces. Consequently, they found themselves highly vulnerable to fraud and intimidation; their resistance slowly collapsed when confronted by the superior resources of their foes. And it was a dilemma that would return to haunt them.

Yet, if by the early 1890s a substantial number of districts in most Upcountry counties had formally adopted the stock law, enforcement could be another matter. A veritable war erupted in some areas after ratification, as embittered farmers turned from the ballot box to individual acts of retaliation. They ripped down newly constructed fences or simply ignored the statute, threatening summary retribution for anyone seeking to implement it. The Carroll *Free Press* charged that "outlaws" lurked in "the dead of the night when all gentlemen were asleep," breaking fences and gates "to smash." "[T]he work of these rascals has been kept up," the editor fretted, "until they have torn up

78. Gwinnett *Herald*, July 14, 1885, July 7, 1891, April 29, 1890; Carroll *Free Press*, July 3, 1885, June 4, 1890.

79. Cherokee *Advance*, August 21, 1891; Gwinnett *Herald*, September 27, 1887; Bonner, *Georgia's Last Frontier*, 142–43.

five gates and torn down 1200 panels of fence. . . . " Here and in sections of other Upcountry counties, "the fence men [were] doing their best to evade the law and warning that if any man takes up their stock, they will turn their little guns on him."[80] The tide of social change swept forcefully, but the embers of resistance still burned.

Fencing stirred heated conflict elsewhere in late-nineteenth-century America, most notably on the Great Plains. Reaping the benefits of federal land policies ostensibly designed to foster homesteading, cattle barons acquired huge tracts and then proceeded to enclose them, thereby curtailing the grazing rights of small farmers and herdsmen, if not squeezing both out entirely. Pitched battles often ensued.[81] But if the details of the struggle varied in different locales and if simple economic interest played a large role, there as in Georgia, clashing ideas about property and use rights proved to be important strains of contention. The open range, in the West and South, represented more than an expedient of scattered settlement; it expressed popular associations of private with productive property and popular predilections against great accumulations of wealth. Western farmers railed against massive enclosures because they engrossed the public domain for speculation rather than for use and because they undermined small-scale enterprise. That such confrontations had parallels in many rural societies as capitalist agriculture expanded should cast the American experience in broader perspective and shed new light on popular protest in the Gilded Age.

80. Carroll *Free Press*, July 12, 1889, March 26, 1886. Also see ibid., April 23, 1886, February 3, 1888, March 14, 1890.

81. Fred A. Shannon, *The Farmers' Last Frontier: Agriculture, 1860–1897* (New York, 1945), 198–218; Robert V. Hine, *The American West: An Interpretive History* (Boston, 1973), 136–38; Lewis L. Gould, *Wyoming: A Political History, 1868–1896* (New Haven, 1968), 137–58.

Epilogue
The Contours of Populism

I

Popular movements normally begin as defenses of traditional rights, standards, and obligations. Whether they remain anchored to the past, committed simply to the restoration of customary relations and values, or chart new and far-reaching courses, hinges on a number of historically discrete conjunctures: their social composition, heritage, leadership, and links with other local and supralocal groups; the character and relative strengths of the dominant classes; the nature, pace, and extent of economic change; wider cultural and political currents. Scholars have come to recognize that rural and urban protests, alike, defy easy categorization; that despite broadly discernible patterns the activities of peasants, workers, or the "crowd" can have different goals and meanings in different settings; that time, place, and other historical circumstances define limits as well as possibilities.[1]

---

1. Henry A. Landsberger, ed., *Rural Protest: Peasant Movements and Social Change* (New York, 1973), 18–64; Eric Wolf, *Peasant Wars of the Twentieth Century* (New York, 1969), 276–302; James C. Scott, *The Moral Economy of the Peasant: Rebellion and Subsistence in Southeast Asia* (New Haven, 1976), 193–240; George Rudé, *The Crowd in History, 1730–1848* (New York, 1964).

Popular ideologies and cultural forms also have a dynamic quality even if their modes of expression remain unaltered. Notions of justice and right, of order and propriety, widely proclaimed and embraced, do not hold the same significance for all social groups. Customs and institutions organizing and governing various aspects of social life not only prove readily adaptable to new conditions but provide powerful means for mobilizing and transforming collective behavior. It was, after all, a preindustrial artisan ideology emphasizing craft pride, cooperative labor, and production for use, along with preindustrial trade and mutual-aid societies, that served as the foundations of later working-class radicalism.[2]

It would be fruitful to reconsider Populism from this perspective. For the long-standing scholarly debate over the movement's character—forward or backward looking, radical or reactionary, liberal or conservative—has been circumscribed, on the one hand, by a tendency to project contemporary ideas about political discourse back into the nineteenth century and, on the other, by a static view of the movement itself.[3] Only quite recently has an effort been made to explore Populism as process, to highlight development and contradiction.[4] Yet it is in this way that the promise and shortfalls, the contours and meanings, of the agrarian revolt can be found. The bitter struggle over grazing rights that stirred the Georgia Upcountry, and other regions like it, during the

2. E. P. Thompson, *The Making of the English Working Class* (New York, 1963), 17–101, 401–29; Sean Wilentz, *Chants Democratic: New York City and the Rise of the American Working Class* (New York, 1984); Leon Fink, "Class Conflict in the Gilded Age: The Figure and the Phantom," *RHR*, III (Fall–Winter 1975), 58–59.

3. See, for example, Richard Hofstadter, *The Age of Reform: From Bryan to F.D.R.* (New York, 1955), 60–93; Norman Pollack, *The Populist Response to Industrial America: Midwestern Populist Thought* (New York, 1962); Walter T. K Nugent, *The Tolerant Populists: Kansas Populism and Nativism* (Chicago, 1963). Southern historians have been more evenhanded and eclectic, though their studies have been informed by and, indeed, generally fail to transcend the boundaries defined by the Midwestern debate. See William Warren Rogers, *The One-Gallused Rebellion: Agrarianism in Alabama, 1865–1896* (Baton Rouge, 1970); William Ivy Hair, *Bourbonism and Agrarian Protest: Louisiana Politics, 1877–1900* (Baton Rouge, 1972); Sheldon Hackney, *Populism to Progressivism in Alabama* (Princeton, 1969). None have surpassed C. Vann Woodward's treatments in *Origins of the New South, 1877–1913* (Baton Rouge, 1951) and *Tom Watson: Agrarian Rebel* (New York, 1938).

4. Lawrence Goodwyn, *Democratic Promise: The Populist Moment in America* (New York, 1976); Bruce Palmer, *"Man Over Money": The Southern Populist Critique of American Capitalism* (Chapel Hill, 1980); Stanley B. Parsons, *The Populist Context: Rural Versus Urban Power on a Great Plains Frontier* (Westport, Conn., 1973).

1880s helped to articulate and politicize the responses of petty producers to disruptive social change. While it generated no program or party for reform, the issue sharpened growing class antagonisms and gave them powerful cultural expression. Had the struggle occurred in isolation, it would have remained defensive, however rich in the language of class conflict its rhetoric. But the appearance of the Southern Farmers' Alliance and then the People's party promised to transform defensiveness into a humane and progressive force—by capturing the tenor of rural disaffection, seeking to link the experiences of small producers throughout the South and West, and attempting to harness those experiences to a platform of mass political action and cooperative economic endeavor. Eventual failure reflected who the Populists were and what they were up against.

II

When the Farmers' Alliance lecturer J. B. Wilkes arrived in Carroll County in August of 1887, the organization had already amassed a considerable following in the old Southwest. After an abortive beginning in east Texas during the late 1870s, a revitalized Alliance had spread throughout that state and into Arkansas, Louisiana, Alabama, and the Indian territory by the mid-1880s. Spurred by a virulent battle on the Texas frontier between farmers and land-engrossing cattlemen, the movement was early marked by fence-cutting wars and vigilantism waged to protect cultivators from ranchers, thieves, and evictions at the behest of land sharks and land companies. Not surprisingly, the Alliance had its greatest initial success in areas where the Greenback party had attracted noteworthy support and nurtured antimonopoly sentiment.[5]

As the Alliance took hold, cooperative buying and selling and the establishment of "trade stores" became the keystone of its appeal to debt-ridden cotton farmers. To these efforts were added overtures to, and increasingly cordial relations with, the Knights of Labor. Indeed, along the route of the Texas and Pacific Railroad and in the mining regions of west Texas, membership in the two orders overlapped. By 1886 the Alliance had fashioned a platform to advance the interests of both agricultural producers and industrial workers. Along with

5. Carroll *Free Press*, August 19, 1887; Robert C. McMath, Jr., *Populist Vanguard: A History of the Southern Farmers' Alliance* (Chapel Hill, 1975), 7–10.

demands for the heavier taxation of railroads and speculative landholdings, for an end to alien landownership and "the dealing in futures of all
agricultural products," and for a federally administered banking
system committed to an expanded and more flexible currency, the
Alliance also called for recognition of trade unions and cooperative
stores, for the creation of a national bureau of labor statistics, and for an
improved mechanics' lien law. These planks, engineered by the
organization's radical wing, prompted a bolt of more conservative
leaders. While a compromise, which still favored the radicals, was soon
effected, such divisions continued to plague the Texas movement and
were reproduced in other Southern states as the Alliance moved
eastward.[6]

Despite their initial skepticism, farmers in Georgia's western
Upcountry greeted the Alliance with mounting enthusiasm. In the fall
of 1887 Wilkes reported "that the order now numbers 400 in Coweta,
between 500 and 600 in Carroll, some 300 in Troup, and about 400 in
Heard [counties]." By the following spring Carroll County alone could
boast thirty-three suballiances with almost 5,000 members, "making
about one-tenth of the numbers in the state." The remainder of the
Upcountry provided equally fertile terrain for the Alliance plant, as the
region came to be an organization stronghold.[7] After "lecturing and
organizing . . . for a short while in Cherokee county," one Allianceman claimed that the order was "on the boom," sprouting nearly
ten suballiances containing over 800 members. Relatively soon
thereafter, the number of suballiances grew to twenty-three. Jackson
County, where an organizing drive began in January 1888, had given
birth to fifteen suballiances by that summer, and within a year the
number had spiraled to seventy-two, with a membership of over 1,200.
And so it went in Gwinnett, Cobb, Milton, Forsyth, and other
Upcountry counties.[8]

6. Goodwyn, *Democratic Promise*, 33–50, 79–82; Woodward, *Origins of the New South*, 188–
92; McMath, *Populist Vanguard*, 23–24, 26–30, 33–35; W. Scott Morgan, *A History of the
Agricultural Wheel and Farmers' Alliance* (Fort Scott, Kan., 1889), 93–146.

7. Newnan *Herald*, quoted in Carroll *Free Press*, October 21, 1887; Carroll *Free Press*,
September 30, 1887, April 6, 1888, June 15, 1888; Robert C. McMath, Jr., "Mobilizing
Agrarian Discontent: The Rise of the Farmers' Alliance in Georgia" (Paper presented to
the Southern Historical Association, Atlanta, November 1973), 1.

8. Cherokee *Advance*, April 27, 1888, May 25, 1888, April 3, 1891; Jackson *Herald*,
January 27, 1888, August 24, 1888; Carroll County *Times*, May 11, 1888; James A.
Furgeson, "Power Politics and Populism: Jackson County, Georgia, as a Case Study"
(M.A. thesis, University of Georgia, 1975), 38–39.

Alliance organizers utilized the forums of popular politics and religion—rallies, barbecues, and camp meetings—to spread the order's gospel. Suballiances met once or twice a month in local district villages and hamlets, while county and regional gatherings took place several times a year at the county seat or convenient camp grounds, where large crowds mixed politicking, socializing, and feasting. Thus, 1,200 Gwinnett County faithfuls assembled in August 1889 for an Alliance picnic at which they heard prominent state leaders discuss "the green back question extensively . . . and the question of labor and capital— the 'robber kings and the money kings,'" followed by dinner, two brass bands, and "more speeches." Another August, "the sturdy yeomanry of Cherokee, with their wives, sons, and daughters . . . reinforced by many good citizens from Cobb, Milton counties and elsewhere, met in Woodstock to spend the day in pleasant social intercourse, listen to alliance speakers, and enjoy a good and sumptuous repast." The Cherokee *Advance* estimated that well over 1,000 attended. An Alliance picnic in Jackson County saw "vehicles of every description . . . winding their way to Wood's Camp Ground," where dinner was coupled with addresses denouncing the "sick condition of farmers, [the] great amount of mortgaged land in Georgia . . . and class legislation, trusts, and monopolies."[9]

As the Cherokee *Advance* suggested, small landowners usually constituted the bulk of Alliance membership. But large landholders and, especially, landless whites also joined the order. Local chapters initially recruited a wide spectrum of rural whites. According to lists from Gwinnett County and Jackson County suballiances, for example, about four members in ten owned no land while about one in ten owned 300 or more acres.[10] Although the Alliance made few overtures to

9. Gwinnett *Herald*, August 13, 1889; Cherokee *Advance*, April 17, 1891, September 4, 1891; Jackson *Herald*, August 2, 1889.

10. Of 110 members from 35 suballiances in Gwinnett and Jackson counties, 52 (47%) owned between 1 and 299 acres, 46 (42%) owned no land, and 12 (11%) owned 300 acres or more. Only 3 had neither real nor personal property, while 67 (61%) claimed total property ranging in value between $1 and $1,000. The Gwinnett County records (63 members) show a greater percentage of farmers with 1 to 299 acres (52%) and a smaller percentage of landless farmers (37%). In the Jackson County records (47 members) there are more landless farmers (49%) and fewer with between 1 and 299 acres (40%), though it is worth noting that several of the former were related to the latter. In both counties 11 percent had 300 acres or more. See Gwinnett County Alliance Minutes, 1889, GDAH; Minutes of the Jefferson Alliance, Jackson County, 1889–1891, GDAH; Gwinnett County Tax Digest, 1889, GDAH; Jackson County Tax Digest, 1890, GDAH.

tenants and croppers, and offered them little in the way of immediate remedies, many either had recently been dispossessed or had landowning relatives, and thereby retained the outlook of petty proprietors. Furthermore, the agricultural depression gripping the South, worsened by high credit and freight rates, squeezed large and small landowners alike. And men of "property and standing" exerted considerable influence on county Alliances at the earliest stages by virtue of officerships and previous experience in the Grange and local agricultural clubs. In the words of the Jackson *Herald*, "the Alliance organization here [is] composed of many of the best men of the community."[11]

These internal divisions were smoothed at first by numerous cooperative ventures designed to ease the plight of all cultivators. The Alliance tapped the "habits of mutuality" deeply embedded in rural social life and sought to broaden them. Steps were taken, with some success, to strike trading agreements with local mercantile firms in the hope of reducing prices through bulk purchasing.[12] But activities soon moved in a more autonomous direction. Upcountry Alliances established cooperative stores and warehouses, set up ginning facilities, and began financing guano, cottonseed oil, and coffin manufactories. "The Cooperative or Carroll County Alliance Store . . . [was] started something over a year ago," the Carroll County *Times* noted, "and now Alliancemen from half a dozen counties buy largely at the Store." "The Farmers' Alliance has done a great deal of good during the past year," the rival Carroll *Free Press* admitted.[13] Local orders also dispensed monetary assistance to trouble-stricken members, and in Hall County "alliancemen . . . resolved not to go to law with a brother," electing instead "a judiciary committee whose duty it shall be to settle all disputes and differences between members, draw wills and deeds, administer on estates, and act as guardians to the wives and children of deceased members." Such was the stuff of a developing "movement culture."[14]

11. Jackson *Herald*, May 17, 1889; Carroll County *Times*, July 23, 1889; McMath, "Mobilizing Agrarian Discontent," 9.

12. Cherokee *Advance*, August 24, 1888; Carroll County *Times*, February 17, 1888, March 2, 1888; Carroll *Free Press*, January 13, 1888.

13. Carroll County *Times*, December 24, 1889; Carroll *Free Press*, December 13, 1889; Gwinnett County Alliance Minutes, April 2, 1891, October, 1891; Cherokee *Advance*, March 14, 1890, August 23, 1890, October 4, 1890; Jackson *Herald*, May 23, 1890.

14. Carroll County *Times*, July 20, 1888; Cherokee *Advance*, November 15, 1889. On the Alliance "movement culture," see Goodwyn, *Democratic Promise*, 47–153.

Alliance cooperative undertakings frequently drew the fire of Upcountry merchants and town interests who were excluded from the organization and feared that their livelihoods would be jeopardized. Insisting that "it is far from our desire to encourage any unnatural prejudice between the people who till our fields and those who reside in commercial centres," the Atlanta *Southern Alliance Farmer* nonetheless found "that in many of the Georgia towns there has been manifest a secret, but bitter and most vindictive animosity against the Alliance movement." Carroll County Alliancemen, calling on storekeepers for the purpose of making trading arrangements, "were treated with contempt." "Our merchants have had the thing their own way," an angry member complained. "They could price the farmers' produce . . . and then price their own goods . . . [and] could demand a mortgage or a waive note and go snooks with the lawyer and bind the poor fellow to pay attornies' fees. . . ."[15] Merchandisers in Milton County successfully blocked the local Alliance cooperative from dealing with Atlanta wholesalers by warning the Atlantans "that they [the merchants] would not purchase any goods from stores that would sell to the Alliance store." In Jackson County an Allianceman could report that "the merchants are . . . fighting us with all the ferocity they can summon . . . pass[ing] ordinances in several towns to keep us from shipping goods into them, or to make us pay a town tax for all goods shipped there." Many a cooperative collapsed under the weight of this determined counterattack.[16]

In important ways, the conflict between the Alliance and the merchants served to exacerbate class divisions within the Alliance itself. The difficulties of organizing and sustaining local cooperative stores, warehouses, and manufactories, due as much to capital shortages as to the merchants' machinations, steered members of the order in new directions and escalated demands for state and national institutions. The Georgia Alliance Exchange, which opened its doors in late 1889, and the subtreasury plan—a proposal for a federally funded system of credit and marketing approved at the Southern Alliance's St. Louis convention that same year—significantly expanded the movement's horizons by offering large-scale cooperative alternatives to established market structures. These alternatives posed serious threats to wealthy

15. Atlanta *Southern Alliance Farmer*, n.d., in Thomas E. Watson Papers, Box 25, Vol. 5, 431, SHC; Carroll County *Times*, March 16, 1888.

16. Cherokee *Advance*, March 29, 1889; Jackson *Herald*, March 7, 1890; Gwinnett *Herald*, September 15, 1891; Carroll *Free Press*, August 31, 1888.

landowners deriving surpluses from liens on their tenants' crops while sweeping the Alliance into political agitation capable of disrupting the Democratic party. One Floyd County landlord, who touted the Alliance's local economic enterprises, reeled in disgust at the order's growing involvement in politics.[17]

By 1890, politics and the subtreasury had begun to rupture Upcountry Alliances. In view of pending state and national elections, militant Alliancemen tried to use the carrot of organized support with the stick of fealty to the order's entire program to win Democratic candidates to their cause, much to the chagrin of conservative elements. When, for example, a group of legislators appeared at a Carroll County Alliance meeting and were asked to commit themselves to Alliance reforms, the protests of a large landholder received applause from other conservatives in attendance. That landholder backed the gubernatorial hopeful John B. Gordon, who styled himself an Alliance advocate but refused to endorse the subtreasury plan. Charging that "conservative aspirants for office in the Alliance [were] left out," like-minded Franklin County members decried the "narrow and unseemly action taken by the Farmers' Alliance . . . in selecting a man [for] . . . the legislature." "This action necessarily places this grand order . . . as political and partisan," these conservatives complained, adding that "secret politics are undemocratic, unsafe, and unclear, and their fruits are disruption and riotous rebellion." There was, they believed, "general dissatisfaction in the order."[18] But while Alliance candidates did obtain more than a healthy share of state-legislative and congressional seats, the organization's rank and file soon discovered that the political offices brought few tangible returns. As Rebecca Latimer Felton later recalled, once many of the self-proclaimed Alliance Democrats took their places, she "heard no more about the subtreasury or government control of the railroad." Small wonder that by 1892, suballiances throughout the Upcountry, convinced that the Democratic party saw "the tariff [as] the only issue," rallied to the banner of Populism.[19]

17. Cottage Home Farm Journal, Floyd County, September 3, 1890, John H. Dent Papers, GDAH; McMath, "Mobilizing Agrarian Discontent," 6; Goodwyn, Democratic Promise, 154–76; Woodward, Origins of the New South, 198–99.

18. Carroll Free Press, October 31, 1890; Carnesville Enterprise, July 4, 1890.

19. Rebecca Latimer Felton, My Memoirs of Georgia Politics (Atlanta, 1911), 645–46; Jackson Herald, August 14, 1891; Atlanta People's Party Paper, January 14, 1892, February 4, 1892, February 18, 1892.

Local issues, like the stock law, also played key roles in splitting Alliances along class lines and pointing the way to the People's party. Although leaders seemed bent upon keeping such potentially explosive matters out of discussions, their interjection was almost unavoidable, stirring up bitterness and further disenchantment with the conservative political course. Thus, a Carroll County Allianceman created rancor in the order when he called for implementation of "the stock law all over the county" and wedded the measure "to the principles of the Farmers' Alliance." A fellow member, in fact, blamed divisions in the ranks on such concerns as whether "somebody is too strong a stock law man."[20] Predicting that "the day the Farmers' Alliance enters politics . . . will its disintegration begin," a cautious Jackson County adherent took pains to warn "of men who have axes to grind." Such men, apparently, as John Grimes of Gwinnett County, who thundered that the Alliance had fallen under the influence of men who "are not the working people . . . who [do not] toil with their hands . . . [who] are really nothing more nor less than Jay Goulds and Vanderbilts on a smaller scale," much to the detriment of "the real farmers of the country . . . [who] are tenants and men who own small farms . . . [with] mortgages over them."[21] Grimes probably found the Populists an attractive alternative.

The stock-law struggle and Populism had additional links. The penchant of newspaper correspondents to write under pseudonyms makes identifications difficult, but available information suggests that active opponents of fencing reform tended to align with the Populists. W. D. Lovvorn of Carroll County, who penned stinging protests against the stock law during the 1880s, for instance, became a local Populist leader in the early 1890s. Vocal supporters of fencing reform, on the other hand, tended to remain within the Democratic party. Such a group of stock-law advocates in Carroll County included numbers of prominent Democrats: the merchant W. C. Adamson, the newspaper editor E. R. Sharpe, the attorney Oscar Reese, and the large landowner G. W. Harper, among others.[22]

Social divisions evoked by the stock-law controversy also persisted

20. Carroll County *Times*, March 30, 1888; Carroll *Free Press*, July 5, 1889; James C. Bonner, *Georgia's Last Frontier: The Development of Carroll County* (Athens, 1971), 145.

21. Jackson *Herald*, March 7, 1890; Atlanta *Southern Alliance Farmer*, n.d., in James T. McElvaney Papers, GDAH.

22. Carroll *Free Press*, July 25, 1890; Carroll County *Times*, November 4, 1892.

into the Populist era. While it might be expected that the leadership of each political party had similar characteristics even if their social bases diverged, notable differences distinguished Populist standard-bearers in the Upcountry from their Democratic counterparts. In Jackson County, leading Populists not only were poorer than rival Democrats; a decided majority had agricultural occupations and rural residences, while most of the Democrats were merchants or professionals and lived in the town districts. Evidence from Carroll County on landownership points to analogous partisan distinctions. Of members on respective party executive committees, Democrats had considerably more substantial landholdings: 40 percent owned real estate assessed at over $1,000, and almost 30 percent owned over 200 acres. Among Populist executive committeemen, however, fewer than one-fourth owned land worth over $1,000, and fewer than one-fifth owned over 200 acres.

Table E.1 Characteristics of Democratic and Populist Leaders, Jackson and Carroll Counties, 1890s

A. Residences and Occupations of Jackson County Democratic and Populist Leaders

	Number	Residence		Occupation	
		Town	Rural	Farm	Non-Farm
Populist	30	27%	73%	63%	37%
Democrat	23	61%	39%	35%	65%

B. Landownership Among Carroll County Democratic and Populist Leaders

	% of Leaders			% of Leaders	
Value of Land	Popu-lists	Demo-crats	Acres	Popu-lists	Demo-crats
$0	24%	16%	0	24%	16%
$1–200	12%	8%	1–100	41%	32%
$201–500	28%	20%	101–200	18%	24%
$501–1,000	12%	16%	201–300	12%	12%
$1,001+	24%	40%	301+	5%	16%
Total	100%	100%		100%	100%
Number	17	25		17	25

Sources: Furgeson, "Power Politics," 50–51; Carroll *Free Press*, April 8, 1892; Carroll County Tax Digest, 1890.

Furthermore, a greater percentage of the Populists was landless (see Table E.1).

Election returns offer even more compelling illustration of the connections between the conflicts of the 1880s and those of the 1890s. Upcountry Democrats, like stock-law proponents, had their base in the town districts. The Populists, like stock-law opponents, had their strength in the countryside and, particularly, in the poorer rural districts. These alignments could be observed as early as the state and national elections of 1892, the first to include People's party candidates. In that year, Jackson County gave the Democratic governor W. J. Northen and the presidential aspirant Grover Cleveland narrow victories, yet most of their votes came from the districts encompassing the towns of Jefferson, Harmony Grove, and Maysville, and the smaller village of Pendergrass. The Populist candidates W. L. Peek (for governor) and James B. Weaver (for president) swept eight of nine and nine of nine rural districts respectively.[23] Two years later, the third-party gubernatorial hopeful James K. Hines and the congressional nominee J. N. Twitty won slim majorities in the county, as did the Populist candidate for sheriff in 1895. But district lineups remained similar: town districts consistently backed the Democrats while most rural districts consistently backed the Populists.[24] Indeed, aggregating ballots cast in six local, state, and national elections between 1892 and 1896 shows that only three town districts maintained a staunch Democratic allegiance; there, Populists obtained less than 30 percent of the votes. In the countryside, on the other hand, Populism reigned triumphant, amassing nearly 70 percent of the votes. And the districts that had raised the strongest opposition to the stock law also raised the strongest support for the Populists (see Table E.2).

In Carroll County, where towns were more numerous and substantial—the county increasingly became a marketing center for surrounding areas of Georgia and Alabama—the Populists did not fare quite as well, though they sent two representatives to the statehouse and filled several local offices. But voting returns also demonstrated clear divisions between town and countryside. While the Democrats rolled up impressive majorities in the town districts, particularly in Carrollton, the third party held sway in many rural districts. Populist office seekers mustered less than 40 percent of the votes in the districts

23. Jackson *Herald*, October 14, 1892, November 11, 1892.
24. Ibid., October 12, 1894, November 9, 1894, January 4, 1895.

Table E.2　District Voting Alignments, Jackson County, 1892–1895 (Six Elections)

District	Per Capita[1] Wealth	Trend[2]	Populist Vote	Democ. Vote	Repub. Vote	Percentage Populist Vote
Town and Village:						
Jefferson	$1,210	D	1,403	2,299	125	37%
Minishes (Harmony Grove)	1,364	D	431	1,892	97	18%
Wilsons (Maysville)	1,055	D	293	813	29	26%
Cunningham (Pendergrass)	777	X	694	816	47	45%
Houses (Winder)	827	P	741	330	8	69%
Rural:						
Hoschton	852	P	1,020	493	7	67%
Newtown[3]	768	P	940	609	41	59%
Millers	765	X	335	406	39	43%
Clarksboro[3]	741	P	683	143	48	78%
Chandlers[3]	592	P	778	312	21	70%
Santafe[3]	554	X	441	190	27	67%
Randolphs[3]	506	P	413	152	2	73%

[1] Total wealth divided by total number of persons on tax rolls.

[2] Indicates voting trend over six elections: D = voted Democratic in each election; P = voted Populist in each election; X = majority shifted at least once.

[3] Denotes district also a strong opponent of the stock law.

Sources: Jackson County Tax Digest, 1890; Jackson *Herald*, October 14, 1892, November 11, 1892, October 12, 1894, November 9, 1894, January 4, 1895.

containing the towns of Carrollton, Villa Rica, Roopville, Bowdon, and Whitesburg, yet won over 70 percent of the combined votes in the rural districts of Turkey Creek, Kansas, New Mexico, Smithfield, Lowell, and Flint Corner, among the poorest in the county and most resistant to the stock law (see Table E.3).

Much the same pattern emerged in other Upcountry counties. Franklin County Populists attained local majorities for state and national candidates in 1892, despite opposition in the town of Carnesville, by winning decisively in most rural districts. A heavy Democratic vote in Paulding County's largest town of Dallas failed to prevent a Populist from capturing a seat in the state legislature that

Table E.3   District Voting Alignments, Carroll County, 1894–1895 (Three Elections)

District	Per Capita[1] Wealth	Trend[2]	Populist Vote	Democ. Vote	Percentage Populist Vote
Town and Village:					
Carrollton	$1,530	D	921	1,866	33 %
Bowdon	985	D	230	339	40 %
Villa Rica	969	X	471	483	49 %
Whitesburg	1,000	X	197	258	43 %
Temple[3]	837	P	472	140	77 %
Roopville[3]	631	D	99	212	32 %
Rural:					
Turkey Creek[4]	686	P	158	29	85 %
Kansas[4]	683	P	162	8	95 %
New Mexico[4]	674	P	143	46	76 %
Lowell[4]	567	X	137	139	49 %
Smithfield[4]	540	P	201	38	84 %
Flint Corner[4]	428	P	101	47	68 %
Shiloh[5]	686	D	69	138	33 %
Fairplay[3]	687	P	130	123	51 %

[1] Total wealth divided by total number of persons on tax rolls.

[2] Indicates voting trend over three elections: D = voted Democratic in each election; P = voted Populist in each election; X = majority shifted at least once.

[3] Based on only two elections.

[4] Denotes district also a strong opponent of the stock law.

[5] Based on only two elections and strong opponent of stock law.

Sources: Carroll County Tax Digest, 1890; Carroll *Free Press*, October 5, 1894, November 9, 1894, January 4, 1895.

Note: County districts went by several names and boundary lines changed during the 1880s and 1890s. This table includes only those districts for which consistent information can be gathered.

same year or from taking nearly every contest for the next three years. In 1894, Gwinnett County voters selected a full slate of Populist state officials by virtually sweeping the rural areas even as the more densely populated town districts of Lawrenceville, Duluth, and Norcross remained in the Democratic camp. And while Cherokee County Populists had greater initial difficulty, they too made real inroads outside of Canton, the county seat and major urban center.[25] In all,

25. Carnesville *Enterprise*, November 11, 1892; Paulding *New Era*, October 7, 1892, May 26, 1893; Dallas *Herald*, October 4, 1894, November 8, 1894; Gwinnett *Herald*, October 2, 1894; Cherokee *Advance*, October 7, 1892, November 11, 1892. Our knowledge of the

Upcountry counties had by 1896 sent twenty-four Populists to the Georgia legislature, roughly one-third of the statewide total, and elected many sheriffs, ordinaries, and other local officials.[26]

The stock-law controversy not only anticipated the social and political contours of Upcountry Populism; it helps elucidate the cultural and ideological contours as well. The defense of private property and common rights illuminates the elements of a nineteenth-century producer ideology embodied in the appeal and program of both the Southern Alliance's radical wing and the People's party. Thus, when Populists assailed the "money kings," the "speculative parasites," the "capitalists" who "grow richer and richer . . . at the expense of those who produce," and associated the third-party cause with "liberty and independence, which can only be realized by giving equal rights to all and special privileges to none," they did not advance a version of political pluralism. They lent wider expression to republican sensibilities founded on social relations quite at odds with the dominant trends of industrializing America—sensibilities at odds with the tenets of bourgeois individualism and the free market. Blaming the concentration of wealth and power on the corruption of the political process, Populists did not wish to unfetter the "invisible hand" of the marketplace; they wished to protect a "liberty tree" rooted in petty ownership of productive resources. The People's party, they proclaimed, "is composed of the yeomanry of the country. The small landed proprietors, the working farmers, the intelligent artisans, the wageworkers[,] men who own homes and want a stable government."[27]

To the hegemony of the marketplace, Populism counterposed the vision of a producers' commonwealth achieved through cooperative enterprise and public regulation of exchange. Included among the party's most far-reaching planks were demands for the Alliance-inspired subtreasury system, for democratization of the money supply

---

sources of Populist support elsewhere in the South remains far from complete, but it is worth noting in this connection that a Texas Democrat claimed, "Where you found the hogs running loose, there were lots of Populists; where you found them penned up, the Democrats were in the majority." See Roscoe C. Martin, *The People's Party in Texas: A Study in Third-Party Politics* (Austin, 1933), 70, n. 21.

26. Atlanta *Constitution*, October 6, 1892, October 4, 1894, October 8, 1896. In the local elections of 1895, for example, Populist candidates swept to victory in Bartow, Carroll, Clayton, Fayette, Haralson, Paulding, Polk, Franklin, Banks, Cherokee, and Jackson counties. See Dallas *Herald*, January 3, 1895.

27. Atlanta *People's Party Paper*, January 14, 1892; Gracewood *Wool Hat*, July 22, 1893.

through the abolition of national banks and the "free and unlimited coinage of silver" so as to increase the "circulating medium . . . to not less than $50 per capita," and for government ownership of the means of transportation and communication. It was a vision informed by historical experience—by the structure and dynamic of the family farm, the shop, and the local market; by notions of government as the repository of the public will and the defender of the public good—and tailored to the exigencies of an expansive society. As one Carroll County yeoman could write, "Competition may be the life of trade, but it is death to the farmer." Not a proletarian movement, Populism spoke for men and women of "small means" who faced and sought to resist the specter of proletarianization, of "be[ing] forced to work at the pleasure of the money lords," of "becom[ing] a nation of shylocks and serfs."[28]

The republican producer ideology embraced by Upcountry supporters of common rights and, later, of Populism at once facilitated and limited the development of a biracial political coalition of poor Southerners. It was, of course, the prominent Georgia Populist Tom Watson who forcefully argued that the economic woes shared by white and black farmers alike demanded cooperative political endeavor. "[T]he crushing burdens which now oppress both races in the South will cause each to . . . see a similarity of cause and a similarity of remedy," Watson contended. "They will recognize that each should help the other in the work of repealing bad laws and enacting good ones." Such "broad lines of mutual interest" did become increasingly apparent to many Upcountry whites in the years after Reconstruction, as the rise of staple agriculture transformed social relations and jeopardized the independence of small landowners. Tentatively during the Independent campaigns of the 1870s and more dramatically during the stock-law conflict of the 1880s, a new political alignment began taking shape. In large part, overtures to the black community reflected its impressive political mobilization; though relatively few in number, the freedmen stood as a force to be grappled with. But, as the arguments of stock-law opponents suggested, a sense of commonly suffered economic exploitation and political misrule gradually emerged as well. While the Farmers' Alliance excluded blacks, relegating them to a separate organization, more than a few Upcountry Populists looked to

28. "The Omaha Platform, July 1892," in George B. Tindall, ed., *A Populist Reader: Selections From the Works of American Populist Leaders* (Gloucester, Mass., 1976), 90–96; Carroll *Free Press*, March 2, 1888; Gracewood *Wool Hat*, July 27, 1892.

narrowing the racial divide. Thus, in an effort to recruit local blacks, the People's party in Jackson County opened meetings to both races, welcomed black delegates at their county conventions, and invited a black speaker from Atlanta.[29]

Blacks contributed significant electoral support to Populist candidates, who were uniformly white. The sympathetic Dallas *Herald* of Paulding County found that the "People's party colored men did splendid work at the polls" in 1894 and 1895 and praised their courage in the face of "protests, persuasions, and the employment of all manner of means by the democrats." The hostile Carroll *Free Press* could blame a local third-party victory in 1894 on a poor Democratic turnout and on blacks who "voted almost solidly for the populists [having been made to] believe that the low price of cotton was attributable to democratic rule."[30] Yet, black political leaders in the Upcountry, and doubtless many of their followers, approached the People's party with some caution and skepticism. For one thing, abandoning the Republican party and its potential network of patronage in favor of a new party whose prospects were uncertain carried risks. Furthermore, numerous blacks justifiably charged that the Populists paid minimal, if any, attention to the special needs of the black community. One announced that he voted for the Democrats in state elections because "Weaver, Watson, and Peek" ignored the issue of public schools, "which is the only hope the colored people can have."[31]

Perhaps more important in steering a considerable number of blacks away from the Populists was the reputation for bitter racism that the party's white constituency had earned. The reign of terror brought upon the freedmen by vigilante bands during Reconstruction left a painful legacy, while Independent efforts to reform the Democratic party led to the establishment of white primaries in the 1880s. And as P. W. Carter, a black Jackson County Republican, roared in 1892, "many who are now Populists were the strongest kind for the primaries because it shut the 'nigger' out." The less-than-courageous response of third-party faithfuls to Democratic accusations that they encouraged racial

29. Atlanta *People's Party Paper*, September 16, 1892; Jackson *Herald*, July 8, 1892; Furgeson, "Power Politics," 85–86.

30. Dallas *Herald*, October 4, 1894, January 3, 1895; Carroll *Free Press*, October 5, 1894.

31. Jackson *Herald*, October 21, 1892; Furgeson, "Power Politics," 83–86; Olin B. Adams, "The Negro and the Agrarian Movement in Georgia, 1874–1908" (Ph.D. diss., Florida State University, 1973), 178–84.

mingling and opened the way for "negro domination" did little to allay the suspicions of men like Carter. Indeed, white Populists could hoist the banner of white supremacy even as they assailed its partisan manifestation. Most state Republican leaders, white and black, along with the head of Georgia's Colored Alliance, endorsed the Populists with good effect; but more than a handful of black voters in the Upcountry and elsewhere chose to abstain or to side with the Democrats, who attempted to lure black support with halfhearted denunciations of lynching.[32]

However much it had a life of its own, the enduring racism of Populism's rank and file was rooted in deeper class relations and attitudes. Though often confronting expropriation, though able to style themselves the "laboring poor" and to feel solidarity with the "toiling masses" throughout the nation, these Southern whites had strong cultural ties, if not direct personal experience, with a community of petty proprietors. They adhered to a popular radicalism—widespread in nineteenth-century America—that linked freedom and independence with ownership of productive resources and looked with fear and contempt upon the permanently dispossessed who fell subject to the wills of other men—precisely the image associated with blacks. Some small landowners in the Upcountry had previously owned, or were members of families that had previously owned, slaves; some had a black cropper or two on their farms; others, including white tenants, occasionally hired black hands for day labor. And when, in 1891, the Colored Farmers' Alliance launched a strike of black cotton pickers across the South, it met with a hostile response from, and often brutal repression at the hands of, the white Farmers' Alliance itself—an episode leaving scars of racial anger. Rather than resolving these tensions and contradictions, the republican producer ideology captured and advanced by Populism served to re-emphasize them. "We have in this country two dangerous classes," a Southern Populist could declare. "One a band of capitalist conspirators who enjoy special advantages which they are determined to maintain and increase even at the cost of involving the nation to ruin. The other, homeless and friendless, goaded to desperation by the teaching of designing men, clamoring for something they do not understand themselves, filled with a desire by a

32. Barton C. Shaw, "The Wool Hat Boys: A History of the Populist Party in Georgia" (Ph.D. diss., Emory University, 1979), 102–6; Jackson *Herald*, October 21, 1892; Adams, "Negro and Agrarian Movement," 142; Palmer, *"Man Over Money"*, 50–66.

reign of riot and confusion, to establish a new order of things based on chimerical values."[33]

The failure of Populism to address the specific plight of blacks and landless farmers generally reflected not only the persisting culture of independent proprietorship but also the particular social relations of the new cotton economy. For if white farmers were increasingly drawn into commercial agriculture and the attendant grip of merchant capital, the household remained the dominant productive unit. Although the raising of staple crops and the acquisition of basic necessities led to spiraling indebtedness and encumbrance and to a growing perception that they "worked for the other fellow" instead of for themselves, heads of farm households continued to rely on family labor. Consequently, they located exploitation in the sphere of exchange rather than at the point of production and looked directly to the credit and money, not the land, question as a solution to their predicament and as a means for rallying political insurgency.[34]

The historical experiences of Southern yeomen that underwrote and gave force to Populism's republican producer ideology created even further obstacles for a movement intent upon reshaping the regional and national landscape in the name of the "laboring classes." A legacy of exclusion from the immediate processes of political decision making, a highly personalized view of economic relations, and a decidedly moral interpretation of political conflict—widely shared by rural folk—made it difficult for the third party to confront the issue of power in an increasingly centralized and bureaucratized society. Nationally, these problems led to dissension, if not confusion, in the ranks when the question of translating the party platform into political reality was faced; and they contributed to the ascendancy of a "shadow movement" committed only to free silver and engineered by political leaders far more interested in electoral success than in radical reform. Locally, these problems hampered the effectiveness of Populist officeholders,

33. Gracewood *Wool Hat,* July 22, 1893; William F. Holmes, "The Demise of the Colored Farmers' Alliance," *JSH,* XLI (May 1975), 196–200. These racial tensions are, in some ways, comparable to the divisions between skilled and unskilled workers which plagued organizations like the Knights of Labor.

34. The Populist platform did include land planks, but they attacked only land held for speculative purposes or by absentee foreign syndicates and railroad companies; the planks did not address the issue of dispossession and accumulation by landlords and merchants. For an important discussion, see James Green, "Populism, Socialism, and the Promise of Democracy," *RHR,* XXIV (Fall 1980), 14–23.

who tended to win on symbolic issues such as abolishing the county courthouse—an action which promised, at best, to reduce taxes and ease the burdens of litigation. And the mixed records that third-party officials compiled hardly offered encouragement to debt-ridden constituents already harassed for their political leanings. Drawing upon the elements of rural disaffection, Populism articulated a bitter critique of capitalist relations and values, but it was no accident that much of its specific program came by way of the Greenbackers and other labor radicals.[35]

What appear to be missed opportunities, of course, can partly be attributed to a rather brief presence. Quite simply, the Populists had precious little time or room in which to move. Although the third party lived on into the early twentieth century, it dissolved as a mass movement after 1896—victimized by the superior resources and intense pressure brought to bear by its opponents. But here, too, internal weakness and contradiction contributed to collapse. Robert Preston Brooks, the economic historian, noted after a research trip through the Georgia Upcountry in 1911 that while black tenants and laborers organized, their white counterparts did not.[36] His caveat could have included yeoman farmers, for this form of self-activity seemed virtually absent among white rural common folk. An explanation may be found, not so much in a legacy of sturdy individualism, as in a complex of social relations that continued to link many of the landed and landless by kinship and that promoted cooperative exchanges between neighboring families. These very networks and norms of the household economy partially disguised class distinctions and probably discouraged reliance on supralocal, unfamiliar, and more formalized organizational structures. In this way, white farmers and tenants could rise to protect customary use rights, could sense and express shared grievances, yet make no attempt to mobilize their forces. If the Farmers' Alliance and the People's party provided an institutional focus for such discontent, they had a tenuous foundation to build upon, leaving the emergent rank

---

35. Goodwyn, *Democratic Promise*, 387–423; Palmer, "*Man Over Money*", 126–37, 199–221; Furgeson, "Power Politics," 57–69. Southern farmers did not fall victim to such weaknesses alone: the weaknesses were, and are, common to peasant movements as well. See Eric J. Hobsbawm, "Peasants and Politics," *Journal of Peasant Studies*, I (October 1973), 7–20.

36. Robert P. Brooks, "Report on District I," Economic Conditions on Georgia Plantations, II, 4–5, UGa.

and file with few means of defense against the fierce, and frequently violent, counterattack of elites who saw in Populism the forebodings of "communism" and "anarchism."[37]

The materials of social unrest, therefore, often flowed into pre-political forms of administering popular justice. As early as the fall of 1893, amid an unfolding nationwide depression, "white-cappers" of distinctly lower-class origin formulated their own remedy for economic distress: they sent anonymous notes to Upcountry merchants and land-lords warning of the torch if cotton were ginned or marketed before the price "reaches 10¢" a pound or if debts were collected before "the monetary stringency is past." The flames that soon engulfed several barns, dwellings, and gins may have evened some personal scores; they signaled the failings of the agrarian movement as well.[38] Only in Texas, where Populism culminated more than a decade of organized activity and benefited from labor support, did the third party show considerable resiliency and unflagging adherence to the full spectrum of Populist demands.

Yet, however beset with contradictions, Populism's commitment to political democracy and cooperative enterprise represented a radical alternative in the Gilded Age and a watershed in the history of industrializing America. On the heels of its demise came formal disfranchisement in the South and a long-range narrowing of political discussion and participation that was national in scope. If later federal farm legislation drew upon Populist programs, it was possible only after the movement's downfall and, not incidentally, served the interests of large landowners. As a further measure of Populism's import and character, defeat gave way to an accelerated process of rural disposses-sion, which left growing numbers of white Southern farmers in a condition of permanent landlessness and turned political protest in new directions. The scattered popular movements of the early twentieth century, especially the Socialist party which spread through the Southwest, set their sights on organizing tenants and laborers and

37. Carroll *Free Press*, August 5, 1892, August 31, 1894; Gwinnett *Herald*, December 20, 1892; Cherokee *Advance*, July 8, 1892.

38. Atlanta *Constitution*, October 25, 1893; Cherokee *Advance*, October 13, 1893, October 27, 1893; Marietta *Journal*, October 26, 1893; Carroll *Free Press*, October 13, 1893, October 27, 1893. Although white-capping erupted throughout the Lower South in the fall of 1893, its incidence in Georgia was confined almost exclusively to the western Upcountry.

evinced an increasingly proletarian sensibility.[39] But theirs was a sensibility owing much to the experiences and struggles of Populist predecessors.

39. James R. Green, *Grass-Roots Socialism: Radical Movements in the Southwest, 1895–1943* (Baton Rouge, 1978); Garin Burbank, *When Farmers Voted Red: The Gospel of Socialism in the Oklahoma Countryside, 1910–1924* (Westport, Conn., 1976).

Appendix
Statistical Methods
and Tables

Many of the statistical data for Jackson and Carroll counties, presented both in the text and in the following tables, are based on samples from the Federal Manuscript Census for the years 1850, 1860, 1870, and 1880. I drew the samples from the population schedule (Schedule I) and used the household as the basic sampling unit. The samples were systematic rather than random, which is to say that I selected every "nth" household on the schedule. The sampling fraction varied by county and year, for I wished to obtain samples of approximately the same size, not the same proportion, for each county in each census year. The approximate sample size was 400, which should leave an error range of ± 4 percent.

For the years 1850 and 1860 the population schedule includes only the households of white and free black inhabitants; slaves appear on a separate schedule. Since Jackson and Carroll counties had only a handful of free blacks, the sample households for these years are almost exclusively white. Sample sizes were as follows:

Year	County	Sample Size	System
1850	Jackson	400	Every 3rd household
1860	Jackson	447	Every 3rd household

Year	County	Sample Size	System
1850	Carroll	460	Every 3rd household
1860	Carroll	433	Every 4th household

In 1870 and 1880, however, the population schedule listed all households, white and black, but I used the identical sampling procedure. The sizes of these samples were as follows:

Year	County	Sample Size	System
1870	Jackson	411 white—292 black—119	Every 5th household
1880	Jackson	388 white—274 black—114	Every 8th household
1870	Carroll	417 white—384 black—33	Every 5th household
1880	Carroll	403 white—360 black—43	Every 8th household

As the sampling proceeded, I first recorded information on the age, sex, occupation, birthplace, and property holdings of the household heads and on the number and characteristics of other household members. Before 1880 the census did not specify kinship relations within the household, although reasonable inferences can be made. Next, I checked the manuscript agricultural schedule (Schedule II) to obtain additional information on those household heads who owned or operated farms. These data included the improved and unimproved acreage, the quantity of various crops produced, the value of farms, machinery, and household manufactures, and the number and value of livestock raised. Only in 1880 did the census record the land tenure of farm units or the acreage planted in different crops.[1] Finally, for 1850

1. The agricultural schedule for the years under consideration lists only farm operators. If an individual owned a farm and rented it out, the renter, not the landlord, would appear on the schedule. This presents special problems for the postbellum period. There is no way of determining the full extent of a landlord's holdings or which tenants worked for which

and 1860, I examined the manuscript slave schedule (Schedule III) to gather information on slaveholdings. The slave schedule does not list the names of slaves; it lists only age, sex, and color (black or mulatto) of each slave under the name of each owner.

Utilizing the data on households, crop production, and livestock, I constructed a "self-sufficiency index" for farm-operating households. The index represents a measure of the foodstuffs available for consumption by household members. I arrived at the index by converting all grain crops into corn-equivalents based on nutritional content, subtracting the seed and livestock-feed requirements, and dividing the residual by the total number of adults plus two-thirds of the children (adults considered as those eighteen years of age and older) in the household. Individuals under the age of eighteen were counted as adults if they were household heads or the spouses of household heads. Thus, the index shows whether a farm household raised surplus bushels of grain (and in the tables, the percentage of farm households raising grain surpluses).[2] For the antebellum period, I tabulated the self-sufficiency index only for slaveless farms, since other studies have shown that slaveowning farm households normally raised food surpluses.[3] For the postbellum period, I tabulated the index for farms operated by owners, share-tenants, and cash-tenants of both races, although from the tenants I subtracted one-third of the consumable grain to account for rent (widely stipulated as one-third of the corn, and perhaps other grain, crops). The postbellum index, it should be said, overestimates the percentage of farmers raising grain surpluses compared with the antebellum period, for the sketchy and often unreliable data on black farm labor in the 1880 census necessitated that I include all farms (whereas only slaveless farms were included for 1850 and 1860). The

---

landlords. Local tax records offer important supplemental data, but do not fully compensate. Due to widely acknowledged inaccuracies, agricultural data from the 1870 census were not recorded. On the problems with the 1870 census, see Roger L. Ransom and Richard Sutch, *One Kind of Freedom: The Economic Consequences of Emancipation* (Cambridge, 1977), 53.

2. For more details, see Ransom and Sutch, *One Kind of Freedom*, 244–53. I estimated subsistence at twenty bushels of grain per capita; additional bushels represented a surplus.

3. Robert Gallman, "Self-Sufficiency in the Cotton Economy of the Antebellum South," *AH*, XLIV (January 1970), 5–23; Raymond C. Battalio and John Kagel, "The Structure of Antebellum Southern Agriculture: South Carolina, a Case Study," *AH*, XLIV (January 1970), 25–37; Gavin Wright, *The Political Economy of the Cotton South: Households, Markets, and Wealth in the Nineteenth Century* (New York, 1978), 57–60.

1880 census, moreover, does not distinguish share-renters (who would usually be left with two-thirds of their grain crop) from sharecroppers (who would usually be left with only one-half of their grain crop), so the further deduction of one-third would be the minimum appropriated by the landlord.

A few words of caution are in order. Aside from the basic sampling error, the statistics have other problematic features. For one thing, county boundary lines occasionally changed from one census year to another (and it is very difficult to take account of this when the changes did not follow previously designated district lines), so the sample universe may not be entirely uniform. This was true for Carroll County, which lost a small section to a newly created county between 1850 and 1860. But since that section was one of the least commercialized areas in Carroll, the error is biased against my general conclusions. Error also derives from the way in which the census data were originally compiled. While the census bureau provided detailed instructions to field-workers, the field-workers often made their own judgments. As a result, there are variations in format from county to county; figures on property holding, crop production, and livestock are commonly estimates; households, especially of poor farmers and laborers, were at times overlooked; and occasionally all relevant information for households was not recorded. Hence it should not be assumed that any variable is a precise measurement. It can be assumed, however, that the census offers reliable indications of general patterns.

The following tables are all derived from the Federal Manuscript Census unless otherwise noted.

Table I Occupations of Household Heads, Jackson and Carroll Counties, 1850–1880

| | % White Household Heads | | | | | | % Black Household Heads | |
| | 1850 | | 1860 | | 1880 | | 1880 | |
Occupation	Jack.	Carr.	Jack.	Carr.	Jack.	Carr.	Jack.	Carr.
Farmer	53.6	52.4	60.5	55.3	49.6	51.1	7.9	10.0
Farmer (No Real Estate)	21.8	22.3	8.7	23.0	18.0	30.4	4.0	40.0
Trade[1]	1.5	2.4	0.7	2.1	2.1	2.7	0.0	0.0
Professional[2]	2.4	2.6	3.7	3.0	2.1	2.7	0.0	5.0
Service[3]	0.3	0.0	0.0	0.2	0.4	0.6	0.0	0.0
Skilled and Semiskilled[4]	8.1	12.6	11.0	11.4	3.3	4.6	3.0	2.5
Unskilled								
—Farm Laborer	11.1	7.5	14.7	4.3	22.9	2.4	81.2	17.5
—Other Laborer	0.6	0.0	0.0	0.7	0.8	5.5	3.9	25.0
Other	0.6	0.2	0.0	0.0	0.8	0.0	0.0	0.0
Total[5]	100.0	100.0	100.0	100.0	100.0	100.0	100.0	100.0
Number	332	454	428	430	240	329	101	40
Agricultural Pop.[6]	288	373	361	357	217	277	94	27

[1] Includes merchants, grocers, and other shopkeepers.

[2] Includes lawyers, physicians, clergymen, teachers, and political officials.

[3] Includes hotel, stable, and saloon keepers.

[4] Includes artisans and helpers likely to acquire a skill such as "works in blacksmith shop".

[5] Does not include household heads reporting no occupation or "keeping house".

[6] Number reporting occupations involved principally with agriculture: farmer, farm laborer, overseer, etc. Includes "laborer" for 1850 since designation "farm laborer" not used in that year.

Table II Cotton and Slaves on Farms, Jackson and Carroll Counties, 1850–1880

Farm Size (Imp. Acres)	Jackson County					Carroll County				
	% Owning Slaves		% Growing Cotton			% Owning Slaves		% Growing Cotton		
	1850	1860	1850	1860	1880*	1850	1860	1850	1860	1880*
1–24	100	0	0	30	68	7	8	28	75	81
25–49	24	24	48	47	95	13	20	49	89	93
50–99	49	59	51	73	95	24	27	48	85	93
100–199	59	77	75	92	100	53	65	33	90	100
200–299	85	100	80	75	100	86	63	43	100	100
300–499	90	100	80	80	—	100	100	100	100	100
500+	100	—	100	—	—	—	100	—	100	—
County Percentages	59	49	66	65	91	22	30	41	87	91
Number of Farms	163	249	163	249	121	240	207	240	207	158

* Includes only owner-operated farms.

Table III Distribution of Slaveholdings Among White Households, Jackson and Carroll Counties, 1850–1860

Number of Slaves	Jackson County				Carroll County			
	% Household Heads		% Landowning Farmers		% Household Heads		% Landowning Farmers	
	1850	1860	1850	1860	1850	1860	1850	1860
0	67.5	68.5	48.3	54.4	85.5	82.7	78.4	72.1
1	7.8	5.7	8.8	7.7	3.7	3.5	5.1	5.8
2–4	7.8	10.1	13.2	14.7	3.7	6.9	5.9	10.1
5–9	7.5	8.1	11.2	11.6	3.9	3.9	6.4	6.6
10–14	4.0	3.7	7.8	5.5	1.4	1.8	1.9	3.0
15–19	1.5	1.3	2.9	2.1	0.6	0.5	1.4	0.7
20–29	2.7	1.8	5.3	2.5	0.9	0.5	0.9	1.4
30–39	1.0	0.6	2.0	1.1	0.0	0.2	0.0	0.3
40–49	0.2	0.2	0.5	0.4	0.0	0.0	0.0	0.0
Total	100.0	100.0	100.0	100.0	100.0	100.0	100.0	100.0
Number of Households	400	447	205	285	460	433	259	254

Table IV Distribution of Slaves Among White Household Heads, Jackson and Carroll Counties, 1850–1860 (By Decile of Real Wealth)

Rank	Jackson County		Carroll County	
	% of Slave Population		% of Slave Population	
	1850	1860	1850	1860
Top Decile	59.7*	53.1*	67.8*	58.3*
Second Decile	19.8*	19.4*	19.1*	16.6*
Third Decile	8.8*	13.2*	4.9*	7.0*
Fourth Decile	3.0*	8.9*	2.8*	9.3*
Fifth Decile	2.1*	2.4*	1.0*	5.2*
Sixth Decile	1.0**	1.7*	0.5**	1.0*
Seventh Decile	0.1	0.2**	0.0	0.6**
Eighth Decile	1.9	0.5	0.3	0.0
Ninth Decile	1.9	0.6	0.8	0.5
Tenth Decile	1.7	0.0	2.8	0.5
Total	100.0	100.0	100.0	100.0
Number of Slaves	1,026	1,015	388	416

* All in decile own real estate.
** Most in decile own real estate.

Table V Production and Property on White Owner-Operated Farms, Jackson County, 1850–1880 (Mean Values)

Item	Farm Size (Improved Acres)								
	1–24			25–49			50–99		
	1850	1860	1880	1850	1860	1880	1850	1860	1880
Number of Farms	1	20	22	21	79	39	47	85	38
Improved Acres (No.)	24.1	15.9	12.7	33.9	33.9	33.1	65.8	65.2	69.2
Unimproved Acres (No.)	0.0	88.6	46.4	111.6	111.4	71.2	131.5	237.7	146.4
Slaves (No.)	1.0	0.0	—	0.6	0.6	—	1.4	2.9	—
Value Farm Machinery ($)	12.0	25.5	18.6	24.9	40.8	37.5	52.9	70.7	53.3
Value Household Mfgs. ($)	11.0	7.0	—	28.8	13.8	—	38.2	23.4	—
Horses (No.)	1.0	1.5	0.6	1.9	1.5	0.8	2.3	2.6	1.1
Asses and Mules (No.)	0.0	0.2	0.4	0.1	0.3	0.7	0.2	0.7	1.1
Oxen (No.)	0.0	0.7	0.0	0.9	0.6	0.2	0.9	1.1	0.2
Milch Cows (No.)	1.0	2.0	0.9	2.2	2.0	1.7	2.9	2.9	2.0
Other Cattle (No.)	3.0	1.8	1.1	4.3	1.6	2.1	3.8	3.0	3.1
Sheep (No.)	0.0	3.0	0.1	5.0	3.5	1.4	5.7	6.3	5.2
Swine (No.)	12.0	7.6	4.6	19.9	10.3	5.8	23.3	15.6	8.9
Wheat (Bu.)	27.0	11.9	11.6	17.3	19.4	31.8	27.4	43.7	34.9
Corn (Bu.)	278.0	115.0	51.0	327.4	202.4	125.0	418.1	360.1	182.8
Oats (Bu.)	0.0	2.1	3.1	50.9	5.5	26.7	65.9	18.0	40.2
Cotton (Bales)	0.0	0.5	2.0	0.7	0.8	4.5	1.0	1.7	6.8
Peas and Beans (Bu.)	0.0	1.3	1.4	7.4	4.5	2.4	12.1	12.4	3.9
Sweet Potatoes (Bu.)	100.0	15.9	4.8	52.5	30.5	12.7	60.9	50.8	17.2
Cotton/Improved Acres*	—	—	47%	—	—	40%	—	—	27%
% Raising Grain Surplus**	—	39%	15%	94%	63%	48%	96%	76%	66%

* Ratio of acreage in cotton to total improved acreage.

** Includes only slaveless farms for 1850 and 1860.

Table V, *continued*

Item	100–199			200–299			300–499		
	1850	1860	1880	1850	1860	1880	1850	1860	1880
Number of Farms	56	47	17	20	8	5	10	10	—
Improved Acres (No.)	129.2	116.1	118.1	233.5	206.3	218.0	338.0	322.0	—
Unimproved Acres (No.)	201.1	293.7	246.7	378.8	621.3	205.8	509.0	978.0	—
Slaves (No.)	4.5	5.3	—	9.6	14.5	—	19.0	23.8	—
Value Farm Machinery ($)	85.3	133.2	95.9	174.1	199.4	112.0	288.5	388.0	—
Value Household Mfgs. ($)	45.1	21.6	—	87.5	40.1	—	95.7	32.3	—
Horses (No.)	3.2	2.9	1.8	5.1	3.1	2.4	6.8	4.8	—
Asses and Mules (No.)	0.3	1.5	2.4	1.1	2.5	3.2	2.0	5.0	—
Oxen (No.)	1.5	1.7	0.4	2.0	1.5	0.8	2.0	2.0	—
Milch Cows (No.)	3.9	3.5	3.9	5.8	5.0	3.4	6.6	7.3	—
Other Cattle (No.)	6.5	3.5	3.9	10.3	5.3	8.2	16.1	7.0	—
Sheep (No.)	9.7	9.2	6.0	10.1	12.5	4.2	13.4	7.1	—
Swine (No.)	31.4	21.1	15.4	50.6	39.1	16.6	63.0	53.8	—
Wheat (Bu.)	40.3	63.0	81.4	62.9	96.9	181.8	65.1	86.2	—
Corn (Bu.)	589.1	546.3	480.6	848.0	875.0	690.0	1,325.0	1,287.0	—
Oats (Bu.)	129.7	17.6	105.2	224.4	91.3	166.0	382.3	57.4	—
Cotton (Bales)	2.4	3.8	13.4	4.6	7.9	29.4	6.4	8.1	—
Peas and Beans (Bu.)	12.7	8.8	8.5	20.4	38.1	20.0	39.6	50.3	—
Sweet Potatoes (Bu.)	77.0	75.4	33.2	197.5	134.4	23.0	180.0	175.0	—
Cotton/Improved Acres*	—	—	31%	—	—	36%	—	—	—
% Raising Grain Surplus**	91%	91%	94%	100%	—	100%	—	—	—

Table V, *continued*

Item	Farm Size (Improved Acres)		
	500 +		
	1850	1860	1880
Number of Farms	8	—	—
Improved Acres (No.)	512.5	—	—
Unimproved Acres (No.)	775.0	—	—
Slaves (No.)	26.5	—	—
Value Farm Machinery ($)	269.5	—	—
Value Household Mfgs. ($)	82.5	—	—
Horses (No.)	6.3	—	—
Asses and Mules (No.)	3.0	—	—
Oxen (No.)	4.8	—	—
Milch Cows (No.)	8.6	—	—
Other Cattle (No.)	25.6	—	—
Sheep (No.)	20.8	—	—
Swine (No.)	62.5	—	—
Wheat (Bu.)	145.1	—	—
Corn (Bu.)	1,843.8	—	—
Oats (Bu.)	343.5	—	—
Cotton (Bales)	9.4	—	—
Peas and Beans (Bu.)	83.8	—	—
Sweet Potatoes (Bu.)	168.8	—	—
Cotton/Improved Acres*	—	—	—
% Raising Grain Surplus**	—	—	—

Table VI Production and Property on White Owner-Operated Farms, Carroll County, 1850–1880 (Mean Values)

| Item | Farm Size (Improved Acres) | | | | | | | | |
| | 1–24 | | | 25–49 | | | 50–99 | | |
	1850	1860	1880	1850	1860	1880	1850	1860	1880
Number of Farms	76	24	42	69	74	57	54	67	40
Improved Acres (No.)	13.6	14.9	15.9	34.6	34.1	34.9	64.4	65.6	64.2
Unimproved Acres (No.)	141.4	91.5	63.9	152.5	109.7	108.1	198.5	140.6	142.8
Slaves (No.)	0.4	0.3	—	0.4	0.4	—	1.0	1.3	—
Value Farm Machinery ($)	19.2	27.8	11.1	33.9	33.7	39.5	61.7	57.1	27.3
Value Household Mfgs. ($)	17.4	10.6	—	20.8	16.3	—	32.5	17.3	—
Horses (No.)	1.3	0.9	0.4	1.5	1.3	0.6	2.5	1.7	1.1
Asses and Mules (No.)	0.2	0.3	0.5	0.3	0.4	0.7	0.4	0.8	1.4
Oxen (No.)	0.6	0.5	0.3	1.1	1.3	0.5	1.4	1.7	0.4
Milch Cows (No.)	2.0	1.8	1.4	2.7	2.4	1.9	3.6	2.8	2.8
Other Cattle (No.)	3.4	2.2	1.7	5.4	3.1	2.5	9.1	4.3	3.5
Sheep (No.)	1.8	1.5	2.5	3.7	4.3	5.9	9.8	7.7	9.1
Swine (No.)	17.5	9.6	6.9	20.9	14.3	9.8	36.3	22.7	10.8
Wheat (Bu.)	8.3	14.5	19.8	15.6	25.1	32.9	35.3	45.1	49.8
Corn (Bu.)	154.9	180.6	100.5	261.5	221.3	251.9	429.5	334.8	249.3
Oats (Bu.)	11.1	3.2	27.7	31.7	6.2	34.6	66.7	15.6	53.3
Cotton (Bales)	0.9	2.2	2.6	1.2	2.4	4.1	1.6	3.6	5.4
Peas and Beans (Bu.)	3.1	0.9	1.0	4.5	1.9	1.8	10.0	3.2	2.4
Sweet Potatoes (Bu.)	41.2	40.5	3.5	45.9	49.1	15.8	84.7	57.8	8.4
Cotton/Improved Acres*	—	—	39%	—	—	30%	—	—	20%
% Raising Grain Surplus**	49%	67%	38%	72%	65%	68%	82%	82%	77%

* Ratio of acreage in cotton to total improved acreage.
** Includes only slaveless farms for 1850 and 1860.

Table VI, *continued*

Item	100–199			200–299			300–499		
	1850	1860	1880	1850	1860	1880	1850	1860	1880
Number of Farms	30	31	13	7	8	5	4	2	1
Improved Acres (No.)	114.5	122.0	112.0	214.3	203.1	211.8	337.5	370.2	350.0
Unimproved Acres (No.)	355.7	293.4	134.9	1,148.6	404.5	414.4	1,412.5	350.0	200.0
Slaves (No.)	4.0	3.9	—	7.0	8.5	—	20.0	17.0	—
Value Farm Machinery ($)	138.2	112.5	44.6	177.1	112.5	108.0	316.3	287.5	0.0
Value Household Mfgs. ($)	37.7	48.7	—	48.6	16.7	—	75.0	50.0	—
Horses (No.)	3.0	2.8	0.5	2.7	3.3	2.2	4.5	2.0	0.0
Asses and Mules (No.)	0.7	1.8	1.0	1.9	1.6	1.2	2.8	6.5	2.0
Oxen (No.)	2.1	2.1	0.3	2.4	2.7	0.8	3.0	5.0	0.0
Milch Cows (No.)	5.0	5.4	2.3	7.7	6.5	2.0	13.3	7.5	2.0
Other Cattle (No.)	14.4	6.4	3.8	20.6	7.7	5.8	36.3	15.5	4.0
Sheep (No.)	9.7	10.3	3.3	13.9	11.2	7.0	41.3	40.5	0.0
Swine (No.)	44.7	27.2	10.2	58.6	35.2	13.0	97.5	75.0	20.0
Wheat (Bu.)	49.2	62.5	69.8	56.6	73.5	32.3	96.5	75.0	480.0
Corn (Bu.)	583.3	562.1	250.0	792.9	887.5	250.0	1,625.0	1,400.0	500.0
Oats (Bu.)	122.0	25.1	136.2	156.4	19.5	62.5	175.0	107.5	15.0
Cotton (Bales)	2.0	7.9	6.4	2.6	11.8	9.3	28.0	31.0	13.0
Peas and Beans (Bu.)	9.2	5.0	4.6	21.7	4.0	10.0	3.8	25.0	0.0
Sweet Potatoes (Bu.)	111.0	82.3	15.8	147.1	91.7	44.0	237.5	125.0	0.0
Cotton/Improved Acres*	—	—	15 %	—	—	12 %	—	—	14 %
% Raising Grain Surplus**	93 %	80 %	92 %	100 %	100 %	100 %	—	—	100 %

Farm Size (Improved Acres)

Table VI, *continued*

Item	Farm Size (Improved Acres)		
	500+		
	1850	1860	1880
Number of Farms	—	1	—
Improved Acres (No.)	—	500.0	—
Unimproved Acres (No.)	—	800.0	—
Slaves (No.)	—	32.0	—
Value Farm Machinery ($)	—	300.0	—
Value Household Mfgs. ($)	—	25.0	—
Horses (No.)	—	4.0	—
Asses and Mules (No.)	—	7.0	—
Oxen (No.)	—	6.0	—
Milch Cows (No.)	—	20.0	—
Other Cattle (No.)	—	20.0	—
Sheep (No.)	—	25.0	—
Swine (No.)	—	150.0	—
Wheat (Bu.)	—	360.0	—
Corn (Bu.)	—	2,000.0	—
Oats (Bu.)	—	50.0	—
Cotton (Bales)	—	47.0	—
Peas and Beans (Bu.)	—	75.0	—
Sweet Potatoes (Bu.)	—	500.0	—
Cotton/Improved Acres*	—	—	—
% Raising Grain Surplus**	—	—	—

Table VII Production and Property on White Tenant-Operated Farms, Jackson County, 1860–1880 (Mean Values)

| Item | 1860 | Farm Size (Improved Acres), 1880 | | | | | | | |
| | | 1–24 | | 25–49 | | 50–99 | | 100–199 | |
		Share Tenant	Cash Tenant	Share Tenant	Cash Tenant	Share Tenant	Cash Tenant	Share Tenant	Cash Tenant
Number of Farms	9	5*	1**	12	2	6	2	1	—
Improved Acres (No.)	NA	17.6	18.0	30.4	43.0	55.0	73.0	100.0	—
Unimproved Acres (No.)	NA	6.0	0.0	63.3	63.0	62.2	188.0	225.0	—
Value Farm Machinery ($)	31.1	2.0	30.0	17.5	7.0	15.8	47.5	100.0	—
Horses (No.)	2.3	0.4	1.0	0.8	2.0	1.3	0.5	1.0	—
Asses and Mules (No.)	0.3	0.0	1.0	0.3	0.0	0.8	1.0	4.0	—
Oxen (No.)	1.0	0.0	0.0	0.1	0.5	0.3	0.1	0.0	—
Milch Cows (No.)	3.2	1.0	1.0	1.5	2.0	2.0	2.5	6.0	—
Other Cattle (No.)	3.3	1.2	1.0	1.3	2.0	2.3	2.5	12.0	—
Sheep (No.)	5.6	0.0	0.0	0.0	0.0	1.7	5.0	5.0	—
Swine (No.)	16.4	5.6	2.0	6.5	7.5	5.7	11.0	8.0	—
Wheat (Bu.)	31.7	3.2	0.0	14.9	7.0	26.5	15.5	29.0	—
Corn (Bu.)	292.2	53.0	40.0	165.4	50.0	213.3	250.0	600.0	—
Oats (Bu.)	0.0	14.0	0.0	8.3	0.0	20.3	14.0	20.1	—
Cotton (Bales)	1.6	2.6	4.0	4.3	3.5	6.5	7.0	16.0	—
Peas and Beans (Bu.)	2.2	0.0	0.0	2.8	0.0	1.5	25.0	8.0	—
Sweet Potatoes (Bu.)	18.6	0.0	0.0	6.2	0.0	15.0	0.0	20.0	—
Cotton/Improved Acres	—	46 %	56 %	42 %	19 %	39 %	24 %	40 %	—
% Raising Grain Surplus	—	0 %	0 %	17 %	0 %	33 %	100 %	100 %	—

* Does not include 4 farms reporting production but no acreage.

** Does not include 6 farms reporting production but no acreage.

NA—Not available. Census normally listed tenant operators in 1860 with crop production, livestock, and equipment values but with no acreage reported. Tenants here would be most comparable to those in the 1–24 and 25–49 improved acres categories.

Table VIII Production and Property on White Tenant-Operated Farms, Carroll County, 1860–1880 (Mean Values)

| Item | 1860 | Farm Size (Improved Acres), 1880 | | | | | | | |
| | | 1–24 | | 25–49 | | 50–99 | | 100–199 | |
		Share Tenant	Cash Tenant	Share Tenant	Cash Tenant	Share Tenant	Cash Tenant	Share Tenant	Cash Tenant
Number of Farms	23	41	7	24	2	9	—	4	—
Improved Acres (No.)	NA	14.7	14.1	28.9	29.0	61.2	—	124.8	—
Unimproved Acres (No.)	NA	3.0	10.3	16.9	3.0	44.4	—	130.0	—
Value Farm Machinery ($)	9.9	6.3	4.7	5.3	2.5	7.4	—	5.3	—
Horses (No.)	0.7	0.1	0.7	0.5	1.5	0.4	—	1.8	—
Asses and Mules (No.)	0.3	0.2	0.2	0.4	0.0	1.1	—	0.3	—
Oxen (No.)	0.7	0.3	0.2	0.3	0.0	0.4	—	0.3	—
Milch Cows (No.)	1.4	1.0	1.2	1.3	0.5	1.1	—	1.8	—
Other Cattle (No.)	1.4	1.0	1.2	1.8	0.5	1.9	—	2.8	—
Sheep (No.)	3.1	0.6	1.6	2.0	0.0	5.1	—	0.0	—
Swine (No.)	9.0	4.3	2.6	4.8	6.0	7.8	—	10.5	—
Wheat (Bu.)	17.2	9.6	5.0	17.7	2.5	59.6	—	38.3	—
Corn (Bu.)	164.7	114.2	109.3	142.3	100.0	231.1	—	243.8	—
Oats (Bu.)	9.0	9.7	9.6	31.5	50.0	26.7	—	41.3	—
Cotton (Bales)	2.2	3.0	4.3	3.5	3.5	4.6	—	5.3	—
Peas and Beans (Bu.)	1.1	0.0	0.0	0.4	4.0	0.6	—	5.5	—
Sweet Potatoes (Bu.)	28.7	4.5	0.0	5.0	4.0	12.8	—	0.0	—
Cotton/Improved Acres*	—	52%	33%	31%	29%	21%	—	11%	—
% Raising Grain Surplus	—	24%	14%	41%	0%	44%	—	50%	—

NA—Not available. Census normally listed tenant operators in 1860 with crop production, livestock, and equipment values but with no acreage reported. Tenants here would be most comparable to those in the 1–24 and 25–49 improved acres categories.

* Ratio of acreage in cotton to total improved acreage.

Table IX Production and Property on Black-Operated Farms, Jackson County, 1880 (Mean Values)

| | Farm Size (Improved Acres) | | | | | | | |
| | 1–24 | | 25–49 | | 50–99 | | 100–199 | |
Item	Owner	Share Tenant	Owner	Share Tenant	Owner	Share Tenant	Owner	Share Tenant
Number of Farms	2	2	2	1	1	1	2	—
Improved Acres (No.)	21.0	19.0	30.0	36.0	50.0	64.0	116.0	—
Unimproved Acres (No.)	29.5	0.0	132.0	114.0	100.0	168.0	185.0	—
Value Farm Machinery ($)	9.0	2.5	22.5	30.0	15.0	60.0	35.0	—
Horses (No.)	1.0	0.0	1.0	0.0	2.0	2.0	2.0	—
Asses and Mules (No.)	0.0	0.5	1.0	1.0	1.0	2.0	1.5	—
Oxen (No.)	0.0	0.0	1.0	0.0	0.0	0.0	1.0	—
Milch Cows (No.)	0.0	0.5	1.0	0.0	1.0	2.0	3.5	—
Other Cattle (No.)	0.5	1.0	1.5	1.0	5.0	4.0	4.5	—
Sheep (No.)	0.0	0.0	0.0	0.0	0.0	0.0	2.0	—
Swine (No.)	0.0	4.0	4.5	0.0	5.0	0.0	16.0	—
Wheat (Bu.)	0.0	1.0	30.9	25.0	9.0	20.0	73.0	—
Corn (Bu.)	5.0	75.0	45.0	100.0	75.0	147.0	575.0	—
Oats (Bu.)	0.0	2.5	0.0	0.0	0.0	9.0	10.0	—
Cotton (Bales)	2.0	2.5	5.5	4.0	6.0	9.0	13.5	—
Peas and Beans (Bu.)	0.0	0.0	0.0	2.0	3.0	0.0	0.0	—
Sweet Potatoes (Bu.)	0.0	0.0	0.0	0.0	8.0	0.0	0.0	—
Cotton/Improved Acres*	38%	37%	55%	40%	50%	33%	26%	—
% Raising Grain Surplus	0%	0%	0%	0%	0%	0%	100%	—

*Ratio of acreage in cotton to total improved acreage.

Table X   Production and Property on Black-Operated Farms, Carroll County, 1880 (Mean Values)

	Farm Size (Improved Acres)			
	1–24		25–49	
Item	Owner	Share Tenant	Owner	Share Tenant
Number of Farms	1	7	1	6
Improved Acres (No.)	20.0	16.0	40.0	34.5
Unimproved Acres (No.)	20.0	0.0	30.0	74.3
Value Farm Machinery ($)	10.0	2.1	5.0	9.5
Horses (No.)	0.0	0.3	0.0	0.3
Asses and Mules (No.)	0.0	0.2	1.0	0.3
Oxen (No.)	2.0	0.0	2.0	0.0
Milch Cows (No.)	0.0	0.9	2.0	1.3
Other Cattle (No.)	0.0	0.7	3.0	1.5
Sheep (No.)	1.0	0.0	1.0	0.0
Swine (No.)	0.0	2.1	0.0	6.3
Wheat (Bu.)	0.0	1.5	24.0	20.3
Corn (Bu.)	0.0	82.5	200.0	109.2
Oats (Bu.)	0.0	13.3	25.0	14.2
Cotton (Bales)	0.0	7.8	5.0	2.3
Peas and Beans (Bu.)	0.0	0.0	0.0	0.0
Sweet Potatoes (Bu.)	40.0	6.7	0.0	5.0
Cotton/Improved Acres*	0%	61%	37%	17%
% Raising Grain Surplus	0%	0%	0%	17%

*Ratio of acreage in cotton to total improved acreage.

Table XI Jackson County Militia Districts, 1890

District:	Per Capita* Wealth	% White	% Land-owners	No. Units 500+ Acres	% Land in Units 500+ Acres
Town and Village:					
Jefferson	$1,210	73%	52%	9	25.9%
Minishes (Harmony Grove)	1,364	80%	49%	10	29.0%
Wilsons (Maysville)	1,055	75%	45%	2	17.9%
Houses (Winder)	827	84%	47%	8	29.9%
Cunningham (Pendergrass)	777	76%	49%	9	31.5%
Rural:					
Harrisburg	866	68%	49%	5	15.4%
Hoschton	852	84%	52%	6	37.9%
Newtown	768	70%	53%	6	21.1%
Millers	765	80%	44%	5	4.9%
Clarksboro	741	64%	53%	5	15.0%
Chandlers	592	75%	46%	1	4.5%
Santafe	554	60%	52%	3	16.7%
Randolphs	506	85%	41%	4	20.5%

*Total wealth divided by total number of persons on tax rolls.

Source: Jackson County Tax Digest, 1890.

Table XII Carroll County Militia Districts, 1890

District	Per Capita* Wealth	% White	% Land-owners	No. Units 500 + Acres	% Land in Units 500 + Acres
Town and Village:					
Carrollton	$1,530	85 %	65 %	17	24.3 %
Whitesburg	1,000	82 %	57 %	6	31.9 %
Bowdon	985	89 %	61 %	6	23.5 %
Villa Rica	969	79 %	55 %	2	7.1 %
Temple	837	78 %	60 %	2	5.9 %
Roopville	631	80 %	62 %	5	20.6 %
Rural					
Cross Plains	1,186	94 %	51 %	3	11.9 %
County Line	1,039	86 %	49 %	0	0.0 %
Fairplay	687	88 %	52 %	0	0.0 %
Turkey Creek	686	98 %	64 %	5	31.8 %
Kansas	683	94 %	53 %	2	14.8 %
New Mexico	674	100 %	69 %	1	11.9 %
Lowell	567	96 %	60 %	0	0.0 %
Shiloh	686	92 %	64 %	0	0.0 %
Smithfield	504	100 %	57 %	2	10.6 %
Flint Corner	428	91 %	68 %	0	0.0 %

*Total wealth divided by total number of persons on tax rolls.

Source: Carroll County Tax Digest, 1890.

Essay on Sources

This study draws upon a considerable array of primary sources, from local records and manuscript collections deposited in numerous archives to published materials of the state and Federal governments and to newspapers and travelers' accounts. It also owes much in inception, perspective, and methodology to the work of previous scholars. Here I should like to discuss those sources found to be most helpful and influential. More complete bibliographic references can be located in the footnotes.

Primary Sources—Unpublished

Local

During the past two decades, historians of urban and rural communities in the North have brought valuable sources for the study of common people to scholarly attention. While Southern historians have only begun to follow their leads, a good deal of pertinent material is available, and I have utilized it extensively. Perhaps the richest is the Federal Manuscript Census, widely accessible on microfilm. Compiled on a decennial basis, the census includes information on individual households and farms: the name, age, sex, occupation, birthplace, and real- and personal-property holdings of household members; the improved and unimproved acreage on farms; the quantities of various crops raised; the value of farm equipment and home manufactures; and the number of livestock present, among other things. Beginning in 1880, the relationships of household members and the land tenure of farm units are also specified, although not until the twentieth century does the census record data for plantations embracing smaller tenant farms. The households are listed by state and county and, for 1860 on, by districts within counties.

This information was supplemented by a variety of local records housed in the Georgia Department of Archives and History in Atlanta and in the Jackson County and Carroll County courthouses. The county tax digests were particularly helpful. They contain listings of real- and personal-property holdings of taxpayers. Since a poll tax was in effect for the entire period under consideration, propertyless adults are included as well, although they are underrepresented. For the antebellum era, the digests are often scattered, but those extant elaborate landholdings in counties other than that of residence along with the locations of all holdings by land lot (neither of which can be found in the census). For the postbellum era, the digests are generally available for the years after 1872 and have the additional merits of being alphabetized and distinguished by race. Thus, I was able to explore the changing structure of landownership in greater detail than the manuscript census (which does not exist for 1890) allowed. For some of these years, moreover, blacks are listed with the name of their employer when appropriate. Caution must, of course, be exercised when using the digests, because property holdings being assessed for tax purposes might be understated.

Much insight into the dynamics of social and economic life in the Georgia Upcountry was provided by voluminous probate records. Along with inventories and appraisements of the deceased's property, they contain wills, store accounts, notes, and sale bills from estate auctions. I found these especially valuable for examining domestic economy, local exchange, and inheritance. Unlike the census or tax digests, which enumerate only the value of most personal property, the probate records delineate specific items and assets: spinning wheels and looms, pots and pans, chairs and tables, hoes and plows, cash on hand, and debts owed the estate, to name just a few. They are also generally indexed. Deed and mortgage records offer further evidence on property transmission and trading relations. The mortgages were extremely helpful for exploring the changing dimensions of credit and exchange, most notably the rise of the lien system during the postwar years. They denote the parties involved, the amount at issue, the property at stake, the schedule of payment, the interest charged, and the nature of the transaction. Before the 1880s, mortgages and deeds were compiled in the same volumes; thereafter, they were separated. While the mortgage books for Jackson County in the 1880s have apparently disappeared, those for Carroll County survive in the vault of the courthouse.

The records of the Inferior and Superior courts proved somewhat disappointing. Though adequate in specifying the cases commonly litigated and in delineating the process of adjudication, they rarely included depositions. I did find the court records useful for understanding public attitudes and customs regarding indebtedness, however. The minutes of the Superior Court, furthermore, contained the presentments of the county grand jury, which convened during twice-yearly court sessions and commented on various local affairs.

State

The Georgia Department of Archives and History contains sizable collections of unpublished state documents which illuminate social and political developments in the Upcountry. The Executive Department Governors' Correspondence varied in usefulness, but that for Governor Joseph E. Brown was immensely valuable, especially for the Civil War period. Hundreds of letters, catalogued in over thirty boxes, had flowed into the governor's office from all over the state and from the troops in the field. These offer, perhaps, the best and most extensive literary evidence regarding the sentiments and values of white common folk to be found for any period during the nineteenth century. Other state records important for this study included the Executive Department listings of County Officers and Officers' Bonds; the Secretary of State Justice of the Peace Commissions; the Legislative Department Incoming Petitions; and the records of the state-owned Western and Atlantic Railroad, which contain schedules of freight shipped from various depots and correspondence pertaining to business and legal concerns of the road.

Federal

Until recently, the records of the Bureau of Refugees, Freedmen, and Abandoned Lands (the Freedmen's Bureau), established by Congress in 1865, lay uncatalogued in the National Archives and virtually untouched by historians. Happily, thanks to a major organizing effort, they are now widely available and have proved to be a gold mine for the early Reconstruction period. While primarily concerned with the ex-slaves, they contain a great deal of information on general social, economic, and political developments for the years 1865–1868. The Records of the Assistant Commissioner for the State of Georgia, both on microfilm and in manuscript, were used extensively. They included monthly reports from bureau agents in several parts of the Upcountry detailing labor arrangements, race relations, economic dislocations, and various social and political conflicts.

The records of two other federal agencies created during Reconstruction also were extremely helpful: the Bureau of Civil Affairs provided much documentation on conditions among Upcountry whites as well as blacks; the Southern Claims Commission, instituted to reimburse loyal Southern whites for damages inflicted by federal armies during the war, took testimony from self-proclaimed Unionists regarding their sentiments towards secession and the Confederacy and their acitivites during the war. The commission files have rarely been tapped by historians, and they must be approached with care. Hoping to win monetary restitutions, many of those submitting claims doubtless exaggerated their wartime fealty to the federal government. But the documents are organized by state and county, and they do provide significant clues to the nature and social bases of opposition to the Confederacy. The records of both the Bureau of Civil Affairs and the Southern Claims Commission are deposited in the National Archives.

Paper Collections

In that little more than functional literacy prevailed among most yeoman farmers, relevant collections of private papers are few and far between; and those turning up generally provide limited rewards. The papers of local planters and substantial farmers, however, have much to say about the texture of social life among rich and poor alike. For the antebellum period, I found several such collections useful. The Thomas Maguire Family Papers from Gwinnett County (AHS) and the James Washington Watts papers from Cass County (GDAH) provide valuable perspectives on class relations. Detailed information on farm tenancy can be uncovered in the Chunn-Land Family Papers from Cass County (GDAH); the John S. Dobbins Papers from Gordon County

(EU); the Lucius H. Featherston Papers from Heard County (EU); the Joseph E. Brown Papers from Cherokee County (UGa); and the George B. Hudson Store and Farm Account Books from Gwinnett County (GDAH).

For local trading relations involving artisans and merchants, one may consult the fascinating account books of the blacksmith Job Bowers from Hart County (GDAH); the Foster and King Mill Account Book from Cherokee County (GDAH); the Thomas Morris Store Ledger from Franklin County (GDAH); and the Fain Account Book from Floyd County (GDAH). The papers of Stephen D. Heard (SHC), an Augusta cotton factor, include information on itinerant cotton buyers in the Upcountry. But the best sources on local merchandisers are the Credit Reporting Ledgers of the R. G. Dun and Company, located in the Baker Library at Harvard University. Beginning in the late 1840s, Dun and Company agents filed reports on storekeepers in every county in Georgia—and the entire United States—that touched upon capital investment, partnerships, the extent and nature of operations, credit ratings, and moral character. The ledgers are available for the years up through 1880.

Three other collections are helpful on the social and economic affairs of antebellum yeomen: the farm journal of Benton H. Miller, a slaveholder from Hancock County in the Georgia Black Belt (GDAH); the Ulrich B. Phillips Collection (YU), which contains notes and newspaper clippings regarding the white lower classes; and the Civil War Questionnaires compiled by the folklorist John Trotwood Moore and deposited in the Tennessee State Archives. Moore sent out inquiries to several hundred Civil War veterans residing in Tennessee at the turn of the century. He asked them about their families and farms, relations between rich and poor, and local politics in the prewar years, and about their experiences during the war. Most of the respondents had been nonslaveholders and many had lived in other Southern states. While the questions were often more interesting than the answers, some of the testimony is extremely pertinent. The questionnaires are available on microfilm.

At no time in the nineteenth century did as many Southerners write as many letters as during the Civil War. Several collections from Upcountry families strikingly detail conditions both in the field and on the home front: the Henry W. Robinson Papers from Gwinnett County (EU); the Richard B. Jett Papers from Fulton County (EU); the James W. Wadkins Confederate Letters from Franklin County (EU); the

W. S. Shockley Papers and Letters from Jackson County (DU); the
Nathan L. Hutchins Papers from Gwinnett County (DU); the William
R. King Diary from Cobb County (SHC); and the Confederate and
United Daughters of the Confederacy Collection from Floyd County
(GDAH).

For the postwar Upcountry a number of paper collections proved
valuable, none more so than the John H. Dent Papers from Floyd
County (GDAH). Dent, a noted agricultural reformer, had moved to
the Georgia Upcountry from the Alabama Black Belt shortly after the
Civil War and kept a farm journal until the early 1890s. The journal
comes to over twenty volumes and covers everything of interest to the
social historian: race and labor relations, general economic conditions,
credit and marketing arrangements, state and local politics, county
agricultural societies, the Grange, and the Southern Farmers' Alliance.
Dent died just as the People's party emerged. Postbellum social and
economic developments can also be traced in the Lucius H. Featherston
Papers from Heard County (EU); the William Beall Candler General
Merchandise Ledger from Carroll County (DU); the R. G. Dun and
Company Credit Ledgers; and the interviews conducted by the
historian Robert P. Brooks during the early twentieth century (UGa).
Brooks spoke with plantation owners across Georgia in an effort to
gather information on the changing structure of agriculture since the
Civil War. The testimony offers considerable detail about shifting labor
relations, prospects for small farmers, the rise of merchants and the lien
system, and the organization of plantations. It is compiled in three
volumes: Economic Conditions on Georgia Plantations, 1911 (2 vols.)
and Inquiries Concerning Georgia Farms Since 1865 (1 vol.). For more
general information, one should examine the life histories collected by
the Federal Writers' Project during the 1930s (SHC). They include a
wide spectrum of Southerners, rich and poor, urban and rural, from all
over the region.

For politics in the postwar Upcountry, I found particularly useful the
Henry P. Farrow Papers (UGa) and the Benjamin F. Conley Papers
(AHS), both prominent Georgia Republicans; the Rebecca Latimer
Felton Collection (UGa), wife of the Independent William H. Felton;
the Minutes of the Agricultural Club of Bartow County, No. 3
(GDAH); the Jefferson Alliance Minutes from Jackson County
(GDAH); and the Gwinnett County Farmers' Alliance Minutes
(GDAH). The papers of the Georgia Populist leader Thomas E.
Watson (SHC) are also excellent for statewide politics during the 1880s
and 1890s.

Primary Sources—Published

State Records and Documents

The publications of the Georgia state government were of aid in studying legal and political matters affecting the Upcountry. Among the most extensively tapped were the *Acts of the General Assembly of the State of Georgia* (Milledgeville, 1850–1861); the *Acts and Resolutions of the General Assembly of the State of Georgia* (Atlanta, 1872–1890); and the various *Codes of the State of Georgia* containing statute laws. The journals of the Georgia House and Senate were used only sparingly, in part because they did not print speeches. Many relevant documents for the Civil War era, including the proceedings of the secession convention, the public correspondence of Governor Brown, and the record of the state constitutional convention of 1868, have been collected, edited, and published in six volumes by Allen D. Candler in *The Confederate Records of the State of Georgia* (Atlanta, 1909). Unfortunately, the secession convention took place behind closed doors and the debates were never transcribed. Other valuable state records were the *Publications of the Georgia State Department of Agriculture* (Atlanta, 1874–1890); the *Annual Report of Thomas P. Janes, Commissioner of Agriculture of the State of Georgia* (Atlanta, 1876); and the *Report of the Comptroller-General of the State of Georgia* (Atlanta, 1870–1890), which lists aggregate county data on landholdings, tax returns, and elections.

Federal Records and Documents

The decennially published returns of the census bureau for the years 1850–1890, tabulated from the manuscript census, were of great importance to this study. They present county-level data on population, farms, crop production, and the like. The *Report to the Commissioner of Patents* (Washington, 1851–1854), issued by the United States Patent Office, contains much information on agricultural and grazing practices for different sections of the antebellum South. Two congressional investigations offer detailed testimony regarding changing social and economic relations in the postbellum South: the *Report of the Industrial Commission on Agriculture and Agricultural Labor*, House Document No. 179, 57th Cong., 1st Sess. (Washington, 1901); and particularly, one volume from the five-volume *Report of the Committee of the Senate Upon the Relations Between Labor and Capital*, Committee on Education and Labor (Washington, 1885). Of special value for the Georgia Upcountry is a survey conducted by the United States

Department of Agriculture during the 1920s: Howard Turner and L. D. Howell, "Condition of Farmers in a White-Farmer Area of the Cotton Piedmont, 1924–1926," U.S.D.A. Circular No. 78 (Washington, 1929). Based on Gwinnett County, this is an intricate account of land tenure, farming patterns, housing, diet, kinship, and mobility. Although confined to the twentieth century, it nonetheless speaks to the entire postwar period.

Other useful Federal documents came from the Reconstruction era, notably a series of congressional inquiries into social, economic, and political conditions in the South: the "Report of Carl Schurz on the States of South Carolina, Georgia, Alabama, Mississippi, and Louisiana," *Senate Executive Documents*, I, 39th Cong., 1st Sess. (Washington, 1866); the *Report of the Joint Committee on Reconstruction*, 39th Cong., 1st Sess. (Washington, 1866); the multivolume *Report of the Joint Select Committee to Inquire Into the Affairs of the Late Insurrectionary States*, 42nd Cong., 2nd Sess. (Washington, 1872), which is the investigation of the Ku Klux Klan; and the Committee on Reconstruction's *Condition of Affairs in Georgia*, House Miscellaneous Documents, No. 52, 40th Cong., 3rd Sess. (Washington, 1869).

Memoirs and Travelers' Accounts

Relatively few Northern or native Southern travelers ventured through the Georgia Upcountry—or indeed through any Backcountry area— between 1850 and 1890. Interest and comfort normally led them to the plantation districts. Nor did many Upcountry residents leave memoirs. But some sources are available and offer helpful descriptions of social and political life. For the antebellum period, one may consult George R. Gilmer, *Sketches of Some of the First Settlers of Upper Georgia* (New York, 1855); Garnett Andrews, *Reminiscenses of an Old Georgia Lawyer* (Atlanta, 1870); George M. White, *Statistics of the State of Georgia* (Savannah, 1849); Rebecca Latimer Felton, *Country Life in Georgia in the Days of My Youth* (Atlanta, 1919); Hiram Bell, *Men and Things* (Atlanta, 1907); Augustus Baldwin Longstreet, *Georgia Scenes*, 2nd ed. (New York, 1875); and Ulrich B. Phillips, ed., *The Correspondence of Robert Toombs, Alexander Stephens, and Howell Cobb* (Washington, 1913). More generally, one may consult the excellent accounts of Frederick Law Olmsted, *A Journey in the Backcountry* (New York, 1859) and *The Cotton Kingdom*, 2 vols. (New York, 1860); Joseph G. Baldwin, *The Flush Times of Alabama and Mississippi* (1853; repr. Gloucester, Mass., 1974); Daniel Robinson

Hundley, *Social Relations in Our Southern States* (New York, 1860); J. F. H. Claiborne, "A Trip Through the Piney Woods," *Publications of the Mississippi Historical Society* (Oxford, Miss., 1906); and William Elliott, *Carolina Sports by Land and Water* (New York, 1859). Elliott's narrative includes a fascinating chapter outlining elite and popular attitudes on hunting rights.

For the Civil War period, I found the following accounts illuminating: John B. Beall, *In Barrack and Field* (Nashville, 1906), which concerns Carroll County; and the military recollections of John B. Gordon, *Reminiscences of the Civil War* (New York, 1904), and Joseph E. Johnston, *Narrative of Military Operations During the War Between the States* (New York, 1874).

Reconstruction brought a flood of travelers and journalists into the South, some of whom either found their way to the Georgia Upcountry or wrote of related developments. Among the best of the narratives are Whitelaw Reid, *After the War* (Cincinnati, 1866); J. T. Trowbridge, *The South: A Tour* (Hartford, Conn., 1866); Edward King, *The Great South* (Hartford, Conn., 1875); and Sidney Andrews, *The South Since the War*, intro. by David Donald (Boston, 1971). Of relevance for the entire period considered are: the Southern Historical Association, *Memoirs of Georgia*, 2 vols. (Atlanta, 1895), a collection of biographical sketches of prominent residents of Georgia counties; Floyd C. Watkins and Charles H. Watkins, *Yesterday in the Hills* (Chicago, 1963), a memoir of life in Cherokee County; the Federal Writers' Project, *These Are Our Lives* (Chapel Hill, 1939), selections from the life histories recorded during the 1930s; and George P. Rawick, ed., *The American Slave: A Composite Autobiography*, 19 vols. (Westport, Conn., 1972), a compilation of the Works Progress Administration interviews with aged ex-slaves, also taken during the 1930s.

Newspapers and Journals

Few Upcountry counties published newspapers before the 1870s, thus hampering the study of local politics during the antebellum and Reconstruction years. Scattered runs of the Rome (Floyd County) *Weekly Courier*, the Cassville (Cass County) *Standard*, the Carrollton (Carroll County) *Advocate*, and the Atlanta *Intelligencer* provided some useful information for the 1850s. Several Cotton Belt newspapers did cover Upcountry affairs to a greater or lesser extent, however, and I drew upon them heavily. Most valuable were the Athens *Southern Banner* and the Athens *Southern Watchman,* but also of aid were the Milledgeville *Federal Union,* the Augusta *Chronicle and Sentinel,* and the Newnan (Coweta County) *Independent Blade.* For the Civil War period the Atlanta *Southern Confederacy* supplemented reports from other documents.

Beginning in the 1870s, Upcountry newspapers proliferated and proved to be of enormous value. I utilized those from Jackson and Carroll counties most extensively: the Jefferson *Forest News* (1875–1881); the Jackson *Herald* (1881–1896); the Carroll County *Times* (1872–1884, 1888–1889); and the Carroll *Free Press* (1884–1896). To these I should add the Gwinnett *Herald*; the Cartersville (Bartow County) *Express*; the Cherokee *Advance*; the Carnesville (Franklin County) *Enterprise*; the Rome *Tri-Weekly Courier*; the Marietta (Cobb County) *Journal*; and the Paulding *New Era*, all of which detailed events during the 1870s, 1880s, and 1890s. The daily Atlanta *Constitution,* which commenced publication in 1868, was used selectively.

Quite a few Upcountry counties boasted Populist newspapers, yet to my knowledge none survive in anything save extremely scattered form, such as the Dallas (Paulding County) *Herald*. Important insight into the state movement, as well as reports from the Upcountry, can be gained from the Atlanta *People's Party Paper* and from the Gracewood *Wool Hat,* which was only recently found and microfilmed.

A number of contemporary Southern farm and commercial journals not only carried agricultural and other economic information but also covered political developments. Most helpful were *The Farmers' Register* (Petersburg, Va., 1833–1834); *DeBow's Review* (New Orleans, 1846–1870); the *Southern Cultivator* (Augusta, 1844–1880); and *The Plantation* (Atlanta, 1871–1873). In addition, the R. G. Dun and Company published an annual Mercantile Agency Reference Book (New York, 1870–90), which listed all merchandising establishments in each county, their capital investment, and their credit rating.

Secondary Sources

Any study of Southern Populism—or, indeed, of the postwar South— must begin with the work of C. Vann Woodward. His *Origins of the New South, 1877–1913* (Baton Rouge, 1951), which amplified themes in his earlier biography, *Tom Watson: Agrarian Rebel* (New York, 1938), has yet to be matched either in scope or analysis. If I have taken a somewhat different perspective at points, my overall debt to Woodward should be readily apparent. The most valuable recent treatment of the Populist revolt in the South, which focuses on ideology but offers a stimulating wider assessment is Bruce Palmer, *"Man Over Money": The Southern Populist Critique of American Capitalism* (Chapel Hill, 1980). Other important works include William Warren Rogers, *The One-Gallused Rebellion: Agrarianism in Alabama, 1865–1896* (Baton Rouge, 1970); Sheldon Hackney, *Populism to Progressivism in Alabama* (Princeton, 1969); William Ivy Hair, *Bourbonism and Agrarian Protest: Louisiana Politics, 1877–1900* (Baton Rouge, 1972); and Roscoe C. Martin, *The People's Party in Texas* (Austin, 1933). Although Alex M. Arnett's rather dated *The Populist Movement in Georgia* (New York, 1922) has long been the only monograph on Georgia Populism, it is now superseded by Barton C. Shaw's *The Wool-Hat Boys: Georgia's Populist Party* (Baton Rouge, 1984).

The finest study of Populism from a national perspective is Lawrence Goodwyn, *Democratic Promise: The Populist Moment in America* (New York, 1976). Although Goodwyn's richest material comes from Texas, his sweep is considerable and his arguments are provocative. *Democratic Promise* is the latest contribution to an extended debate over Populism's character that began with John D. Hicks, *The Populist Revolt* (Minneapolis, 1931), which Goodwyn takes to task for equating Populism with the free-silver movement. For a useful summary of the historiographical controversy, and especially of recent state and local studies utilizing quantitative techniques and suggesting that Populism drew its strength from rural areas with the deepest precapitalist traditions, see James Turner, "Understanding the Populists," *JAH*, LXVII (September 1980), 354–83. David Montgomery's critical review, "On Goodwyn's Populists," *Marxist Perspectives*, I (Spring 1978), 166–73, calls for greater attention to class divisions in the countryside and points to links between Populism and labor.

The historical experiences of Southern Populism's white rank and file are drawing new interest, though the literature is still scarcely developed. The most substantial body of scholarly work was completed during the 1940s by Frank L. Owsley and his students, who used impressive statistical data to argue for an emerging economic democracy in the Old South: Owsley, *Plain Folk of the Old South* (Baton Rouge, 1949); Blanche Clark, *The Tennessee Yeomen, 1840–1860* (Nashville, 1942); and Herbert Weaver, *Mississippi Farmers, 1850–1860* (Nashville, 1945). Fabian Linden's devastating critique of their findings, " 'Economic Democracy' in the Slave South," *JNH*, XXXI

(April 1946), 140–89, demonstrated that agricultural wealth was concentrated in relatively few hands, but unfortunately closed off further inquiry for more than two decades and relegated to obscurity some other important insights of the Owsley school.

New investigations of the lives of Southern white "plain folk" are now beginning to bear fruit. Two collections of essays include some of these: Edward Magdol and Jon L. Wakelyn, eds., *The Southern Common People* (Westport, Conn., 1980) and Robert C. McMath, Jr., and Vernon Burton, eds., *Class, Conflict, and Consensus* (Westport, Conn., 1982). Also of considerable value are James D. Foust, *The Yeoman Farmer in the Westward Expansion of United States Cotton Production* (New York, 1975); David Weiman, "Petty Production in the Cotton South" (Ph.D. diss., Stanford University, 1982); John M. Allman, "Yeoman Regions in the Antebellum Deep South" (Ph.D. diss., University of Maryland, 1979); Forrest McDonald and Grady McWhiney, "The Antebellum Herdsman," *JSH*, XLI (May 1975), 147–66; Dickson D. Bruce, *And They All Sang Hallelujah: Plain Folk Camp-Meeting Religion, 1800–1845* (Knoxville, 1974); Bertram Wyatt-Brown, "Religion and the Formation of Folk Culture," in Lucius F. Ellsworth, ed., *The Americanization of the Gulf Coast* (Pensacola, Fla., 1972); and Eugene D. Genovese, "Yeoman Farmers in a Slaveholders' Democracy," *AH*, XLIX (April 1975), 331–42. Some of this material is assessed in Ira Berlin's excellent review essay, "White Majority," *Social History*, V (May 1977), 653–59.

Studies of rural communities in the antebellum South are now appearing in some volume and bear on the subject at hand. One may start with three of the oldest, but still very important: James C. Bonner, "Profile of a Late Antebellum Community (Hancock County, Georgia)," Edward W. Phifer, "Slavery in Microcosm: Burke County, North Carolina," and John M. Price, "Slavery in Winn Parish (Louisiana)," all of which are reprinted in Elinor Miller and Eugene D. Genovese, eds., *Plantation, Town, and County* (Urbana, Ill., 1974). Among the more recent are John T. Schlotterbeck, "Plantation and Farm: Social and Economic Change in Orange and Greene Counties, Virginia, 1716–1860" (Ph.D. diss., Johns Hopkins University, 1980); J. William Harris, "A Slaveholding Republic: Augusta's Hinterlands Before the Civil War" (Ph.D. diss., Johns Hopkins University, 1981); John S. Otto, "Slaveholding General Farmers in a Cotton Country," *AH*, LV (April 1981), 166–79; and especially Rachel N. Klein, "The Rise of the Planters in the South Carolina Backcountry, 1760–1808"

(Ph.D. diss., Yale University, 1979), a pioneering analysis of the development of white class relations in an emerging plantation area.

Much about the experiences and roles of yeomen and lower-class whites in the Old South can, of course, be learned from the more general literature. Of special significance are Eugene D. Genovese, *The Political Economy of Slavery* (New York, 1965); Gavin Wright, *The Political Economy of the Cotton South* (New York, 1978); Lewis C. Gray, *History of Agriculture in the Southern United States to 1860* (Gloucester, Mass., 1958); Roger W. Shugg, *Origins of Class Struggle in Louisiana* (Baton Rouge, 1939); Harold D. Woodman, *King Cotton and His Retainers* (Lexington, Ky., 1968); Sam B. Hilliard, *Hogmeat and Hoecake: Food Supply in the Old South* (Carbondale, Ill., 1972); and Morton Rothstein, "The Antebellum South as Dual Economy," *AH*, XLI (October 1967), 373–82.

The place of yeomen and the Upcountry in the antebellum political system is at least touched upon in Charles S. Sydnor, *The Development of Southern Sectionalism, 1819–1848* (Baton Rouge, 1948); Ulrich B. Phillips, *Georgia and State Rights* (repr.: Antioch, Ohio, 1968); Richard H. Shryock, *Georgia and the Union in 1850* (Philadelphia, 1926); Donald A. DeBats, "Elites and Masses: Political Structure, Communication, and Behavior in Antebellum Georgia" (Ph.D. diss., University of Wisconsin, 1973); and William L. Barney, *The Secessionist Impulse: Alabama and Mississippi in 1860* (Princeton, 1974). More directly relevant are Ralph A. Wooster, *The People in Power: Courthouse and Statehouse in the Lower South* (Knoxville, 1969); and especially J. Mills Thornton III, *Politics and Power in a Slave Society: Alabama, 1800–1860* (Baton Rouge, 1978), and Michael P. Johnson, *Toward a Patriarchal Republic: The Secession of Georgia* (Baton Rouge, 1977), which are the freshest and most thought-provoking accounts of the coming of the Civil War in the South now available.

Several studies of the Civil War, itself, offer important perspectives on the attitudes and aspirations of plain folk. The finest is Bell I. Wiley, *The Life of Johnny Reb: The Common Soldier of the Confederacy* (New York, 1943). Also of interest are Charles Ramsdell, *Behind the Lines in the Southern Confederacy* (Baton Rouge, 1944); Albert B. Moore, *Conscription and Conflict in the Confederacy* (New York, 1924); Ella Lonn, *Desertion During the Civil War* (Gloucester, Mass., 1966); Georgia L. Tatum, *Disloyalty in the Confederacy* (Chapel Hill, 1934); and Stephen E. Ambrose, "Yeoman Discontent in the Confederacy," *Civil War History*, VIII (September 1962), 259–68.

Scholarly treatments of white yeomen, tenants, and sharecroppers in the postwar South are still few and far between, but a growing literature on the period contains a wealth of information on the changing structure of agriculture. Two of the most useful are older studies of Georgia: Robert P. Brooks, *The Agrarian Revolution in Georgia, 1865–1912* (Madison, Wis., 1914), and Enoch Banks, *The Economics of Land Tenure in Georgia* (New York, 1905). Other related monographs include Anthony Tang, *Economic Development in the Southern Piedmont, 1860–1950* (Chapel Hill, 1958); Thomas D. Clark, *Pills, Petticoats, and Plows: The Southern Country Store, 1865–1900* (Norman, Okla., 1944); and Roger W. Shugg, *Origins of Class Struggle in Louisiana* (Baton Rouge, 1939), which remains a pioneer in conception and methodology.

Drawing heavily upon quantification, several recent studies are reshaping the way we think about the postbellum economy and have already stirred heated controversy. While focusing largely on planters, freedmen, and the Black Belt, their approaches also hold important implications for yeomen and the Upcountry. Particularly significant are Jonathan Wiener, *Social Origins of the New South: Alabama, 1860–1885* (Baton Rouge, 1978); Roger L. Ransom and Richard Sutch, *One Kind of Freedom: The Economic Consequences of Emancipation* (Cambridge, 1977); Stephen J. DeCanio, *Agriculture in the Postbellum South* (Cambridge, Mass., 1974); Robert Higgs, *Competition and Coercion* (Cambridge, 1977); Jay R. Mandle, *The Roots of Black Poverty* (Durham, N. C., 1978); Dwight Billings, *Planters and the Making of a "New South"* (Chapel Hill, 1979); Michael Wayne, *The Reshaping of Plantation Society: The Natchez District, 1860–1880* (Baton Rouge, 1983); and Harold D. Woodman, "Post–Civil War Southern Agriculture and the Law," *AH* LIII (January 1979), 319–37. Woodman also surveys much of this literature in his excellent review "Sequel to Slavery," *JSH*, XLII (November 1977), 523–54. Robert Gilmour's "The Other Emancipation: Studies in the Society and Economy of Alabama Whites During Reconstruction" (Ph.D. diss., Johns Hopkins University, 1972) and Frank Huffman's "Old South, New South: Continuity and Change in a Georgia County" (Ph.D. diss., Yale University, 1974) are both limited in conceptualization but contain useful material. Far more promising are forthcoming studies of the South Carolina piedmont by Lacy Ford and the Hill and Wiregrass regions of Alabama by Michael Hyman.

Relevant postwar political developments are considered in Elizabeth Studley Nathans, *Losing the Peace: Georgia Republicans and Reconstruction*

(Baton Rouge, 1968); C. Mildred Thompson's still valuable *Reconstruction in Georgia* (New York, 1915); Armstead L. Robinson, "Beyond the Realm of Social Consensus: New Meanings of Reconstruction for American History," *JAH*, LXVIII (September 1981), 276–97; J. Morgan Kousser, *The Shaping of Southern Politics* (New Haven, 1974); Judson C. Ward, "Georgia Under the Bourbon Democrats, 1872–1890" (Ph.D. diss., University of North Carolina, 1948); Lewis N. Wynne, "Planter Politics in Georgia: 1860–1890" (Ph.D. diss., University of Georgia, 1980); Charles L. Flynn, "White Land, Black Labor: Property, Ideology, and the Political Economy of Late-Nineteenth Century Georgia" (Ph.D. diss., Duke University, 1980); George L. Jones, "William H. Felton and the Independent Democratic Movement" (Ph.D. diss., University of Georgia, 1971); and Randolph D. Werner's provocative "Hegemony and Conflict: The Political Economy of a Southern Region, Augusta, Georgia, 1865–1895" (Ph.D. diss., University of Virginia, 1977). Two recent works discuss the Southern Farmers' Alliance in detail: Michael Schwartz's stimulating *Radical Protest and Social Structure* (New York, 1976), which nonetheless has some glaring deficiencies, and the fine monograph by Robert C. McMath, Jr., *Populist Vanguard* (Chapel Hill, 1975).

We are very much in need of more research on race relations in the rural—and particularly the nonplantation—South during the nineteenth century. One must, of course, begin with C. Vann Woodward's classic *The Strange Career of Jim Crow* (New York, 1955). But a foundation also should include Ira Berlin's outstanding *Slaves Without Masters* (New York, 1974); Barbara J. Fields's challenging and insightful "Ideology and Race in American History," in J. Morgan Kousser and James M. McPherson, eds., *Region, Race, and Reconstruction* (New York, 1982); W. McKee Evans, *Ballots and Fence Rails: Reconstruction on the Lower Cape Fear* (Chapel Hill, 1969); Vernon Burton, "Race and Reconstruction," *Journal of Social History*, XII (Fall 1978), 31–56; Edward Magdol, "Against the Gentry," *Journal of Social History*, VI (Spring 1973), 259–83; Lawrence C. Goodwyn, "Populist Dreams and Negro Rights," *AHR*, LXXVI (December 1971), 1435–56; Edward L. Ayers, "Crime and Society in the Nineteenth Century South" (Ph.D. diss., Yale University, 1980); and Eugene D. Genovese, " 'Rather Be a Nigger Than a Poor White Man': Slave Perceptions of Southern Yeomen and Poor Whites," in Hans L. Trefousse, ed., *Toward a New View of America* (New York, 1977).

Much of the literature pertaining to Georgia has been mentioned, though some additional state and local studies merit note: Amanda Johnson, *Georgia as Colony and State* (Atlanta, 1938); James C. Bonner, *A History of Georgia Agriculture, 1732–1860* (Athens, 1964); Willard Range, *A Century of Georgia Agriculture, 1850–1950* (Athens, 1954); Peter Wallenstein, "From Slave South to New South: Taxes and Spending in Georgia From 1850 Through Reconstruction" (Ph.D. diss., Johns Hopkins University, 1973); James C. Bonner, *Georgia's Last Frontier* (Athens, 1971); and James A. Furgeson, "Power Politics and Populism" (M.A. thesis, University of Georgia, 1975).

Finally, I should like to take note of a few broader works which have significantly influenced my thinking on the subject at hand and on its place in American history. On the South: Eugene D. Genovese, *Roll, Jordan, Roll* (New York, 1974), and Edmund S. Morgan, *American Slavery, American Freedom* (New York, 1976). On the rural North: Michael Merrill, "Cash Is Good to Eat," *RHR*, III (Winter 1977), 42–66; James A. Henretta, "Families and Farms," *WMQ*, 3rd ser., XXXV (January 1978), 3–32; and Jonathan Prude, *The Coming of Industrial Order* (New York, 1983). On the Civil War and Reconstruction: Eric Foner, *Politics and Ideology in the Age of the Civil War* (New York, 1980); Lawrence N. Powell, *New Masters* (New Haven, 1980); and David Montgomery, *Beyond Equality* (New York, 1967). On labor: Herbert G. Gutman, *Work, Culture, and Society in Industrializing America* (New York, 1976); Eric Foner, *Tom Paine and Revolutionary America* (New York, 1976); and Leon Fink, *Workingmen's Democracy* (Urbana, Ill., 1983).

I have also benefited enormously from readings on rural peoples, the working classes, and capitalist development in other parts of the world. Among the most valuable for this study were Eric J. Hobsbawm, *The Age of Capital, 1848–1875* (New York, 1975); idem, *Primitive Rebels* (New York, 1965); idem, *Captain Swing*, with George Rudé (New York, 1968); E. P. Thompson, *The Making of the English Working Class* (New York, 1963); idem, *Whigs and Hunters* (New York, 1975); idem, "The Moral Economy of the English Crowd in the Eighteenth Century," *Past and Present*, no. 50 (February 1971), 76–136; Barrington Moore, Jr., *Social Origins of Dictatorship and Democracy* (New York, 1965); C. B. Macpherson, *The Political Theory of Possessive Individualism* (New York, 1962); Edward W. Fox, *History in Geographic Perspective* (New York, 1971); David Brion Davis, *The Problem of Slavery in the Age of Revolution* (Ithaca, 1975); Sidney Mintz, "The Rural Proletariat and the Problem of Rural Proletarian Consciousness," *Journal of Peasant Studies*, I (April 1974), 291–323; and Hans Medick, "The Proto-Industrial Family

Economy," *Social History*, III (October 1976), 291–315. To these I might add numerous studies of peasant societies in Europe, Latin America, and Asia which hold much of value for students of rural America. Fittingly, two Southern historians—C. Vann Woodward and Eugene D. Genovese—have been particularly vocal in emphasizing the need for a comparative approach to American history. They are right.

Index